Advances in Spatial Science

The Regional Science Series

This series contains scientific studies focusing on spatial phenomena, utilising theoretical frameworks, analytical methods, and empirical procedures specifically designed for spatial analysis. Advances in Spatial Science brings together innovative spatial research utilising concepts, perspectives, and methods relevant to both basic science and policy making. The aim is to present advances in spatial science to an informed readership in universities, research organisations, and policy-making institutions throughout the world.

The type of material considered for publication in the series includes: Monographs of theoretical and applied research in spatial science; state-of-the-art volumes in areas of basic research; reports of innovative theories and methods in spatial science; tightly edited reports from specially organised research seminars.The series and the volumes published in it are indexed by Scopus.

More information about this series at http://www.springer.com/series/3302

Roger R. Stough • Karima Kourtit • Peter Nijkamp •
Uwe Blien

Editors

Modelling Aging
and Migration Effects
on Spatial Labor Markets

 Springer

Editors
Roger R. Stough
Schar School of Policy and Government
Arlington
Virginia, USA

Peter Nijkamp
Tinbergen Institute
Amsterdam, The Netherlands

JADS (Jheronimus Academy of Data
Science), 's-Hertogenbosch,
The Netherlands

Karima Kourtit
KTH Royal Institute of Technology
Stockholm, Sweden

JADS (Jheronimus Academy of Data
Science), 's-Hertogenbosch,
The Netherlands

Uwe Blien
Institute for Employment Research (IAB)
Nuremberg, Germany

Otto-Friedrich-University of Bamberg
Bamberg, Germany

ISSN 1430-9602 ISSN 2197-9375 (electronic)
Advances in Spatial Science
ISBN 978-3-319-68562-5 ISBN 978-3-319-68563-2 (eBook)
https://doi.org/10.1007/978-3-319-68563-2

Library of Congress Control Number: 2018951473

This Springer imprint is published by the registered company Springer Nature Switzerland AG
The registered company address is: Gewerbestrasse 11, 6330 Cham, Switzerland

Preface

There is no question that contemporaneous demographic developments, notably ageing and international migration, exert a decisive influence on the level and growth of welfare in all countries, regions and cities. These two mega-trends, the structural rise of the share of elderly people and the rapid increase in cross-border (temporary or permanent) movements of people, have led to intensified interest—from both the scholarly community and policymaking bodies—in the system-wide implications of these two mega-trends for our societies. The rise of the 'silver generation' has far-reaching labour market participation effects and induces an intensive discussion on compensating mechanisms such as migration.

In recent years, we have witnessed unprecedented spatial-demographic dynamics in many parts of the world as a result of political tensions, war conditions, income and employment disparities, ageing societies or fortune-seeking behaviour. The resulting migration flows—in the form of job migrants, refugees, asylum seekers, illegal migrants, or temporary migrants—have had far-reaching consequences for labour markets and regional welfare conditions in the receiving countries. The phenomenon of the 'homo mobilis' has at times also prompted public and political resistance against open orders and has played a critical role in the outcomes of recent democratic choice situations (such as the presidential elections in the USA or the Brexit referendum in the UK).

The Regional Science Academy (TRSA)—a recently established scholarly institution in the field of the spatial sciences with the aim to act as a catalyst for innovative thinking in regional science and related disciplines—has made an ambitious attempt to address these issues by organizing a so-called Advanced Brainstorm Carrefour (ABC) in May 2016 at the Tinbergen Institute in Amsterdam. Several well-known scholars expressed their views on the issues concerned at this scientific gathering. These presentations and discussions formed the source of inspiration for the present volume on *Modelling Aging and Migration Effects on Spatial Labor Markets*, supplemented with editorial contributions by other scholars. The additional wish to thank the Tinbergen Institute for providing hospitality for this meeting, the Institut fuer Arbeitsmarkt- und Berufsforschung (IAB—Institute for Employment

Research) in Nurnberg for its support for this meeting and the secretaries Elfie Bonke and Jenny Wiersema for their unrivalled help in organizing this unforgettable scientific venue.

Wien, Austria   Manfred M. Fischer
Charlotte, NC   Jean-Claude Thill
Groningen, The Netherlands   Jouke van Dijk
Jönköping, Sweden   Hans Westlund

Contents

About the Authors

Uwe Blien is Professor at the Otto Friedrich University in Bamberg, Head of the Department of Regional Labour Markets at the Institute for Employment Research (IAB), Fellow of the Labor and Socio-Economic Research Center (LASER) within the Friedrich-Alexander-University of Erlangen-Nuremberg, and Research Fellow of the Institute of Labor Economics (IZA) in Bonn. He received a Doctor in Economics from the University of Regensburg and a habilitation (postdoctoral degree) from the Technical University of Kaiserslautern. From 2010 to 2014, he was President of the "Gesellschaft für Regionalforschung" (GfR), the German-speaking section of the European Regional Science Association (ERSA), and he was a member of the ERSA Council. Uwe Blien's research interests concern among others regional labor markets, the effects of technical progress on labor markets, the effects of labor market policy, and the development of South-East Asian societies. He has published over 50 articles in refereed journals and 14 books (including edited volumes) and written over 100 book chapters and articles in other journals. In Germany, he has done manifold consulting work for the Federal Ministry of Labour and Social Affairs, for the Federal Employment Services, and for other official institutions (also in other countries).

Karima Kourtit is at the Jheronimus Academy of Data Science (JADS) of the division Smart Cities, at the Eindhoven University of Technology and Tilburg University, 's-Hertogenbosch, the Netherlands. She has worked at the Centre for the Future of Places (CFP) of the Department of Urban Planning and Environment, School of Architecture and Built Environment at KTH Royal Institute of Technology, Stockholm, and Adam Mickiewicz University, Poznan, Poland. She holds two PhDs, in economics and geography (with distinction), and has a profound interest in regional and urban topics. Her research interest focuses on the emerging *"New Urban World."* Her main scientific research is in the field of creative industries, urban development, cultural heritage, digital technology, and strategic performance management. Lately, she has also been involved in the implementation of several national and international research projects and initiatives. Furthermore, she has been an editor of several books and guest editor for many international journals and has published a wide array of scientific articles, papers, special issues of journals, and edited volumes in the field of geography and the spatial sciences. She is also managing director of *The Regional Science Academy*.

Peter Nijkamp is emeritus Professor in regional and urban economics and in economic geography at the VU University and associated with the Jheronimus Academy of Data Science (JADS) of the division Smart Cities, 's-Hertogenbosch (the Netherlands); Royal Institute of Technology (KTH), Stockholm (Sweden); and A. Mickiewicz University, Poznan (Poland). He is a member of editorial/advisory boards of more than 30 journals. According to the RePec list, he belongs to the top 30 of well-known economists worldwide. He is also a fellow of the Royal Netherlands Academy of Sciences and past vice-president of this organization. He has served as president of the governing board of the Netherlands Research Council (NWO). In 1996, he was awarded the most prestigious scientific prize in the Netherlands, the Spinoza award.

Roger R. Stough is in the Schar School of Policy and Government at George Mason University, USA. His research specializations include innovation and entrepreneurship as drivers of economic develop, leadership in regional economic development, economic modeling, and transport analysis. During the past two decades, Dr. Stough has been heavily involved in development-related research in China, Korea, India, Pakistan, Turkey, and Europe. More recently, he has been involved in the development and application of indexes to measure and evaluate regional innovation and entrepreneurship ecosystems. During his Presidency of the Technopolicy Network in Europe, he was involved in the development of an index designed to measure and evaluate innovation levels and processes. Further, he has advised officials in Turkey on the adoption of open innovation processes and management of intellectual property. In China, he has evaluated and advised various innovation policies at the subnational regional level concerning the Torch, Technology Incubation, and Innovation Parks. His publication record includes several hundred scholarly and professional publications and 43 books (including edited volumes).

Chapter 1
Geographic Labor Markets, Aging and Migration: A Panoramic Perspective

Roger R. Stough, Karima Kourtit, Peter Nijkamp, and Uwe Blien

1 Introduction

Older population cohorts are growing disproportionately faster than younger cohorts. This is a trend that is affecting countries and regions to different extents. At the same time, another demographic process that is also impacting on many regions is migration. Today, many migration movements are episodic and thus more

R. R. Stough (✉)
George Mason University, Arlington Virginia, USA
e-mail: rstough@gmu.edu

K. Kourtit
JADS (Jheronimus Academy of Data Science), 's-Hertogenbosch, The Netherlands

Uppsala University, Uppsala, Sweden

KTH Royal Institute of Technology Stockholm, Sweden

Adam Mickiewicz University, Poznan, Poland
e-mail: k.kourtit@jads.nl

P. Nijkamp
JADS (Jheronimus Academy of Data Science), 's-Hertogenbosch, The Netherlands

Center for the Future of Places (CFP), KTH Royal Institute of Technology, Stockholm, Sweden

Adam Mickiewicz University, Poznan, Poland

Tinbergen Institute, Amsterdam, The Netherlands
e-mail: p.nijkamp@jads.nl

U. Blien
Institute for Employment Research (IAB), Nuremberg, Germany

Otto-Friedrich University Bamberg, Bamberg, Germany
e-mail: uwe.blien@iab.de

© Springer International Publishing AG, part of Springer Nature 2018   1
U. Blien et al. (eds.), *Modelling Aging and Migration Effects on Spatial Labor Markets*, Advances in Spatial Science,
https://doi.org/10.1007/978-3-319-68563-2_1

unstable than in the past (e.g., from famines, war, political turbulence and natural disasters), as illustrated by the growth of return, circular and temporary or chain migration. In fact, at the same time these growing and emerging types of migration are occurring the distinction between migration and commuting is blurring, e.g., those who are commuting across continents and intercontinentally might also be viewed as temporary migrants. As with aging, there are great differentials in the manifestation of these processes across places, regions and nations and in turn in their impact on regional labor markets.

The dynamics of these major demographic and population processes (aging and migration) have become topics of considerable concern for researchers and policy makers (Turchin 2003). This book provides not only summary and descriptive contributions about these trends and labor market stability/instability, but also modelling and policy-centric empirical chapters that includes new and expanded knowledge about their effects on geographic labor markets. The contributions are focused in part on the European context, however they also provide broader insight from empirical analyses drawing on data from North and South America, and Australasia.

Aging has become a universal megatrend in many countries, with far-reaching consequences for the welfare state, public finance, consumption and mobility patterns, and labour force participation (Guerin et al. 2015 and UNICEF 2015). It is increasingly recognized that the consequences of an aging society may exhibit different patterns on a regional system, depending on the demography, quality of life and economic resilience of these regions. For example, declining labour force participation as a result of the aging process may be compensated for through other demographic factors such as international migration, extended participation of older cohort members, higher productivity of younger cohorts and application of productivity enhancing new technologies.

It is noteworthy that the spatial distribution of migration flows shows also heterogeneous patterns in national-regional and regional systems, so that migration is not by definition a panacea for solving the aging issue. For a regionally heterogeneous labor market, aging and migration may sometimes be mutually complementary and sometimes mutually conflicting phenomena. Overall the research presented underscores findings that show the current and future powerful driving force that migration and aging are having on spatial labor markets; but the nature of the effects is heterogeneous across nations and subnational regions.

The aging and migration megatrends and their impact on spatial—regional and local—labor market performance is the core theme of this book and thus together define its scope and range. A number of basic thematic efforts appear in the various contributions. These are:

- An informed and broad inventory of aging and migration issues in various countries.
- Analysis of the heterogeneous impacts of these developments in regional labor markets.
- Systematic examination of data bases and related empirical analyses that enable mapping out the complex and dynamic nature of these developments.

- Utilization of various contemporary economic and modelling techniques to analyse the above referenced complex regional labor market developments.
- Critical review and assessment of various policy measures that are or may cope with the effects of aging and migration effects on regional labor markets.

At the same time, while these themes are prominently represented, there are two additional recurring themes that also cut cross the contributions and their findings: technological change and forced migration (International Organization for Migration 2016 and Turchin 2003). Technological change in such areas as IT, biotechnology, and robotics are impacting and will continue to affect not only the structure and performance of regional labor markets but also many real-world elements of society, e.g., transportation and logistics, social relations, shopping and procurement, work, retirement, entrepreneurship and innovation. Forced migration from war, political turbulence and natural disasters, the second recurring theme in this volume is creating major impacts on labor market performance and dynamics in both emerging and developing economies as well as in developed economies. Most of the forced migration effects will continue to be negative. So, technology and technological change, and forced migration are also factors that may be seen as intervening variables in a world where aging and migration are impacting regional labor market performance and stability.

The idea and motivation for this book stem from various systemic and general changes in demographic structure and migration patterns and the unprecedented effect these changes are having and will have on regional labor markets. Two general demographic structural changes that are occurring broadly in the world are considered in the various contributions in this volume. The first of these is a disproportionate growth of seniors in the populations of many countries. This aging trend means that other cohorts, usually the working age cohorts, are experiencing relative contraction. Such change alters the structure of labor markets and thus can lead to major disturbing effects which in turn can impact a host of other processes including labor supply and demand, economic development, employment and unemployment, welfare, health, public finance, consumption, mobility and immigration. The other structural change is the growth of large youth (ages 18–29) cohorts, especially in developing countries (and to some extent also in developed countries) that are underemployed or unemployed. Clearly, this pattern is of huge importance, but it is not the primary focus of this book, although several of the contributions consider related issues.

The importance of migration is, among other things, its potential to offset effects of aging in regional labor markets. While migration can be a policy focus for managing labor market effects of aging, its ability to do this must be viewed in the context of the nature of migration in contemporary times where its forms include temporary, circular, return and chain migration. The motivation for this book is then to examine the effects of aging (and to some extent growing youth population cohorts) on regional labor markets and the role migration is playing and may play in softening the disruptive effects of demographic structural changes in regional labor markets.

Gaining an improved understanding of the impact that aging is having on regional labor markets and how migration may be a mitigating factor are the primary motivations for this book. However, given the relatively unique nature of the potential aging impact, it also seeks to bring new and creative conceptual frameworks and methodologies to facilitate greater insight into the aging impact and migration. Along with new theoretical and conceptual views and methodologies and new empirical findings policy lessons were also envisaged. In short, the editors expect that the aging impact on regional economies and migration themes would not only motivate, but also lead to new developments, methods, insights, policy and management views on regional labor market functionality.

2   Organization of the Book

The reader will find a rich inventory of the various aging and migration issues and their expression in the opening chapters of the book, **Part A** of this volume. Their heterogeneous impacts on regional labor markets are analysed in subsequent chapters. Furthermore, many of the papers in this volume systematically map out the complex and dynamic nature of these impacts and their related public policy implications. In **Part B**, the focus of the chapters narrows, as these contributions employ contemporary economic and statistical modelling techniques to bring greater analytical clarity to the range and diversity of the impacts of aging and migration effects on regional labor markets. Moreover, in **Part C**, the chapters provide empirically based policy analyses and proposals for coping with the impacts of changing aging and migration behavior. In short, the book provides a descriptive and definitional inventory of aging and migration driven problems and modelling and empirical analyses of the driving effect of aging and migration on regional labor markets along with an assessment of relevant public policies on regional labor markets.

The book is organized around three major topical areas in a total of 16 chapters including this Introduction. First, **Part A** offers a general framing of issues and addresses aging and migration problems (the aging-migration nexus) as well as the implications these processes are having in particular on regional labor markets. Short summaries of the two chapters that contribute to and define this part of the book are presented hereafter. Next, **Part B** addressing intriguing issues on advanced modelling of modern population geography focuses specifically on modelling approaches and associated statistical analyses in six chapters. These offer contemporary—and/or adaptations of more traditional modelling—approaches for examining the impacts of aging and migration, often from a policy perspective, on spatial labor markets and spatial development. Finally, six papers provide the content of **Part C** which consists of empirical analyses of aging and migration and their impact on geographic labor markets and relevant policy issues. Abstracted versions of each of the chapters for **Parts A**, **B** and **C** appear below. The title and authors' names for each chapter are also presented.

3 The Century of Migration and Aging: A Review of Labor Market Effects

The first paper in **Part A**, Chap. 2, is by Bruce Newbold and is entitled "Aging and Migration: An Overview". Newbold argues that aging is a growing global phenomenon, with some countries already seeing dramatic aging, and others just starting to see their populations age. With older cohorts representing an increasingly large proportion of the world's population, the implications of aging societies include a diverse set of issues and processes such as economic development, welfare, public finance, consumption, mobility patterns, migration and immigration. This chapter covers the demography of aging before moving on to consider the linkages between migration, immigration and aging along with policy options associated with aging societies. As societies age, larger numbers of the old will be mobile, although it is unlikely that the mobility rate will increase. Although internal migration can redistribute older populations across space, with implications for sending and receiving regions, Newbold concludes that this will not change the overall population profile of a country. Instead, immigration is the most likely option to reduce or slow the aging of a population, but it too is limited in its effect.

The second paper, "Fortunado's, Desperado's and Clandestino's in Diaspora Markets: The Circular 'Homo Mobilis'", Chap. 3, is authored by Karima Kourtit, Peter Nijkamp and Masood Gheasi, and examines how world demographic patterns (e.g., aging processes, birth and death rates) are increasingly influenced by migration movements. Rising numbers of people are 'on the move', in search of better fortunes elsewhere. It is noteworthy that nowadays many migration movements no longer show stable patterns, but reflect a high degree of dynamics, for instance, in the form of return migration, circular and temporary migration, or chain migration. There is also great heterogeneity in the motivations of many migrants that may have significant impacts on the migration choice, the destination place, the migrant's status, and the duration of stay. Consequently, return migration, temporary migration and circular migration have in recent years become important research and policy issues. This chapter offers a review of the dilemmas and assessment issues inherent in the effects of non-structural or temporary migrants (the so-called cross-border 'movers') on host economies. Particular attention is paid to circular migration policy in Europe as a vehicle to both mitigate temporary tensions on regional labor markets of host economies and to provide a solid base for sustainable growth in the sending countries. Various research and policy challenges are also considered.

4 The Dynamics of Modern Population Geography

Bo Feng, Mark Partridge and Mark Rembert provide the first paper in **Part B**, Chap. 4, entitled *"The Perils of Modelling How Migration Responds to Climate Change"*. The authors begin with the observation that the impact of climate change has drawn growing interest from both researchers and policymakers. Yet, relatively little is known with respect to its influence on interregional migration. The surge of extreme weather conditions could lead to the increase of forced migration from coastal to inland regions, which normally follows different patterns than voluntary migration. However, recent migration models tend to predict unrealistic migration trends under climate change in that migration would flow towards areas most adversely affected. Given the great uncertainty about the magnitude and distribution of severe weather events, it is nearly impossible to foresee migration directions by simply extrapolating from the data on how people have responded in the past to climate and weather. For example, weather events will likely occur far outside of what has been observed. Other issues include poor climate measures and a poor understanding of how climate affects migration in an entirely different structural or institutional environment. Unintended consequences of public policies also contribute to the complication of predicting future migration patterns. In this paper, the authors survey the limitations of the existing climate change literature, explore insights of regional economic studies, and provide potential solutions to those issues.

Tomaz Ponce Dentinho provides the next paper, Chap. 5, in **Part B**, entitled "*Migration Pressures and Responses in South Asia*". Globalization involves also a group of poor and nearby nations in South and Southeast Asia that send migrants to rich countries in the western world, to dependent countries in the Middle Eastern Gulf area and to emerging and developed economies in Asia. These patterns influence the way we see and react to migration from these poor and developing nations. The aim of the chapter is to examine and understand the impact of institutional barriers in migration in this context. The chapter examines several research questions: What are likely effects if institutional barriers cease to exist? What will happen with the collapse of the oil rents in the Middle East? What might happen with a development take-off of some countries in the region? To answer these questions the paper presents a contextualization of South Asia in the World, uses a migration model to identify the demographic, economic and institutional factors that push and pull migration in the region. The conclusion proposes an interpretative synthesis of the research results and future work on the impact of institutional barriers on migration.

Ana Maria Bonomi Barufi examines "*Lagging Regions and Labor Market Dynamics in Brazil*" in the next Chap. 6. She observes that agglomeration economies reinforce the concentration of economic activity that in turn stimulate unbalanced growth and uneven development. In this context, she argues that the development of lagging regions will largely depend on government intervention, as market forces by themselves are unlikely to overcome polarization effects and may actually increase regional inequality. Given these circumstances, migration helps to explain the spatial distribution of workers and the skill composition of the local labour force. At a first glance, migration should be able to equalize real regional wages, but instead, it ends up reinforcing regional disparities. Therefore, this chapter aims to examine the main behavioral and policy implications from the regional concentration of production resources of lagging regions in Brazil. More specifically, the composition of the local labour force is dependent on pull factors for specific skills that may arise from agglomeration economies. Consequently, this chapter also explores the probability of losing or attracting workers with different skill levels, given an initial level of local development.

The next paper, Chap. 7, focuses upon *"Migration and Aging in Expanding and Shrinking European Regions"*. It is authored by Mats Johansson, Pia Nolsson and Hans Westlund. At the outset, the authors note that Europe is in a phase of vast transition seen from both demographic and economic-structural perspectives. Studies have shown that demographic development differs considerably when comparing urban regions with more sparsely populated and peripheral regions. Such patterns are shown to be especially strong in the northern and eastern parts of Europe, where a redistribution of people has been contributing to concentration in metropolitan or big cities and to shrinkage and depopulating of rural and peripheral areas. This chapter empirically examines these differing demographic development paths by analysing the influence of key underlying demographic factors on population change across European regions. Typologies based on both economic and demographic structure and cross-regional regression modelling are employed to examine these patterns. The economic-structural typology developed within a European project is used to describe and analyse economic-structural factors. A typology based on demographic characteristics that classifies regions as either shrinking or expanding in terms of population is deployed in the empirical assessment. The findings support a conclusion that age structure is of importance with regard to population changes and that there exists an east–west divide between the growing west and declining east where the declining sectors are more frequent. It is also shown that large and densely populated regions have better preconditions for growth and less risk of shrinking than small and sparsely populated ones.

The next paper in **Part B,** Chap. 8, is entitled "More pensioners, less income inequality? The impact of changing age composition on inequality in big cities and elsewhere", and is authored by Omoniyi B. Alimi, David C. Mare, and Jacques Poot. Like most of the developed world, New Zealand's population is aging both numerically and structurally. Population aging can have important effects on the distribution of personal income within and between urban areas. The age structure of the population may affect the distribution of income through the life-cycle profile of earnings but also through the spatial-temporal distribution of income within the various age groups. By decomposing New Zealand census data from 1986 to 2013 by age and urban area, this chapter examines the effects of population aging on spatial-temporal changes in the distribution of personal income to better understand urban area-level income inequality (measured by the Mean Log Deviation index). The authors focus explicitly on differences between metropolitan and non-metropolitan urban areas. New Zealand has experienced a significant increase in income inequality over the last few decades, but population aging has slightly dampened this trend. Because metropolitan areas are aging slower, the inequality-reducing effect of ageing has been less in these areas. However, this urban-size differential-ageing effect on inequality growth has been relatively small compared with the faster growth in intra-age group inequality in the metropolitan areas.

The 'pensionado society' does not only have implications for regional labour market conditions, but also for the demand for 'pensionado' amenities. Robert J. Stimson and Tung-Kai Shy are the authors of Chap. 9 which is entitled "*Analysing the Demand for Retirement Housing: The Australian Context*". They begin by observing that population aging, which is being driven-up as the 'baby boomer' generation reaches the traditional retirement age, is expected to generate an increased demand for housing alternatives that are more suitable for older people, including retirement village living. Key questions that are asked in this chapter are: (a) what will be the level of propensity for older people to seek to 'downsize' rather than 'age in place'? (b) what will motivate them to do so?; (c) what role will retirement villages play as a housing alternative for older people and what will be the level of demand?; and (d), what will be the locations that are best for the development of new retirement villages? Demographic and spatial modelling approaches as developed by regional scientists are helpful to address these questions, including how to assist retirement village developers identify where optimal locations might be for developing new retirement villages that would maximize proximity to the likely aged cohorts that have a high propensity to choose to relocate to live in a retirement community; and to estimate the likely take-up rate that might occur if a new retirement village was to be developed on a specific site that is available to a developer.

Population dynamics may also leave a footprint in a firm's productivity achievement. The final chapter in **Part B**, Chap. 10, is entitled "*Demographic Transition and Firm Performance: An Empirical Analysis for Germany*", addresses this issue. The authors are Stephan Brunow and Alessandra Faggian. This paper presents an original analysis of the channels that reduce the dependency ratio on plant productivity in Germany. Of the three channels considered: (1) increasing female participation; (2) increasing elderly participation; and (3) immigration, the least problematic for increasing productivity appears to be female participation, although the effect of part-time work is unclear and needs to be further examined. The results of the other two channels, especially immigration, are more mixed and require additional research to better determine their effects, for example, decomposing the analysis by specific industries and/or occupations rather than a broader whole economy study. The insignificant findings in this study, for especially immigration, may be due to heterogeneity among immigrant workers in terms of the jobs and sectors chosen or to a differential selectivity of immigrants by potentially less productive firms.

5   Regional Labor Market Transitions, Aging and Migration

Thomas de Graaff, Daniel Arribas-Bel and Ceren Ozgen are the authors of the first chapter in **Part C**, Chap. 11, "*Demographic Aging and Employment Dynamics in German Regions: Modeling Regional Heterogeneity*". The authors observe that the persistence of high youth unemployment and dismal labor market outcomes are imminent and current concerns for most European economies. The relationship between demographic aging and employment outcomes is even more worrying, once the relationship is examined at the regional level. The authors focus on modelling regional heterogeneity. They argue that an average impact across regions is often not very useful, and is conditional on the region's characteristics resulting in measured impacts that may differ significantly. To address this issue, the authors advocate the use of modelling varying level and slope effects, and specifically, to cluster them by the use of latent class or finite mixture models (FMMs). Moreover, in order to fully exploit the output from the FMM, self-organizing maps are presented to help understand the composition of the resulting segmentation and as a way to depict the underlying regional similarities that would otherwise be missed if a standard approach was adopted. The proposed method is applied in a case-study of Germany where the analysis shows that the regional impact of young age cohorts on the labor market is indeed very heterogeneous across regions and the results are robust against potential endogeneity bias.

The next chapter by Vicente Rios and Roberto Patuelli, Chap. 12, entitled *"What is the Effect of Population Aging in Regional Labor Market Fluctuations of Germany? A SVAR with Zero-Sign Restrictions Approach"*, is adopted for examining this research question. The authors observe at the outset that population and workforce aging have been shown to have a major influence on growth paths and public finance, as different demographic compositions affect productivity and innovative capacity, and therefore potential growth, as well as macroeconomic processes such as public spending for health, welfare, or tax collection. The relationship between aging and labor market variables has been studied before, but always using a single equation analytical method, where only one particular labor market outcome has been related to aging. The problem of such analyses is that labor markets are multivariate systems and their related variables are closely linked with each other through supply and demand. Therefore, neglecting potential endogenous interactions between them may induce bias in the results of empirical analyses. This study examines and aims to fill this gap, as it analyses the role of population aging in the labor market dynamics of West Germany, and subsequently for a sample of ten West German NUTS-1 regions during the period 1970 to 2014. To that end, a Bayesian Structural Vector Autoregressive (SVAR) model is calibrated which includes the following variables: wages, participation rates, unemployment rates and the working-age dependency ratio as an indicator of population aging. Structural labor market shocks are identified using zero-short run restrictions and the assumption that aging is the most exogenous variable in the system. The findings suggest that labour demand shocks have a relevant effect in the short run, while labour supply explains the largest extent of uncertainty over longer periods. The role of wage-bargaining and population-aging shocks appear to be less important, although specific periods show an increased role for such shocks in determining labor market outcomes.

The next chapter in **Part C**, Chap. 13, estimates the effect that changes in the size of the youth population have on the wages of young workers. The chapter is entitled *"Regional Population Structure and Young Workers' Wages"*, and is authored by

Alfred Garloff and Duncan Roth. Assuming that differently aged workers are only imperfectly substitutable, economic theory predicts that individuals in larger age groups earn lower wages. A test of this hypothesis for a sample of young, male, full-time employees in Western Germany during the period 1999–2010 is conducted. Based on instrumental variables estimation, it is observed that an increase in the youth share by one percentage point is predicted to decrease a young worker's wages by about 3%. Moreover, the results suggest that a substantial part of this effect can be ascribed to members of larger age groups being more likely to be employed in lower-paying occupations.

The authors of Chap. 14, Marco Modica, Aura Reggiani, Nicola De Vivo and Peter Nijkamp, entitle their study as *"Aging and Labor Market Development: Testing Gibrat's and Zipf's Law for Germany"*. Gibrat's and Zipf's laws describe two very well-known empirical regularities in the distribution of settlements. Many studies have focused on the analysis of both of these regularities, stimulated by the idea that an accurate description of the distribution of people in space is important for both policy-relevant purposes and for specifying more appropriate theoretical models. However, the existing literature provides an analysis of Gibrat's and Zipf's laws without taking into account the demographic characteristics of the population under analysis. Given the fact that many countries, and especially those in Europe, will become aging societies in the decades to come, the aim of this chapter is to provide a more accurate description of the distribution of people, taking into account the demographic differences between people. In this analysis, the focus is on both municipal population (place of residence) and employment (place of work) data for Germany between the years 2001 and 2011. Evidence of different behaviour in the cohorts of older people is provided as well.

The authors of Chap. 15, entitled *"Career Moves: Migration Histories of Selected Regional Workforces in Bendigo, Australia"*, are Fiona McKenzie and Jonathan Corcoran. The mobility of young adults is often related to education and employment. In Australia, there is a strong regional dimension to this mobility, with state capital cities like Melbourne attracting people from non-metropolitan regions. Spatial patterns of skills accumulation and deficit arise from youth migration to cities, and this continues to be a concern for regional policy makers seeking to boost non-metropolitan growth. However, despite the net flows of human capital towards capital cities, many regional centres still maintain diverse economies and many professional workers choose to locate there. To better understand the characteristics and migration histories of these professional workers, a survey of three workforce samples was undertaken in the city of Bendigo (150 km from Melbourne). While it was expected that metropolitan areas would play a role in migration pathways and skills acquisition, variation was found between the workforces, with one proving to be very regional in its character while the others drew workers from both metropolitan and rural areas. Spatial patterns of human capital accumulation are explored in this paper with a view to understanding where such capital is developed and where it is subsequently located. Such analyses can assist policy makers in developing more effective attraction and retention strategies for regional Australia.

Both aging and migration induce unprecedented dynamics on regional labour markets. Clearly, these megatrends are not exclusively separate factors operating independently of the remaining part of the economy. On the contrary, labour markets are increasingly operating in a new technological and institutional arena where next to population dynamics also productivity-enhancing technologies and economic perturbations play a key role. Consequently, population dynamics, technological progress and spatial labour markets are mutually process-interwoven phenomena. Against this background, Uwe Blien and Oliver Ludewig are the authors of Chap. 16, the final chapter of **Part C**, which is entitled *"Compensation or Substitution: Labor Market Effects of Technological Progress and Structural Change"*. The authors note that technological progress can have contradictory effects on employment development and hence on spatial labor markets. On the one hand, there is a substitution effect, because the same product can be produced with less labour. On the other, there is a compensating effect, because prices will be decreased and therefore product demand and also labour demand will be increased. In this study, the relative strength of the two effects is discussed and a brief empirical analysis for Germany is given.

In summary, the present volume presents a range of new perspectives and advanced modelling experiments on the nexus of aging, migration and local or regional development, in particular labor markets. This nexus appears to be a complicated phenomenon, in which the different vectors in this force field are not easy to disentangle. Solid statistical data bases and modern statistical econometric tools are a *sine qua non* for an enhanced understanding of the complexity of labor markets in an aging and open world. Similarly, labour market policy is fraught with many uncertainties and contradictory forces, which can only be unravelled by using sophisticated research tools.

6   Value of the Book and Its Contributions

The book provides value added contributions to the literature on labor market functionality, aging and migration research. Here, we provide encapsulated examples from the book that illustrate its important contributions. Clearly, one of these appears in Chap. 2 which provides a literature review on migration, aging and the confluence of these with regional labor market processes. Others are elaborated in the following paragraphs.

6.1   Conceptual and Framework Contributions

There are several places in this book where new and improved conceptual framework contributions appear. For example, Chap. 3 shows the diversity or heterogeneity of motivations that drive migration behavior including the more traditional goal to permanently relocate. However, more recent types of migration where motivations are more complex such as return, circular, chain and temporary moves are also examined. It is also observed that the more recent forms of migration might be used to mitigate temporary and possibly longer-term tensions in the regional labor markets of Europe and elsewhere. Another novel conceptual contribution, migration motivated by climate change, is examined in Chap. 4, where it is concluded that climate change is difficult to predict and thus also any associated migration response. Consequently, linking migration to climate change is difficult to achieve with any accuracy, particularly at the local and regional level. The authors conclude that future effort should be focused on improving climate change measurement and policies to guide community adaptation and resilience in the face of extreme climate events.

Another interesting contribution is presented in Chap. 5 where the institutional barriers to migration are examined in the face of physical, and human and societal pressures such as famine, war, poverty and so on in South Asia. South Asia is a fruitful context for this research given the huge divergences between poverty and development among nations and regions which produce a variety of motivations for migration.

A final example is presented in Chap. 15 where career moves (and migration) of different workforce professionals to the Bendigo Region in Australia are examined. This research shows that bank employee career changes tend to result in moves in and about the Bendigo Region, while health/hospital and council sectors in Bendigo tend to draw employees from broader metropolitan and rural areas and locations outside the region. The difference in these career type groups migration behavior is partly in keeping with the general trend for professionals to migrate to metropolitan centers but also indicates that not all professional types of behavior can be explained by metropolitan population center pull forces. These examples illustrate some of the novel thinking and research concepts and frameworks that appear in the present book.

6.2 Methodological Contributions

There are also new methodological contributions, not the least of which are illustrated by the research methodology used and introduced in the Bendigo analysis above (Chap. 15) and by the examination of the relationship between climate change and migration (Chap. 5). However, there are several others. For example, research reported in Chap. 14 which shows that traditional applications of Gibrat's and Zipf's laws to a set of regional units vary, when they are recalibrated for sub-populations such as the aged cohort. Further, it is observed that population and employment do not vary evenly across spatial units, so that results of applications of Gibrat and Zipf laws will differ depending on the variable used to calibrate their applications. This provides evidence for the importance of considering these and other variables in the interpretation of the results of applications of Gibrat's and Zipf's Laws.

Another example (Chap. 11) is a case where different methodologies are combined to examine the relationship between demographic aging and regional labor market employment levels. The authors hypothesize that there is considerable variance in the nature of this relationship across regions in Germany, i.e., heterogeneity is likely a key factor. Regression techniques combined with Finite Mixture Modeling (FMM) are used to create self-organizing maps of regions with similar relationships between demographic aging and employment. This synthesis of modeling techniques is used to examine the impact of young age cohorts on regional labor markets which are shown to be heterogeneous and that exhibit different levels of resilience. These are samples of some of the creative methodological approaches used in the book.

The book also offers a wide and diverse array of empirical findings regarding the dynamic relationship between aging and dynamic demographic structural elements, as they impact regional labor markets. Some of these findings have been referenced in the discussions above on new conceptual and methodological contributions of the book. The focus here is largely on empirical findings and their policy implications.

6.3   Empirical Contributions

A collage of empirical findings is presented below drawing from several different chapters along with their policy implications. Here the focus is on empirical findings related to the relationship between structural demographic change, for example, in aging and youth cohorts and labor market functioning. Other empirical and policy related findings are presented above in the examples provided.

Several chapters argue conceptually and on the basis of empirical research that the impact of aging and other structural demographic elements will be heterogeneous across regions. One of the most emphatic is Chap. 11, in which an analysis of German regional data reveals that the impact of youth cohorts on labor market performance is heterogeneous across regions. While heterogeneity is usually an assumption in studies of groups of regions, this is not always true. But the work in the book clearly demonstrates the importance of variability across regions.

In Germany and other countries where the population is expected to decline in the near future, the working age population is expected to shrink faster than the aged or pensioner cohort which will put pressure on the welfare system. Analysis of a policy of exhausting the available labor from such sources as females, older workers and immigration finds that this policy would not harm firm productivity, despite the absence of a strong positive relationship of such a policy and firm level productivity (Chap. 10).

Population aging is often assumed to be associated with increased worker participation and reduced unemployment levels. However, research presented in Chap. 12 finds that the initial effect is as expected, but that later the participation rate decreases and the unemployment level increases, i.e., the pattern reverses over time. Also, this work finds that the impact of a larger aging cohort on the regional economy is felt most in the wage effect. This study uses data from ten federal states of Germany between 1970 and 2014.

An examination of survey responses from a sample of West German young male full-time employees over the period 1999–2010 finds that an increase of 1% in the youth share of employment is associated with a 3% decrease in youth wages (Chap. 13). Further analysis suggests that the above result occurs due to spillover effects: members of larger age groups likely move relatively into lower paying occupations.

6.4   Policy Contributions

Both aging and migration are vectors that are disequilibrating forces impinging on regional labor markets. While these factors are not problematic forces in all regional labor markets, they are impacting factors for many. Disproportionate aging changes the source of labor and thus the structure of the labor market. As seniors become a more dominant element of the population, the proportion of the traditional working age cohort will decrease which implies that maintenance of the regional economy must change. The various changes that might be considered in a seniors-dominated region could be via technological change (e.g., robotics), extending employment age of the seniors-cohort, expanding employment of other cohorts, e.g., women, younger cohorts (via lowering the child labor age for seasonal work), selective migration, and possibly structural economic change to less labor intensive activities. Many of the chapters provide policy suggestions aimed at use of these various adjustment approaches and for managing the institutional barriers (see Chaps. 4 and 5) to their deployment, e.g, see chapters and the unexpected effects that occur in some cases (see e.g., Chaps. 6, 7, 8, 12, 13 and 15).

The changing nature of migration includes not only permanent moves but also temporary, return, circular and chain moves thus creating new alternatives for using migration policy as a novel way to adjust regional labor markets. Most of the chapters in keeping with this view of migration, view it as an adjustment mechanism for addressing labor market disequilibria (see for example, Chap. 10). At the same time, migration can also be seen as a disruptive force, e.g., when migration leads to labor market dysfunctionality due to an excess of in-migration leading to higher dependency levels. The contributions included here have only to a limited extent considered this role of migration in labor market performance.

Some of the chapters in this volume examine the appropriateness of labor market policy in other ways. For example, Chap. 2 in the context of sustainable growth, Chap. 4 in the context of climate change, Chap. 6 in the context of lagging regions, and Chap. 15 in the context of relationships between migration of young adults and occupational structure and performance of regional labor markets.

As illustrated with these examples, aging and other structural changes in the population distribution are impacting and will impact efficiency and equity in the operation of regional labor markets. But these are only illustrative examples from the great many contributions in the book. There are of course many other findings beyond these examples.

7   New Research Pathways and Data Bases

New findings regarding the performance of regional labor markets in response to aging and other structural changes lay a foundation for future research. Clearly, other topics such as the role of migration in labor markets and change are examined and provide a basis for future research into how the evolution in migration types (temporary, circular, chain and return) might offer instruments for managing disequilibria in labor markets. On the other hand, such new contemporary migration forms could also be the source of such labor market disequilibria.

Beyond these general observations on possible future directions that the research reported here might take, there are several specific topics that are worthy of comment. One of these is that more than half of the papers in the book are empirical, which most of these use German regional data for the empirical analysis. Future research is needed using data from other countries and regions to test for the generalizability of the new findings presented herein.

Further, there are perhaps other novel ways to obtain data for research examining the interface between population structural changes and the performance of labor markets in this era of big data. Such data which is not only large but often is in a state of continuous growth and evolution rather than fixed data sets, as in the past, offers a variety of alternative ways to construct research into the topics addressed in this volume. Moreover, there are ways using social media and communication in the form of near or real-time data to conduct quasi-experimental analyses or to draw numerous samples that enable producing many analyses and tests of hypotheses. In short, future research that seeks to test or extend the results presented in this book can not only use different existing data sets, but may also use different approaches given the nature of data sets that are continuously expanding.

Most of the papers presented in this collection offer various policy lessons or prescriptions. However, these are often presented in light of the immediate research findings and not integrated into a broader policy framework. This suggests that there is an opportunity for examination of broader public policy analyses. For example, a policy-oriented workshop and associated edited book or a journal special edition might be undertaken to examine the public policy issues and approaches to the impact growing aging and/or youth cohorts are having on geographic labor markets. Similarly, a focus on the evolving nature of migration and how this may impact economic performance of labor markets begs for more empirical and related policy analysis in different parts of the world.

References

Guerin B, Hoorens S, Khodyakou D, Yaqub O (2015) A growing and ageing population: global societal trends to 2030: thematic report 1. Rand Corporation, Santa Monica, CA. https:www.rand.org/pubs/research_reportsRR92031.html. Accessed 23 June 2018

International Organization for Migration (2016) Global migration trends factsheet 2015. International Organization for Migration, Geneva. https://gmdac.iom.int/global-migration-trends-factsheet. Accessed 23 June 2018

Turchin P (2003) Complex population dynamics: a theoretical/empirical synthesis. Princeton University Press, Princeton, NJ

UNICEF (2013) Population dynamics: international migration, children & adolescents. UNICEF, New York, NY. https://www.unicdf.org/socialpolicy/files/Populations_Dynamics_and_Migrations(1).pdf. Accessed 23 June 2018

Part I
The Century of Migration and Aging: A Review of Labor Market Effect

Chapter 2
Aging and Migration: An Overview

K. Bruce Newbold

1 Introduction

For decades, global population concerns have focused on rapid population growth, driven by high birth rates and young populations, resulting in a global population explosion that saw the world's population grow from approximately 2 billion in 1900 to over 7.4 billion by 2016. Despite the assurance of continued population growth over the coming decades due to population momentum and persistently high fertility in some countries (notably sub-Saharan Africa), population aging—whereby the median age of a country or region increases due to declining fertility rates and increased life expectancy—has now emerged as *the* global population concern (Harper 2014).

Below replacement fertility levels and longer life expectancies have resulted in shrinking populations and aging populations. Japan, which is the world's 'oldest' country when measured by median age (46.9 years) has a total fertility rate of 1.5 (recalling that a fertility of 2.1 is typically considered to be required for replacement). With its low fertility rate, Japan's population is projected to decline from 125.3 million in 2016 to just slightly greater than 100 million by 2050, assuming no significant changes in fertility or international migration (Population Reference Bureau 2016). But Japan is far from alone: With the major exception of much of sub-Saharan Africa, the majority of the world's countries have either nearly or fully completed the demographic transition, transitioning from a high fertility and mortality regime to a low fertility and mortality regime (Franklin and Plane 2017). Fertility rates below replacement level are the new norm. Even in China, where concerns with high fertility and rapid population growth led to the implementation

K. Bruce Newbold (✉)
School of Geography & Earth Sciences, McMaster University, Hamilton, Canada
e-mail: newbold@mcmaster.ca

© Springer International Publishing AG, part of Springer Nature 2018   19
U. Blien et al. (eds.), *Modelling Aging and Migration Effects on Spatial Labor Markets*, Advances in Spatial Science,
https://doi.org/10.1007/978-3-319-68563-2_2

of the one-child policy to hasten fertility reduction, concerns have turned to an aging population and its support given the rapid increase in the proportion of its population that is over 65 years.

Although aging is a global phenomenon, it will occur at a different pace and with varying intensities across countries and regions (Kim and Hewings 2013), with some countries already seeing dramatic aging, and others just starting to see their populations' age. Regardless, the old will represent an increasingly large proportion of the population, with implications for economic development, the welfare state, public finance, consumption and mobility patterns, communities, and labor force participation. Drawing upon multiple examples, the following chapter explores some of these issues, with the intent of setting the background for the balance of the book by providing the reader with an overview of aging and migration issues.

2 The Demography of Aging

Aging populations can be characterized by different demographic measures. Globally, the proportion of the population over 65 is expected to represent over 20% of the world's population by 2050. Being amongst the first to complete the demographic transition, western, developed countries have grown increasingly older, characterized by older median ages and larger proportional shares of their older populations (65+). For example, 18% of the developed world's population is now 65 years old or greater, compared to just 7% in the less developed world (PRB 2016). Many European Union countries, along with Japan, have some of the highest proportions of older populations, with 27% of Japan's population aged 65 or older, and 19% of the population in the European Union over age 65. Meanwhile, the median age (2016) in the EU is 42.7 years. Similarly, life expectancies are typically the greatest in the developed world, averaging 79 years compared to just 68 years in less developed countries.

Population aging is further demonstrated in the shift in old dependency ratios, defined as the ratio of the older (65+) 'dependent' population relative to the labor force aged population (aged 15–64) which can 'support' the older, dependent population. When there are fewer working-age adults relative to the old, the labor force age group has a greater dependency burden: more people to support with the same income and assets. Between 1960 and 2015, the proportion of dependents in the European Union (those 65 and over) increased from 15% to 29%, pointing to a shrinking labor force that is able to support the old (World Bank). In the United States, the old dependency ratio is expected to increase from the current (2015) ratio of 23% to 30% by 2020, reflecting the aging of the US population (Ortman and Velkoff 2014). At the global scale, the proportion of dependents per 100 workers has risen from 9% to 13% in the same period.

When we refer to an aging population, the literature has tended to define and focus on those who are 65 years old or greater, with 65 being the typical retirement age. But this single 65+ age group is far from homogenous. Increasingly, discussions around aging societies have focused on the 'old-old', often defined as those who are 80 and over, while younger cohorts (i.e., 65–79) are the 'younger old', a group that typically retains a high quality of life, good health, either full or partial engagement in the labor force, and are more likely to move as compared to their older counterparts (Statistics Canada 2011). Beyond these usual dividers, it is also important to consider who *will* be old. The aging of the baby boom cohort, particularly in North America, parts of Europe, and Australia has been described by some as an approaching tsunami (Frey 2001), given the relative size of this cohort and their ability to shape the political and economic structure of their respective societies. Baby boomers have, for instance, strained health and education systems, and their movement in the United States has contributed to population growth in the Southwest, population decline of the Northeast, and the 'rural renaissance' as they passed through their most migratory years (Plane and Rogerson 1991; Plane 1992; Pandit 1997).

Although population aging reflects broad demographic processes, it has clear spatial patterns and ultimately implications, with rapidly aging regions and metropolitan areas reflecting both aging-in-place and the out-migration of younger cohorts (Frey 2001, 2011). In the United States, for example, northern rustbelt cities are, on average, older than their counterparts in the west and south, which have experienced in-migration of younger cohorts, driven by amenities and job opportunities. Typically, areas experiencing the fastest growth of the old are located in America's Sun Belt. At smaller spatial scales, a growing number of older households are found in suburban locations, a legacy of residential preferences amongst aging boomers and aging-in-place (Frey 2011). Similar patterns are found elsewhere, with large cities often having comparatively younger populations, while rural and smaller cities are often characterized by older populations.

3   Migration, Immigration and Aging

Although aging populations broadly represent the outcome of long-term population processes and fertility choices, an important exception is the impact of migration and/or immigration and the ability to (comparatively) rapidly change the demographic profile of a region. Countries such as Canada have used immigration to forestall population decline, with immigration now accounting for approximately two-thirds of Canada's population growth (Statistics Canada 2016). Immigration's impact can be dramatic, as illustrated by population projections reported by the Population Reference Bureau (PRB): In its 2007 World Data Sheet, the PRB projected that Germany's population would shrink from over 82 million in 2007 to 71.4 million by 2050. In its 2016 World Data Sheet, however, the PRB estimated Germany's population would decline to just 81.0 million by 2050, with the difference largely attributable to its intake of refugees in 2015 and 2016.

Reflecting the well-known mobility patterns across the life course (Rogers et al. 1978), increasing age is associated with lower propensities to migrate relative to younger cohorts, an outcome observed regardless of location, time, or geographic scale. With increasing age, migrations become more difficult and costly (both physically and emotionally) as employment, families, other household assets or declining health tie individuals to their location. Many of the reasons for declining migration propensities by age can be attributed to life-cycle changes such as marriage, children, and empty nesting (i.e., Goetzke and Rave 2013; Plane and Jurjevich 2009), concepts made popular by Rossi (1955). Sjaastad's (1962) human capital theory also helps to explain differing migration rates by age, with young adults having a longer career time to recoup the costs of moving than older individuals.

The implication of the age-migration schedule is twofold. First, younger adults will typically migrate for economic reasons (Partridge and Rickman 2003) and to maximize their returns to human capital (Brown and Scott 2012). In doing so however, age-selective out-migration from a region (especially of younger labor force participants) can leave behind a smaller, older, poorer and less healthy population, a situation experienced across rural areas and small communities over-and-over again and reinforcing the spatial differences in the age structure of populations. Population loss, along with the loss of income, savings, and related human capital (Nelson 2005; Newbold and Meredith 2012) has implications for service delivery and the fiscal capacity of communities (Davenport et al. 2009). Concurrently, schools and other services or programs directed toward younger age cohorts may be forced to close or reduce the range of services offered in areas with shrinking and aging populations. Receiving communities, on the other hand, may benefit from in-migration by gaining human capital, transferable income (i.e., retirement), and offsetting population loss.

Second, lower mobility rates amongst the old mean that the majority of the old prefer to age-in-place, retaining local capital and relationships (i.e., Davis 2013). Between 2009 and 2010, for example, only 5.8% of older persons in the US moved, compared to 16.9% of the under 65 population. Amongst the old that moved, most (58.7%) stayed in the same county, and 78.2% remained in the same state (Administration on Aging 2011). For those that do relocate, their destination choices and the motivations for moving are often different from their younger counterparts.

Movement amongst the old reflects a series of moves that is frequently age dependent, often leading to a small 'retirement peak' observed at or around age 65—the typical retirement age, as individuals adjust their location and transition from work to retirement. Free from labor market or economic needs, the old typically migrate for a different set of reasons as compared to those still in the labor force. Amongst the young-old, migrations are often driven by amenities and 'down the urban hierarchy' into smaller urban or rural areas as evidenced by research in the United States (Karner and Dorfman 2012; Plane et al. 2005; Plane and Jurjevich 2009) and Canada (Newbold 2011). Migration decisions within this demographic typically reflect the desire for lower costs of living, reduced congestion, or to be closer to amenities and/or family (children and their own aging parents), along with knowledge of specific places such as where they grew up, vacationed, or worked, with a well-established literature that discusses the concept of return migration amongst the old to their places of birth or long-term residence (see, for example, Newbold and Bell 2001). Amongst the old-old, late-life migrations are often associated with health issues, bringing individuals closer to family or into institutions for care.

With aging, patterns of labor force participation will change, leading to differential migration patterns. In some regions, the primary effect will be changes in the age structure, with concomitant declines in labor force participation rates. In other cases, migration will alter the number of people not in the labor force. The diversity of changes in participation pose different challenges for regions (Nichols et al. 2015). Declines in mobility rates and shifting labor market opportunities will have spatial effects. In the US and other countries, rates of migration at all spatial scales have declined, in part owing to population aging, with Karahan and Rhee (2014) estimating that population aging accounts for approximately 50% of the observed decrease in inter-state migration in the United States owing to a general equilibrium effect. But population aging is not the only reason for this decline, with Molloy et al. (2014) suggesting that part of the reason for the observed decline is due to a reduced net benefit to changing employers, making relocations (for employment reasons) less attractive. That is, a prime reason for the decline in movement is related to labor market opportunities. Evidence from Denmark (Mitze and Schmidt 2015) suggests that agglomeration economies are key drivers of migration, as compared traditional labor market and housing effects. Importantly, both studies suggest that the determinants of migration, and concomitantly the spatial effects of migration, are changing.

4   The Economics of Aging

With the share of its older population projected to increase from 8.3% in 2010 to nearly 24% in 2050 (Kochher and Oates 2014), China's rapidly aging population has raised concerns about its ability to support its older population given a shrinking workforce. At the same time, projections suggest that its economic growth will be reduced by as much as three percentage points per year in the coming years because of its shifting population structure (Sheets and Sockin 2013). But, while China may be an extreme example of the economic implications of an aging society given the pace of aging in the country, it is not alone: Shrinking populations and aging will challenge economies, social welfare systems, healthcare systems and labor markets across the globe. More broadly, because the old are generally less economically productive than the young, a growing older population suggests that economic growth will be slower than in the past and that the comparatively smaller labor-force aged cohorts will be required to support the older population. In turn, pressure will be exerted on pensions, health and long-term care with a smaller labor force supporting such programs, ideas which are explored further in the following paragraphs.

Reflecting shifting dependency ratios, one of the most visible outcomes associated with population aging will be the aging of the labor force and a comparatively smaller labor force relative to the old. Already, baby boomers have started to leave the work force and the size of the cohorts following baby boomers—or more precisely the workers and the taxpayers that will support baby boomers in their old age—are smaller. The loss of the working age population could have a significant impact on per capita income, unless the loss of labor can be compensated through other means, such as increased productivity (Park and Hewings 2007a) or through migration and/or immigration. Retirements will potentially result in a shortage of skilled labor, with a lack of middle-aged employees ready to fill senior management positions. The same problem is observed in health care, the resource sector, finance, teaching and education, with a bi-modal workforce of older, senior and experienced employees, fewer workers in the middle cohorts, and young and much less experienced workers. Immigration can help offset declines associated with an aging population, but only after immigrants acquire skills and experience to increase their productivity (Park and Hewings 2007b).

Aging populations may also have a significant impact on savings and capital accumulation. Older cohorts are less likely to spend on consumer goods as they move into retirement, despite having higher accumulated savings per capita than younger cohorts. At the same time, they tend to dissave by spending down their savings. While individuals may also save more for retirement expecting a longer lifespan, reductions in spending may be compounded by the fact that many baby boomers are heading into retirement carrying a larger debt load that has been encouraged by low interest rates and a culture of spending. The debt that boomers carry, along with their fixed incomes, will incentivize reduced consumer spending. Aging populations may be associated with declining economies, given reduced incentives to invest in new stores and housing and reduced infrastructure investment (Yoon and Hewings 2006).

If the workforce is not being replaced, then taxes and consumer spending that are part of this group are not being replaced. Future taxpayers will need to carry a heavier load as they pay for pensions, health plans and other services, assuming that the same level of services is maintained or desired. Consequently, aging populations are expected to increase fiscal burdens to governments (Park and Hewings 2007a). Population aging is expected to push public pensions and health care programs to consume greater proportions of gross domestic product (GDP), with changing demographics a concern for governments and employers alike. Nationally, expenditures associated with pensions and health care are projected to increase as a share of GDP, with public pension expenditures expected to represent approximately 15% of GDP in several European countries by 2050 (Kochher and Oates 2014). In the United States, the impact is less severe, with pension expenditures estimated to only increase from 6.8% of GDP in 2010 to 8.5% in 2050. Like many other countries, the US Social Security system is based on the taxation of workers to support the older, retired generation (Silverstein 2008). Given a smaller workforce and increased life expectancy, the number of beneficiaries has grown, leading to concerns that the Social Security system will be depleted or will offer smaller benefits. For many employers, especially those that provide defined benefit plans to their employees (Silverstein 2008), pensions remain a high cost, even as many employers have moved toward defined contribution plans whereby the employee shoulders investment risks.

Concerns also revolve around public health care expenditures. In the U.S., public health expenditures are projected to more than double to 14.9% in 2050 (Kochher and Oates 2014). Large increases in expenditures related to health care are also expected in multiple countries due to the increased demands that will be placed on a range of services that are important to older cohorts, including health and long-term care. Household finances may also be stressed, forcing people to work into their retirement (Clements et al. 2012; OECD 2012, 2013). While this sounds problematic, it is important to realize that seniors are experiencing longer, healthier lives on average, with the greatest pressures on the health care (and other sectors) amongst the oldest old. Beyond health services, the range of community services that people require after they retire differs from that during other stages of life.

The age-structure of the older population at any particular geographic scale will have an impact on service demand and delivery. Older cohorts typically demand and use a different range of services as compared to younger cohorts, with the old typically being significant users of recreation services, public transit, affordable housing, and long-term care, amongst other services. Perhaps not surprisingly, older populations will likely demand changes in the allocation of public investments, including the reallocation of resources from children to meet the needs of the old. At smaller spatial scales, regional (i.e., state or provincial) and local social services and infrastructure needs will consequently change with the aging of the population. Coupled with employment loss, out-migration could have important implications for service delivery, economic development and planning. For example, the selective out-migration of workers along with relatively healthy and wealthy new retirees can leave behind an older, poorer and less healthy population, with implications for service delivery and fiscal capacity of communities (Davenport et al. 2009), while services geared toward younger cohorts, including schooling, will be forced to close.

Finally, with higher levels of savings and social welfare systems in place, developed nations are comparatively well prepared for an aging population. For them, the question is whether aging populations will lead to increasingly larger proportional shares of GDP. Emerging countries, on the other hand, typically spend much less on social welfare and health programs. The challenge for these countries is to build their social welfare and health programs to meet the needs of their aging populations even as they experience slowing economic growth (Clements et al. 2012; Kochher and Oates 2014).

5 Policy and Aging Populations

Although there are comparatively few tools, including changing labor policies, fertility preferences, migration, and immigration, population aging can be offset or minimized. But, the effectiveness of each of these tools is limited. For example, changes to labor policies such as delayed retirement, changes in the eligible age for retirement benefits, or reductions in benefits could offset or diminish some of the impacts of an aging population (i.e., Park and Hewings 2007c). Several countries, including the United States, Canada, the United Kingdom and Australia, have raised the age at which individuals are eligible for state-funded pension plans, and/or have abolished mandatory retirement ages. However, such policy changes may be tinkering at the margins, and also have negative effects in terms of overall losses to welfare (Park and Hewings 2007c).

Second, changes to fertility, and specifically policies, programs and incentives aimed at increasing fertility levels can reduce the median age of the population by increasing the fertility rate and hence the proportion of the young. But, programs or policies meant at enhancing fertility levels are long-term and have a poor track record: the province of Quebec in Canada, France, and other countries have tried to enhance fertility but with relatively little success (Haub 2008). Attempts to increase fertility levels through the provision of various financial incentives such as paid maternity and paternity leave, free or reduced-cost childcare and tax benefits, have some (albeit limited) impact on fertility rates (Haub 2008), although increased fertility may just reflect a change in the timing of fertility, but no real increase in the number of desired children. Even in China, which is facing the prospect of the very rapid aging of its population owing to its one-child policy, anxiety over its expanding elderly population and smaller labor force led the Chinese government to abandon its one-child policy in 2014. To date, China's fertility rate has not changed dramatically, suggesting that low fertility is here to stay. Moreover, altering fertility choices tends to be a rather long term approach to offset aging, not to mention the fact that you need to mess with social conventions and needs.

Third, migration and immigration are potentially the most viable options for altering age profiles over the short-term. Internal, domestic migration could offer relief, but only at the regional level, given population gain in one region implies population loss in another. While the old have relatively low rates of mobility, a growing older population means by default that more old will move, even if migration rates stay the same. That is, there is an important distinction between the rate of migration and the population that is at-risk of moving, with the growth of the 65+ demographic ensuring that the number of older migrants will increase. Migration will likely have the greatest impact at the municipal scale, leading some communities to market themselves as retirement destinations and attracting migrants to amenity rich areas (Kupiszewski et al. 2001a), access to health care, and/or lower housing costs and lower taxes (Karner and Dorfman 2012; Kupiszewski et al. 2001a, 2001b; Kawase and Nakazawa 2009).

Certainly, the ability to attract seniors may be beneficial in the face of long-term population aging, with the intent of maintaining or growing a population and utilizing existing infrastructure. However, it has not been established that promoting the concentration of retirees in a community is an effective economic development policy, despite the impact of their local expenditures and taxation (Serow 2003). Further, while communities that can attract in-migrants may benefit from the in-flow, these migrants must come from somewhere, meaning that communities that experience out-migration are placed at a disadvantage. In the Canadian context, for example, western provinces tend to have younger median ages, while the eastern, Maritime provinces tend to be older, reflective of decades of out-migration from the economically depressed east and in-migration to the resource rich western provinces, particularly Alberta (Statistics Canada 2012). In both cases—receiving and sending centers—changing age profiles will have implications including for the location and types of services provided (Gaigné and Thisse 2009). Inevitably, however, everyone ages, and unless a community is able to maintain the inflow of younger migrants, the economic benefits of being an aging community could turn to an overall cost, given the demand on related programs and services as noted earlier in this chapter.

This therefore leaves immigration as an option to reduce or slow the aging of a population. But such a policy can only work if immigrants younger than the median age of the population are encouraged to immigrate. Immigration can aid population growth, but countries cannot offset aging without tremendous increases to annual immigration flows (United Nations 2001), a policy that is problematic as governments seek to integrate newcomers, with tensions over immigration highlighted in European elections in 2016 and the rise of anti-immigrant parties. Moreover, even immigrants will age and join the ranks of the retired, meaning that the flow of younger immigrants must be sustained.

6 Conclusions

Population aging will have significant effects on local, regional and national economic systems and policies. Although the impacts of population aging can be minimized, policy options are limited given the inability, slow response times, or minimal impact of programs focusing on increasing fertility rates or labor market policies to offset population aging. Of all the policy options, migration and/or immigration appear to offer short-term solutions to population aging. But neither option will alleviate or solve population aging, especially in a regionally heterogeneous labor market where aging and migration may be both complementary and conflicting phenomena.

Proportionately, migration by the old is not a significant phenomenon given low migration rates amongst this group. However, aging populations mean that larger numbers of seniors will be on the move in the coming years. As noted elsewhere in the literature (i.e., Newbold and Meredith 2012), policy concerns associated with the migration of the old will be primarily located at the local level, where recreation, community, and other services are delivered and urban planning and housing policies are created and implemented. Conversely, the labor and economic impacts of aging will be both regional and national in scope.

Regardless of whether communities are gaining or losing older populations, there is a need for communities and governments to be proactive in planning and program development to meet the needs of an aging population. Developed by the World Health Organization (2007), concepts such as "Age Friendly Communities" can be employed to incorporate "active aging practices" into the local context, including areas such as transportation and the built community. The question is, however, whether communities are adequately prepared to address the needs of an older population, regardless of whether they are net receivers or senders of older migrants.

Despite the interest and attention given to aging and shrinking populations over the past decade, substantive questions remain, with additional research and insight required in a number of areas, some of which the balance of this book cover. Topics such as the impact of migration on the labor market, population movements, housing, pension systems, and differences in the experiences between the developed and developing world require additional insights. The unprecedented changes to the population structure of many countries pose huge challenges for their economies and their aging populations, and have prompted questions including:

- Will their capacity to support a growing number of retirees and fund long-term health care for those of advanced age prove sufficient?
- How will domestic migration respond to changing demographics?
- Can immigration offset population aging and how will it reshape society?
- What other demographic or socioeconomic policies can be used to decrease the impacts of an aging society?
- What policy implications are associated with aging populations, and how can policy best address aging?

The following chapters explore some of these ideas in greater detail.

References

Administration on Aging (2011) A profile of older Americans: 2011. U.S. Department of Health and Human Services, Washington, DC http://www.aarp.org/content/dam/aarp/livable-communities/learn/demographics/a-profile-of-older-americans-2011-aarp.pdf Accessed 28 Nov 2016

Brown WM, Scott DM (2012) Human capital location choice: accounting for amenities and thick labor markets. J Reg Sci 52(5):787–808

Clements B, Coady D, Eich F, Gupta S, Kangur A, Shang B, Soto M (2012) The challenge of public pension reform in advanced and emerging market economies, International Monetary Fund, Occasional Paper 275 (2012)

Davenport J, Rathwell T, Rosenberg MW (2009) Aging in Atlantic Canada: service-rich and service-poor communities. Health Policy 5(1):145–160

Davis LS (2013) Aging in place suburban style. J Am Plan Assoc 79(6):24–28

Franklin RS, Plane DA (2017) The view from over the hill: regional research in a post-demographic transition world. In: Jackson R, Scheaffer P (eds) Regional research frontiers. Springer, Cham

Frey WH (2001) The baby boom tsunami. The Milliken Institute Review. http://www.frey-demographer.org/briefs/B-2001-5_BabyBoomTsunami.pdf. Accessed 23 Nov 2016

Frey WH (2011) The uneven aging and 'younging' of America: state and metropolitan trends in the 2010 census. https://www.brookings.edu/research/the-uneven-aging-and-younging-of-america-state-and-metropolitan-trends-in-the-2010-census/

Gaigné C, Thisse J-F (2009) Aging nations and the future of cities. J Reg Sci 49:663–688

Goetzke F, Rave T (2013) Migration in Germany: a life cycle approach. Int Reg Sci Rev 36(2):167–182

Haub C (2008) Tracking Trends in Low Fertility Countries: An Uptick in Europe? Population Reference Bureau. http://www.prb.org/Publications/Articles/2008/tfrtrendsept08.aspx

Harper S (2014) Economic and social implications of aging societies. Science 346(6209):587–591

Karahan F, Rhee S (2014) Population aging, migration spillovers, and the decline in interstate migration. Federal Reserve Bank of New York Staff Reports, no. 699

Karner A, Dorfman J (2012) Retiree migration: considerations of amenity and health access drivers. Presented at the annual meeting of the Agricultural and Applied Economics Association, August 12, Seattle. Available at: http://ageconsearch.umn.edu/bitstream/124606/2/AAEA_Amenity_Migration_Retirees.pdf. Accessed 24 Nov 2016

Kawase A, Nakazawa K (2009) Long-term care insurance facilities and interregional migration of the elderly in Japan. Joint discussion paper series in economics, no. 39. MAGKS Network of the Universities of Aachen, Giessen, Göttingen, Kassel, Marburg and Siegen. Available at: https://ideas.repec.org/a/ebl/ecbull/eb-09-00561.html. Accessed 24 Nov 2016.

Kim T-J, Hewings GJD (2013) Endogenous growth in an aging economy: evidence and policy measures. Ann Reg Sci 50(3):705–730

Kochher R, Oates R (2014) Attitudes about aging: a global perspective. Pew Research Foundation. http://www.pewglobal.org/2014/01/30/attitudes-about-aging-a-global-perspective/. Accessed 28 Nov 2016

Kupiszewski M, Illeris S, Durham H, Rees P (2001a) Internal migration and regional population dynamics in Europe: Denmark case study. Working paper. University of Leeds, School of Geography, Leeds

Kupiszewski M, Borgegard L-E, Fransson U, Hakansson J, Durham H, Rees P (2001b) Internal migration and regional population dynamics in Europe: Sweden case study. Working paper, University of Leeds, School of Geography, Leeds

Mitze T, Schmidt TD (2015) Internal migration, regional labor markets and the role of agglomeration economies. Ann Regional Sci 55:61–101

Molloy R, Smith CL, Wozniak A (2014) Declining migration in the US: The role of the labor market. NBER Working Paper 20065, Cambridge MA. http://www.nber.org/papers/w20065

Nelson PB (2005) Migration and the regional redistribution of non-earnings income in the United States: metropolitan and nonmetropolitan perspectives from 1975 to 2000. Environ Plan A 37:1613–1636

Newbold KB (2011) Migration up and down Canada's urban hierarchy. Can J Urban Res 20(1):131–149

Newbold KB, Bell M (2001) Return and onwards migration in Canada and Australia: evidence from fixed interval data. Int Migr Rev 35(4):1157–1184

Newbold KB, Meredith T (2012) Migration among Canadian seniors: implications for public policy. IRPP Study 36. Institute for Research on Public Policy, Montreal

Nichols A, Martin S, Astone NM, Peters HE, Pendall R, Hildner KF, Stolte A (2015) The labor force in an aging and growing America. Mapping America's futures, Brief 4, Urban Institute, Washington DC

OECD (2012) Looking to 2060: Long-term global growth prospects. OECD Economic Policy Papers No. 03 (November 2012)

OECD (2013) Public spending on health and long-term care: a new set of projections. OECD Economic Policy Papers, No. 06 (June 2013)

Ortman JM, Velkoff VA (2014) An aging nation: the older population in the United States. US Census Bureau, New York

Pandit K (1997) Cohort and period effects in U.S. migration: how demographic and economic cycles influence the migration schedule. Ann Assoc Am Geogr 87:439–450

Park S, Hewings GJD (2007a) Aging and the regional economy: simulation results from the Chicago CGE model. Discussion paper 07-T-4, Regional Economics Applications Laboratory, University of Illinois, Urbana IL. www.real.uiuc.edu. Accessed 24 Nov 2016

Park S, Hewings GJD (2007b) Immigration, aging, and the regional economy. Discussion Paper 07-T-5, Regional Economics Applications Laboratory, University of Illinois, Urbana, IL. www.real.uiuc.edu. Accessed 24 Nov 2016

Park S, Hewings GJD (2007c) Does a change in retirement age affect a regional economy? Evidence from the Chicago economy. Discussion paper 07-T-6, Regional Economics Applications Laboratory, University of Illinois, Urbana IL. www.real.uiuc.edu. Accessed 24 November 2016

Partridge M, Rickman DS (2003) The waxing and waning of regional economies: The chicken-egg question of jobs versus people. J Urban Econ 53:76–97

Plane DA (1992) Age-composition change and the geographical dynamics of interregional migration in the U.S. Ann Assoc Am Geogr 82:64–85

Plane DA, Jurjevich JR (2009) Ties that no Population Reference Bureau, 2016

Plane DA, Rogerson PA (1991) Tracking the baby boom, the baby bust, and the echo generations: how age composition regulates US migration. Prof Geogr 43:416–430

Plane DA, Henrie CJ, Perry MJ (2005) Migration up and down the urban hierarchy and across the life course. PNAS 102(43):15313–15318

Population Reference Bureau (2016) World population data sheet, 2016. Population Reference Bureau, 2016, Washington DC

Rogers A, Racquillet R, Castro LJ (1978) Model migration schedules and their applications. Environ Plan A 10:475–502

Rossi PH (1955) Why families move: a study of the social psychology of urban residential mobility. Free Press, Glencoe, IL

Serow WJ (2003) Economic consequences of retiree concentrations: a review of North American studies. Gerontologist 43(6):897–903

Sheets N, Sockin R (2013) Global demographics: emerging markets to the rescue? Citi GPS. https://www.citivelocity.com/citigps/OpArticleDetail.action?recordId=301. Accessed 28 Nov 2016

Silverstein M (2008) Meeting the challenges of an aging workforce. Am J Ind Med 51(4):269–280. https://doi.org/10.1002/ajim.20569

Sjaastad LA (1962) The costs and returns of human migration. J Political Econ 70:80–93

Statistics Canada (2011) Delayed retirement: a new trend? Component of statistics Canada catalogue no. 75-001-X, Perspectives on labour and income. Available at: http://www.statcan.gc.ca/access_acces/alternative_alternatif.action?l=eng&loc=2011004/article/11578-eng.pdf. Accessed 26 Nov 2016

Statistics Canada (2012) http://www.statcan.gc.ca/pub/91-215-x/2012000/part-partie2-eng.htm. Accessed 5 Dec 2016

Statistics Canada (2016) http://www.statcan.gc.ca/pub/11-630-x/11-630-x2014001-eng.htm. Accessed 24 Nov 2016

United Nations (2001) Replacement migration: is it a solution to declining and ageing populations? Population Division, Department of Economic and Social Affairs, New York, NY

World Bank http://data.worldbank.org/indicator/SP.POP.DPND.OL?end=2015&start=1960. Accessed 17 Nov 2016

World Health Organization (2007) Global age friendly cities: a guide. World Health Organization, Geneva

Yoon SG, Hewings GJD (2006) Impacts of demographic changes in the Chicago Region. Discussion paper 2006-07-T-6, Regional Economics Applications Laboratory, University of Illinois, Urbana. www.real.uiuc.edu. Accessed 17 Nov 2016

Chapter 3
Fortunado's, Desperado's and Clandestino's in Diaspora Labour Markets: The Circular 'Homo Mobilis'

Karima Kourtit, Peter Nijkamp, and Masood Gheasi

1 Introduction: People on the Move

The wealth of nations and regions is often explained from the availability and efficient use of productive resources, such as human capital or material inputs. The volume and quality of human capital in a given region is co-determined by socio-demographic factors, such as natural growth, migration, age composition and education. One of the founding fathers of regional economics, August Lösch, has written in 1936 a seminal contribution on the impact of population dynamics on economic growth, in particular in relation to business cycles. It seems plausible that changes in the quantity and quality of human capital—in the form of either cross-border population movements ('migration') or changes in the composition of the productive population ('ageing')—will have profound impacts of the functioning

K. Kourtit (✉)
JADS (Jheronimus Academy of Data Science), 's-Hertogenbosch, The Netherlands

Adam Mickiewicz University, Poznan, Poland

Tinbergen Institute, Amsterdam, The Netherlands

Uppsala University, Uppsala, Sweden
e-mail: k.kourtit@jads.nl

P. Nijkamp
JADS (Jheronimus Academy of Data Science), 's-Hertogenbosch, The Netherlands

Adam Mickiewicz University, Poznan, Poland

Tinbergen Institute, Amsterdam, The Netherlands
e-mail: p.nijkamp@jads.nl

M. Gheasi
VU University, Amsterdam, The Netherlands
e-mail: m.gheasi@vu.nl

© Springer International Publishing AG, part of Springer Nature 2018
U. Blien et al. (eds.), *Modelling Aging and Migration Effects on Spatial Labor Markets*, Advances in Spatial Science,
https://doi.org/10.1007/978-3-319-68563-2_3

of local or regional labour markets, and hence on the competitive position of regions. In this chapter we will address in particular migration—notably, temporary and circular migration—and changing age cohorts as determinants of regional development.

We live in the 'age of migration' and in the 'age of ageing'. The population dynamics resulting from a migrating and ageing society leads to far-reaching structural impacts on our contemporaneous space economy all over the world including regions. Human settlement patterns are decisively influenced by demographic evolution (e.g., ageing) and migration movements (Kourtit 2014, 2015). Both phenomena are drivers of local and regional labour markets and run parallel to socio-economic dynamics. Our contemporary world is in full swing. Ups and downs in socio-economic systems have become a structural feature of our modern society: rise is often accompanied—or followed up—by fall. It seems as though the general product life cycle theory manifests itself in many multi-faceted specific cycles: economic turbulence, demographic evolution, political fluctuations, urban dynamics, and so forth. The cyclicity of many socio-economic phenomena (in particular, population demography in the form of migration and refugee movements)—with greatly varying fluctuations in amplitude and time coverage, ranging from short-term cycles to long-range cycles—prompts a variety of intriguing research and policy questions on social and spatial dynamics in a modern open society. A prominent and pressing issue is of course whether cross-border migration will prompt economic growth and spatial-economic convergence (see Fratesi and Percoco 2014; Kanbur and Rapoport 2005; Kubis and Schneider 2016; Ostbye and Westerlund 2007; Ozgen et al. 2010). There is an extant literature on the theory of international migration. We refer here in particular to a recent interesting and informed study on international population movements from an analytical economic perspective, written by Kondoh (2016).

One of the most prominent phenomena which prompt nowadays splintering views on a modern society and its cohesiveness is without any doubt cross-border or international migration (see for a detailed overview Chiswick and Miller 2015). Clearly, unforeseen spatial-demographic developments and socio-economic disruptions caused by a massive influx of migrants or refugees is often seen as a tragedy for both sending and receiving countries, but may also be seen as an unprecedented and innovative opportunity for individuals to improve their own economic fortune ('fortunado's'). It is in the meantime broadly recognized that innovative behaviour and economic progress in a host economy depend also on a favourable local absorption capacity for migrants. Do such seedbed conditions also hold for contemporaneous large-scale migration movements? Can heterogeneity and fluctuation in migration inflows create an unstainable situation or, inversely, stabilize a local labour market? And which are the conditions to create a balanced migration situation that increases welfare in both a sending and a receiving country or region? These questions will be highlighted in the present paper.

We live nowadays in the 'age of migration' or the age of the 'homo mobilis', but this does not necessarily mean that migration is a uniform social-demographic phenomenon in space. It is clear that migration may have many 'faces', but a standard UN interpretation is that foreign migration means a cross-border movement from country A to B for a time span of at least half a year, irrespective of their motivation.

Some people deliberately leave their country of origin to seek for better opportunities elsewhere (the so-called *'fortunado's'*), but other people—refugees— are forced to leave their country of origin involuntarily as a consequence of war, political or religious suppression, natural disaster, or poverty (the so-called *'desperado's'*). Clearly, in the latter case they have to look for better living conditions elsewhere, so that at the end the search pattern and motivation of *'desperado's'* for an attractive host country resembles that of the *'fortunado's'*. In addition, there are in an open world with more healthy and wealthy people in an aging society, also many people who decide to spend the final part of their life in climatologically attractive places (the so-called *'pensionado's'*). The same may hold for the 'happy few' who have sufficient resources and leisure time to spend part of life elsewhere under favourable climatological conditions (see Suchecka and Urbaniak 2016). And finally, there is also an increasingly large share of cross-border migrants who have moved to another country (either as fortunado's or as desperado's) without being in the possession of the legally required documents in the form of visa, working permits or residential permits (the so-called *'clandestino's'*) (see also Leerkes et al. 2007).

In recent years the issue of illegal versus legal migration has gained much interest, especially because temporary migrants who normally stay in a host region for a limited time seem to care less about formal entry and labour market regulations. In most cases, two main types of restriction policies are employed, viz. border enforcement and internal enforcement (see Ethier 1986; Djajic 1997; Kondoh 2017). It is well-known that illegal (or undocumented) migrants often find a job in the grey or informal economy (e.g., daycare, restaurants). In a review article, Orrenius and Zavodny (2015) provide an overview of various theories on undocumented migration, e.g., risk-aversion job search theories, enforcement cost theories, unauthorized migration theories, self-selection theories, life-cycle theories, etc. It turns out that duration of stay is in many cases a critical variable for the decision in favour of illegal, often temporary border crossing (Reyes 2001).

It is noteworthy that the two demographic phenomena, viz. an aging society and the 'age of migration', may become mutually interwoven phenomena, since a lower labour force participation in a host country or region as a result of aging may prompt the need for a compensating socio-demographic mechanism in the form of immigration to meet the needs of labour markets in host regions. Clearly, education and skills of immigrants are also critical conditions in this context (see Newbold 2017).

It should be noted that in the history of migration many migration movements show a bilateral or two-sided nature of these flows. There are people moving from country A to B, but there are often also people going from country B to A. In an article published by Lutz et al. (2014a), the authors map out bilateral migration flows between many countries in our world in a 5-year time span (2005–2010), using a so-called circular plot. These bilateral migration plots display at a global level a rather robust pattern over the relevant period, although there are large variations among continents. Circular migration as organised labour migration with a frequent return character (from county A to B and visa vera) is an increasing popular phenomenon (e.g., from India and Malaysia to the Gulf states), especially for construction workers and educated migrants. It also turns out that over the relevant period concerned, Europe was the biggest receiver of migrants, while South Asia was the bigger sender. It is noteworthy that in all these migration plots schooling appeared to be a major determinant for the size of flows and the duration of stay. Finally, it should also be noted that for Europe in-migration is the major determinant of a (slight) population increase in various countries (see also Lutz et al. 2014b).

In the light of these observations, it is important to regard migration not exclusively as a structural one-directional flow between countries, but as a potential bilateral or symmetric flow (in the form of return migration or circular migration) or even as a multi-lateral flow (in the form of stepwise or chain migration). Income differences, cultural and geographic proximity, and education/schooling appear to be the critical factors for this pluriformity in migration behaviours (see Tubadij et al. 2015).

The present paper aims to provide a review of bilateral or multi-lateral migration flows, with particular emphasis on temporary circular migration as an organized mechanism for regional or national labour markets. After a broad description of some important facts, trends and underlying mechanisms for migration movements in Europe, we will zoom in here on circular migration as a vehicle for a balanced labour market policy in the EU. In the present study, circular migration policy will be evaluated from the perspective of a triple-win situation (viz. with benefits for the temporary migrants, for the sending country, and for the receiving country), using The Netherlands as an example.

This paper is organized as follows. After this introductory section, Sect. 2 will briefly describe the constellation of the migration system from the perspective of structural or temporary migration. The next section, Sect. 3, will offer a few illustrative statistical facts on the migration scene in Europe, and in particular on circular migration. In Sect. 4, some outcomes of a policy and applied research experiment and its implementation in the area of circular migration for The Netherlands will concisely be presented. The paper will be concluded with a policy perspective.

2   Structural or Temporary Migration

Population dynamics is one of the drivers of spatial and socio-economic dynamics in our world. This concept does not only refer to growth and decline of population as a result of births and deaths or of migration, but also of societal developments reflected in spatial aging patterns. Since aging means lower labour force participation rates, the question of compensating inflows into the labour market of aging host regions through a rise in immigration flows links population changes to migration.

Migration—both domestic and international—is not an exclusive phenomenon of the past decades. People all over the world have been moving around in search of better opportunities, sometimes forced by famine, natural disaster, war or religious suppression (desperado's), sometimes also driven by better economic conditions elsewhere (fortunado's) or by family formation or family re-unification. In the context of foreign migration, in the aftermath of WWII various immigration countries have emerged, such as the United States, Canada, South Africa, Australia, New Zealand or Brazil. But in the past decades, the flows of migration have been widened to virtually all countries in the world. This does not only hold for European countries, but also for Asian, African and Latin-American countries. In addition to the scope of migration, also the size of international migration has significantly increased. In the year 2010, the World Bank reported that more than three percent of the world population may be classified as migrant, and this share is steadily rising.

From a purely economic perspective, migration may be considered to be an equilibrating mechanism to match supply and demand on national labour markets. It is thus a phenomenon that has a welfare-enhancing effect. Notwithstanding this positive interpretation of migration, reality is often more complicated and harsh. In various cases, migrant sending countries are concerned about the loss of qualified labour force and about the waste of public expenditures for education of talented people leaving the country, even though remittances may offer a financial compensation for the loss of talent. On the other hand, migrant receiving countries complain about adjustment costs for migrants, tensions on local housing and labour markets, relatively high unemployment figures for migrants and associated high social welfare transfers to migrants, ethnic segregation and ghetto formation, as well as relatively high crime rates for specific cohorts of some ethnic groups (see for an overview Nijkamp et al. 2012). The socio-economic picture of foreign migration is thus by no means unambiguously positive, as is witnessed in recent political elections in various countries.

Over the past years, the awareness has grown that we need a trustworthy, systematic assessment of the various social-economic impacts of international migration. A first analytical framework and various empirical examples of this so-called *Migration Impact Assessment* (MIA) can be found in Nijkamp et al. (2012). In their study the authors provide the foundations and operational tools for a quantified estimation of a great diversity of migration effects on the receiving country, such as labour market effects, growth effects, innovation effects, trade and tourism effects, and cultural diversity effects (see also e.g., Combes et al. 2008, Ottaviano and Peri 2006, Suedekum et al. 2014). Various research tools are presented in this MIA book, such as econometric analysis, micro-based surveys, comparative case studies, and so forth. MIA is based on the availability of quantitative information on distinct groups of migrants.

A major problem clearly emerges if we are faced with unknown migrants. This group is—as mentioned above—often called undocumented migrants, unregistered migrants, illegal migrants or 'clandestino's'. They comprise illegal seasonal workers, illegal permanent workers, undocumented refugees, unregistered opportunity seekers, unregistered knowledge workers, informal businessmen, informal long-term visitors such as relatives or friends etc. The assessment of the socio-economic effects of the latter class of (structural or temporary) migrants is fraught with many difficulties due to lack of reliable data (Gheasi et al. 2014; Kondoh 2016). Yet, the order of magnitude of this group tends to increase. This is partly due to the emergence of open borders in many countries, the rise of globalization and world-wide communication systems (including the Internet), the substantial decline in the costs of geographical mobility, and large-scale flows of refugees in countries suffering from war conditions. There is an increasing concern on the problematic phenomenon of such unknown migrants. Particularly important issues related to such migrants in the host economy are:

- job risks related to a less protected position on the labour market;
- higher probabilities for wage exploitation of illegal migrant workers;
- unfair competition in the business sector, if migrant entrepreneurs do not respect taxation, employment or safety rules or regulations;
- loss of tax revenues for the public sector due to income tax evasion (or no income tax payments at all);
- emergence of a 'grey economy' in case of informal ethnic entrepreneurship;
- high expenditures for the health care system if no insurance premiums are paid;
- high claims on the social welfare system in case of loss of jobs by foreign migrants;
- relatively low degree of loyalty of migrants regarding the host country.

It is thus clear that the intriguing phenomenon of informal and unknown migration will be prominent on the political agenda in the years to come. Informal and unknown migration will also form a tremendous challenge for a reliable socio-economic impact assessment in a diaspora world (see Gheasi et al. 2014).

As mentioned, as a result of many structural factors in a globalizing economy, rising volumes of people are nowadays on the move (for both the short and the long term). And despite various observed negative impacts, the positive effects seem to prevail, so that in our 'age of migration' it is foreseeable that global migration flows will continue to be an established fact in the future. This migration phenomenon exhibits rather complex behavioural patterns, as economic motives are only a partial determinant. Other drivers may be social capital and network attractiveness, or cultural similarities (bonding and bridging, e.g. through a common language) (see e.g. Wang 2016). One important factor is the attraction force of large cities for migrants (the 'urban magnetism'). Cities have become a last resort for people on the move. This does not only hold for knowledge migrants, but also for migrant entrepreneurs and unskilled workers. Big cities offer also a shelter for illegal migrants, because it is so much easier to be hidden in large population concentrations and nevertheless to find a living there. Consequently, international migration and urban cultural diversity are two parallel phenomena (see Nijkamp et al. 2015).

The complex socio-economic position of migrants in urban areas has prompted various research and policy concerns on key elements of immigration in cities in the receiving countries, notably the social costs of migrants, the economic-political risks of a high share of undocumented migrants, the general perceived negative image of migrants, the competition on scarce knowledge migrants, the counterfactual question what the economy would have looked like in case of zero immigration (the 'dead weight' effect), local tensions on housing and labour markets, and the growing importance of informal migrant business. Clearly, MIA aims to map out the various consequences of these migration flows for the receiving country, but the assessment of all relevant effects of a variety of migrants is a real challenge.

In addition, it is increasingly recognized that an important source of trans-border migration is found in climatological change and related territorial and social tension. People are for their well-being and economic survival depending on the physical resources of our planet. Destruction or decay of these resources erodes the basis of their existence and will by necessity lead to cross-border migration movements. This phenomenon is not new in the history of our world, but is intensified by the high population density and scarce resources in many countries. Climate change may thus act as an important cause for migration across borders, both directly (people leave their country to seek for better opportunities elsewhere) and indirectly (population groups fight for scarce resources, with the consequence that several people have to move out of their region because of socio-political tensions or even war conditions).

Europe—with its relatively stable political climate and its relatively high welfare profile—becomes increasingly a magnet for international migrants and refugees, not only from within Europe (e.g., the Balkan region), but also from outside (e.g., the Middle-East or Africa). Sometimes this influx is caused by forced migration (e.g. climatological conditions, famine, war), but at times also by opportunity seekers, often in the form of fortunado's, but sometimes also in the form of forced migrants (refugees) desperately seeking for a living (desperado's). This diffuse flow of immigrants leads to increasing concern on the social and political instability in European countries and induces more and more security issues, originating from socio-economic discrepancy and cultural diversity among this large influx of people (Nijkamp et al. 2015). A major problem is that a migrant—once he/she has decided to leave the country and to find his/her fortune in another host country—becomes almost automatically a labour migrant (or an opportunity seeker) who cannot— or hardly—be distinguished anymore from other job seekers. Consequently, the demarcation line between voluntary and forced migrants becomes very thin, as soon as such migrants enter the host economy or labour market of another country. In addition, the distinction between temporary and structural migrants becomes also increasingly vague, as an increasing number of people on our planet is 'on the move'. Especially in the younger age cohorts we observe an increasing share of temporary workers for a limited number of years (e.g., knowledge workers). This phenomenon of the 'homo mobilis' will certainly be one of the greatest challenges in the age of globalization.

Many advanced countries have put in operation a variety of temporary worker programmes and regulations. A rich source of information on guest workers and temporary workers, notably on the US side, can be found in Martin (2015), who offers informed insights into the order of magnitude of these flows and on the regulatory aspects (e.g., contracts, free agents) of these temporary migration flows.

His contribution provides also some evidence on European guest workers. This study offers a new systematics on migration issues by introducing the 3-R model (recruitment and selection of appropriate migrants, remittances by migrants to their country of origin, and return decisions of temporary migrants back to their home country). It turns out that skills and education levels are in many cases the critical factors for the social benefit conditions related to this 3-R model.

3 Europe: A Migration Challenge

Europe has over the past decades exhibited two interesting demographic changes: (1) it has largely moved into an 'ageing' society (except only a few countries); (2) it has exhibited a high degree of complex (cross-border) population movements in the form of rural to urban migration, internal European migration (especially from East to West), and external immigration (mainly from the Middle East and Northern African countries). Clearly, Europe shows clear signs that the spatial mobility of people is increasing, while the costs of geographical mobility are decreasing. The high cross-border mobility of people in Europe means that population dynamics is nowadays more determined by migration (and refugees) than by fertility patterns.

It ought to be recognized that the share of foreign-born people in Europe varies a lot across countries in Europe (see OECD Factbook 2016; Wittgenstein Centre 2016). For instance, countries like Hungary, Finland, the Czech Republic or Slovakia have relatively low shares (about 5%), while Germany, Sweden, Austria, Ireland or Switzerland have relatively high shares (about 10–15% or higher) of foreign people.

Europe has also shown the fastest growth in foreign-born population among all world regions in the past decades (with an average annual change of 4–5%). Furthermore, these shares—and their growth rates—vary considerably between regions in these countries. Consequently, also cultural diversity among these regions in Europe does vary significantly.

It is noteworthy that most cross-border migration in Europe comes from inside Europe, even though migration between European countries is lower than domestic migration in European countries. As mentioned, significant cross-border migration flows in Europe are now taking place from Central and Eastern European countries to Western European countries, though the recent recession has also prompted some return migration (e.g. to Poland).

The World Economic Forum (2016) has recently produced some very interesting information on migration flows in Europe, which sheds new light on bilateral migration flows. For example, the highest proportion of immigrants to the UK in 2015 originated from its former colony, India, while most of Ireland's foreign-born population comes from the UK. Colonial and cultural linkages appear to dominate also for the cases of France, Spain and Portugal, with most immigrants coming from Algeria, Morocco and Angola. It is also noteworthy that the countries with the highest percent point change in immigrant population are Norway, Switzerland,

Belgium, Austria and Sweden. And finally, it turns out that migration is a selective geographic choice process, as is witnessed inter alia by the following figures: the highest rise of immigrants (2010–2015) into France is caused by Algerians, in the UK by Indians, in Sweden by Syrians, in Germany by Poles, in Austria by Germans, in Belgium by French, and in Italy by Romanians.

It is thus clear that Europe has become a migration continent with a mixed nature. The current migration pattern falls somewhere in between purely international migration patterns and domestic migration patterns, with different national migration rules. The recent refugee crisis has brought to light the vulnerability of the present heterogeneous European migration system.

From an economic perspective, labour migration is usually seen as a long-term investment which leads to high costs at the beginning for a migrant, but may generate benefits in the form of higher wages or better prospects in the future (Chiswick and Miller 2015). Costs items of migration comprise normally transport, removal, housing as well as loss of social capital and identity, while benefits comprise higher long-range earnings as well as (perhaps) better career opportunities, amenities and living conditions. A major problem inherent in any migration decision (at least in the past) is its irreversible nature. If a migration fails, the movement costs may be very high. It is therefore, no surprise that in our contemporaneous world—with its open character and worldwide information flows—the migration risk may be considerably lowered by a combination of comprehensive information supply on the place of destination as well as by more flexibility in return migration in case the movement was not successful. Consequently, there are many more migration opportunities nowadays, for instance temporary migration, return migration or chain migration (from A to B to C etc.). The distinction between long-range commuting and temporary migration becomes even blurred. More contemporaneous forms of non-structural migration are nowadays arising that may form a meaningful vehicle for coping with temporal tensions or job needs on regional labour markets, while they may also mitigate the disadvantages of brain drain or loss of skills in the sending countries. Therefore, in recent years several ideas have been developed to create flexible forms of temporary migration, not only for seasonal workers (e.g., in agriculture), but also for short-term migrant workers for a limited number of years (e.g., in the construction industry or in the medical care sector). The remaining part of this paper will address in particular such new forms of temporary migration in Europe, which might mitigate some of the former migration tensions in the past.

4 Temporary and Circular Migration

International migration has in recent years become one of the most debated and controversial topics—social, economic and political—in many countries, both the developed and developing world. There are apparently ambiguous and contrasting views on the flows of migrants from the perspective both sending and receiving countries. Host countries are concerned about the broader social and economic

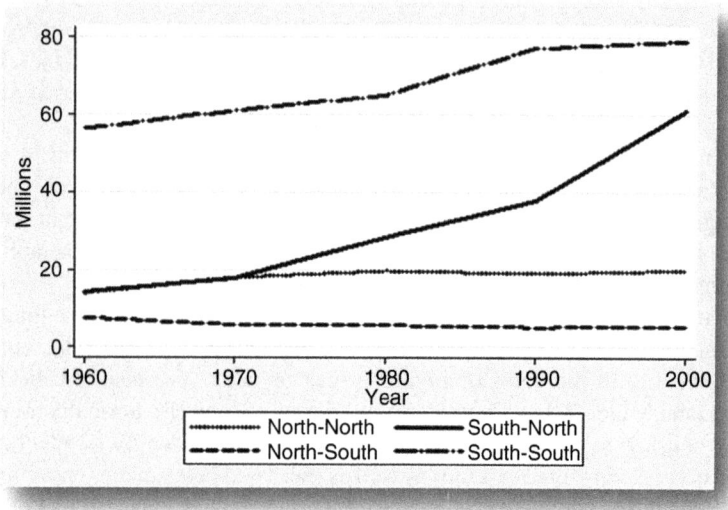

Fig. 3.1 Stock of migrants by country of origin and destination. Source: Özden et al. (2011)

effects of foreign immigration, while countries of origin are concerned about brain-drain effects. there is a broadly shared belief that migration flows are larger from developing countries to developed ones, but surprisingly actual figures indicate that the migration pattern is stronger between developing countries themselves or between developed countries. Figure 3.1 shows some development patterns of international migration in Europe between the years 1980 and 2015.

Although South-South migration dominates international migration, it share is falling. Özden et al. (2011) indicate that the South-South migration share has decreased by 13% between 1960 and 2000, while the South-North migration share has increased during the same period. It is, for instance, illustrative that opportunities for migrants from third countries to enter Europe and to find legally employment opportunities are rather unfavourable, while only a very limited group of people—highly educated and skilled—have this possibility. However, restricted migration policies have not been very efficient to stop the flow of migrants in this region. This is clearly demonstrated in a more up-to-date figure (see Fig. 3.2) which maps out the world development of foreign migration over the years 1980–2015. The stock of migrants world-wide is structurally rising.

Historically, it is believed that migrating people will structurally leave their country of origin and will resettle on a permanent basis in a host country. This was certainly the case in the period until 1980s. However, nowadays most people migrate only for work purposes and their intention for migration is often temporary. Furthermore, an OECD report (2008) indicates that depending on the country of destination, around 20% to 50% of immigrants leave again their destination countries within 5 years of stay. They either return to their country of origin or

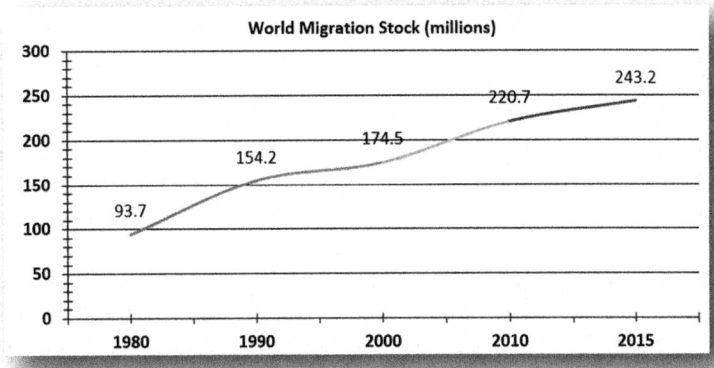

Fig. 3.2 World Bank figures on international migration. Source: The World Bank (2016), International Migrant Stock

to a third country. Since 2000, there has been a gradual shift in European policy thinking with increasing attention for the re-opening of borders and the management of migration flows. While most EU states still reject the idea of providing legal entry on a permanent basis (particularly for lower skilled workers), there has been a flowering of schemes to allow a temporary (including seasonal) entry of limited numbers of migrants, in most cases to fill specific needs in the labor market by sector or by skill level. Schemes are, for instance, put in place in Germany, the Netherlands, Norway, the UK, Ireland, Belgium, Sweden, Greece, Italy and Spain (see Plewa and Miller 2005; OECD 2005).

Circular migration provides a new interest in an old form of migration; the most common example of this type of migration is internal migration where people move from rural to urban areas due to better job opportunities, without changing their residential place. Circular migrants are temporary migrants who move back and forward between origin and destination. This type of migration has not only happened inside the countries—rural to urban—, but also at the international level (Fargues 2008, p. 5).

If we review the history of immigration, we can also find many examples of seasonal or circular migration in the contemporary history of society. For example, Meillassoux (1975), a French anthropologist, explains the interaction between capitalist employers and circular migrant workers in the traditional economies of Western Africa. He indicates that at that time workers were employed on a seasonal basis and after each period of employment, they had to return back to their homes. Through this mechanism of employment, the wealth was transferred from a subsistence-crops sector to export-oriented capitalist areas (Fargues 2008). This type of migration was a very common type of people mobility in Western Africa, Eastern Africa and Indonesia. In Asia, the two-way mobility of people has been a potential topic of research for three decades (Bovenkerk 1974). Another example of circular or return migration happened in Europe after World War II, where some European countries signed a bilateral agreement with Maghreb and Turkey, to fill their labor shortages on a temporary basis, in the understanding that migrants would return to their home country after a couple of years.

For the US, Tienda and Diaz (1987) argued that circular migration to the US decreased the employment opportunities for those circular migrants who returned back to Puerto Rico, and were consequently almost forced to re-migrate again. They also indicated that circular migration increased the number of female-headed families and led to higher school-dropout rates. In a more recent study, Porter (2003) related circular migration to illegal migration, and indicated that circulation of migrants—going back and forth—between Mexico and the United States happens often illegally. The increasing legal and border restrictions on international migration have not stopped people from moving to developed countries, but it rather stopped a circulation of migrants. It was found that on average an illegal Mexican migrant stayed for about 3 years in 1980s, while during the 1990s an illegal Mexican stayed on average 9 years in the United States (Constant and Zimmermann 2011). Furthermore, evidence from Bulgarian migrants to Greece shows that the benefit gained by Bulgarian migrants in Europe after joining the EU was the freedom of movement enabling them to travel to Bulgaria to visit their families and friends. Evidence on Bulgarian migrants also shows that legalization of their movement strengthened their bonds with their country of origin (Newland 2009).

Circular and temporary migration is not only beneficial to the host country, but as Zimmermann (2014) argues, it is a win-win-win situation. It means that the host country can fill its labor shortages without an increase in population, while legally the host country also can restrict the employment opportunities to specific jobs. Clearly, in case of permanent migration such measures are not possible. Secondly, there are advantages for the country of origin, such as benefits from the knowledge gained and remittances of circular migrants. And thirdly, the migrant himself/herself can benefit from various locational opportunities without a permanent relocation and without suffering from psychological costs of structural movement (see also Martin 2015).

In general, circular migration can be divided into spontaneous and managed (or controlled) circular migration. The first type of circular migration includes less mobility limitations, as then migrants usually go back and forth between their country of origin and country of destination. An example of such migration flows can be found between Asian and the Gulf countries, where many migrants circulate more than once between their country of origin and the Gulf countries. However, circularity of Asians in the Gulf states is not freely chosen, because the regulations in the Gulf states do not grant these migrants a long-term permit, and also the savings that these migrants make during their stay in a host society are not always sufficient to support them for a longer time in their countries of origin. Therefore, they emigrate again, and this situation creates circular migration, with frequent flows of return movements. In Europe, the flows of people from new EU members to more developed EU countries also include elements of spontaneous circular migration, where workers come for temporary or seasonal jobs and return back to their country of origin after some time.

The next type of circular migration, legally managed circular migration, usually refers to official governmental programs, bilateral agreements, and migration policies of the country of origin or destination or by both countries. Circular migration has different definitions and interpretations, and mostly there is not a clear distinction between circular migration and temporary migration. The interchangeable usage of these two terms can also be observed in different definitions. For example, the International Organization for Migration (IOM 2016) defines circular migration as *"the fluid movement of people between countries, including temporary or long-term movement which may be beneficial to all involved, if occurring voluntarily and linked to the labor needs of countries of origin and destination"*.

Given the definition of circular migration mentioned above, it is difficult to distinguish between circular migration and temporary migration. For example, The Netherlands defines temporary migration as *"migration for specific motivation and/or purpose with the intention that afterwards there will be a return to the country of origin, or onward movement to another country."* Both definitions—circular and temporary migration—share the same formal obligation for the migrants, namely the return of migrants at the end of their rights. It is the essential part of the process, and according to Dutch migration policy, the return means repatriation from the Netherlands. In many definitions nothing—or hardly anything—has been mentioned on the duration of stay. This makes the differentiation between these two types of people's mobility more difficult. The only difference we can extract from these two definitions—circular and temporary—is the possibility of multiple entries for circular migrants, while such rights would be limited to temporary migrants. However, in practice there are no official programs or bilateral agreements between the Netherlands and third countries to allow circular migration.

Wickramasekara (2011) presents the commonalities and differences between circular and temporary migration programs, as described in Table 3.1. From the commonalities and differences, it seems that temporary migration is a more general concept, while circular migration is a part of it. On the other hand, it also suggests that not any type of temporary migration can be counted as circular migration, because of a multiple involvement of the same person in circular migration, while for temporary migration it can be once in a lifetime. In terms of duration of stay, it is still difficult to differentiate between these two types of migration.

Apart from the difficulties in distinguishing circular migration from temporary flows, there is also a statistical problem in the identification of circular migrants at national and international level; the term circular migration hardly appears in any national and international data system, while most countries even lack an official definition of this term. This adds to the above mentioned difficulties in estimating flows of circular migrants between countries, as will be illustrated in a subsequent section.

Table 3.1 Commonalities and differences between circular and temporary migration programs

Common	Different
Temporariness: both involve temporary stays with no pathway to permanency	Circular migration programs allow for frequent temporary stays abroad, whereas temporary migration programs are based on a one-time only temporary stay and return which usually closes the migration cycle-single migratory cycle
Both can be components of broader patterns of loose or formal (backed by bilateral agreements) bilateral cooperation	Repetition of movements possible in spontaneous circular migration and regulated circular migration
Often involved countries that are characterized by large differentials in terms of economic and social development	a. Circular migration programs are more resource-intensive in terms of financial and logistical resources required for implementation than temporary migration schemes
	b. Circular migration programs usually involve the same groups of persons (migrants who are invited back), while temporary migration programs often involve different groups
Returns may be voluntary and forced	a. Circular migration schemes are based on professional mechanisms aimed at selectively organizing the mobility of foreign workers and at securing the return of migrant workers (related to above point)
	b. One pillar of circular migration programs is the outward circular migration to home countries for varying duration by diaspora settled in destination countries
Similar benefits claimed: remittances, bringing back skills and mitigating brain drain	Involves specifically diaspora contributions

Source: Wickramasekara (2011, pp. 11–12)

5 Circular Migration: Experiences from the Netherlands

In this section we will address some recent experiences and policy initiatives on circular migration in Europe, and in particular in The Netherlands. Circular and temporary immigration is in recent years a highly debated topic by the European Commission and various EU member countries, because especially the population decline and the ageing process in many EU countries call for new labour market perspectives. Therefore, there is increasingly a need for migrants—skilled and unskilled—to fill temporary labour market shortages in various countries. In this context, Germany and The Netherlands, for instance, have developed various initiatives on welcoming highly educated (skilled) migrants and also on stimulating circular and temporary migration from specific target groups (e.g., in agriculture). We will present here some evidence on such initiatives, with particular emphasis on The Netherlands.

The economic literature has argued that human capital is a significant and determining factor for long-term economic growth and development (see e.g., Borjas 1989; Mellander et al. 2011). For this reason, the return of skilled migrants is often considered as the main factor to turn the vicious circle of brain drain into a virtuous circulation of the production factor labor (Card 2001). However, large-scale flows of return migrants, especially less skilled workers, can cause adverse economic outcomes, if they cannot be absorbed in the local labor market of the original country and if a sudden decrease in remittances would affect the economic conditions of family members in sending countries.

One of the biggest concerns on circular and temporary migration usually refers to the question whether migrants return back to their country of origin after a period of employment or not. Migrants are heterogeneous in terms of skills, age, nationality etc, and therefore their willingness to return is also based on different motives, which includes both possibilities and constraints (see Longhi et al. 2008, 2010). In this context, Gmelch (1980, p. 135) has defined return migration as: *"the movement of emigrants back to their homeland to resettle"*. From this definition it can be derived that, when an emigrant returns back to his/her country of origin, this means the end of the migration story. This forms a contrast to recent migration movements which show that migration is an open-ended human behaviour in space, so that a return is often only a step within a continued migration movement. A number of studies has tried to explain the return behavior of migrants from different motivations. For example, Dustmann and Weiss (2007) indicate that migrants might return to their country of origin, once they have accumulated the knowledge and skills that have a higher return in their country of origin. Furthermore, migrants may also return after they have accumulated sufficient savings in the country of destination and return to establish a business to secure themselves and their family future (see Bellemare 2007; Kirdar 2004 for more information).

One of the countries with an officially adopted circular migration policy is the Netherlands. We will concisely outline here this scheme of circular migration from third countries into the Netherlands. The only official dedicated circular migration program that the Dutch government has implemented for low and medium skilled occupations from third countries is the so-called '*Blue Birds*' program. This programme aims to attract on a temporary basis (max. 2 years normally) foreign workers under strictly controlled support conditions, with a guaranteed return scheme to their country of origin. However, this program failed to bring a sufficient number of low and medium skilled migrants; instead, most candidates were highly educated—mostly, engineers, researchers and creative professions—migrants. It is important to add here that in general the Dutch government had already a rather open migration policy toward highly educated and highly skilled migrants. Migrants from third countries who are involved in temporary occupations are usually highly educated migrants. Low and medium skilled positions are mostly filled either by third country nationals who have a permanent residence, or by migrants from new EU member states (e.g., Poland, Romania). Furthermore, third country nationals are also heavily involved in low-skilled jobs, such as domestic work or the care sector. However, these migrants are mostly undocumented, and do not qualify for the terms and conditions of official Dutch circulation migration projects. Given the scope and limitations of this programme, the anticipated quantitative target levels for circular migrants was by far not reached. Several assessments studies have been undertaken to test the success of this programme (see for an overview Gheasi et al. 2015a, 2015b). The *'Blue Birds'* programme, at the end, did not have a significant outreach and impact, and may therefore, be regarded as a failure. In general, such programmes do not boost a high degree of success.

It is likely that more flexible and tailor-made circular migration arrangements—for instance, focused on specific target groups of temporary migrants and serving the a priori articulated needs of the host society—are needed. A practical illustration of the latter situation is circular migration of employees of multi-national firms. Another good example of circular or temporary migrants is formed by the class of young knowledge workers (e.g., Ph.D. candidates, post-docs). These migrants stay normally only for a limited period in a knowledge institution in a foreign country and return usually after a limited time span. In various cases, they may return to the host country in order to work on a common temporary research project. Return migration to the country of origin is often stimulated through a bonus system (like the case of China) or a contractual incentive (like in the Marie Curie programme of the EU).

It is plausible to assume that organized public circulation migration programmes for skilled workers will not boost a great success. It is even likely that some sort of formal quota systems for target groups may provide more favourable outcomes; in such a setting, the private sector might play a more active role.

6 Lessons

International migration may be seen as an innovative decision and a creative act or state of mind of millions of (potential or actual) migrants. They do unusual things in an attempt to improve their welfare position and career or to avoid a dramatic decline in their well-being. In addition, as a result of the rise in smart specialization and in cultural diversity induced by rising volumes of migrants, their position on the local or regional labour market or in the business sector in the host economy may induce new ways of operating, working or doing business, and may hence lead to various types of innovation (see Falck et al. 2012). Migration and innovation are thus often mutually intertwined phenomena.

Empirical research has clearly demonstrated the rise in innovation potential as a result of a diversified labour market or local business environment from an innovation perspective. The long-run benefits of both formal and informal migration are most likely significant (Olfert and Partridge 2011; Alesina and La Ferrara 2005). Consequently, international migration should not be seen as a threat causing socio-economic disaster, but more as a 'blessing in disguise' (Nijkamp et al. 2012).

Globalisation, development in information technology, and cheap transportation/communication have extended and intensified the network ties between migrants and their countries of origin. Digital technology is a tool for migrants to maintain social economic linkage and provides potential migrants with a customer-based information on job opportunities and life styles in the destination country, as well as on how to enter a destination country. Cheap international transportation has also facilitated return migration or circular migration nowadays.

On the basis of the observations in the present study, a few set of provisional policy lessons and recommendations may be put forward (see for details Gheasi et al. 2015a, 2015b):

- Government policies may focus more on the visibility and feasibility of official circulation migration programs, such as the '*Blue Birds*', in The Netherlands and the countries of origin. By making such programs more visible and attractive in the future, it might stimulate a situation of a more intense talent competition based on human capital quality; this might also give to the host country a fair chance to select the best possible candidates, and to migrants the possibility to find the best possible employment option in a host country.
- A close collaboration on temporary and circulation migration strategies and rules between the sending and receiving countries is needed to improve the understanding about the needs of both countries and to enhance mutual benefits.
- Circular migration programmes need to be well articulated. The Dutch '*Blue Birds*' program was officially a circular migration pilot program, but from the implementation perspective it was a temporary migration program. Future circular migration programs need to ensure the circularity of brains as well.
- The recruitment of migrants from third countries always deals with the recognition of the migrants' qualifications and the resulting selection of migrants. In practice, more freedom of choice might be needed for employers and recruiters in the receiving country to fill their labor shortages by recruiting the skills and qualifications they need. This can bypass many unnecessary regulations for a legal recognition of qualifications including official government employment agencies.
- Given the above observation on the recruitment of migrants, it is also important to note that many migrants are happy to work in host countries for lower wages. This needs further harmonization of labour market rules and contracts, for instance, on minimum wages.
- Recent experiences from the impact of diaspora on social-economic development in developing countries show that the stock of diaspora can play a significant role in the social-economic development of their country of origin (see Gheasi 2015). Therefore, policies to make these migrants more mobile are needed.
- At present, female migrants are increasingly recognized, not as dependents or passive follows—as part of a family reunification process or as forced migrants in a problem situation—, but as independent actors and/or family supporters. Therefore, gender composition needs more focus and policy interest at the outset.
- Social integration is an important issue, as it turns out that temporary migrants experience often loneliness; therefore, social integration and social capital aspects should not be ignored in the policy development for future circular migration programs.

- Highly educated and talented migrants tend to show a strong commitment to return back to their country of origin. Therefore, better articulated policies (or improvement of current policies) are needed to focus more on increased mobility and social participation of these migrants.
- Circularity of migrants is not only a matter of public concern; it can also flexibly be organised inside large multinational companies. This does not only decrease the concerns on the mismatch of the migrants' qualifications for jobs in the host country, but needs also less political concern. Therefore, policies to encourage such companies and to provide technical support (in the form of advice and guidance) are desirable to reconcile the ambitions of migration and development goals of a country or region.
- Finally, circular and temporary migration appears to have a clear bias towards younger age cohorts. From this perspective, aging and migration are again two mutually compensating mechanisms.

In conclusion, more empirical insights on exploratory circulation programs are needed to develop sustainable/mobility policies in the context of circular and temporary migration. Our findings from the Netherlands show a considerable diversity in life style, working and learning patterns, communication, values and preference systems, as well as in needs and decisions of circular and temporary migrants in the Netherlands. These differences are not sufficiently addressed in current policies and related programmes on circular and temporary migration and their communication strategies. This evidence calls for more emphasis on 'ethno-marketing' and 'diversity policy' for circular and temporary migration policy, so as to strengthen and expand 'bonding and bridging' strategies in order achieve the above-mentioned 'win-win-win' situation that would favour all interested parties, in particular, the country of destination, the country of origin, and—last but no least—the migrants themselves.

Acknowledgement The authors acknowledge support of the EU 'Mobile Identities' project and wish to thank the participants for their support to the publication. Website: http://www.iprs.it/pubblicazione/mobile-identities-background-paper/. This paper is being issued simultaneously as *Global Labor Organization (GLO)* Discussion Paper No. 39, https://www.econstor.eu/handle/10419/156159.

References

Alesina A, La Ferrara A (2005) Ethnic diversity and economic performance. J Econ Lit 43(3):762–800
Bellemare C (2007) A life-cycle model of outmigration and economic assimilation of immigrants in Germany. Eur Econ Rev 51:553–576
Borjas GJ (1989) Economic theory and international migration. Int Migr Rev 23(3):457–485
Bovenkerk F (1974) The sociology of return migration: a bibliographic essay. Martinus Nijhof, The Hague

Card D (2001) Immigrant inflows, native outflows, and the local market impacts of higher immigration. J Labor Econ 19(1):22–64

Chiswick BR, Miller PW (eds) (2015) Handbook of the economics of international migration. Elsevier, Amsterdam

Combes P-P, Duranton G, Gobillon L (2008) Spatial wage disparities: sorting matters! J Urban Econ 63(2):723–742

Constant A, Zimmermann K (2011) Circular and repeat migration: counts of exits and years away from the host country. Popul Res Policy Rev 30:495–515

Djajic S (1997) Illegal immigration and resource allocation. Int Econ Rev 38:97–117

Dustmann C, Weiss Y (2007) Return migration: theory and empirical evidence from the UK. Br J Ind Relat 45(2):236–256

Ethier WJ (1986) Illegal immigration. Am Econ Rev 76:56–71

Falck O, Heblich S, Lameli A, Suedekum J (2012) Dialects, cultural identity, and economic exchange. J Urban Econ 72:225–239

Fargues F (2008) Circular migration: is it relevant for the south and east of the Mediterranean? CARIM Analytic and Synthetic Notes 2008/40, Rober Schuman Center for Advanced Studies, European University Institute. Florence, Italy

Fratesi U, Percoco M (2014) Selective migration, regional growth and convergence: evidence from Italy. Reg Stud 48(10):1650–1668

Gheasi M (2015) The social-economic aspects of the diaspora world. Ph.D. Dissertation, VU University Amsterdam

Gheasi M, Nijkamp P, Rietveld P (2014) A study on undocumented migrant workers in the Dutch household sector. Int J Manpow 35:103–117

Gheasi M, Nijkamp P, Kourtit K (2015a) Mobile identities: migration and integration in transnational communities, Final National Report – Netherlands. VU University, Amsterdam

Gheasi M, Nijkamp P, Kourtit K (2015b) Mobile identities: migration and integration in transnational communities, Final National Policy Recommendations. VU University, Amsterdam

Gmelch G (1980) Return migration. Annu Rev Anthropol 9:135–159

International Organization for Migration (2016) Key migration terms. http://www.iom.int/key-migration-terms. Accessed 5 Dec 2016

Kanbur K, Rapoport H (2005) Migration selectivity and the evolution of spatial inequality. J Econ Geogr 5(1):43–57

Kirdar MG (2004) An estimable dynamic model of asset accumulation and return migration. ERC Working Papers in Economics 04/16

Kondoh M (2016) The economics of international migration. Springer, Tokyo

Kondoh K (2017) The frequency of migration and optimal restriction policies. In: Kondoh K (ed) The economics of international immigration, New frontiers in regional science: Asian perspectives, vol 27. Springer, Singapore

Kourtit K (2014) Competitiveness in urban systems – studies on the 'urban century'. VU University, Amsterdam

Kourtit K (2015) The 'new urban world' – economic-geographical studies on the performance of urban systems. Adam Mickiewicz University, Poznan, Poland

Kubis A, Schneider L (2016) Regional migration, growth and convergence – a spatial dynamic panel model of Germany. Reg Stud 50(11):1789–1803

Leerkes A, Engbersen G, van San M (2007) Shadow places. Patterns of spatial concentration and incorporation of irregular immigrants in The Netherlands. Urban Stud 44(8):1491–1516

Longhi S, Nijkamp P, Poot J (2008) Meta-analysis of empirical evidence on the labour market impact of immigration. Région et Développement 27(1):161–191

Longhi S, Nijkamp P, Poot J (2010) Meta-analyses of labour-market impacts of immigration: key conclusions and policy implications. Env Plan C Gov Policy 28(5):819–833

Lösch A (1936) Population cycles as a cause of business cycles. Q J Econ 31:649–662

Lutz W, Butz WP, KC S, Sanderson WC, Scherbov S (2014a) Population growth: peak probability. Science 346(6209):561

Lutz W, Butz WP, Samir KC (2014b) World population & human capital in the twenty-first century: executive summary. IIASA, Laxenburg, Austria

Martin P (2015) Guest or temporary foreign worker programs. In: Chiswick BR, Miller PW (eds) Economics of international migration. North-Holland, Amsterdam, pp 717–776

Meillassoux C (1975) Femmes, Greniers et Capitaux. Maspero, Paris

Mellander C, Stolarick K, King K (2011) What you do, not who you work for: a comparison with the United States, Canada and Sweden. Martin Prosperity Institute Working Paper Series, Martin Prosperity Institute, Rotman School of Management, University of Toronto

Newbold B (2017) Ageing and migration: a review. In: Blien U, Nijkamp P, Kourtit K, Stough R (eds) The Pensionado-Migration Nexus in regional labour markets. Springer, Heidelberg

Newland K (2009) Circular migration and human development. Migration policy, Institute Research Paper (2009/42)

Nijkamp P, Poot J, Sahin M (eds) (2012) Migration impact assessment: new horizons. Edward Elgar, Cheltenham

Nijkamp P, Poot J, Bakens J (eds) (2015) The economics of cultural diversity. Edward Elgar, Cheltenham

OECD (2005) Trends in international migration: annual report 2004. OECD, Paris

OECD (2008) Temporary labour migration: an illusory promise? International Migration Outlook, SOPEMI, Paris

OECD (2016) OECD factbook 2015–2016: economic, environmental and social statistics. OECD, Paris. https://doi.org/10.1787/factbook-2015-en

Olfert MR, Partridge MD (2011) Creating the cultural community: ethnic diversity vs. agglomeration. Spat Econ Anal 6(1):25–56

Orrenius P, Zavodny M (2015) Undocumented immigration and human trafficking. In: Chiswick BR, Miller PW (eds) Economics of international migration. North-Holland, Amsterdam, pp 659–716

Ostbye S, Westerlund O (2007) Is migration important for regional convergence? Comparative evidence for Norwegian and Swedish Counties 1980–2000. Reg Stud 41(7):901–915

Ottaviano GIP, Peri G (2006) The economic value of cultural diversity: evidence from U.S. cities. J Econ Geogr 6(1):9–44

Özden C, Parsons CR, Schiff M, Walmsley TL (2011) Where on earth is everybody? The evolution of global bilateral migration 1960–2000. World Bank Econ Rev 25:12–56

Ozgen C, Nijkamp P, Poot J (2010) The effect of migration on income convergence: meta-analytic evidence. Pap Reg Sci 89(3):537–561

Plewa P, Miller MJ (2005) Postwar and post-cold war generations of European temporary foreign worker policies: implications from Spain. Migraciones Internacionales 3:58–83

Porter E (2003) Tighter border yields odd result: more illegals stay. Wall Str J October 10, 2003

Reyes BI (2001) Immigrant trip duration. Int Migr Rev 35(4):1185–1204

Suchecka J, Urbaniak B (2016) Determinants of healthy ageing for older people in european countries – a spatio-temporal approach. Reg Stat 19(5):157–178

Suedekum J, Wolf K, Blien U (2014) Cultural diversity and local labour markets. Reg Stud 48(1):173–191

The World Bank (2016). International migrant stock, total. Available online: http://data.worldbank.org/indicator/SM.POP.TOTL?end=2015&start=1960&view=chart. Accessed 12 Jul 2017

Tienda M, Diaz W (1987) Puerto Rican circular migration. N Y Times, August 28, p A31

Tubadij A, Gheasi M, Nijkamp P (2015) Immigrants' ability and welfare as a function of cultural diversity: effect of cultural capital at individual and local level. IZA Discussion Paper No. 8460

Wang Z (2016) People on the move. Ph.D. Dissertation, VU University, Amsterdam

Wickramasekara P (2011) Circular migration: a triple win or a dead end, global union research network. Discussions Papers No. 15, International labour Organization, Geneva

Wittgenstein Centre (2016) European demographic data sheet 2016, Vienna

World Economic Forum (2016) The global competitiveness report 2016–2017, Geneva

Zimmermann KF (2014) Circular migration: why restricting labour mobility can be counterproductive. IZA World of Labor: Evidence-Based Policy Making. Nr. 1

Part II
The Dynamics of Modern Population Geography

Chapter 4
The Perils of Modelling How Migration Responds to Climate Change

Bo Feng, Mark Partridge, and Mark Rembert

1 Introduction

We live in an age of accelerating climate change. According to the National Climate Assessment report, the average U.S. temperature has increased by 1.3 °F to 1.9 °F since 1895.[1] Global warming has accelerated in the most recent decade, with the highest average global temperature ever recorded being in 2015. Extreme weather conditions including intense heat waves, flooding, hurricanes and severe storms, are expected to increase in frequency due to climate change, affecting people living in both coastal and inland areas (Melillo et al. 2014). Because firm and household migration is a key adaptive response to climate change, we need accurate predictions of migration to assess the future costs of climate change in order to craft effective policy. Though our emphasis is on the United States, the points we make about modeling and research needs apply to all affected countries.

First, issues arise when studies on the cost of climate change fail to accurately incorporate the adaptive mechanisms into their model for how households and

---

[1]Melillo, Jerry M., Terese (T.C.) Richmond, and Gary W. Yohe, Eds., 2014: Climate Change Impacts in the United States: The Third National Climate Assessment. U.S. Global Change Research Program, 841 pp. doi:10.7930/J0Z31WJ2. http://nca2014.globalchange.gov/report.

B. Feng (✉) · M. Rembert
AED Economics, The Ohio State University, Columbus, USA
e-mail: feng.411@osu.edu; rembert.16@osu.edu

M. Partridge
School of Economics, Jinan University, Guangzhou, China

AED Economics, The Ohio State University, Columbus, USA

Urban Studies, Gran Sasso Science Institute, L'Aquila, Italy
e-mail: partridge.27@osu.edu

© Springer International Publishing AG, part of Springer Nature 2018
U. Blien et al. (eds.), *Modelling Aging and Migration Effects on Spatial Labor Markets*, Advances in Spatial Science,
https://doi.org/10.1007/978-3-319-68563-2_4

businesses are likely to behave, most notably by migration to less affected regions. When facing climate change, people can choose either to stay in the most affected areas and pay a higher price to mitigate such change through certain adaptive technology, or to migrate to other locations less negatively impacted by climate change. The ultimate decision depends on the relative costs of adaptive technology versus migration costs.[2] People would choose to stay instead of migrating if adaptation is less costly (Reuveny 2007). Just as the spread of air conditioning and improved public health efforts—such as controlling malaria—has contributed to the population growth in the American South (Rappaport 2007; Sledge and Mohler 2013), new technologies could lower future adaptation costs and enhance human ability to cope with extreme climate events.

When an analysis does attempt to incorporate migration into climate change models, it often relies upon assumptions that can produce misleading results. For example, it is often assumed that migration will continue based on past trends regardless of how climate change alters the attractiveness of destinations and origins. Technological development, government policy, and improving relative climate conditions in other parts of the country are all factors that could impact how climate change affects migration and the costs incurred by households and businesses; yet these factors are absent in our current migration models. Likewise, an understanding of how to measure climatic attractiveness to business and households is typically based on prior climate behavior; yet climate change will produce negative events outside of the range of previous experience, making it hard to model without knowing how people respond. Current migration models are unable to incorporate the more extreme possibility of massive forced climate migration away from areas that are severely impacted.

In general, we have a good understanding of the response of migration to natural amenities for the latter twentieth century and early twenty first century. However, while it is tempting to simply apply what we have observed from the second half of the twentieth century and the first part of the twenty first century to make our climate-change migration predictions, we should do so with caution. Indeed, as we will discuss, if we had asked economists in 1940 to predict U.S. regional population dynamics up through 2016, they would have been very wrong. Why do we think that economists of today would do much better in making long-run forecasts of events that are so much more challenging due to the distinctive features of climate change as well as the normal "unknowable" features of future economic and technological events? Even with new insights into the drivers of U.S. migration patterns in recent decades, unforeseen innovations that will affect migration are difficult to anticipate and incorporate into our models. Indeed, the climatic changes on the horizon are so structural, that previous reduced form findings unlikely apply.

Researchers and policymakers are left with analysis that is incomplete and inaccurate. Yet, there is no easy solution to the dilemma. For example, imagine regional economists of the early 1940s trying to understand regional growth and

---

[2]Monetary cost and social cost, such as loss of social networks and family.

migration 75 years in advance. Economists of the early twentieth century believed that the primary (if not only) factor behind differential regional performance was relative incomes and job growth—i.e., a narrow firm-side perspective. However, technological innovations like air conditioning and advancements in public health along with rising incomes that allow households to "consume" more natural amenities (a normal good) have resulted in U.S. regional economic growth that has been dominated by natural amenity migration to nice climates, mountains, nice landscapes, lakes, and oceans (Partridge 2010). Partridge (2010) notes that models that stress job creation or agglomeration such as the New Economic Geography would have predicted exactly the opposite of what actually happened. Fortunately, there is the spatial equilibrium model which has served economists well in understanding U.S. migration.

Even with better theoretical models, the large structural changes in climate, technology, and possibly even in governance means that we still do not know the parameters to put into the underlying structural equations that may form an analytic model. While forecasting future migration is a "wicked problem," we will highlight the need to incorporate adaptive behavior like migration into our climate change models, and then discuss where some of our blind spots might lie so that we can make more accurate future predictions.

In Sect. 2, we first discuss the spatial equilibrium model as a guide to understanding regional economic patterns in advanced countries. Then we will highlight a related household decision-making model proposed by Kahn (2014) as a way to model decisions under climate change. Section 3 will discuss how past and current trends fit into the spatial equilibrium model and then describe why these *past* regional trends do not help us understand how *future* migration will respond to *future* climate change. We then assess how recent climate change research allows us to understand the linkage between migration and climate change. Section 4 then describes some other migration and policy issues that will further affect how future regional forecasts are modelled. The final section discusses priorities for future research.

2 Theoretical Framework: Spatial Equilibrium Model

We begin our discussion by introducing the Spatial Equilibrium Model (SEM) as the workhorse theoretical framework in understanding regional (subnational) migration patterns. The impetus for a new theoretical framework that became the SEM occurred as economists theoretical a priori prediction that relative employment and productivity growth (solely) drove regional migration patterns was contradicted by the early Post War movements to the Sunbelt and Mountain West (e.g., Graves 1976, 1979). One big theoretical addition is that households maximize utility and not just some simple function of income. While income is one component of utility, there clearly are other quality of life factors that affect household utility.

Spatial equilibrium is a condition that neither households nor firms have the incentive to relocate to another location. Simply, households' utilities are equalized across space in equilibrium. The simplest structural SEM can be explained by the equilibrium of labor demand and supply in a locality (e.g., Roback 1988; Partridge and Rickman 2003, 2006). Following on the work of Graves (1976, 1979) and others, this idea was first fully formalized by Roback (1982) followed by many subsequent improvements (e.g., Beeson and Eberts 1989; Glaeser and Gottlieb 2009). Of course, it is unlikely that a regional system is fully in equilibrium at a given moment, but the SEM has proved invaluable to predicting regional growth paths and net migration patterns in response to SEM disequilibrium.

The SEM is based off of the assumptions are that (1) workers are identical and completely mobile;[3] (2) firms produce a numeraire traded composite good X, the price of which is determined on an international market; (3) return of capital is equalized everywhere; and (4) workers consume X and non-traded housing land (Beeson and Eberts 1989). Then in spatial equilibrium, the indirect utility function can be written as

$$V_i(w, r; S) = V_N$$

Where i is region, w is wage rate, r is the price of housing land, and S is site-specific amenities. V_N is the representative national utility level. The equation shows that if there is perfect mobility of households and firms, then prices will adjust and households will move until equilibrium is reached and utility equals the national average across all locations. Indeed, a key feature that determines the accuracy of the SEM model for prediction and policy is the degree that households (and firms) are perfectly mobile to arbitrage utility (and profit) differentials.

Since the production is assumed to be constant returns to scale, the cost function (or the profit function works as well) can be normalized to a unit cost function without loss of generality. Thus, the unit cost function for region i can be written as

$$C_i(w, r; S) = 1$$

in which the notation is the same as above. Likewise, because of perfect mobility of factors of production, firms will move between regions to arbitrage differences in the cost of productions until the unit cost function for a region i equals one across the country.

Figure 4.1 shows the equilibrium for two locations 1 and 2, in which the difference is that the site specific amenity for 2 is greater than for 1 ($S_2 > S_1$). By assumption $V_S > 0$ and $C_s > 0$ or S is a household amenity and a firm disamenity—e.g., something like clean air and costly pollution regulations). The iso-indirect utility function is upward sloping as households are willing to accept higher wages

---

[3]The assumptions that workers can be heterogeneous can be easily incorporated in the model at the expense of mathematical tractability (Roback 1988).

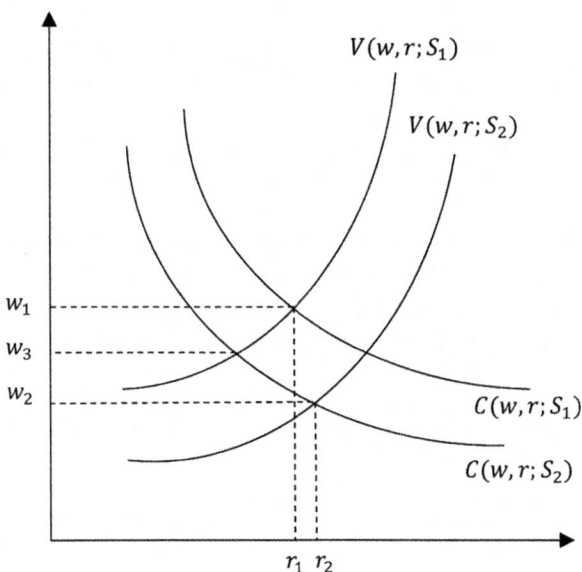

Fig. 4.1 Determination of equilibrium wages and rents (Author's Own Figure). * See Beeson and Eberts (1989)

as a tradeoff for higher housing costs, all else equal. The iso-cost function is downward sloping in that if land costs fall, then wages will have an offsetting increase to keep costs constant at one. In the equilibrium, wages and rents are such that the indirect utility function crosses the unit cost function.

It is easy to see that places with natural amenities tend to have higher housing costs and lower wages. However, migrants are not necessarily drawn to places with high nominal or real wages, which could imply a significant compensating differential for site-specific disamenities. Shocks to the system lead to price changes as well as migration/relocation of factors of production to restore equilibrium (Glaeser and Gottlieb 2009).

Kahn (2014) extends the SEM by modeling the decision of households to avoid the negative effects of climate change by either moving or adopting measures which reduce climate disamenities in their current location. In Khan's model, each household i at location j at time t chooses a combination of location, private consumption, and investments in self-protection to maximize its utility:

$$U(i, j, t) = \max\ p\left(risk_{ijt}, e_1\right) * U\left(C, h\left(amenity_{ijt}, e_2\right)\right)$$

$$s.t.:\quad C = income_{djt} - rent_{ijt} - \delta_t * e_1 - \gamma_t * e_2$$

$risk_{ijt}$ and $amenity_{ijt}$ are attributes of a location. The possibility of avoiding certain location specific life threatening risk, $p(risk_{ijt}, e_1)$ is a function of both risk and investment e_1 in self-protection measure e_1 at price δ_t, to reduce risk, such as insurance. $h(amenity_{ijt}, e_2)$ is the Becker Household Production function, which describes how household produces "comfort" by selecting a combination of amenities. The comfort of a household can also be improved by investing in a disamenity reducing technology e_2 price γ_t, such as air conditioning (Kahn 2014).

Based on Kahn's model, the appropriate way to analyze the impact of climate change is through an expenditure function approach and estimating individual willingness to pay (WTP) to change disamenities (migration, self-protection investment e_1, and technology investment e_2), because climate change will inevitably shift the distribution of locational attributes, $risk_{ijt}$ and $amenity_{ijt}$ (Kahn 2014). Kahn's extension of the SEM model is useful in that it directly incorporates how investment, risk, and changing amenities affect location decisions. Yet, while this extension provides an improved framework for modeling how households might behave in response to climate change, applying the model to develop predictions faces several challenges addressed in the next section.

3   Recent Migration Trends

We now discuss migration patterns since the 1950s to illustrate the connection to the SEM and to appraise whether these trends are consistent with adaptive responses to emerging climate change. A key pattern of U.S. migration flows is long-term persistence. Places that grew fast in the mid-twentieth century were (are) also likely growing fast in the twenty first century. Figure 4.2 shows that much of the population growth between 1950–2000 occurred in Southern Sun Belt states, the Mountain West, and high-amenity coastal areas in the South Atlantic and Pacific coasts. Likewise, the growth of the largest core cities such as New York, Boston, Chicago, and Detroit greatly slowed as population redistributed west and south to new cities such as Orlando, Phoenix, and Atlanta (Partridge 2010). Figure 4.3 shows that this trend continued unabated into the early 2000s up to the housing bust beginning in 2007. During the Great Recession, a pause took place because the most affected places hit by the housing crash were typically high-amenity areas. Yet, we show that after the housing market and economy stabilized in *circa* 2012, the same persistent trends emerged.

Figures 4.4 and 4.5 illustrate the persistence in migration. Even after the major shocks of a housing bubble/bust and the Great Recession, long-term migration patterns reasserted themselves after about 5 years. At least superficially, this may suggest that it will take a massive shock to reverse such trends, at least until we fully reach spatial equilibrium. Figure 4.4 shows that the 2000–15 growth patterns mimic the 2012–15 growth patterns—which follow closely the 2000–07 and 1950–2000 patterns. The only exceptions is that during the circa 2005–2015 period, much of the Great Plains experienced a positive commodity boom including agriculture, oil and natural gas. Thus, those regions had much more positive growth rates than its norm. With the recent conclusion of that commodity super-cycle, those patterns should revert in the long term.

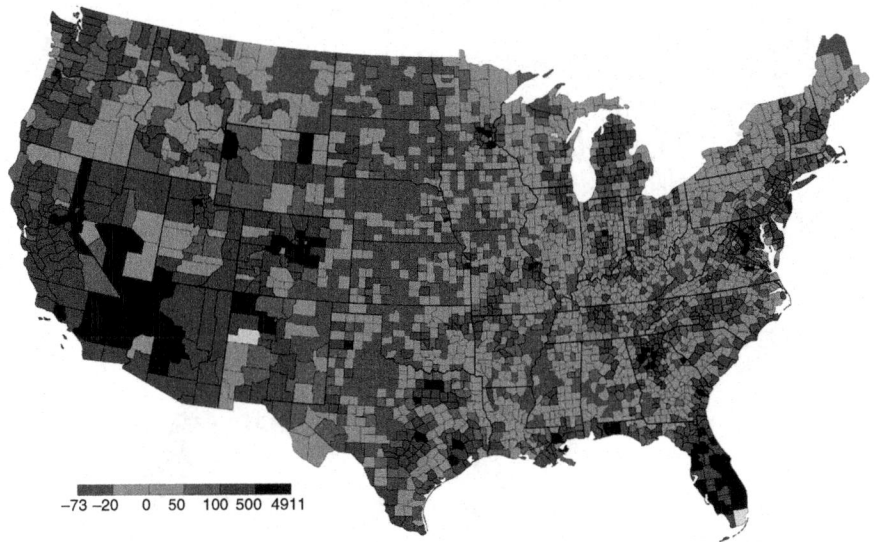

Fig. 4.2 1950–2000 population growth (percentage change). * Source: U.S. Census Bureau

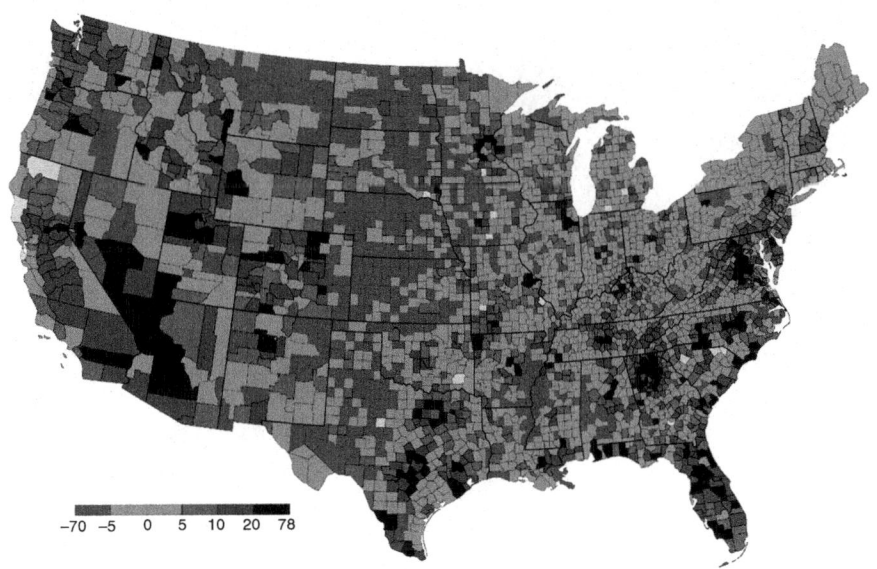

Fig. 4.3 2000–2007 population growth (percentage change). * Source: U.S. Census Bureau

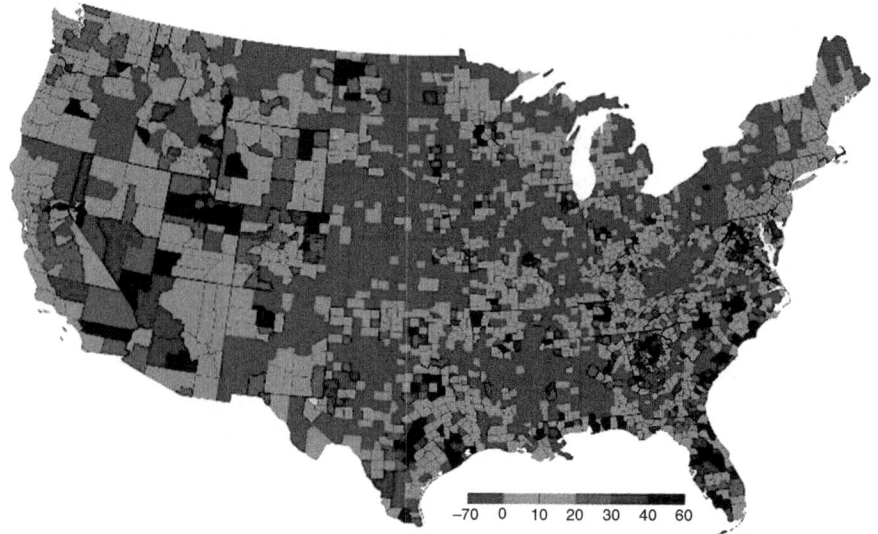

Fig. 4.4 2000–2015 population growth (percentage change). * Source: U.S. Census Bureau

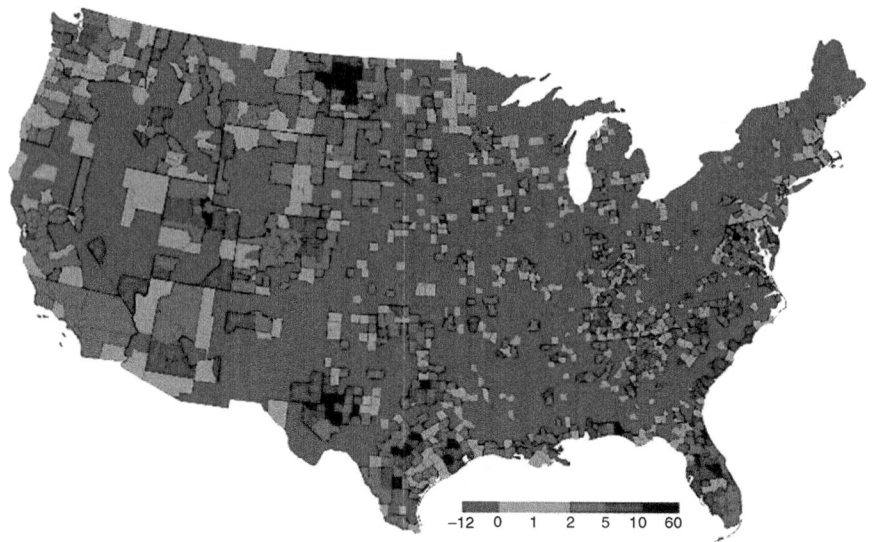

Fig. 4.5 2012–2015 population growth (percentage change). * Source: U.S. Census Bureau

Table 4.1 The correlation of state population growth rates over time

Period 1	Period 2	Pearson correlation of state population growth rates	Spearman rank correlation of state population growth rates
1950–2000	2000–2015	0.71	0.71
1950–2000	2012–2015	0.49	0.51
2000–2014	2014–2015	0.82	0.83
2000–2007	2012–2015	0.56	0.63
2005–2006	2014–2015	0.51	0.72

Source: US Census Bureau Population Estimates Program

Table 4.1 shows that at the state level, correlations of population growth and the respective state rank correlations over several different time periods over 1950–2015. The results illustrate that modern U.S. regional growth patterns are very persistent even when considering growth in the 1950–2000 period to growth in the 2012–2015 period. This strong correlation prevails even with the super-commodity boom leading to faster than normal growth rates in the interior of the country. These persistent patterns are consistent with the SEM, in which natural amenities attract people to areas that are relatively "nice." Conversely, they are inconsistent with disequilibrium economic demand shocks driving these regional growth patterns; that would suggest very random distributions as regions and their businesses experience shocks at a different pace—i.e., it is not that actors aren't responding to differential regional economic shocks, rather if differential economic shocks were *primarily* at work, then the growth patterns would be much more random.

Table 4.2 shows the importance of amenities using the 1950–2000 population growth results from Partridge et al. (2008). We compare outcomes of places that have the same "low-natural amenity" values such as Detroit to places with the "high-natural amenity" values of Orlando, Florida. The table uses the amenity values for Detroit and Orlando and then applies these values to Partridge et al.'s (2008) population change regression coefficients from nonmetropolitan, small metropolitan (counties in metropolitan areas with less than 250,000 people in 1990) and large metropolitan samples (counties in metropolitan areas with more than 250,000 people in 1990).

The results consistently show large statistically significant differences between places with amenity characteristics of Detroit and Orlando. For example, the average differences in January temperature is associated with 135% faster growth in non-metro counties that had Orlando's January temperatures versus Detroit's, with corresponding gaps of about 750% for the metro samples. However, some differences are offset by summer temperatures and humidity in places like Orlando.[4] In fact, it is apparent that urban areas are much more affected by climate effects,

---

[4]Rappaport (2007) also shows that while hot humid summers are a repellent to net migration patterns, they are overwhelmed by the positive net-migration effects of warm winters.

Table 4.2 Difference in population growth over 1950–2000

Variables\Samples	Non-metro	Small metro	Large metro
Mean pop growth %	32.20	122.47	138.00
Jan temp (diff Detroit − Orlando)	**−135.58**	**−768.63**	**−731.88**
July temp (diff Detroit − Orlando)	**94.87**	**323.93**	**255.89**
July humidity (diff Detroit − Orlando)	**57.61**	**215.23**	**162.94**
Sunshine hours (diff Detroit − Orlando)	7.69	**−257.88**	**−248.06**
Percent water area (1 std. dev.)	**11.03**	0.53	−3.04
Great Lakes (within 50 kms)	**−45.19**	37.25	52.44
Atlantic Ocean (within 50 kms)	**56.09**	**205.85**	**133.31**
Pacific Ocean (within 50 kms)	−28.28	−162.18	**−177.55**
Typography (most mtn. to coast plain)	**26.1**	24.6	22.29
Amenity rank (diff between Detroit (3) and Orlando (5) on a 1–7 amenity scale	**−69.74**	**−153.05**	**−143.11**

* Source: Partridge et al. (2008)

Note: Boldface indicates significant at 10% level. The difference between Detroit and Orlando uses their actual values. "1 std. dev." represents a one-standard deviation change in the variable. The models were re-estimated with USDA ERS amenity rank replacing all nine individual climate/amenity variables to calculate the amenity rank effects (available online at ERS). The amenity scale is 1 = lowest; 7 = highest

which means urban growth patterns will likely see the biggest migration adjustments due to climate change.

As indicated above, strong underlying pressures cause migration to the Sun Belt, the arid Mountain West, and to coastal regions that are likely to be the most exposed to excessive heat, large storms, and periods of extensive drought from future climate change. Thus, people are moving to the exact places that will experience the highest costs of climate change, meaning that migration patterns since 1950 are exacerbating the future costs of climate change with more people living in affected areas. It is too early to make simplistic claims that as the effects of climate change will be more apparent, people will begin to reverse trends and begin (net) migration to the Northern areas and places that will be less affected by climate change. However, these patterns do suggest that current migration patterns are unsustainable, at least in some dimension.

For public policy purposes, it is urgent to determine when migration trends will slow down and reverse due to ongoing climate change as well as to find the right market signals to better incentivize these movements—e.g., higher housing insurance premiums on the exposed South Atlantic and Gulf coasts, higher state and local taxes to provide adaptive infrastructure and public services, etc.

There are several factors that will make it challenging for economists and planners to predict future migration patterns. In Sect. 4, we will discuss some challenges that will need to be much better addressed if economists are going to produce migration forecasts that are precise enough to be useful to policymakers.

4   Challenges to Predicting Future Migration Flows

The first challenge economists face is the difficulty of predicting future *technological changes* and *productivity changes* that will affect real household income, in which natural amenities being a normal good, would affect how fast and to what extent households will respond to future climate change through migration.

The second challenge facing economists is developing new *climate measures*. In order to parametrize a model like Khan's, detailed data on climate and preferences is needed. Accurately estimating a location's *risk$_{ijt}$* and *amenity$_{ijt}$* requires detailed data, though at the moment, we are not exactly sure what measures we need. Similarly, economists currently rely on climate measures such as average daily-high January or July temperature, number of precipitation days, or temperature variation—which works very well in explaining how weather has affected utility and migration since World War II. While average July temperature, for example, is very highly correlated with measures of extreme heat or other "unpleasant" climate events associated with climate change, backward looking research would not be very useful in developing the right measures of whether extreme heat is an accurate measure—i.e., is it numbers of days over (say) 30 °C or 40 °C, does it include heat indices with humidity, or is average July high temperature sufficient? We simply do not know the right measures for excessive heat episodes that seem to be in our future and looking backward is unlikely to provide much guidance because excessive heat has not been anywhere near the issue that it will become.

Using the empirical results produced by current migration models, increasingly warm weather in the Sunbelt, Gulf, and Mountain West would attract population and people would keep swarming to places experiencing relatively rapid climate warming (and other issues), which does not seem plausible if climate forecasts are accurate. Thus, it is urgent to discover to what degree do negative hot-summer effects begin to overwhelm the positive effects of warm winters in terms of net-migration. We simply do not know given that such a figure is far outside the range of past observations.

Another seeming feature of climate change is greater variability of adverse events such as droughts, storms, tornados, hurricanes, etc. However, droughts are associated with clear skies and low humidity that is currently associated with *positive* net migration. Likewise, given the pattern of hurricanes of the last 50 years or so, places with more hurricanes tend to be the same places that attract people today in the Gulf and South Atlantic regions. That is, based on current empirical modelling, areas facing the most severe effects of climate change would still attract migrants.

Thus, we need to know two things in order to understand how climate change will directly affect migration as an adaptation response. First, we need to develop better measures of the climatic conditions associated with climate change. Second, with such measures, we can better assess the tipping point where these conditions are associated with positive migration to where they become a net negative.

A third challenge in modelling the long-term migration effects of climate change is incorporating *external unknowns like government interventions* that could have a significant impact on the predictions that we might draw from a model such as Kahn's (2014). Given that public policy is inherently endogenous to many of the same unknown factors including the exact climate change effects, technological change, and other factors, it is nearly impossible to model the effects and unintended consequences of public policies.

One particular important issue is the degree that all levels of government, but especially the federal government, subsidizes and supports infrastructure development and rebuilding in the most affected areas. Such policies would subsidize and maybe even reinforce population movements that encourage more people to reside in the most adversely affected areas, which is exactly the opposite of what is good public policy—i.e., more people and economic activity is then exposed to adverse climate change effects, further increasing losses and government expenditures. For example, if the federal government builds a seawall to protect Florida, that would encourage more people to live there. Such moral hazard effects are particularly exacerbated when the central/federal government pays for such disaster prevention or disaster recovery efforts. If local taxpayers and households faced the costs of living in hazard prone areas, then fewer people would move to places, reducing the adaptation and mitigation costs.

Further complicating matters is the contradictory desire of many state and local politicians to develop their local economy and create jobs in the short term (or perceived to have created jobs), potentially impairing the interest of the general public in the long run. That is, rather than focusing on long-term policies that may help their local communities address climate change and community resilience, they instead focus on efforts to boost short-term job creation. For example, they may encourage short-term economic development and infrastructure provision even if those plans run counter to the needs to shift activity from the most affected areas such as along South Florida beach-front property. Overall, this means that key parameters of government policy responses to climate change are unavailable in modelling climate-change adaptation migration.

The lack of key individual-level and household data has also limited the possibility to effectively make predictions using a model such as Kahn's (2014) because we are unable to precisely estimate a household's migration, self-protection investment e_1, and market investment e_2. Most studies estimating the WTP to avoid the effects of climate change only adopt first-stage hedonic model, in which e_1 and e_2 are assumed to be constant over time (Kahn 2009; Burke et al. 2009; Deschênes and Greenstone 2011; Albouy et al. 2016).[5] Yet, this approach will overestimate the costs of climate change because it fails to model the fact that household behavior will change as the "rules of the game" change—i.e., Kahn's (2014) Lucas Critique

---

[5]This model is primarily a framework to analyze the future impact of climate change, not anchoring spatial equilibrium. Another complication is that much of investment needs to be done in advance while the benefits are for future generations, making modeling even more complex.

that reduced-form parameters from a hedonic model will change as structural conditions change. Factors like the changing climate or technological change will cause the structural parameters to change and households will alter their investment in self-protection and disamenity migration responses (e_1 and e_2). Unfortunately, more data alone is likely to solve this problem. Instead, we would need data on future technology and future preferences (and preferably actual observations), which is impossibly unavailable at the moment. While simulations can "plug" in some values, they are educated guesses at best if not outright misleading in other cases.

5 Existing Research in Light of Theoretical and Methodological Concerns

Given these concerns we raise, we now examine how these concerns relate to the existing related climate change literature. In this, we are not necessarily questioning the technical rigor of this research, rather we comment on the data and assumptions employed. The existing literature paints a gloomy picture of our future under climate change in which temperature outside a narrow range (18 20°C) would reduce labor productivity (Heal and Park 2015), raise mortality rate (Deschênes and Greenstone 2011), reduce agriculture and industrial production (Dell et al. 2009, 2012; Park 2015), decrease national income (Hsiang 2010; Deryugina and Hsiang 2014; Dell et al. 2009, 2012; Colacito et al. 2016), slow economic growth (Dell et al. 2009, 2012) and even increase social instability (Burke et al. 2009).

Dell et al. (2009) use subnational data for 12 countries in Americas and find that in 2000, national income drops 8.5% per degree Celsius rise in temperature. Dell et al. (2012) take advantage of year-to-year temperature fluctuation within countries and find one degree Celsius increase in temperature on average reduce GDP growth by 1.3% in a given year. Their results seem to confirm the long observed relationship that hot-climate countries tend to be poor (Dell et al. 2009).

Attributing a low economic growth to the weather oversimplifies the relationship between climate and human activities. For example, predicting the cost of climate change should not be based on past correlations that will likely change, but a genuine causal relationship. More importantly, such results for the U.S. are inconsistent with the SEM. Again, there is evidence that under contemporaneous weather conditions, people trade off lower incomes to live in nice warm weather (especially in the winter), as predicted by the SEM. That is, people in Southern U.S. climates would have lower income than those who live in more harsh climates (cet. par.), but in spatial equilibrium, utilities are equalized across the country. Thus, the lower incomes in warm Southern climates are **not** associated with lower welfare.

It can be extremely misleading to interpret subnational correlations between income and climate as causal in a spatial equilibrium context because income serves as a compensating differential. Additionally, there is likely further heterogeneity because wealthy countries are much more likely to adapt better and/or affordable technologies (e.g. air conditioning) to offset the negative effects of high temperatures (Kahn 2005). Indeed, a simple example can show why such analysis is not applicable.

Assume that in a location with a temperate climate, the average summer temperature is 25 °C with a relatively small variation. Of course, given the current climate, businesses would not find it profitable to find ways to operate efficiently if a heat wave of 40 °C took hold because it is so rare. However, in a climate change regime, future businesses in this location would adapt and be much more prepared for heat waves and any output declines would be limited.

Deryugina and Hsiang (2014) apply a difference-in-difference approach to estimate annual income growth of U.S. counties during 1960–2000. Finding a negative link between average daily temperature and productivity, they claimed the results are causal, though again the results can easily be explained in a SEM framework to warm southern weather. They also separately estimate income-temperature relationship for each decade in fear that might be affected by adaptation strategies, and find no significant difference from pooled estimation, though it is unclear what adaptation strategies were being taken in the twentieth century to the very initial signs of climate change.

Colacito et al. (2016) also examine how temperatures have historically impacted the U.S. economy. With both time-series and panel-data approaches, they find that higher average summer temperature reduces the growth rate of state-level output. More importantly, they also predict a one-third reduction in U.S. economic growth would result from rising temperatures over the next century. Again, interpreting these results in the context of spatial equilibrium can produce a completely different interpretation about welfare. In addition, during the past with a more climate-stable history, such relationships may appear, but again there is a need to be cautious as consumers and producers adapt new (unknown today) technologies. Increasing awareness of changing climate and the demand for related technological innovations are more likely to shift household behavior and lower the cost for future adaptation technologies to a degree that one degree temperature increase will not be as significant as in the past, though it would be very hard to predict how that might affect migration patterns. For instance, one extremely simple change that we expect is that rather than the winter months being when employment and production tend to fall, it will be the summer period when this lull takes place in many industries.

There have been several hedonic studies of the effects of climate change. For one, Kahn (2009) estimates a first-stage hedonic model (Rosen 1974; Roback 1982) to find the impact of climate change on the real estate market. The impact is calculated by multiplying a hedonic real estate gradient with the difference between the future and current climate index, under the assumption that household behavior is held constant. Albouy et al. (2016) developed a quality of life index to measure WTP for nicer weather, and finds an annual 1–4% of income loss by 2100 given no change of technology and preference. Deschênes and Greenstone (2011) and Burke et al. (2009) adopt similar approach and estimate the climate change effect on mortality rate and civil war occurrence separately. Deschênes and Greenstone (2011) also predict an increase of location specific mortality rate by 3% at the end of the century under climate change, while Burke et al. (2009) claim the climate change will very likely cause social instability and induce more civil war in Sub-Saharan Africa. Yet again, following Kahn (2014), such reduced-form approaches overestimate the cost of climate change, as households will be able to foresee the change of locational attributes and adjust their self-protection investment, and the market will be able to invest in new technology to offset negative impact of climate change. Likewise, hedonic models are only accurate for marginal changes, which do not describe climate change.

Fan et al. (2016) use 2-stage random utility sorting model to estimate the WTP to avoid additional day of extreme weather. While such results potentially improve upon first-stage hedonic estimation, there remains the other problems we mentioned about not knowing what the future entails.

In summary, the existing literature estimating the costs of climate change are primarily static using backward-looking parameters and measures, as well as quite often not incorporating the implications of the SEM for an advanced economy such as the U.S. As more people make their decisions based on climate change, more R&D into new adaptive technologies will take place, causing a drop in adaptation costs to a degree that it may be lower than migration costs. In such a scenario, very little migration may occur. Nonetheless, we simply do not know what will happen.

6   Climate Change in Light of the Related Economic Shock Literatures

The relationship between natural amenities and migration is well established, but there are other related literatures that may help inform how climate change will affect migration. For example, the persistence of returning to long-term economic growth paths after regions are impacted by extreme shocks has been demonstrated in a variety of cases.

For example, during the late 1980s and 1990s, Congress established a process for realigning military bases known as BRAC (Base Realignment and Closure). This process led to the reduction or closure of 97 major military installations across the US, with net loss of military and defense civilian employment of more than 4000 employees per base, representing significant economic shocks to local economy where the bases were located (especially in rural communities where many of the bases were located). In a representative study in this literature, Poppert and Herzog Jr. (2003) consider the effect of these closures on local employment. They find that within 2 years, the downsized employment at the military facility produced positive in-direct employment effects. This was particularly true when former military facilities were repurposed for other uses that were better connected to the regional economy. One implication is that communities can recover from large economic shocks; another is that the persistence behind regional economic growth could hamstring the needed adjustments from most to least affected areas.

There has been significant research on the effects on natural disasters on economic events such as how storms and droughts will impact migration patterns. Fussell et al. (2014) explore how the pre-storm migration systems related to the post-disaster mitigation system following Hurricane Katrina and Rita. They find that the migration system following the storms became more concentrated and intense. In-migration from nearby counties to disaster affected counties increased significantly during the recovery period as displaced households returned home and new in-migrants migrated to the disaster affected areas (likely for the rebuilding). Migration from rural areas to urban areas intensified within the disaster areas during the recovery period. These findings challenge fears that extreme weather events like storms will permanently displace large populations. Instead, they suggest that the effects of even large shocks like Hurricane Katrina tend to be temporary. While such results may have implications for regionally concentrated storm events, they are considerably less applicable to widespread natural disasters with geographic reaches beyond the impact of a storm or earthquake. For example, displaced people from New Orleans could easily move to undamaged Houston or Atlanta, for example.

The disaster literature indicates that in the long-term, places hit by natural disasters tend to recover to their pre existing long-term GDP rate, with the rebuilding process helping to create new jobs (e.g., Xiao 2011). For climate change, this suggests a possibility that if mass migration (or rebuilding) takes place, this may have a simulative effect on GDP growth as it opens up considerable demand for new homes, new furniture and appliances, and for communities to construct new infrastructure to support this influx of people. However, GDP growth is not the same thing as improved welfare, which like in the case of disasters and wars, there is a massive destruction of *wealth* along with the welfare losses associated with the changing climate.

Evidence pointing to the persistence growth of regions impacted by severe shocks has been widely explored in the context of war and large scale employment shocks. War shocks have commonalities with climate change in that wars are more severe (in the short term) than climate change and unlike hurricanes, climate change creates stress fto the entire country. Two noted papers consider how population responded to the severe damage, casualties, and population displacement suffered by cities in Japan and Germany during World War II (WWII). Davis and Weinstein (2002) consider the effect that the bombings of Japanese cities during WWII, including dropping nuclear bombs on Hiroshima and Nagasaki. They find that Japanese cities suffering massive damage from bombings displayed remarkable resilience, and recovered from the devastation within 12 years.

Brakman et al. (2004) consider the population response in Germany to WWII bombing. They find that the damage and population loss caused by the war was only temporary for cities in West Germany, while the effects had a permanent effect in East Germany. These differences are attributed to the policy regimes in each country. West Germany's market based economy coupled with policies which incentivized home reconstruction helped to increase housing demand and housing values, creating conditions that supported the redevelopment of the cities. The centrally planned economy in East Germany did not create the same conditions or incentives to promote the reconstruction of cities that suffered severe damage during the war, permanently affecting the growth paths of these cities. These results are indicative that better governance and economic systems make a difference in how fast regions can recover from disasters, but there are still some questions about the broad scale applicability because they did not exactly identify the key socioeconomic institutions that aided West Germany's recovery. Like climate change, wars have more global or national common effects that may hamper recovery efforts after major events such as bombing or large increases in sea levels. Thus, they seem to paint an optimistic picture for climate change's long-run effects, but again there are the same caveats about technological change and other factors that may produce wildly different effects from climate change than the effects of past wars.

Each of these studies offer insights into regional system recovery after being impacted by severe shocks. They point to the persistence and even resilience of regional economies, and suggest that given the right conditions, population and economic activity will bounce back and return to a previous growth path following a shock. Thus, this can be a positive finding pointing to the resilience of communities and regions hit by economic shocks. On the other hand, they may suggest that reversing migration patterns to support climate change mitigation and adaption may be very difficult. Yet, given that the these studies tend to focus on singular events, we should be hesitant when drawing conclusions about how migration might be affected by an increase in the frequency of extreme weather events brought on by climate change.

One critical, yet unanswered, question is the degree to which climate change will make regions less-productive versus being almost uninhabitable. If the latter is the case, then it is expected to be much larger migration flows away from regions adversely affected by climate change. If it is just drop in productivity, population declines will be much smaller as real estate prices and wages adjust to re-achieve spatial equilibrium. Glaeser and Gyourko (2005) find that when a region experiences a relative decline in productivity and amenities, highly-skilled workers are likely to migrate away to areas with stronger jobs markets while large declines in housing costs attract lower earning, lower skilled households seeking inexpensive housing. In this scenario, regions adversely affected by climate change would experience less population decline, while poverty and urban decay would increase, which together with the decline in human capital would result in less resilient regions that face even larger economic declines due to the feedback effects. In some sense, such a vicious circle is reminiscent of the decline of Rust Belt regions in the second half of the twentieth century (Glaeser and Gyourko 2005). In the absence of catastrophic climate events that make areas of country uninhabitable, Glaeser and Gyourko (2005) suggest that the effects on the distribution of income and wealth across regions might be more significant than the patterns of net-migration flows, increasingly the complications in predicting the migration response to climate change. Indeed, changes in the distribution of income also has feedback effects on the effectiveness of federal, state and local governments if policies are more aimed at the elite who provide critical help in election campaigns.

7   Other Complicating Factors that Affect Migration Under Climate Change

While climate and landscape were the most important factor driving migration for the past 75 years, it is uncertain whether these factors will continue driving large volumes of migrants in the future. A central question that needs to be explored is how close U.S. regions are to spatial equilibrium. At equilibrium, the amenity driven benefits have been fully capitalized into housing prices and wages, which would end or slow the long-term migration patterns of the last 70 years. When spatial equilibrium is reached, migration patterns might look very different as other factors will emerge as the central drivers of migration.

Partridge et al. (2012) explore this question by considering the considerable slowing in migration flows in the US over since the early 1990s. Is it due to U.S. regions reaching spatial equilibrium or is it due to other factors such as a decline in migrant response to economic conditions? They attribute much of the decline to a slowdown in "economic" migration in response to local economic shocks. They do find a very slight ebbing in migration driven by amenities, suggesting that amenities are increasingly being capitalized, but they find that migration away from rural areas to be nearer larger metropolitan areas continuing (though this is not the same thing as people moving to live *in* the largest cities).

While these findings suggest that the US has not yet reached a spatial equilibrium in which growth rates are equalized across regions, Partridge et al. (2012) offers evidence that the structures that drove migration during the twentieth century are evolving, and might continue to do so into the future with less responses to economic conditions, which may slow climate-change related migration related to changing economic conditions.

Figure 4.6 shows migration rates by age group over several periods from 1990 to 2015. The figure shows the standard human capital theory that young adults are far more likely to migrate than any other age group. However, while the figure shows that all cohort groups have experienced migration declines, both in terms of migration rates and in absolute terms, the biggest declines are among young adults. Figure 4.7 shows between migration rates by level of educational attainment going by to the early 1990s. At every level of educational attainment, migration rates have declined since 1991, with the largest decline among the population with a bachelor's degree. Both of these patterns suggest that migration rates are declining among the what have historically been the most mobile populations—young people and college graduates. If these patterns continue, migration as an adaptive response to climate change may be much slower than past migration rates would have suggested.

Another set of policy issues that will likely have a significant impact on future migration patterns are land-use and building regulations. While preferences for better climate has driven much of the migration to Sunbelt states, these migration patterns were facilitated by land use and building regulations that were supportive of a rapid increase in housing supply (Glaeser and Tobio 2007). Conversely, some expensive coastal cities have artificially limited in-migration by driving a wedge

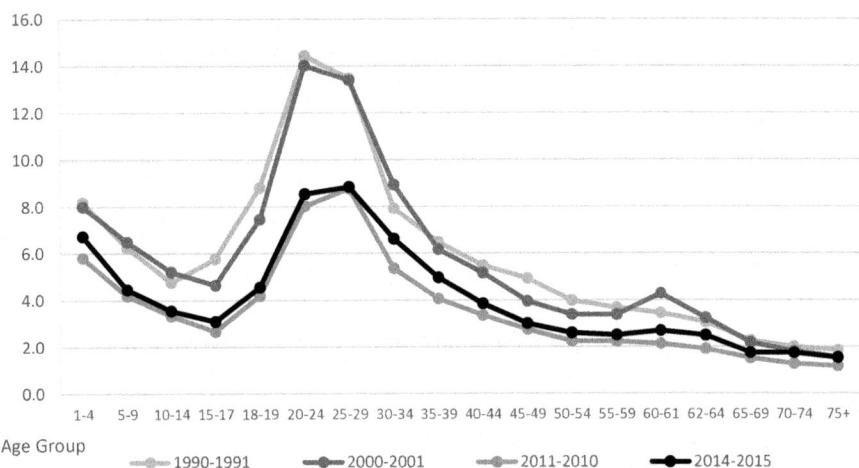

Fig. 4.6 Between county migration rates by age group. * This figure does not include movers in Puerto Rico. * Source: U.S. Census Bureau

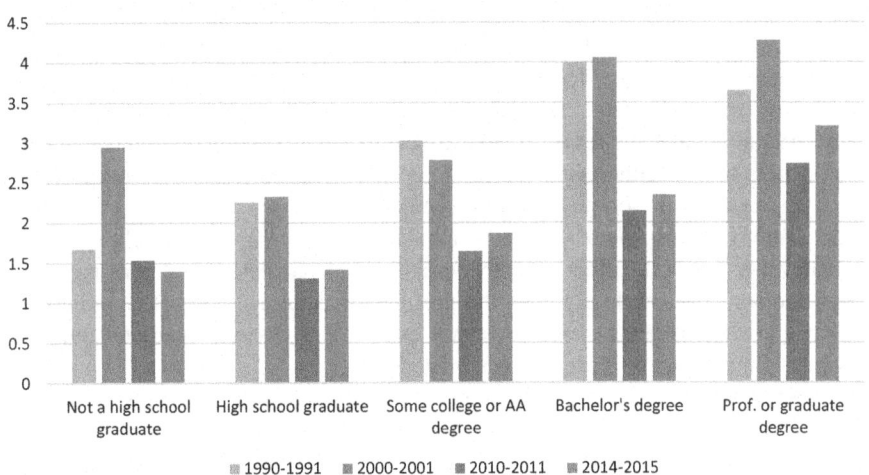

Fig. 4.7 Between state migration rate by education attainment. * This figure does not include movers in Puerto Rico. * Source: U.S. Census Bureau

between the cost of housing production and housing prices using restrictive building and land use policies (Glaeser et al. 2005). Yet, in general, land-use policies have typically allowed residences and businesses to build and operate very near the coast—being vulnerable to growing intensity of storms and sea rise—further subsidized by the placement of necessary infrastructure. Such policies will increase the costs of adapting to climate change and slow the needed adjustments. However, such policies should be unwound to reduce their adverse effects. Nonetheless, in predicting future migration and future costs, economists need to understand the role of land-use policy, which is further complicated by the fact that land-use policy and migration are simultaneously determined.

8 Conclusion

Predicting the future is extremely difficult. Projecting future migration under climate change is not straightforward in nature. In general, we are skeptical about current research on climate change impact because of overwhelming uncertainty. Contemporaneous studies seem to oversimplify the casual relationship between climate conditions and human activities. Some examples include a poor understanding of the SEM model; not recognizing that structural relationships will change from current linkages; lacking measurement of key climate data; or understanding how actual climatic events affect socioeconomic behavior; and not considering technological change and future adaptive measures. In this sense, simply extrapolating from past patterns is naïve. Even assuming people will move to the less affected areas is over-simplistic without an understanding about how future government policy incentivizes moving to the most affected areas through taxes, infrastructure placement, land-use policy, etc. At least at the moment, researchers still lack the necessary knowledge and tools to make a meaningful prediction on climate change induced migration. Rather than focusing on some neat experimental design from some past event or a complex structural model to forecast the effects of climate change, more effort should simply go into the measurement of the climate (and other) events that will affect future household and business settlement patterns. These factors can completely limit the usefulness of future migration predictions due to climate change, and we have not even noted that the predicted climate changes themselves are imprecisely estimated.

Future research on this topic could also focus more on policy aspects of climate change. More efforts should be given to develop flexible institutions to address these issues in a centralized or decentralized system, which appears to underlie West Germany and Japan's recovery from WWII. The optimal mix of federal intervention versus state and local interventions to climate change also deserve more research attention. More precise prediction can be achieved in the future with better understanding of policy consequences, as well as extra weather measures, more individual-level data on risk and clarity of our limitations.

Other areas that should be at a higher priority are efforts to help increase the resilience of regions to withstand the stresses of long-term climate change (Martin and Sunley 2014). Resilience is something that is currently poorly understood including clear definitions. For example, it is not just simply a rapid recovery from adverse economic events as any boomtown mining town or recession ravaged manufacturing town tends to experience "V" shaped recoveries due to the highly cyclical nature of their industries. Yet, such industries face long-term employment declines if simply due to rapid productivity growth (Partridge and Rickman 2002). Resilience in that sense does not seem to be welfare enhancing.

Thus, future research priorities should focus on the factors that improve community "resilience." We mean beyond the notion that diverse economies fare better in response to economic shocks (Partridge and Olfert 2011). In particular, it would be best to focus on the institutions that facilitate resilience. For example, does the widening income distribution reduce the effectiveness of governments to holistically respond to major adverse events or are they captured by the interests of the elite class? Likewise, issues of fragmented local governance will likely reduce a region's ability to respond to future stresses as "small-box" local governments pursue their myopic self-interest rather than focus on the broader needs of the region.

Another area ripe for research is the proper "pricing" of climate change into economic actors' relocation decisions. In particular, should new residents pay impact fees for the increase in externalities and costs they cause by migrating to affected areas? Likewise, how much of protective and adaptive government expenditures in affected locations will be paid for by local taxpayers. The more such costs are passed onto the federal government and national taxpayers, the more that people are be incentivized to live in such areas, increasing the costs of climate change. Finally, another area of urgent research interest is how international immigration should be regulated under climate change. Should immigration policies be relaxed to let in future "climate migrants" or will such policies place heavy strains on an already stressed system?

References

Albouy D et al (2016) Climate amenities, climate change, and American quality of life. J Assoc Environ Resour Econ 3(1):205–246

Beeson PE, Eberts RW (1989) Identifying productivity and amenity effects in interurban wage differentials. Rev Econ Stat 71:443–452

Brakman S, Garretsen H, Schramm M (2004) The strategic bombing of German cities during World War II and its impact on city growth. J Econ Geogr 4(2):201–218

Burke MB et al (2009) Warming increases the risk of civil war in Africa. Proc Natl Acad Sci 106(49):20670–20674

Colacito R, Hoffmann B, Phan T (2016) Temperature and growth: a panel analysis of the United States. Inter-American Development Bank, Washington, DC

Davis DR, Weinstein DE (2002) Bones, bombs, and break points: the geography of economic activity. Am Econ Rev 92(5):1269–1289

Dell M, Jones BF, Olken BA (2009) Temperature and income: reconciling new cross-sectional and panel estimates. No. w14680. National Bureau of Economic Research

Dell M, Jones BF, Olken BA (2012) Temperature shocks and economic growth: evidence from the last half century. Am Econ J Macroecon 4:66–95

Deryugina T, Hsiang SM (2014) Does the environment still matter? Daily temperature and income in the United States. No. w20750. National Bureau of Economic Research

Deschênes O, Greenstone M (2011) Climate change, mortality, and adaptation: evidence from annual fluctuations in weather in the US. Am Econ J Appl Econ 3(4):152–185

Fan Q, Allen Klaiber H, Fisher-Vanden K (2016) Does extreme weather drive interregional brain drain in the US? Evidence from a sorting model. Land Econ 92(2):363–388

Fussell E, Curtis KJ, DeWaard J (2014) Recovery migration to the City of New Orleans after Hurricane Katrina: a migration systems approach. Popul Environ 35(3):305–322

Glaeser EL, Tobio K (2007) The rise of the sunbelt. No. w13071. National Bureau of Economic Research

Glaeser EL, Gottlieb JD (2009) The wealth of cities: agglomeration economies and spatial equilibrium in the United States. J Econ Lit 47(4):983–1028

Glaeser EL, Gyourko J (2005) Urban decline and durable housing. J Political Econ 113(2):345–375

Glaeser EL, Gyourko J, Saks R (2005) Why is Manhattan so expensive? Regulation and the rise in housing prices. J Law Econ 48(2):331–369

Graves PE (1976) A reexamination of migration, economic opportunity and the quality of life. J Reg Sci 16(1):107–112

Graves PE (1979) A life-cycle empirical analysis of migration and climate by race. J Urban Econ 6(2):135–147

Heal G, Park J (2015) Goldilocks economies? Temperature stress and the direct impacts of climate change. No. w21119. National Bureau of Economic Research

Hsiang SM (2010) Temperatures and cyclones strongly associated with economic production in the Caribbean and Central America. Proc Natl Acad Sci U S A 107(35):15367–15372

Kahn ME (2014) Climate change adaptation: lessons from urban economics. No. w20716. National Bureau of Economic Research

Kahn ME (2009) Urban growth and climate change. Annu Rev Resour Econ 1(1):333–350

Kahn ME (2005) The death toll from natural disasters: the role of income, geography, and institutions. Rev Econ Stat 87(2):271–284

Martin R, Sunley P (2014) On the notion of regional economic resilience: conceptualization and explanation. J Econ Geogr 15:1–42

Melillo JM, Richmond TC, Yohe GW (eds) (2014) Climate change impacts in the United States: the third national climate assessment. U.S. Global Change Research Program, 841 pp. https://doi.org/10.7930/J0Z31WJ2

Partridge MD (2010) The duelling models: NEG vs amenity migration in explaining US engines of growth. Pap Reg Sci 89(3):513–536

Partridge MD, Olfert MR (2011) The winners' choice: sustainable economic strategies for successful 21st-century regions. Appl Econ Perspect Policy 33(2):143–178

Partridge MD, Rickman DS (2002) Did the new economy vanquish the regional business cycle? Contemp Econ Policy 20:456–469

Partridge MD, Rickman DS (2003) The waxing and waning of U.S. regional economies: the chicken-egg of jobs versus people. J Urban Econ 53:76–97

Partridge MD, Rickman DS (April 2006) Fluctuations in aggregate U.S. migration flows and regional labor market flexibility. South Econ J 72:958–980

Partridge MD, Rickman DS, Olfert R, Ali K (2008) Lost in space: population growth in the American hinterlands and small cities. J Econ Geogr 8:lbn038

Partridge MD et al (2012) Dwindling US internal migration: evidence of spatial equilibrium or structural shifts in local labor markets? Reg Sci Urban Econ 42(1):375–388

Poppert PE, Herzog HW Jr (2003) Force reduction, base closure, and the indirect effects of military installations on local employment growth. J Reg Sci 43(3):459–482

Rappaport J (2007) Moving to nice weather. Reg Sci Urban Econ 37(3):375–398

Reuveny R (2007) Climate change-induced migration and violent conflict. Polit Geogr 26(6):656–673

Roback J (1982) Wages, rents, and the quality of life. J Political Econ 90:1257–1278

Roback J (1988) Wages, rents, and amenities: differences among workers and regions. Econ Inq 26(1):23–41

Rosen S (1974) Hedonic prices and implicit markets: product differentiation in pure competition. J Political Econ 82(1):34–55

Sledge D, Mohler G (2013) Eliminating malaria in the American South: an analysis of the decline
of malaria in 1930s Alabama. Am J Public Health 103(8):1381–1392
Xiao Y (2011) Local impacts of natural disasters. J Reg Sci 51:804–820

Chapter 5
Migration Pressures and Responses in South Asia

Tomaz Ponce Dentinho and Patricio Aroca

1 Introduction

Globalization involves the general mobilization and transportation of resources, goods and services: natural, technological, financial and human. They flow from where they are abundant and available to where they are in much need and demand, moulding channels and adapted spaces, affecting ecosystems and institutions, generating and distributing wages, rents, profits and interests across space and time. Globalization reinforces the driving forces of migration (Hatton and Williamson 2011). Demographic transitions increases population in developing regions and decreases in the more developed ones, improvement of migrants' human capital and poverty reduction in the developing world rises the capacity of the population, namely those that are more gifted (Grogger and Hanson 2011) to search, move and integrate in better places. On the other hand diminishing transport costs and the improvement of communication links between migrants, reduces the attrition of distance and relocation costs, and moderates family and community disarrays. (Hatton and Williamson 2011) suggest that most of Asia, Latin America, and the European periphery have finished their emigration life cycles, and only sub-Saharan Africa lagged behind. Nevertheless associated with globalization process (Abel and Sander 2014) estimate that large movements will tend to occur in South and East Asia, from Latin to North America, and within Africa.

Migration have significant effects in the labour markets both in the source and in the sink countries. Taylor and Williamson (1997) estimate that the migration phenomena from Europe to North American between 1870 and 1913 raised wages in the source countries by 32% in Ireland and by 28% in Italy whereas wages

T. P. Dentinho (✉) · P. Aroca
University of Azores, Azores, Portugal
e-mail: tomas.lc.dentinho@uac.pt

© Springer International Publishing AG, part of Springer Nature 2018   77
U. Blien et al. (eds.), *Modelling Aging and Migration Effects on Spatial Labor Markets*, Advances in Spatial Science,
https://doi.org/10.1007/978-3-319-68563-2_5

become lower in the countries of destiny by 16% in Canada and by 8% in America. Reduction of wages and increase of unemployment in the country of destiny occurred also in France when Portuguese and Spanish emigrants arrive in the country in the sixties and seventies of the twentieth century (Hatton and Williamson 2011). According to (Winters et al. 2003), in OECD countries, 1 percentage point increase in the immigrant share increases native unemployment by 0.3 percentage points. All of this in a very dynamic process where different generations and sources of migrants adjust (Akresh 2008) and move (Zorlu 2013) across sectors of activity and society in the more developed world that attract migrants.

Not surprisingly, popular opinion on immigration pressures tend to be protectionist (Freeman 1995) with the low skilled workers concerned with labour competition (O'Rourke and Sinnott 2006) and the more wealthy worried with the tax effects (Boeri 2010). Understandably, the current scale of immigration matters too (Sides and Citrin 2007). Policy responses—in Europe, America, Japan and Australia— maintain and create border barriers (Baldwin-Edwards and Arango 1999) whenever it is possible to do it (Orn et.al. 2015). These attitudes and gestures regarding newcomers lead to migrants struggling for recognition in informal and formal low paid jobs in construction, agriculture, domestics, tourism, factory work and street hawking, remotely controlled by the authorities. There they fill the gaps of labour market inefficiencies and hope to get amnesties and family reunion (Carella and Pace 2002) but quite often, they are unable to build relationships and coherent communities (Dayaratne and Raja 2003).

In countries with loose controls in Africa, India and South America, migrants agglomerate in the slumps of major towns that, some argue, are the landscape of poverty reproduction (Gugler 1997; Davis 2006). Others hope that the formation of slums is just a phase of the urbanization and development process somehow manageable by appropriate planning tools or by wiser deployments of housing in urban areas (Antrop 2004; Ooi and Phua 2007). Nevertheless, even in very well planned rich cities, there are empty new houses where without jobs in the proximities, signs of slum resilience and developments in unplanned locations (Ooi and Phua 2007). Still others argue that spatial redistribution of public investment can ensure politically tolerable income disparities (Scott and Storper 2003) but agglomeration economies force the concentration in the larger cities many time reinforced urbanization policies followed by more concentration of public and private investments (Seto 2011). On the other side of the world, there are always those who are unable to migrate remaining detached in their poor landlocked places or suffering in the border wars for the control of rents from natural resources.

Migration models evolve according to theoretical background, the aim of the study, the available techniques and the quality of the data. The gravity type model proposed in (Zipf 1946) assumed that the volume of migration between two locations depends directly on their populations and inversely by the distance between them. This is a long-term perspective that does not take into account the changes in the labour markets (Jerome 1926) and the impact of migrant policies (Kuznets and Rubin 1954). More recently migration models based on human capital begun to appear and stated that people adjust their skills to where they are better rewarded, but those decisions are many times taken by families (Mincer 1978). Within the family and community context, where remittances play an important role (Katz and Stark 1986), the modelling can include the phenomenon of circular migration and the possibility of a stationary dynamic equilibrium (Harris and Todaro 1970).

Adam Smith (1776) suggested that spatial differences in the returns to labour pressures migration but high costs of international migration reduces the strength of that force. Authors along history followed this reasoning highlighting the factors that have positive and negative effects on migration, differences in labour retributions on the one hand and transport and communication costs on the other. Nevertheless, the strong reduction of transportation and communication costs is influencing the system dramatically which, associated with popular resistance to migrants, stimulate the creation of institutional barriers that are substituting distance and cultural barriers. International barriers are relatively recent in world history (Orn et al. 2015) but can become more and more present when the effect of their collapse rises with the differences in income around the world (Clemens et al. 2009). Until recently, developed countries tend to facilitate the entry and stay of immigrants but this enablement has probably been reversed (Ortega and Peri 2012).

Summing up, migration is the result of many drivers: policies and public investments, source and destination institutions, urbanization policies and the geographic concentration investments and growth very much related to regional development. The conceptual migration model proposed in this paper relates to a regional development model that highlights by two geographical attributes: scale and accessibility (Krugman 1991). Scale, associated with productive capacity and access, associated with the expenditure possibility, can be different and define, not just two, but four types of development processes somehow stimulated by geography: developed, underdeveloped, dependent and exploited (Dentinho 2012).

Developed regions are the ones that have productive and consumptive capacity; in these regions virtuous circles of development function as expected, with increasing productivity sustaining growing consumption and investment, allowing innovation and snowballing productivity. Poor places are those that suffer from vicious circles of poverty many times because they lack of scale and accessibility, observed in many poor regions with reduced productivity constrained consumption and limited investment, that discourages innovation and keeps income at subsistence levels. Emerging regions have productive capacity but part of the income generated go outside; in these cases, the consumptive part of the virtuous cycle of development runs outside the region that receives investment. Finally, dependent regions receive systematic unilateral transferences from outside which strengthen the consumptive capacity without reinforcing the productive capacity. Migration flows mainly from poor to emerging, dependent and developed regions and countries (Fig. 5.1).

The integrated model proposed above identifies, from the perspective of a poor region, various migration factors. From the source any change in income and access will increase migration pressures because better off individuals and families chose to

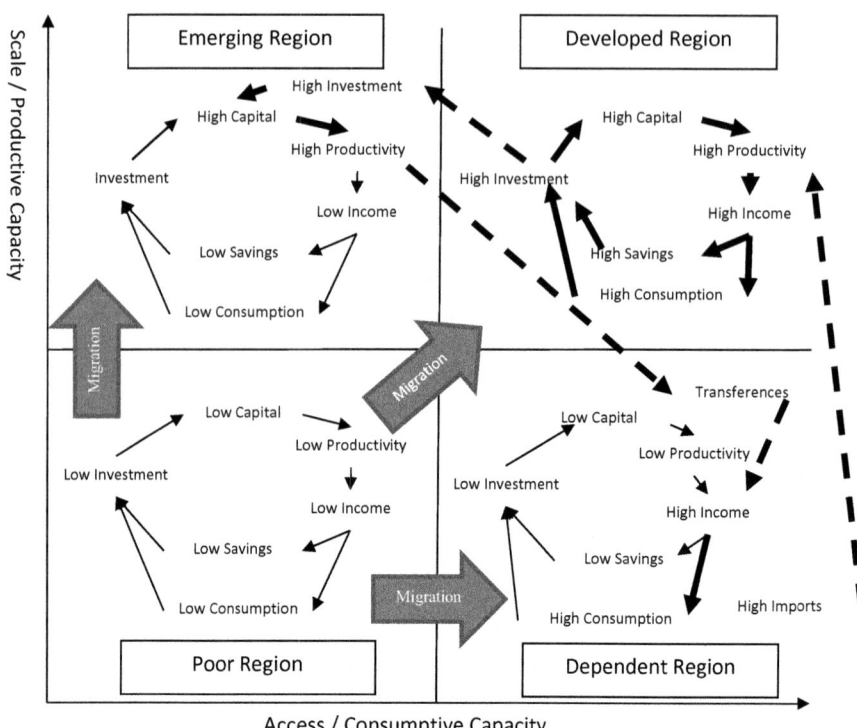

Fig. 5.1 Typology of regional development and migration pressures

get rewards from their skills in the dependent, emerging or developed world and be part of one possible emerging development story in their home countries by sending remittances owned outside. Nevertheless, quite often, these financial resources go to investments on non-tradable activities with reduced impact on local development. From the sink regions perspective, all of them have low paid jobs to fulfil by people coming from poor regions.

The aim of the paper is to understand the effect of those institutional barriers in migration looking at South Asia, a group of migrant developing and nearby nations that send migrants to depend, emerging and developed countries. These countries send migrants to the Golf area that depends on the rents of the oil, to emerging countries in South East Asia, and to the developed Western World. Nevertheless, the countries of South Asia do not share many migrants between themselves due to long lasting conflicts that divide them. What will be the effect if those barriers ceased to exist? What will happen with the collapse of the oil rents in the Middle East? What might happen with the take-off of some countries in the region?

To answer these questions for South Asia we first put South Asia in the World context in terms of development and migration. Then we estimated the migration model to simulate various scenarios for the migration factors including institutional barriers. The conclusion proposes some synthesis and future work on the impact of institutional barriers on migration.

2   South Asia Context

South Asia forms a quite clear group of countries in the World, with very low income per capita, strong rural population and high urbanization rates. Those countries also have reduced health care expenditures, high levels of remittances and small amount of rents from natural resources. Young population, reduced amount of trade in services, poor logistics and very low level of governmental expenditure complete the image of the regions based on treated data from the World Bank (Fig. 5.2 and Table 5.1).

The countries of South Asia are relatively poor compared to others and have large parts of their population still leaving in a vicious circle of poverty. Nevertheless, the opening of their economies to external trade and investment would bring those countries to a status of exploited and still more developed societies. Furthermore, the reduced weight of rents from natural resources refrains the path to a dependent situation based on those rents. Nevertheless, some dependency can occur associated with the importance of workers remittances tend go to urban areas, reinforcing dependent urbanization and rural poverty (Fig. 5.3).

In all, the intuition for this region is that the development process based on increasing flows of trade, investment and people is certainly better than isolationist's policies. In this paper we focus in migration and in the institutional barriers that limits them.

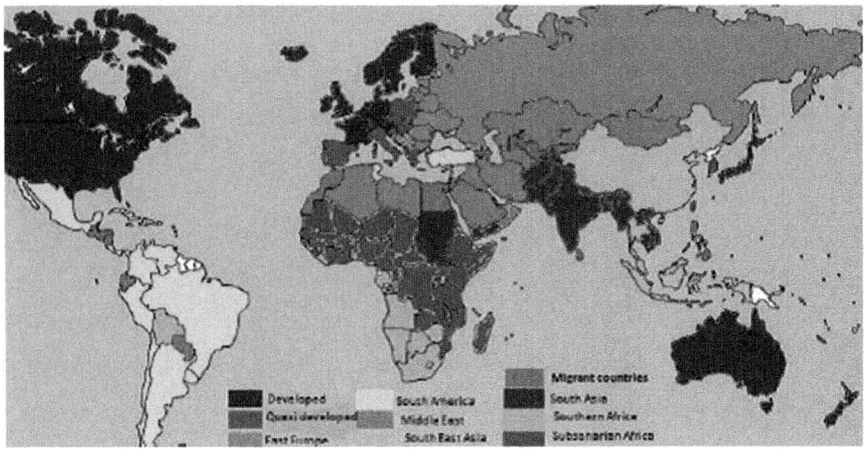

Fig. 5.2 Typology of countries

Table 5.1 Typology of countries (Treatment of data from the World Bank)

	Developed	Quasi developed	East Europe	South America	South East Asia	Middle East	Migrant countries	South Asia	Sub Saharan	Southern Africa
GNP per capita US$	46.263	19,816	5490	6022	3468	5498	2957	349	569	3318
Urban population %	80.40	64.63	23.61	78.64	19.03	64.38	54.87	29.85	34.41	44.19
Urban growth %	1.14	0.74	0.19	1.57	2.74	2.32	1.92	2.61	3.84	3.45
Heath expenditures %	9.64	7.65	6.11	6.73	3.88	4.07	6.50	4.49	6.57	6.61
Workers remittances %	0.59	1.27	4.62	2.61	1.36	1.98	12.37	10.34	3.00	9.90
Natural resources rent %	1.49	0.50	5.58	9.57	12.37	44.10	4.33	7.77	10.03	16.91
Population over 65%	15.73	14.92	14.10	7.21	6.10	5.17	5.83	4.22	3.05	3.67
Trade on services %	32.76	21.65	18.87	10.95	20.73	16.20	26.41	14.57	14.85	17.78
Logistic performance I	3.93	3.19	2.57	2.83	3.53	2.31	2.45	2.51	2.33	2.62
Governmental consumption %	19.14	18.39	15.56	12.71	12.55	13.56	13.33	10.68	12.84	22.66

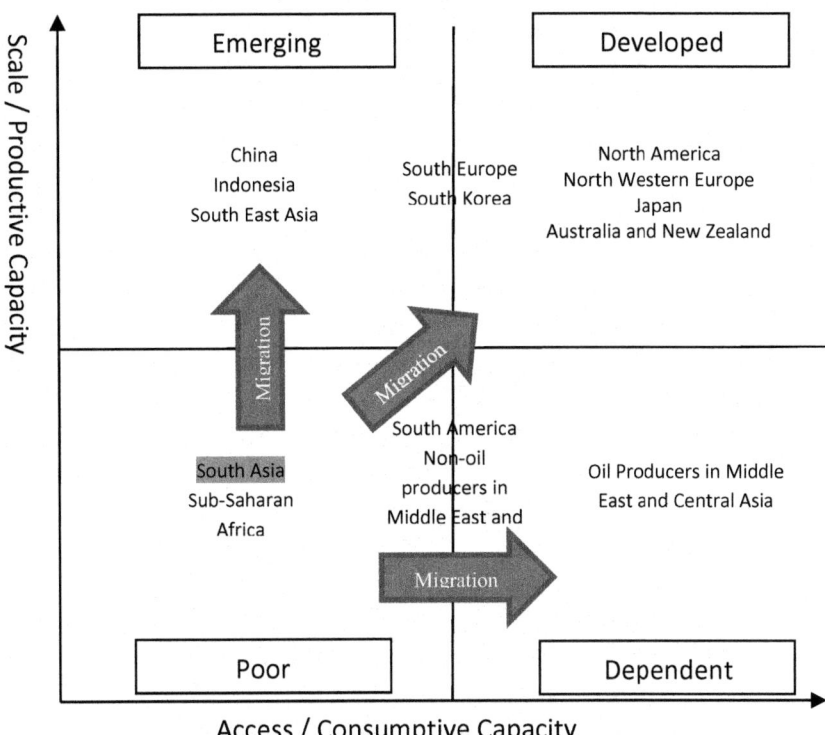

Fig. 5.3 Typology of regional development and migration pressures for South Asia

3   Migration Pressures and Responses in South Asia

Table 5.2 presents the migration flows to and from South Asian countries. A preliminary analysis of this table allows some intuitive comments: First, most emigrants (69%) go out of the region but 40% of them go to the nearby Middle East indicating that both income attraction and distance play a crucial role in migration flows. Second, as expected, more populated countries have more migrants than less populate ones. India, Bangladesh and Pakistan count for 71% of the emigrants of South Asian countries. Nevertheless, the proportion of emigrants per population is much bigger in countries experiencing conflicts like Afghanistan or in countries quite open to the outside in terms of migrants such as Bangladesh.

Furthermore, there seems to be many migration barriers between the different countries of the area; Afghanistan only receives migrants from Pakistan; Bhutan and Sri Lanka are only open to Indian migrants; the more open countries are certainly India and Bangladesh. Finally, it is quite common to have bilateral migration flows indicating that there is a strong return movement or even commuting migrations.

There are interesting patterns of migration flows in the area. Migrants from Afghanistan go to Pakistan but also to former Soviet Union. Bangladesh population

Table 5.2 Migration movements to and from South Asia countries

	Afghanistan	Bangladesh	Bhutan	India	Iran	Maldives	Nepal	Pakistan	Sri Lanka	Africa	Asia	Middle East	Europe	Latin America	North America	Oceania	IMMIGRANTS
Afghanistan								348,369			15,782						364,151
Bangladesh				34,431			39,059				939,753	30,160	47,781	36,583	46,008	0	1,173,775
Bhutan		52		44,732			717	22	33		1198	0	211		173	51	47,189
India	8086	3,171,022	6647		1706	199	542,947	1,106,212	155,195	4714	104,059	23,145	9659		4364	835	5,138,790
Iran	2,348,369							28,402			4901	102,456					2,484,128
Maldives		53,565		22,120				167	9448	49	1891	14	1119		177	131	88,681
Nepal		233	28,740	446,491				1268	46		20,308						497,086
Pakistan	1,618,687			2,000,908	2301				578		3202	251					3,625,927
SriLanka	128	653	227	10,460	102	1364	334	803		446	5886	7125	7876	37	839	570	36,850
Africa	677	13,166		103,582	1550	126	307	17,870	5346								
Asia	9306	477,853		402,032	9029		243,840	207,105	65,708								
Middle East	395,295	2,824,948		8,211,884	94,770		602,948	2,798,650	681,526								
Europe	313,229	386,095	2211	1,231,390	451,247	603	79,876	875,740	402,064								
Latin America	330	210	17	14,858	2018	14	82	1191	99								
North America	108,988	237,255	2519	2,591,284	508,502		84,734	500,660	195,072								
Oceania	40,022	40,358	3829	461,552	52,158	538	34,462	48,734	122,270								
EMIGRANTS	4,843,117	7,205,410	44,190	115,575,724	1,123,383	2844	1,629,306	5,935,193	1,637,385								

spreads around the World but have a major presence in India. Bhutan chooses Nepal. Indians have a considerable presence in Bhutan, Nepal, Sri Lanka, Africa, Australia and North America. Nepalese go to India and Asia and Pakistanis are the only ones that go to Afghanistan. Finally, people from Sri Lanka do migrate to Asia especially Japan.

There are signs that South Asian migrants in Europe and in South East Asia tend to stay where they migrate more than expected whereas South Asian migrants in China, Japan, North America and Russia tend to go back to the region more than would have been expected.

Trying to find the relative importance of factors that influence migration, we estimate a model that has, as dependent variable, the Natural Logarithm of Migrants from country (i) in country (j). The explanatory variables are the population in the origin (PopOriM), the population at the destiny (PopDesM), the ratio between the Product per Capita at the destiny and the Product per capita at the origin (GDPDes-Ori), the distance (Dist1000), and the square distance (Dist10002) between the origin and destiny. Furthermore, we introduce a set of dummy variables to capture the institutional relations from and between countries. With 3969 observations for 2015 cross section data, and with disaggregation for the countries of Western Asia, East Asia and South East Asia, the specified model has an Adjusted R2 of 0.18 that is relatively low indicating that there are any other factors that can add explanation to the existing migration patterns. Nevertheless all the explanatory variables present robust coefficients and with the expected signs:

- The variable (GDPDesOri) has significant coefficient. It shows that, on the one hand, economic convergence between countries and regions, mainly between emerging and developed places, will reduce migration pressures. On the other hand, the concentration of rents in dependent countries—like the Middle East—will attract migrants to those places mainly from poor countries that continue to expel the best human resources and fail to attract suitable Foreign Direct Investment.
- The Population at the origin (PopOriM), has relatively more influence that the population at destiny (PopDesM) which somehow explains the worries of host countries.
- Distance (Dist1000) has the expected negative effect on migration although far away countries be less penalized shown by the counterbalance effect of distance square (Dist10002). Necessarily, lower costs of transport and communication will increase the pressure of migrants.
- Finally, there are clear signs that there are institutional effects presented in the signals and in the significance of the dummy variables. On the one hand, there are strong migrant interactions centred in Afghanistan both with Iran (IRAAFG) and with Pakistan (AFGPAK, PAKAFG) related to the existence of conflicts and exiled people around this region. On the other hand, there are also some stronger interactions between India and Nepal (INDNEL), Pakistan and India (PAKIND), India and Nepal (INDNEL) and Nepal and Bhutan (NELBHU) (Table 5.3).

Table 5.3 Migration model estimates

R	R square		Adjusted R square		Std. error of the estimate	
0.431[a]	0.185		0.180		4.07370	
	Sum of squares	Df	Mean square	F	Sig.	
Regression	14,893.709	25	595.748	35.899	0.000[b]	
Residual	65,434.209	3943	16.595			
Total	80,327.917	3968				
Coefficients	Unstandardized		Standardized	*T*	Sig.	
	B	Std. error	Beta			
(Constant)	4.959	0.195		25.420	0.000	
PopDesM	0.004	0.000	0.189	10.240	0.000	
PopOriM	0.005	0000	0.279	15.171	0.000	
Dist1000	−0.642	0.054	−0.604	−11.973	0.000	
GDPDesOri	0.037	0.005	0.114	7.743	0.000	
Dist10002	0.031	0.003	0.479	9.547	0.000	
AFGor	−3.389	0.524	−0.094	−6.465	0.000	
AFGde	−1.125	0.520	−0.031	−2.164	0.031	
BANor	−2.232	0.520	−0.062	−4.289	0.000	
BANde	−3.990	0.663	−0.111	−6.018	0000	
BHUor	−3.001	0.523	−0.083	−5.736	0.000	
BHUde	−1.773	0.520	−0.049	−3.411	0.001	
INDor	−2.939	0.524	−0.082	−5.607	0.000	
INDde	−3.384	0.529	−0.094	−6.401	0.000	
NELor	−2.455	0.664	−0.068	−3.698	0.000	
PAKor	−1.957	0.519	−0.054	−3.768	0.000	
MALde	−2.253	0.523	−0.063	−4.304	0.000	
MALor	1.336	0.522	0.037	2.558	0.011	
SRIde	2.168	0.519	0.060	4.180	0.000	
AFGPAK	8.250	4.141	0.029	1.992	0.046	
PAKAFG	12.117	4.109	0.043	2.949	0.003	
IRAAFG	12.821	4.108	0.045	3.121	0.002	
PAKIND	8.503	4.141	0.030	2.053	0.040	
INDNEL	8.004	4.108	0.028	1.948	0051	
NELBHU	10.639	4.141	0.038	2.569	0.010	

- Finally—looking at the dummies specific to the countries—Iran, other Asian countries and blocks around the world has no difference from the constant whereas most of the countries of South Asia seem to present barriers to entry and to go out. The exception is to move from the Maldives or to go into Sri Lanka.

The results of this simple exercise provide some guidance for future work. First demographic, geographic and economic factors although having a robust explanatory impact on migration they are not able to explain most of the observable variance. Second, there are clear signs that conflicts of proximity do play a role in the migration patterns. Thirdly, most of the region has clear restrictions on the movement of people with the few exceptions of the Maldives, Sri Lanka and Iran.

Those are eventually the first barriers to overcome, because they would allow better interactions across borders but also because the reduction of barriers stimulates the adaptation of the skills to the place where they get more rewards. In fact, higher GDP in the relatively poor South Asia and in the emerging South East Asia will improve migration and at least theoretically higher incomes and lower unemployment back home, at least if there are lower barriers to move out and to move in.

4 Conclusions

The aim of the essay was to perceive the impact of institutional barriers in migration looking at South Asia, a group of migrant poor and nearby nations that send migrants to rich countries in the western world, to dependent countries in the Golf Area and to emerging economies in South East Asia. The question was to know the impact of the change of the institutional boundaries that limit the movement of people within and from South Asia.

The main argument of the paper is that globalization is strengthening migration factors with reduced transport and communication costs, increased demographic complementarities between sending and receiving countries and accumulated pressures from potential migrants to better use their skills. These causalities reinforce themselves in South Asia because there is no control on the migration from rural to urban areas and many times across loose borders. Also because many types of alternative migrations are possible: to developed countries in the Western World with long established communication links; to dependent countries in the Golf area, and to emerging countries in South East Asia. The enormous scale of the Subcontinent associated with a considerable degree of isolationism refrains the movement of more people to the outside world. The issue is to know how this enormous scale and isolationism can feed an endogenous process of development; so far, it did not, at least when the performance of the region compares with South East and East Asia. Institutional factors in the migration policies might play a role.

References

Abel GJ, Sander N (2014) Report: quantifying global international migration flows. Science 343(6178):1520–1522
Akresh IR (2008) Occupational trajectories of legal U.S. immigrants: downgrading and recovery. Popul Dev Rev 34(3):435–456

Baldwin-Edwards M, Arango J (eds) (1999) Where free market reign: Aliens in the Twilight Zone. Page 1 to16 of immigrants and informal economy in the Southern Europe. Frank Cass, London

Carella M, Pace R (2002) Some migration dynamic specific to Southern Europe: South and East-West Axis. Int Migr 39(4):63–99

Clemens MA, Montenegro AC, Pritchett L (2009). The place premium: wage differences for identical workers across the U.S. Border, Centre for Global Development Working Paper 148, Washington

Dayaratne R, Raja S (2003) Empowering communities: the Peri-urban areas of Colombo. Environ Urban 15(1):102

Dentinho T (2012) New challenges for sustainable growth. In: Capello R, Dentinho TP (eds) Networks, space and competitiveness, evolving challenges for sustainable growth. Edgar Elgar, UK, pp 276–290

Grogger J, Hanson G (2011) Income maximization and the selection and sorting of international migrants. J Dev Econ 95:42–57

Harris J, Todaro M (1970) Migration, unemployment and development: a two-sector analysis. Am Econ Rev 60:126–142

Hatton TJ, Williamson JG (2011) Are third world emigration forces abating? World Dev 39:20–32

Jerome H (1926) Migration and business cycles. National Bureau of Economic Research, New York

Katz E, Stark O (1986) Labour migration and risk aversion in less developed countries. J Labour Econ 4(1):134–149

Kuznets S, Rubin R (1954) National Bureau of Economic Research Occasional Paper 46. Immigration and the Foreign Born. National Bureau of Economic Research, New York

Mincer J (1978) Family migration decisions. J Polit Econ 86(5):749–773

Orn BB, Nicole BS, Chad S (2015) Migration theory. In: Chiswick BR, Miller PW (eds) Economics of international migration, vol 1A. North Holland, Oxford

Ortega F, Peri G (2012) The effect of income and immigration policies on international migration, NBER Working Paper 18322, Boston

Ooi GL, Phua KH (2007) Urbanization and slum formation. J Urban Health 84(1):27–34

Pace M (2006) The politics of regional identity: meddling with the Mediterranean. Routledge, New York

Scott AJ, Storper M (2003) Regions, globalization and development. Reg Stud 6 & 7:579–593

Smith A (1776) An Inquiry into the nature and causes of the Wealth of Nations, 1937 edn. Modern Library, New York

Taylor AM, Williamson JG (1997) Convergence in the age of mass migration. Eur Rev Econ Hist 1:27–63

Winters LA, Walmsley TL, Wang ZK, Grynberg R (2003) Liberalising temporary movement of natural persons: an agenda for the development round. World Econ 26:1137–1161

Young A (2013) Inequality, the urban-rural gap, and migration. Q J Econ 128(4):1727–1785

Zipf G (1946) The [P(1)P(2)/D] hypothesis; On the intercity movement of persons. Am Sociol Rev 11:677–686

Chapter 6
Lagging Regions and Labour Market Dynamics in Brazil

Ana Maria Bonomi Barufi

1 Introduction

Regional disparities in Brazil are still very pronounced, albeit the significant income inequality reduction in the country as a whole in the past 15 years. The average wage in the Northeast region of the country amounted to 0.65 of the national level, while in the Southeast it was 1.14 times higher than the national level in 2015. Moreover, college degree holders represented 17.2% of total workers in the Southeast and 9.6% in the Northeast. Unemployment rates reached 10.5% and 10.1% in these regions in the same year, respectively.

Labour mobility should be an important ingredient for the dynamics of regional inequalities. The literature of internal migration has two markedly distinct perspectives on this relationship. Traditional neoclassical models conclude that migration should respond to and decrease regional inequalities. In this way, the impact of migration is strong in labour supply and almost negligible in labour demand (Niebuhr et al. 2012). However, the persistent regional inequalities do not seem to be encompassed by these conclusions (Greenwood 1997).

An alternative explanation for migration movements comes from convergence and divergence forces. On this verge, agglomeration effects advocated by the New Economic Geography literature represent divergence forces, increasing real income differentials. Eventually, congestion costs will impose a limit on migration and to the attraction of workers to a large city. In this context, migration affects labour demand, since the inflow of workers strengthen agglomeration economies (Niebuhr et al. 2012). An alternative explanation for growing regional disparities comes from the selective migration (Kanbur and Rapoport 2005). Potential migrants are

A. M. B. Barufi (✉)
Economics Department – FEA, NEREUS – The University of São Paulo Regional and Urban Economics Lab, São Paulo, Brazil

© Springer International Publishing AG, part of Springer Nature 2018   89
U. Blien et al. (eds.), *Modelling Aging and Migration Effects on Spatial Labor Markets*, Advances in Spatial Science,
https://doi.org/10.1007/978-3-319-68563-2_6

heterogeneous and they may be affected by the incentives to migrate in a unique way. As a consequence, the characteristics of those who remain are different from those of the original pool of individuals. If there is positive selection in migration, origins from migratory movements are expected to become less developed and to show lower income levels.

This chapter aims at investigating the role migration had on the skill composition of the labour force in Brazil in the past few decades, highlighting the main differences for lagging and developed regions. Next, the relationship between migration movements and labour market outcomes is explored, focusing on the effects of skilled and unskilled migration flows over local wages.

The main results indicate that regional disparities are reinforced by migration flows in Brazil. There are two main channels through which this effect is generated: (1) more educated workers are more likely to migrate and usually move to more developed labour market areas; (2) these are the same areas in which local wages are positively affected by the arrival of skilled individuals. Lagging regions are directly affected only by migration flows of low-skilled individuals (positive effect for their departure, negative effect for their arrival). This result is in accordance to the results found by the agglomeration economies literature, according to which migration reinforces regional disparities.

The remaining of the text is organised as follows. The next section presents empirical findings on labour mobility and regional disparities, with a brief review of migration studies for Brazil. The third section outlines the empirical strategy. Then, the fourth section presents the data and the main descriptive statistics, with an analysis of recent migration flows and their relations with local skill composition. The fifth section discuss the main estimation results of regression analysis and the sixth section presents the final remarks.

2 Empirical Literature

The distribution of population in space has been changing in the past few decades, and this process relates to increasing urbanisation, ageing population and agglomeration forces which lead to concentration and higher inequality. The rise in agglomeration (Glaeser 2011) can be associated to a decline in transportation costs, new infrastructure, increasing returns to scale (sharing, matching and learning— Puga 2010), more attractive amenities, and the sorting of more productive firms and workers (Combes et al. 2008), among other factors, according to Poot and Pawar (2013). On the other hand, many cities saw a population decline and an ageing process, given local disamenities (congestion, crime, pollution) and higher life costs.

Labour migration is key to this process, as it proves to be one of the main channels through which regional equilibrium is pursued over time. There is a plethora of methods and strategies to investigate the interaction between regional inequality and labour flows, with varying conclusions. Following a strand of the literature that explores migration's role in promoting interregional labour-market flexibility, Partridge and Rickman (2006) find that less than half of migration fluctuations were responses to demand shocks. This type of flow should be the channel through which migration could reduce regional disparities, meaning that the impact of total mobility on regional inequality was somewhat limited in the US. Migration timing to local labour demand shocks may vary according to the skill level (Mauro and Splimbergo 1999). For Spain, the authors find that highly skilled people adjust more rapidly to those shocks, a movement that is associated to the persistence of geographical disparities.

Migration generates opposing forces, some increasing and others reducing spatial differentials. Among the former, there are the traditional negative impacts of brain drain, and the latter include the creation of business and trade networks through return migration and remittances. In the context of endogenous skill formation, Kanbur and Rapoport (2005) focus on the effects of migration selectivity over the origin region, and show that migration may be an additional factor to explain why spatial disparities either persist or diminish over time.

High-skilled workers benefit more from migration to rich regions, while low-skilled workers tend to migrate to poor regions to decrease their life costs (Giannetti 2003). On the same direction, Borjas et al. (1992) find that places which offer higher returns to skills will attract skilled workers, and individuals who face a severe mismatch of their skills with the reward structure will most likely relocate to achieve a better matching in the labour market. These mechanisms seem to reinforce regional disparities, as high-skilled workers will tend to move to richer regions. The results found by Arntz (2010) for Germany reinforce this perspective that high-skilled individuals are more likely to relocate in response to interregional income differentials, while low-skilled workers go after a larger number of job opportunities.

A third literature strand explores labour market effects of migration. For instance, Huber and Tondi (2012) find that unemployment is not significantly related to migration, while GDP per capita and productivity are positively affected by labour flows. Niebuhr et al. (2012) find that for Germany, distinguishing by in-flow and out-flow movements, there is no effect of migration over wages and they can only find an effect over unemployment disparities, which seems to be in line with the neoclassical reasoning previously mentioned. Moreover, Østbye and Westerlund (2007) aim to identify whether regional convergence of GDP per capita is facilitated by migration in Norwegian and Swedish counties. Their results indicate that in Norway there seems to be a centripetal force against regional convergence, while in Sweden migration works in the opposite direction.

This study will aim to implement an empirical strategy that is similar to the one adopted by the third literature strand aforementioned. Given the lack of a conclusion of the potential effects of migration over local labour markets, there is room to contribute to this subject and provide further empirical elements for the posterior formulation of theoretical models.

2.1 Migration Analysis in Brazil

The literature on internal migration in Brazil is significantly large, mapping the most recent developments of interregional and rural-urban flows. These migration movements are directly related to the heterogeneous regional development of the country, both as cause and consequence. Migration can be investigated on the basis of aggregated flows as well as at the individual level. In the Brazilian case, Justo and Silveira-Neto (2006) follow the former approach, estimating a panel model for the net migration rate at the state level (1992–1997–2002), including local characteristics (labour market conditions – expected income, geography, climate, criminality, and inequality) and the spatial lag of all these independent variables. Their main conclusion is that the coefficient for expected income increases whenever further controls are included in the regression from 0.3401 to 0.4677.

Dos Santos Júnior et al. (2005) use cross-section state-level data to show that migrant workers are positively selected from non-migrants both at the origin and the destination. Among the main controls included in their analysis, local life cost (ICV), schooling level, age, age-squared, occupation, residence zone, race, gender, sector of activity, union status, and state of residence. A similar exercise is conducted by Silva and Silveira-Neto (2005) for a longer period (1993–2003). They find a lower effect of migration over wages than the previous study, and this selection seems to decrease over time.

Ramalho and Queiroz (2011) find that return migrants are negatively selected in relation to permanent migrants. Moreover, among those who return, individuals that are more qualified obtain wage increases by returning (probably because they find a more suitable occupation for their qualification). With a slightly different methodology, Santos and Ferreira (2007) evaluate the relationship between interstate migration and regional income distribution. Migration seems to be related to an increase of 13.7% on individual income. Furthermore, their results over a counterfactual analysis indicate that migration seems to increase average income of most states and of the country as a whole.

More recently, there has been an effort to include not only observed but also unobserved individual characteristics as controls for a migration decision analysis, considering longitudinal databases. In Brazil, RAIS-MIGRA is the main data source with these characteristics. Based on this database, Taveira and Almeida (2014) show that the main determinants of migration flows of qualified migrants between municipalities in Brazil are expected income in the destination, population, GDP per capita, the degree of industrialisation and better amenities. They also find that the characteristics of neighbouring areas are relevant in this migration decision. Even after controlling for individual fixed effects, Freguglia, Gonçalves and Silva (2014) find that wage differentials between origin and destination states are very relevant in determining the migration of skilled workers. In addition, these migrants look for states with higher prosperity, higher population density, better urban amenities and higher dynamism.

Finally, the results found by Freguglia and Procópio (2013) indicate that after controlling for individual unobserved characteristics, regional wage differentials are largely affected by changing jobs and interstate migration. Furthermore, the effect on wages of getting a job in a different firm is lower than the effect of moving to another municipality.

3   Empirical Strategy

The analysis presented here aims to investigate whether regional migration increases or decreases inequalities in the labour market, promoting regional divergence or convergence. The empirical approach is based on different aspects of Østbye and Westerlund (2007) and Niebuhr et al. (2012). These authors explore migration effects over GDP per capita, and over unemployment rate and wages, respectively. The focus of this paper will be solely on the real wage, given its direct relationship with regional inequalities and the fact that this variable meets consistency requirements for Brazilian databases over time.

The basic model to be estimated is the following:

$$w_{rt} = \beta_1 w_{rt-10} + \beta_2 imr_{rt-5} + \beta_3 omr_{rt-5} + \sum_{k=1}^{K} \delta_k x_{k,rt} + \mu_r + \varphi_t + \varepsilon_{rt}$$

(6.1)

where w_{rt-10} is the average wage for the same region in the previous census, the in-migration rate is defined as $imr_{rt-5} = im_{rt-5}/pop_{rt-5}$ and the out-migration rate can be obtained through $omr_{rt-5} = om_{rt-5}/pop_{rt-5}$. There are potential endogeneity issues for these migration ratios that are treated with the estimation of instrumental variables models. More specifically, the instruments considered here are based on 10-year lags of the same in and out-migration rates. One of the main contributions of this work is the estimation of the model outlined in (6.1) for different education attainment levels.

Furthermore, $x_{k,rt}$ includes a set of controls at the local level, such as the composition of the labour force in terms of sectors and occupations, the education level of local workers, the percentage of male individuals in the population and the percentage of people living in urban areas.

Finally, no spatial effects are considered in this study, apart from region dummies. Elhorst (2003) points out that commuting should be explicitly considered in a model for regional labour markets. However, the unit of analysis here is the labour market area (LMA), which comprises daily commuting flows. In this sense, local labour markets are supposed to be somehow independent among these areas, given their size and the fact that administrative regions were already aggregated to form LMAs.

3.1   Lagging Regions

The definition of a lagging region can be based on a comparative analysis of a specific indicator of economic activity. Camagni (1995) points out that successful new industrial regions may present the main characteristics to be an *innovative milieu*, among which there are district economies, proximity economies, and synergy elements. Lagging regions, on the other hand, can potentially house an *innovative milieu*, but they do not present these elements yet.

Farole (2012) associates these spatial disparities within countries to an accelerated growth pattern of well-located metropolitan regions in comparison to peripheral areas that fall further behind. According to Farole (2013, p. 2), growing regional disparities may challenge social and political cohesion, especially when factor markets are not fluid enough and tax and transfer policies do not work efficiently to reduce inequalities. Migration flows from lagging to leading regions may deepen this process.

The World Bank's World Development Report (2009) brought attention to the fact that agglomeration economies may exacerbate regional divergence. Apart from structural factors (location, agglomeration potential), other barriers such as government failures may frustrate integration and growth prospects. The United Nations strongly advised governments to remove this type of barrier to the deconcentration of the economic activity (political, institutional, lack of infrastructure, etc.). In the same direction, governments should promote investments to start growth poles in lagging regions and should facilitate migration of individuals to areas of rising well-being (Kanbur and Venables 2005).

There are different criteria to define lagging regions. To the World Bank (2009), a lagging area is a place distant from density. The European Union applies a simple definition to identify which areas require assistance to achieve the interregional convergence objective: lagging areas are those whose GDP per capita is lower than 75% of the EU average[1]. In Mexico, the basic measure is a marginalisation index, which is a composed indicator of access to drinking water and electricity, quality of the dwelling, and the percentage of the working population that is poorly paid, focusing on remote rural areas of the south (OECD 2003).

The analysis conducted here will compare lagging and leading regions by analysing labour market areas according to their position on the GDP per capita distribution. Then, five different groups will be defined: labour market areas with less than 100,000 inhabitants, and among labour market areas with at least 100,000 inhabitants, they are divided in quartiles based on their GDP per capita.

4   Data

Every 10 years the Brazilian Institute of Geography and Statistics (Instituto Brasileiro de Geografia e Estatística – IBGE) conducts the Demographic Census, which covers the whole country with regional disaggregation at the municipal level

---

[1]http://www.europedia.moussis.eu/books/Book_2/5/12/01/01/?all=1 , accessed on 25/04/2016.

(or at the neighbourhood level for bigger municipalities). This survey investigates the main characteristics of individuals and households (education, migration, labour market supply aspects, family composition, living conditions, among others).

The analysis that follows was based on information obtained from the demographic censuses of 1991, 2000 and 2010. Over this period, there has been a significant change in the number of municipalities in Brazil, with the emancipation and consequent foundation of new local administrations. In 1991, there were 4491 municipalities; in 2000, 5507; and in 2010, 5565 municipalities. Any analysis involving data over this time period should take into consideration the fact that the borders of municipalities have been changing, due to merging or splitting processes to create new municipalities (Reis et al. 2011). Therefore, 4258 Minimum Comparable Areas (MCAs) for the period 1991–2010 were defined keeping, constant the borders and areas of each regional unit of analysis.

Then, these MCAs were put together to form labour market areas (*Regiões de Influência de Cidades*), a compound of municipalities aggregated on the basis of the flow of goods and services (IBGE 2007) for the 2010 municipal configuration. Their configuration was harmonised with the 1991–2010 MCAs previously defined, obtaining 478 LMAs (from originally 482).[2] Here, they will form the basic unit of analysis.

Wages in LMAs are calculated over individuals aged 25 or more, working in the private sector, and were deflated by the national consumer price index (INPC-IBGE). Data is obtained at the LMA for 2000 and 2010, and some variables are calculated for 1991 as well to be used as instruments. Migration data in the census refers to the residential location 5 years before the interview. Therefore, it does not identify the exact moment the individual moved.

As discussed above, lagging regions are defined according to their population size and GDP per capita. The reference year is 1999, as it is the first year for which IBGE calculated the municipal GDP and it is prior to 2000, the first year of our regression models. Then, there are two types of lagging regions: those with population lower than 100,000 inhabitants and the ones with a higher population, but with a GDP per capita ranked among the lowest quartile of the LMAs with a population of 100,000 or more. Table 6.1 presents the main descriptive characteristics of these LMAs' groups.

The criteria outlined above generates a very clear regional distribution of each class. The upper group (higher GDP per capita and large population) is concentrated in the Southeast and the South, with some LMAs in the North and the Centre-West. On the other hand, lagging regions are scattered all over the Northeast and in parts of the Centre-West, apart from some LMAs in the South (Fig. 6.1).

---

[2]The definition of the 1991-2010 MCAs and respective LMAs can be made available by the author upon request.

Table 6.1 Descriptive statistics of the five groups of LMAs

	Average GDP per capita (R$ 1999)	Average population	Number of LMAs
Less than 100,000 inhabitants	R$ 3932	60,126	162
More than 100,000 inhabitants			
First quartile GDP pc	R$ 1441	256,950	79
Second quartile GDP pc	R$ 2933	469,828	79
Third quartile GDP pc	R$ 5144	307,063	79
Fourth quartile GDP pc	R$ 8627	978,982	79
All LMAs	R$ 4331	353,041	478

Source: Author's elaboration

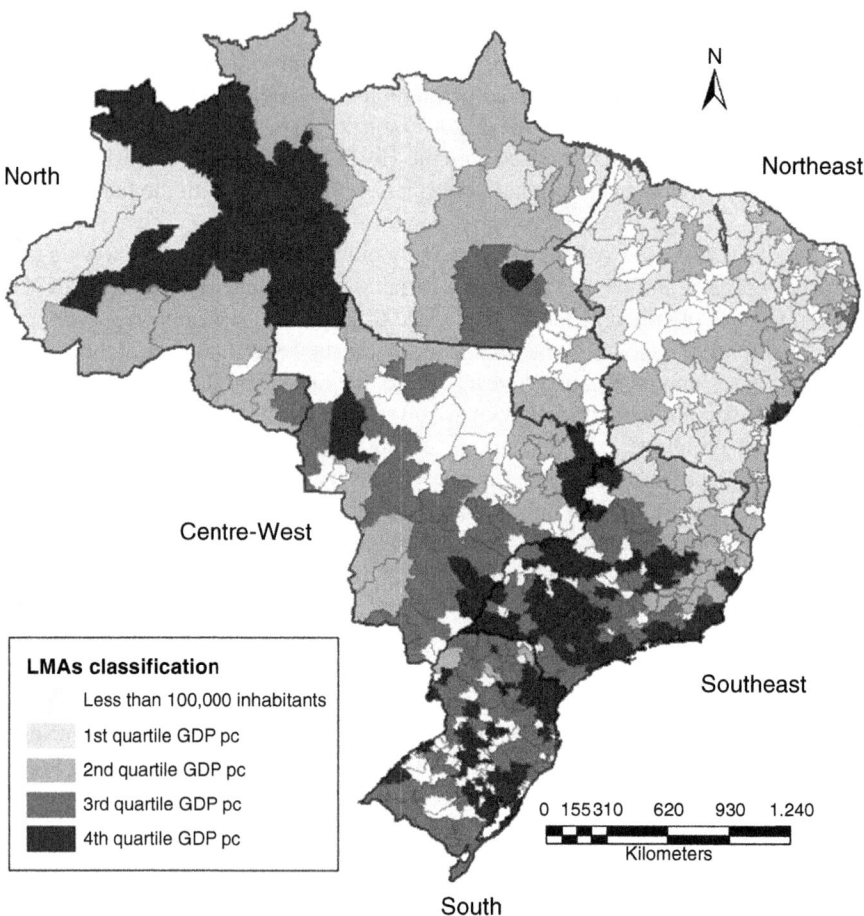

Fig. 6.1 Classification of LMAs. Source: Author's elaboration

4.1 Descriptive Statistics

The main descriptive statistics presented in Table 6.2 show that wages grew in real terms between 2000 and 2010. In addition to that, migration seems to have decreased, but is higher in relative terms for workers with tertiary education. The education level of the population has increased significantly over the decade, with the percentage of individuals with tertiary degree almost doubling. Women also increased their participation in the labour market.

A more detailed analysis of migration flows is presented in Table 6.3. Skilled individuals (with at least a completed secondary degree) are more prone to migrate, and the difference between in and out-migration is larger for lagging regions (lose more people than attract). In LMAs with less than 100,000 inhabitants, there is almost one percentage point of difference between those who leave and whose who arrive these places. In LMAs in the first quartile of GDP per capita, this difference almost reached three percentage points in 1991, and decreased over time (but still amounts to 1.7 percentage point).

The most interesting result is presented in Table 6.4. Even in lagging regions people who move in and out the LMA are more qualified than those who stay. However, the composition of the labour force in general terms is less favourable

Table 6.2 Main descriptive statistics

	2000	2010
ln(hourly wage)	1.65	1.73
ln(hourly wage) $(t-10)$	1.43	1.65
In-migration rate—educ1	6.3%	4.8%
In-migration rate—educ2	9.4%	6.8%
In-migration rate—educ3	10.0%	7.4%
In-migration rate—educ4	17.9%	10.4%
Out-migration rate—educ1	6.6%	4.9%
Out-migration rate—educ2	10.5%	7.4%
Out-migration rate—educ3	10.9%	8.3%
Out-migration rate—educ4	13.9%	9.7%
Total in-migration rate	7.3%	5.9%
Total out-migration rate	7.7%	6.2%
% male	67.2%	61.1%
% urban population	72.9%	78.4%
% complete primary or incomplete secondary education	11.5%	15.0%
% complete secondary or incomplete tertiary education	16.5%	24.6%
%complete tertiary education	5.4%	10.9%
ln(population density)	3.21	3.30

(*) edu1-educ4 refer to the different education levels: no schooling or incomplete primary education, complete primary education or incomplete secondary education, complete secondary education or incomplete tertiary education, and complete tertiary education, in the same order
Source: Author's elaboration

Table 6.3 Share of in and out-migrants, for skilled and total population, by LMA class

	Less than 100,000 inhabitants (%)	First quartile GDP pc (%)	More than 100,000 inhabitants			Fourth quartile GDP pc (%)
			Second quartile GDP pc (%)	Third quartile GDP pc (%)		
1991% of out-migrants—total	10.8	7.7	6.9	7.5		4.9
% of out-migrants—skilled	15.9	13.5	8.8	10.2		6.2
% of in-migrants—total	8.9	4.7	6.8	7.5		5.8
% of in-migrants—skilled	15.0	10.5	9.4	11.1		6.1
2000% of out-migrants—total	9.0	6.5	5.8	6.4		4.7
% of out-migrants—skilled	12.9	10.6	7.6	8.9		5.6
% of in-migrants—total	8.1	4.6	5.9	6.4		5.2
% of in-migrants—skilled	11.7	8.6	7.9	8.8		5.8
2010% of out-migrants—total	7.4	5.3	4.6	5.2		3.8
% of out-migrants—skilled	10.1	7.7	5.7	7.2		4.6
% of in-migrants—total	7.0	3.6	4.5	5.5		4.2
% of in-migrants—skilled	9.7	6.0	5.8	7.2		4.7

Source: Author's elaboration

Table 6.4 Educational attainment of individuals who arrive, leave or stay in different LMAs

	Less than 100,000 inhabitants		More than 100,000 inhabitants—1st quartile		More than 100,000 inhabitants—2nd quartile		More than 100,000 inhabitants—3rd quartile		More than 100,000 inhabitants—4th quartile	
	No schooling or incomplete primary education (%)	Complete tertiary education (%)	No schooling or incomplete primary education (%)	Complete tertiary education (%)	No schooling or incomplete primary education (%)	Complete tertiary education (%)	No schooling or incomplete primary education (%)	Complete tertiary education (%)	No schooling or incomplete primary education (%)	Complete tertiary education (%)
1991 Outflow	78.1	3.1	82.2	1.9	71.9	5.2	66.4	7.8	56.6	11.6
Inflow	75.3	4.5	78.5	3.5	69.8	5.6	63.8	8.4	64.0	9.1
Stayers	85.7	1.8	90.8	0.8	78.2	3.4	74.5	4.8	63.9	7.9
2000 Outflow	68.0	4.6	73.8	2.3	61.8	6.7	54.1	10.6	48.9	12.6
Inflow	68.1	5.3	71.5	4.0	60.6	7.0	53.9	10.0	52.3	11.3
Stayers	78.0	2.6	84.9	1.2	70.0	4.2	65.2	6.1	54.9	9.0
2010 Outflow	51.1	10.4	57.1	5.5	45.4	13.4	36.8	20.7	33.5	22.1
Inflow	50.5	11.2	53.4	9.7	44.6	14.1	39.1	18.0	36.2	20.2
Stayers	63.7	6.6	71.0	3.9	55.4	8.2	50.7	10.9	41.0	14.3

Source: Author's elaboration

in these regions. The aforementioned improvement in education attainment is also shown in this table, given the significant change of skill composition in all LMAs. People who arrive in lagging regions are relatively more qualified than those who leave, and in more developed LMAs, the percentage of individuals with tertiary education is lower among those who arrive than between the group of people that leaves. This is an indication that the group of individuals that decides to leave a developed area must have found a better opportunity, and may be even more qualified than those who arrive. For all cases, stayers are less qualified than people who move (in accordance with the literature).

The next section will explore how different types of migration flows affect wages in Brazilian LMAs.

5   Results

Table 6.5 summarizes the main results of the pooled cross-section model for average wages in LMAs. In all the specifications, whenever the wage lag is significant, it is positive. Migration flows refer to the past 5 years before the survey, but it is not possible to assert when the individual actually moved. In-migration has a positive and significant sign for smaller LMAs, and for larger LMAs in the upper quartiles. In fact, wage growth in lagging regions with lower GDP per capita is not significantly affected by in-migration flows. Out-migration is negative and significant only in Models 4 and 5, but its general indication is of a reduction in the current wage level of the origin.

In Models 7–12, out-migration of low-skilled workers (*educ1*) leads to an increase in local wages, while the fact that individuals with an intermediate education attainment (*educ2*) leave the LMA decreases local wages. This result is valid for small LMAs and the whole dataset. For LMAs in the first quartile, the entrance of low-skilled workers decreases local wages while their exit has the opposite effect. For LMAs in the third quartile, the effect is the opposite. The arrival of more skilled workers increases local wages, while their departure has an opposite sign. This set of models indicate that the labour market of less developed LMAs is more affected by low-skilled workers, while in more developed LMAs it is the flow of high-skilled workers that matters.

The final set of models brings an attempt to deal with the potential endogeneity of migration flows mentioned in Sect. 4. However, when 10-year lags of migration flows are used as instruments, the effects of in and out-migration rates of each skill group no longer exist. Some of the models lose their aggregated explanatory power (Models 14, 15 and 17), which is a sign that these instruments may not capture adequately the relationship between migration rates and wages.

Then, in Table 6.6 the same models are estimated, but now exploring the longitudinal structure of the database. It is worth mentioning that the two observations considered here are separated by a 10-year period, which may be too long for a local unobserved effect to be valid. It would mean that in 10 years unobserved

Table 6.5 Pooled cross sections for the logarithm of the hourly wage in LMAs, 2000 and 2010

	OLS regressions												IV regressions					
	Total	Less than 100,000 inhabitants	More than 100,000 inhabitants				Total	Less than 100,000 inhabitants	More than 100,000 inhabitants				Total	Less than 100,000 inhabitants	More than 100,000 inhabitants			
			First quartile GDP pc	Second quartile GDP pc	Third quartile GDP pc	Fourth quartile GDP pc			First quartile GDP pc	Second quartile GDP pc	Third quartile GDP pc	Fourth quartile GDP pc			First quartile GDP pc	Second quartile GDP pc	Third quartile GDP pc	Fourth quartile GDP pc
	Model 1	Model 2	Model 3	Model 4	Model 5	Model 6	Model 7	Model 8	Model 9	Model 10	Model 11	Model 12	Model 13	Model 14	Model 15	Model 16	Model 17	Model 18
Wage ($t-10$)	0.467***	0.407***	0.338***	0.331***	0.429***	0.398***	0.465***	0.401***	0.341***	0.312***	0.407***	0.360***	0.491***	-1.584	0.671	0.006	0.573	0.373***
In-migration rate	0.556***	0.519**	0.227	0.333	1.106***	0.634***												
Out-migration rate	0.175	0.465	0.186	-0.679*	-0.910**	-0.223												
In-migration rate_educ1							0.063	0.502	-2.257**	0.101	0.281	0.920	-0.774	-166.380	-13.249	0.335	-1.748	0.112
In-migration rate_educ2							0.197	-0.055	0.428	-0.514	0.295	-0.069	0.801	160.212	-6.054	0.914	-2.958	3.952
In-migration rate_educ3							0.159	-0.025	1.067**	0.654	0.036	-0.114	-0.879	-10.462	6.438	-3.880	7.983	-2.961
In-migration rate_educ4							0.041	0.070	0.002	0.001	0.403**	0.057	0.654	10.129	0.664	1.981	-5.116	-0.022
Out-migration rate_educ1							1.000***	1.316***	1.331*	0.086	0.635	0.449	4.319	-49.347	5.097	7.691	22.564	-2.740
Out-migration rate_educ2							-0.630***	-0.724**	-0.429	-0.336	-0.068	-0.447	-5.299	192.090	-0.685	4.871	-31.732	-1.316
Out-migration rate_educ3							0.034	0.133	0.511	-0.571	-1.490***	-0.341	3.093	-60.081	3.608	-11.102	13.058	2.461
Out-migration rate_educ4							0.048	0.114	-0.026	0.102	0.203	0.039	-0.291	-58.994	-3.185	0.912	1.778	0.085
Year dummy	Yes	Yes	Yes	Yes	Yes	Yes	Yes	Yes	Yes	Yes	Yes	Yes	Yes	Yes	Yes	Yes	Yes	Yes
N	956	324	158	158	158	158	956	324	158	158	158	158	956	324	158	158	158	158
Adjusted R2	0.918	0.860	0.804	0.879	0.853	0.879	0.919	0.862	0.816	0.877	0.861	0.875	0.823	0.6	.	0.085	.	0.782
Wald test													5173.3	837.9	112.2	201.1	41.9	837.9

Obs: additional controls: percentage of workers in economic sectors and occupations, % of rural workers, % of people living in urban areas, % of people with each education attainment. Instruments: 10-year lag of in and out-migration rates for each education group (Models 13–18)

Obs1: edu1–educ4 refer to the different education levels: no schooling or incomplete primary education, complete primary education or incomplete secondary education, complete secondary education or incomplete tertiary education, and complete tertiary education, in the same order

Source: Author's elaboration

Table 6.6 Panel models for the logarithm of the hourly wage in LMAs, 2000 and 2010

	FE models						FE models						IV FE models					
	Total	Less than 100,000 inhabitants	More than 100,000 inhabitants				Total	Less than 100,000 inhabitants	More than 100,000 inhabitants				Total	Less than 100,000 inhabitants	More than 100,000 inhabitants			
			First quartile GDP pc	Second quartile GDP pc	Third quartile GDP pc	Fourth quartile GDP pc			First quartile GDP pc	Second quartile GDP pc	Third quartile GDP pc	Fourth quartile GDP pc			First quartile GDP pc	Second quartile GDP pc	Third quartile GDP pc	Fourth quartile GDP pc
	Model 1	Model 2	Model 3	Model 4	Model 5	Model 6	Model 7	Model 8	Model 9	Model 10	Model 11	Model 12	Model 13	Model 14	Model 15	Model 16	Model 17	Model 18
Wage (t–10)	−0.158***	−0.294***	−0.106	−0.218**	0.046	0.098	−0.149***	−0.296***	−0.038	−0.257***	0.011	0.033	−0.210***	−0.295***	−3.095	−0.281	−1.316	0.231
In-migration rate	0.446**	0.756*	−0.990	0.019	0.471	0.384												
Out-migration rate	−0.642**	−0.230	0.050	−1.009	−2.849***	0.432												
In-migration rate_educ1							0.256	0.719	−1.182	0.388	0.400	1.218	0.289	1.590	−10.212	−2.541	−22.171	−8.755
In-migration rate_educ2							−0.016	−0.159	0.632	−0.571	0.075	−0.220	−0.493	−0.867	−21.996	0.284	16.390	5.882
In-migration rate_educ3							0.147	0.194	0.196	0.180	−0.601	−0.409	−0.284	0.260	−49.299	1.107	−8.597	−2.306
In-migration rate_educ4							0.035	0.009	0.159*	0.043	0.525	0.450	0.046	0.007	0.822	−0.264	18.477	1.734
Out-migration rate_educ1							−0.324	1.190	−1.660	−1.768	−2.257*	3.066*	0.184	−0.544	−31.283	−2.316	6.458	11.001
Out-migration rate_educ2							−0.557**	−0.844**	0.116	−0.339	0.740	−2.112**	0.373	0.286	−3.384	1.090	−14.743	−3.821

(continued)

Table 6.6 (continued)

	FE models												IV FE models					
	Total	Less than 100,000 inhabitants	More than 100,000 inhabitants				Total	Less than 100,000 inhabitants	More than 100,000 inhabitants				Total	Less than 100,000 inhabitants	More than 100,000 inhabitants			
			First quartile GDP pc	Second quartile GDP pc	Third quartile GDP pc	Fourth quartile GDP pc			First quartile GDP pc	Second quartile GDP pc	Third quartile GDP pc	Fourth quartile GDP pc			First quartile GDP pc	Second quartile GDP pc	Third quartile GDP pc	Fourth quartile GDP pc
	Model 1	Model 2	Model 3	Model 4	Model 5	Model 6	Model 7	Model 8	Model 9	Model 10	Model 11	Model 12	Model 13	Model 14	Model 15	Model 16	Model 17	Model 18
Out-migration rate_educ3							0.077	−0.156	0.948*	0.557	−2.518***	−0.911	0.312	0.298	5.054	1.870	−27.026	−1.146
Out-migration rate_educ4							0.111	0.068	0.025	0.532**	0.164	0.494	0.432	0.267	1.796	0.238	19.232	−0.939
Year dummy	Yes	Yes	Yes	Yes	Yes	Yes	Yes	Yes	Yes	Yes	Yes	Yes	Yes	Yes	Yes	Yes	Yes	Yes
LMAs FE	Yes	Yes	Yes	Yes	Yes	Yes	Yes	Yes	Yes	Yes	Yes	Yes	Yes	Yes	Yes	Yes	Yes	Yes
N	956	324	158	158	158	158	956	324	158	158	158	158	956	324	158	158	158	158
Adjusted R2	0.203	0.245	0.710	0.296	−0.410	−0.726	0.206	0.247	0.742	0.312	−0.286	−0.583						
Wald test													377,417.8	75,711.5	416.2	106,635.4	1273.2	67,041.6

Obs: additional controls: percentage of workers in economic sectors and occupations, % of male workers, % of people living in urban areas, % of people with each education attainment. Instruments: 10-year lag of in and out-migration rates for each education group (Models 13–18)

Obs1: edu1–educ4 refer to the different education levels: no schooling or incomplete primary education, complete primary education or incomplete secondary education, complete secondary education or incomplete tertiary education, and complete tertiary education, in the same order

Source: Author's elaboration

characteristics of each LMA do not change. This may be true for some geographical characteristics, but is unlikely to be valid for all local heterogeneity.

The inclusion of LMA fixed effects change the sign of the time lag of local wages (whenever its coefficient is significant, it becomes negative). In general, out-migration rates have a negative relation with local wages, and on average in-migration rates are positive whenever significant. Once again, the inclusion of instruments in Models 13–18 leads to non-significant coefficients for all migration variables. These results should be analysed carefully, as it is not clear whether fixed effect for such a long time period should be included.

6 Conclusion

Internal migration flows represent one of the main factors of adjustment of regional labour markets. In the literature, there is no clear conclusion on whether such flows increase or decrease regional disparities. This chapter aims to shed light on the Brazilian case, investigating specific effects for high and low-skilled workers, for LMAs with different development levels. This is achieved through the analysis of the effects of in and out-migration rates over local wages.

The first set of conclusions come from the descriptive statistics. Skilled individuals are more likely to migrate even if they are in less developed LMAs. Furthermore, lagging regions seem to lose more population than to attract. People who migrate to a lagging region are in general more qualified than those who leave, and the educational attainment of out-migrants from more developed regions is higher than the one of the group of people who arrive there.

Moving to the estimation results, on average, the arrival of new workers in a local labour market has a positive effect, while the out-migration rate has a negative effect. However, the positive effect of in-migration is mainly felt in more developed LMAs, while the negative effect of out-migration is concentrated in LMAs with intermediate development level. Therefore, positive selection seems to work only in LMAs in the upper part of the development distribution, while the wage in lagging regions is negatively affected by the departure of workers who move elsewhere. In this sense, migration seems to reinforce regional inequality.

For less developed LMAs, the arrival of low-skilled workers has a negative impact on local wages, while their departure has the opposite effect. On the other hand, migration flows of highly educated workers is only relevant for more developed LMAs, with their in-migration presenting a positive effect over local wages and their out-migration leading to lower wages.

In summary, migration flows seem to increase regional disparities, with the highest benefits being captured by more developed LMAs, which are actually the main destinations of the group of more educated workers.

References

Arntz M (2010) What attracts human capital? Understanding the skill composition of interregional job matches in Germany. Reg Stud 44(4):423–441

Borjas GJ, Bronars SG, Trejo SJ (1992) Self-selection and internal migration in the United States. J Urban Econ 32:159–185

Camagni RP (1995) The concept of *innovative milieu* and its relevance for public policies in European lagging regions. Pap Reg Sci 74(4):317–340

Combes PP, Duranton G, Gobillon L (2008) Spatial wage disparities: sorting matters! J Urban Econ 63:723–742

Dos Santos Júnior ER, Menezes-Filho N, Ferreira PC (2005) Migração, seleção e diferenciais regionais de renda no Brasil. Pesqui Planej Econ 35(3):299–331

Elhorst PJ (2003) The mystery of regional unemployment differentials: theoretical and empirical explanations. J Econ Surv 17(5):709–748

Farole T (2012) Competitiveness and connectivity: integrating lagging regions in global markets. Economic Premise, vol 93. The World Bank, Washington, DC, pp 1–5

Farole T (2013) The internal geography of trade: lagging regions and global markets. The World Bank, Washington, DC

Freguglia RS, Procópio TS (2013) Efeitos da mudança de emprego e da migração interestadual sobre os salários no Brasil informal: evidências a partir de dados em painel. Pesqui Planej Econ 43(2):255–278

Freguglia RS, Gonçalves E, Silva ER (2014) Composition and determinants of the skilled out-migration in the Brazilian formal labour market: a panel data analysis from 1995 to 2006. EconomiA 15:100–117

Giannetti M (2003) On the mechanics of migration decisions: skill complementarities and endogenous price differentials. J Dev Econ 71(2):329–349

Glaeser EL (2011) Triumph of the city: how our greatest invention makes us richer, smarter, greener, healthier, and happier. Macmillan, London

Greenwood MJ (1997) Internal migration in developed countries. In: Rosemberg MR, Stark O (eds) Handbook of population and family economics, vol 1B. North Holland, Amsterdam, pp 647–720

Huber P, Tondi G (2012) Migration and regional convergence in the European Union. Empirica 39(4):439–460

Justo WR, Silveira Neto RM (2006) Migração inter-regional no Brasil: evidências a partir de um modelo espacial. EconomiA 7(1):163–187

Kanbur R, Rapoport H (2005) Migration selectivity and the evolution of spatial inequality. J Econ Geogr 5:43–57

Kanbur R, Venables AJ (2005) Rising spatial disparities and development. Policy Brief United Nations University 3:1–7

Mauro P, Splimbergo A (1999) How do the skilled and the unskilled respond to regional shocks? The case of Spain. IMF Staff Pap 46(1):1–17

Niebuhr A, Granato N, Haas A, Hamann S (2012) Does labour mobility reduce disparities between regional labour markets in Germany? Reg Stud 46(7):841–858

Østbye S, Westerlund O (2007) Is migration important for regional convergence? Comparative evidence for Norwegian and Swedish counties, 1980–2000. Reg Stud 41(7):901–915

Partridge MD, Rickman DS (2006) An SVAR model of fluctuations in U.S. migration flows and state labor market dynamics. South Econ J 72(4):958–980

Poot J, Pawar S (2013) Is demography destiny? Urban population change and economic vitality of future cities. J Urban Manag 2(1):5–23

Puga D (2010) The magnitude and causes of agglomeration economies. J Reg Sci 50(1):203–219

Ramalho HMB, Queiroz VS (2011) Migração interestadual de retorno e autosseleção: evidências para o Brasil. Pesqui Planej Econ 41(3):369–396

Reis EJ Pimentel M, Alvarenga AI, Santos MCH (2011) Áreas mínimas comparáveis para os períodos intercensitários de 1872 a 2000. 1° Simpósio Brasileiro de Cartografia Histórica

Santos C, Ferreira PC (2007) Migração e distribuição regional de renda no Brasil. Pesqui Planej Econ 37(3):405–425

Silva TFB, Silveira Neto RM (2005) Migração e seleção no Brasil: evidências para o decênio 1993–2003. In: Encontro Regional de Economia, 10, Fortaleza. *Anais*

Taveira JG, Almeida E (2014) Os determinantes regionais da atração do migrante qualificado. Análise Econômica, Ano 32, N. 69, p 199–224

The World Bank (2009). Reshaping economic geography, World Development Report, No. 43738

Chapter 7
Migration and Ageing in Expanding and Shrinking European Regions

Mats Johansson, Pia Nilsson, and Hans Westlund

1 Introduction

The purpose of this paper is to analyze demographic- and economic structural changes across regions in Europe, as well as the connections between these two types of processes. The relations between urban and rural areas are given a special focus, as population changes in rural areas cannot be analyzed without taking the urban population development into account and vice versa. This is particularly important with regard to migratory movements where urban in-migration, in many cases, is dependent of rural out-migration. It has also been shown that rural areas have different migration patterns where many areas in the surroundings of big cities have experienced a positive population development as an effect of both natural population increase and net in-migration. The opposite is, however, the case in peripheral and remote rural areas where contrary development paths often seem to be the case. Moreover, out-migration also results in eroding reproduction potentials as out-migration of young women accentuates the effects of the drops in fertility. Natural population change has, thus, lost its primacy as the dominant factor behind regional population development both in positive and negative ways as the European

M. Johansson (✉)
Royal Institute of Technology (KTH), Stockholm, Sweden
e-mail: mats.johansson@abe.kth.se

P. Nilsson
Jönköping University, Jönköping, Sweden
e-mail: pia.nilsson@ju.se

H. Westlund (✉)
Royal Institute of Technology (KTH), Stockholm, Sweden

Jönköping University, Jönköping, Sweden
e-mail: hans.westlund@abe.kth.se

© Springer International Publishing AG, part of Springer Nature 2018   107
U. Blien et al. (eds.), *Modelling Aging and Migration Effects on Spatial Labor Markets*, Advances in Spatial Science,
https://doi.org/10.1007/978-3-319-68563-2_7

regions—urban as well as rural—have been transformed from high fertility societies to low fertility ones. Instead, migration has become the main driver with regard to population development. These processes are all related to the economic-structural changes taking place in both urban and rural regions, which is the focus of this paper.

In order to describe and empirically address the differing demographic development paths and altered preconditions for transformation the paper applies typologies based on both economic and demographic structure and a cross regional regression model. In a first step, a typology based on demographic characteristics that classifies regions as either shrinking or expanding in terms of their population base is used in a descriptive analysis that illustrate sustainable and unsustainable population changes across rural Europe. The unit of analysis is the NUTS 3 regional level and the time dimension is 2001–2012. The economic-structural typology developed within the ESPON/EDORA-project is then used to expand the analysis in terms of economic-structural factors.[1] The purpose is to examine how these two typologies relate to each other and how they can be used jointly in empirical analyses of the factors influencing population change across Europe. Hence, one of the central questions addressed in this paper is whether the relative importance of key determinants of population change varies across regions defined as either shrinking or expanding. In order to answer this question, we use the analyzed sample of NUTS 3 regions in a cross-regional regression framework to estimate a growth equation that indicate the economic and statistical significance of the different underlying components that explain population change.

The paper is organized in the following way: Sect. 2 provides a background to the paper by analyzing demographic trends in Europe using both the demographic and the economic-structural typology. Sections 3 and 4 summarize some of the relevant literature and present the theoretical framework of the underlying factors presumed to influence regional population growth and shrinkage. Section 5 describes the data used in the empirical analysis followed by a description of empirical methodology and regression results.

2   Shrinking Regions: A Long Term Structural Phenomenon?

When analysing shrinking regions in Europe it seems natural to focus on population change. Maps 7.1 and 7.2 show the general pattern of demographic change based on the demographic equation during the period 2001–2012 concerning growth as well as decline. It would of course be better with a longer time-span but the data

---

[1]ESPON is a research programme that started 2002 and named European Spatial Planning Observatory Network. It changed name 2007 to European Observation Network for Territorial Development and Cohesion. EDORA (European Development Opportunities in Rural Areas) was an ESPON project that was running between 2008 and 2010. This article is not an EDORA project but we use the EDORA typology for the classification of differing regions within the ESPON Space, i.e. the EU plus Iceland, Liechtenstein, Norway and Switzerland but here minus Denmark and Croatia, which was excluded as a consequence of data shortage.

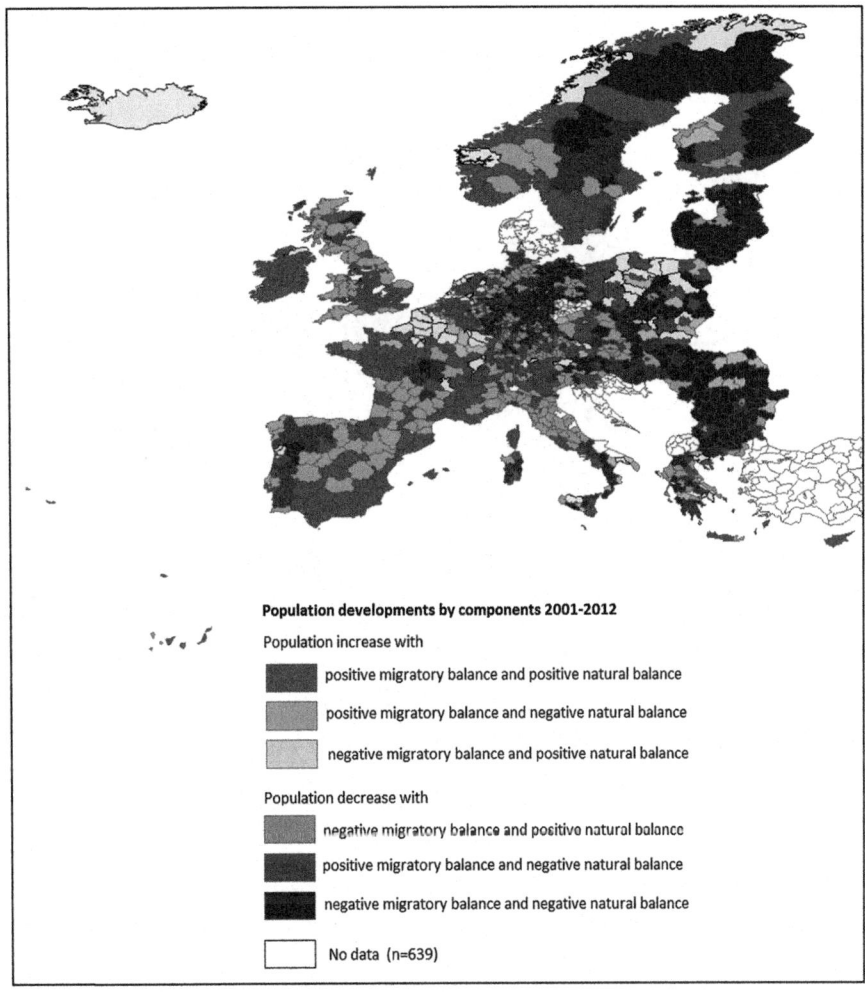

Map 7.1 The demographic typology for the period 2001–2012 (NUTS3, N = 1294). Based on annual population change 2001–2012. Source: Estimations based on data from Eurostat

series from Eurostat and changing regional delimitations hindered this with regard to NUTS3-levels. Both the central European growth zones and the peripheral edge areas with declining population are clearly identifiable even at a first glance. A lot of studies have shown a polycentric development within the Pentagon, while there instead are indications of monocentric development with respect to demographic development in more sparsely populated peripheral areas. This phenomenon has been and still is especially strong in the northern and eastern parts of Europe where a redistribution of people contributes to a concentration process to the metropolitan or big city areas as well as to shrinkage and depopulating.

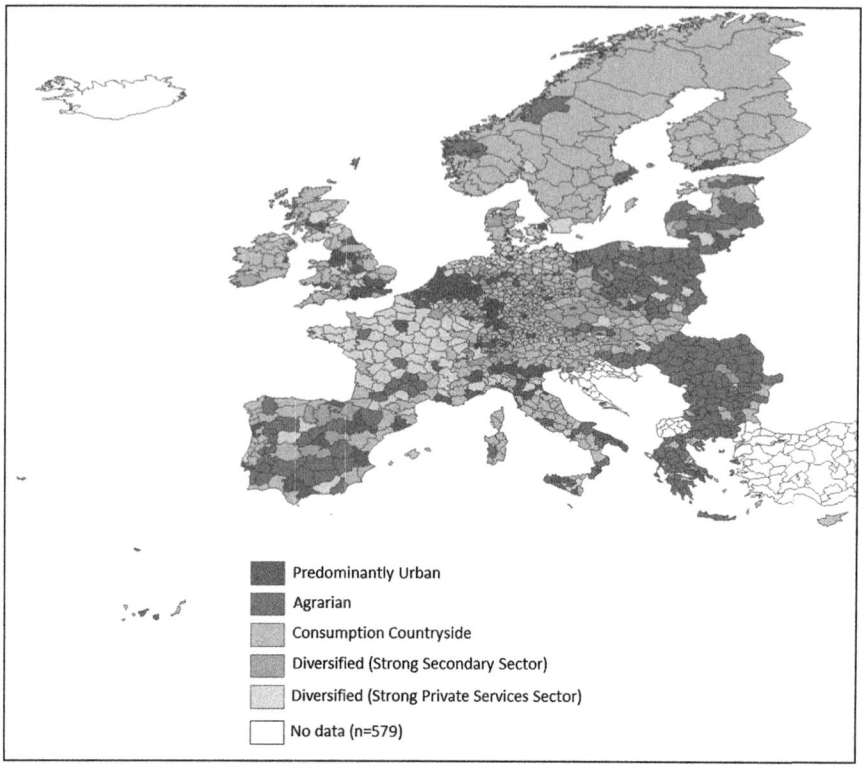

Map 7.2 The EDORA structural typology, 2011 version

Economic growth is often consequence of structural changes and this has a key place in the theory of economic growth. This means picking out that part of economic growth that has a connection with a transfer of the production factors—usually labour—from the less productive to the more productive parts of the economy. Of course growth effects of structural change do not have to be a consequence of transfer of labour in the literal sense but may equally good result from different parts of the economy, with different productivities, developing in dissimilar ways. The classical example is the transition from an agricultural society to an industrial society where the "transfer gains" explained much of the economic growth. This transformation process can even be applied to the development in Europe today and then also in disadvantaged or lagging regions. Here it must be kept in mind that most of the disadvantaged regions in Europe can be characterized as rural areas and many localized in the "new member states".

A lesson to be learned from the narrative above is that when discussing shrinkage from a territorial point of view it is more or less necessary to use a long-term perspective and to differ between structural transformations and business cycles. The structural perspective is, thus, the primary reason for choosing a period as long as possible, in this paper the years 2001–2012 depending of the possibility/impossibility to construct continuously available data series and then to minimize the number missing data at NUTS3-level. A longer time perspective would of course be preferred but data problems stopped this.

In order to compare growing and shrinking regions the development paths concerning population sizes and the social-economic structures are used. The first typology is based on the demographic equation and the second typology is the EDORA economic-structural typology where the rural Europe is split in four different types with differing rural characteristics (for a more in-depth description see Copus et al. 2010; Copus and Johansson 2010).

2.1 Sustainable and Unsustainable Population Changes: A Demographic Typology

In the ESPON 2006 project 1.1.4; "Spatial effects of demographic trends and migration", a typology based on the demographic equation (i.e. *regional population change* = *natural population change* + *net-migration*) was produced. The sixfold typology comprised of combinations of the three demographic components—total population development, natural development and net-migration. The result is a summary of the demographic situation in each region and the preconditions with regard to future population trends, shedding light on issues such as sustainability, population growth, depopulation and ageing. The typology was first presented in ESPON 1.1.4 and covered the period 1996–1999. It has since then been updated, developed and extended in relation to the period 2000–2005, in Copus (2006), Johansson (2009) and in combination with the EDORA Structural Typology in Copus and Johansson (2010). In this study the estimations have been developed to include almost every NUTS3-region (N = 1294) within the "ESPON space". As "shrinkage topics" are a relatively new in regional science any explicit and straightforward common definition of "shrinkage" is not stated. Instead operational definitions are used as a consequence of the topics that are analyzed (for a discussion see e.g. Ubareviciene et al. 2014; Hoeckfeld 2012; Haase et al. 2013). The demographic typology has been used here in order to identify growing and shrinking regions (types 1–3 and 4–6 respectively, see Map 7.1).

From Table 7.1 it seems obvious that Type 1 is the most frequent, both with regard to number of regions and size of population. Growing regions take the lion's share—61.5% of the regions consisting of 72.1% of the population within the ESPON. This means that the size has some importance for growing or might be an effect of growth in the long-term. 'Big is beautiful' seems then to have some relevance even for growing.

The contrary is also clearly illustrated by Type 6 that is the worst case from a sustainable point of view. Total population decrease in combination with natural population decrease and net out-migration is not a good starting point in order to

Table 7.1 The distribution among the types with regard to number of regions and population size

2001–2012	Type 1	Type 2	Type 3	Type 4	Type 5	Type 6
Number of regions (N = 1294)	31.5	25.1	4.9	3.0	11.5	24.0
Population size (N = 1294)	42.7	20.4	9.0	3.4	7.0	17.5
Size/numbersIndex: 100 = neither/nor	135.3	81.6	185.1	111.4	60.6	72.9

SI = size/numbers. Source: Estimations based on data from Eurostat
Note: Denmark and a few other NUTS 3 regions are not included due to missing data

create good possibilities for sustainable population development. Many of these regions are located in the European periphery. Many of these are also characterized as some form of rural areas. The common dominator with regard to these rural shrinking regions is sparse population and few inhabitants.

2.2 The Regions of Europe: An Economic/Structural Typology

In the ESPON/EDORA-project an economic/structural typology with regard to the ESPON Space was clustered based on 18 economic and structural variables. For a more in-depth discussion about the variables and the clustering can be seen in Copus et al. (2010) and Copus and Johansson (2010).

The principal findings with regard to the EDORA-types are (see also Map 7.2):

Predominantly urban regions are primarily localized in Pentagon—the area that is delimited by London–Paris–Milan–Munich–Hamburg–London. Other predominantly urban regions are often to be found in capital regions and larger city regions. This localization pattern contrasts to the *Agrarian regions* that are concentrated in a peripheral eastern and southern arc. The rest of the European space seems to be characterized by a patchwork of three types of rurality, *Consumption Countryside*, *Diversified (with Strong Secondary Sector)* and *Diversified (with Strong Private Services Sector)*. Consumption Countryside regions are often closely associated with Agrarian ones but are also populated by people employed in the industrial and service sectors where a large share of the working people is dependent of wages and salaries.

The Diversified (Strong Secondary Sector) regions are found in various regions in the Mid-Europe. These regions can also be seen as industrial regions that in many cases are in a state of deindustrialization and transformation. Especially in the "new" member states they seems to be in a stagnating or retarding phase and lose people both as a consequence of natural population decrease and out-migration.

The last category—Diversified (Strong Market Services) is evident especially in northern and central France, northern Germany and southern Denmark. This type is the one that is most associated with the New Rural Economy (NRE).

2.3 The Demographic and the EDORA Economic/Structural Typologies: Different Types, Different Outcomes

In this part of the study the Demographic types are cross-tabulated against the Structural types in order to investigate the differences between the five Structural types for sustainable population development and depopulation. Some conclusions can be drawn based on the tables below and consisting of almost all regions within the ESPON Space with the exception of Iceland. The number of regions and the size of the different Structural types are shown in Table 7.2 below.

Three Structural types are "overrepresented" in Type 1—the most favorable type from a sustainable demographic point of view concerning the numbers of regions. These are the" Predominantly Urban" and the two "Diversified rural types". All three have a higher share of regions in Type 1 compared to the total share of all ESPON regions (see Table 7.3). When the size aspects are taken on board in the analysis the Structural type 3" Diversified with strong secondary sector" is dropping off (Table 7.4).

The relatively good population development in the diversified countryside with a strong secondary sector is perhaps less expected. This type of region accounts for only 7.2% of the regions and 6.6% of the population within the ESPON Space, and are concentrated in the Czech Republic, Poland and Spain. The diversified countryside with a strong secondary sector has in many cases gone through a

Table 7.2 Size distributions of the five structural types

Structural types, N = 1294	% of N	% of size	Size index
0. Predominantly urban	31.2	42.6	136.4
1. Agrarian	16.3	14.0	85.8
2. Consumption countryside	33.7	23.5	69.9
3. Diversified (strong secondary sector)	7.2	6.6	91.7
4. Diversified (strong market services)	11.5	13.2	114.8

*Based on numbers of regions (NUTS3) and population size (%). Size index, over- or underrepresented with regard to size (index = 100, neither nor)

Table 7.3 The distribution of the demographic types with regard to the five structural types (Color figure online)

Structural Types	% Demographic Types, N=1294					
	Type 1	Type 2	Type 3	Type 4	Type 5	Type 6
Structural Types Total	31.5	25.1	4.9	3.0	11.5	24.0
0. Predominantly Urban	42.1	26.4	6.0	1.7	10.5	13.2
1. Agrarian	15.7	13.8	5.7	6.7	13.8	44.3
2. Consumption Countryside	27.0	27.3	2.3	2.1	12.9	28.4
3. Diversified (strong secondary sector)	37.6	21.5	4.3	4.3	6.5	25.8
4. Diversified (strong market services)	33.8	35.1	8.8	2.7	10.8	8.8

*Number of regions (%). Period 2001–2012. Combinations highlighted in grey are those where the share (%) exceeds the average for all Structural types

Table 7.4 The distribution of the demographic types with regard to the five structural types (Color figure online)

Size: % Structural and Demographic Types, N=1294, NUTS3							
		Type 1	Type 2	Type 3	Type 4	Type 5	Type 6
StructuralTypes	Total	42.6	20.5	9.0	3.4	7.0	17.5
0. Predominantly Urban		52.2	19.4	11.4	2.6	5.4	8.9
1. Agrarian		17.2	7.4	8.5	8.5	9.1	49.3
2. Consumption Countryside		38.7	27.9	3.0	2.3	10.3	17.8
3. Diversified (strong secondary sector)		35.6	18.9	6.0	5.0	5.6	28.9
4. Diversified (strong market services)		47.7	26.4	14.2	1.5	4.7	5.5

Based on population size (%) 2001. *Size of regions (%). Period 2001–2012. Combinations highlighted in grey are those where the share (%) exceeds the average for all structural types

deindustrialization process with the result that these regions have experienced a vicious circle with regard to migration and natural population development. More than one third of these regions (34.4%) experienced net out-migration during the period 2001–2012—perhaps a low figure for regions dependent on the declining manufacturing industries.

The diversified countryside with strong market services structural type accounts for 11.5% of the regions within the ESPON Space and 13.2% of the population. This category shows good population development, as does the Consumption Countryside group which accounts for 33.7% of the regions and 23.5% of the population. The prime driver behind the good demographic development in these categories is—as usual—in-migration.

These high figures might be an effect of the 'new rurality'" or the 'New Rural Economy' that has changed the performance of the countryside in many European countries and especially then in densely populated rural areas in the surroundings of big urban agglomerations. The densely populated rural regions are in a more favorable position with regard to population change than other more peripheral rural regions. This is not especially surprising as densely populated rural regions have experienced a relatively positive population development during the past decades (Copus 2006; Johansson and Kupsiszwski 2009). Shrinking rural regions in this type were—and still are—often remote and sparsely populated ones already from the beginning and then with bad preconditions for growth and development. The regions in the eastern part of Europe show similarities with the agrarian regions in the same areas. This will result in a future precarious situation for these regions in general and for the rural ones especially.

This can be contrasted to the figures in the 'diversified countryside with strong market services' where only 8.8% of the regions with 5.5% of the population are in Demographic Type 6 (see Tables 7.3 and 7.4). These rural areas are predominantly localized in the western part of Europe—and then especially in France—and it might also be in this kind of rural areas where the NRE has been established. It seems, however, also in this case to be small peripheral and sparsely populated rural regions that is hurt mostly by the demographic development with ageing and depopulation as one result (Johansson 2009, see also Map 7.3 and Tables 7.3 and 7.4). The few blue spots are to be found predominantly in the eastern part of Europe.

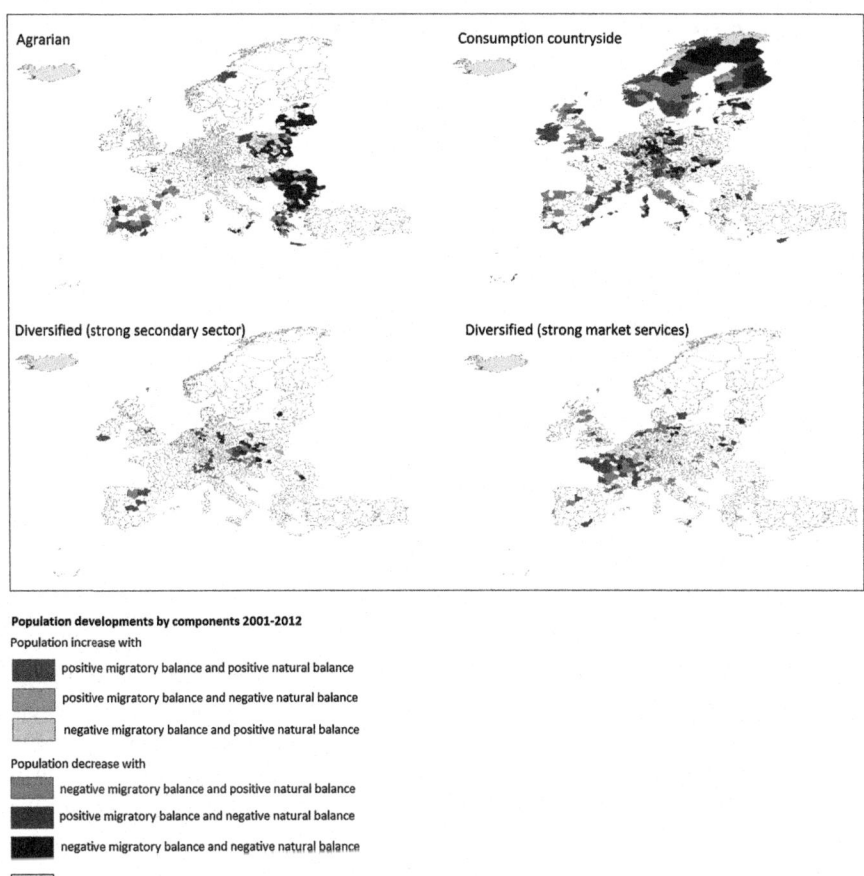

Agrarian

Consumption countryside

Diversified (strong secondary sector)

Diversified (strong market services)

Population developments by components 2001-2012

Population increase with

positive migratory balance and positive natural balance

positive migratory balance and negative natural balance

negative migratory balance and positive natural balance

Population decrease with

negative migratory balance and positive natural balance

positive migratory balance and negative natural balance

negative migratory balance and negative natural balance

No data (n=639)

Map 7.3 The demographic typology applied on the four non-urban EDORA Structural types for the period 2001–2012 (NUTS3)

The rural category with the most negative demographic development was the Agrarian and these regions are in a very problematic situation from a sustainable demographic point of view. The active component here is once again migration—internal as well as external—that is the prime driver in this downgrading process. The agrarian regions seem here—as in many other countries—thus to be involved in processes dominated by viscous circles and negative development spirals.

2.4   Large Regions: Better Preconditions

There are studies that have shown no correlations between growth and shrinkage on the one hand and on population density on the other. Instead the history can witness about both growing and shrinking regions on densely populated areas as well the contrary—sparsely populated regions might experience "explosive" growth (European Parliament 2008, pp. 34–35). This is, however, not the same as size has no importance for population growth and shrinkage. Already Ravenstein highlighted that the mass was pull and push factors depending of the size in in- and out-migration areas and, then consequently, also for demographic development (Ravenstein 1885, 1889).

In order to investigate the relation between population size and demographic development the size index (SI) has been used here (Table 7.6) in order to investigate if the size has importance for the demographic development in the differing Structural types. SI is estimated as the following formula:

$$SI = (P_i R_i) * 100 \tag{F1}$$

SI (Size Index) = weighted index according to size
P_i = share of the total population in type i (percent)
R_i = share of all regions in type i (percent)

By combining the size of the regions with the numbers it seems obvious that large regions are in better positions concerning sustainable demographic development than small ones. As can be seen from Table 7.5 large regions are overrepresented in growing regions and underrepresented in shrinking ones. The overrepresentation in the growing Demographic types is valid for almost all Structural types except the diversified countryside with a strong secondary sector—in all other types are large regions overrepresented in the growing Demographic Type 1 (Table 7.5).

Table 7.5 Over- and underrepresentation of the various demographic (ESPON) types with regard to population size 2001 in the differing Structural types (Color figure online)

Size/numbers: Edora/Demographic Types, N=1294. NUTS3. Over 100 = large regions overrepresented, under 100 = large regions underrepresented						
Demographic Types	**Type 1**	**Type 2**	**Type 3**	**Type 4**	**Type 5**	**Type 6**
Structural Types Total	135.3	81.6	185.1	111.4	60.6	72.9
0. Predominantly Urban	123.9	73.4	191.2	148.6	51.8	67.5
1. Agrarian	109.4	53.4	149.5	127.7	65.8	111.3
2. Consumption Countryside	143.2	102.2	129.8	110.3	80.0	62.7
3. Diversified (strong secondary sector)	94.6	87.7	139.9	116.1	87.3	112.0
4. Diversified (strong market services)	141.2	75.1	161.5	56.8	43.1	62.7

Period 2001–2012. *Combinations highlighted in grey are those where large regions are overrepresented

3 Regional Characteristics Behind Growth and Shrinkage

Besides the demographic and economic-structural factors discussed above there are a number of additional regional characteristics that may influence regional population growth, and shrinkage, in regions classified as both urban and rural. It is for example well established that the level of human capital in a region is one significant factor that influence growth in income and population. In all its essence, people are a significant part of the wealth of regions in terms of what labour contributes to output. The productive capacity of the regional population is known to be larger than other forms of wealth taken together and a primary factor that influence regional growth patterns (Barro 1991; Rauch 1993). Moreover, many of the key factors that drive regional growth can be related to the existence of knowledge spillovers and supply of human capital (Becker 1962; Asheim 1999). Hence, as people invest in themselves by acquiring education and experience they augment not only their own productivity and income, but also the capacity of the region to grow. In the view that individuals drive regional growth, the overall level of human capital in a region becomes a central factor, in the perspective of population development, since differences across regions can influence regional growth patterns. However, human capital does not only produce externalities in terms of productivity but also in terms of consumption that are of importance in this perspective (Haveman and Wolfe 1984). Such consumption externalities capture a wide range of welfare effects in the social environment that benefit the majority of the regional population. Two such benefits are the democratic involvement and social cohesion, which are both functions of the education level and literacy rate (Blundell et al. 1999).

As stated by the endogenous growth theory, a higher initial level of human capital can bring a one-time increase in the income level or increase the income growth rate (Romer 1990). This implies that enhancements in human capital have both a level and/or a growth effect. What follows from this is that a region with a larger share of highly educated individuals will successively grow to be wealthier compared to regions that have lower shares (Becker 1962; Blundell et al. 1999; Funke and Strulik 2000). Besides level effects, regions that have a high overall level of human capital are also shown to experience a cumulative process of higher growth in the human capital level (Moretti 2004). However, the influence of human capital on growth does not only depend on individual characteristics but also on the presence of both demand and supply effects. These effects mainly appear in the form of educational infrastructure and the presence of knowledge intensive firms that influence the regional ability to produce human capital, to replace any that it might lose through migration and to prevent human capital from exiting the region (Rauch 1993). Hence, there are reasons to believe that the influence of human capital on growth varies depending on regional characteristics with regards to industry structure and degree of urbanity.

The contrary to growth is shrinkage and what is said above is then also relevant for shrinking regions but in the opposite way. Shortage of human capital is often seen as a central factor behind shrinkage and stagnation. This kind of reasoning has much in common with the product-life cycle theory and development can be seen as a consequence of the spatial product-life cycles that transform the economic landscape and where the shrinking regions often are in the matured phases (Friedrich 1993). One effect is the increased polarization between growing and shrinking regions and 'brain-drain' to the expanding knowledge-based areas. This 'cumulative causation' process is often a central ingredient in differing kinds of transformation and polarization processes where the 'backwash effects' are larger than the 'spread effects' (Myrdal 1957, see also McCann 2001, pp. 197–200). History can also stand witness to this kind of processes with e. g. industrialization and de-industrialization as obvious and illustrative cases where differences and changes in human capital are both causes to and effects of growth and decline.

The size of human capital is also a function of the demographic structure in a region as human capital in many ways is a cohort phenomenon. Regions with young population differ from regions with an ageing population with regard to human capital. For our purpose it is then interesting to check if the age structure is of importance for regional growth and shrinkage. For checking the effects the age groups −15, 16–35 and 65+ have been used in the regressions in Chap. 5. The problem here is to isolate causes and effects. A changed age structure is often an effect of in- or out-migration but it has also impact on the preconditions for growth and the risk for shrinkage. It is also a well-known fact that various cohorts have differing migration patterns and this might also have impact on the level of human capital and the production factor of labour (ESPON 1.1.4 2005). It shall also be kept in mind that different age groups have differing consumption patterns and demands with regards to different kinds of products seen from a local and regional point of view and then different impact on growth and decline. This means that the age structure has differing impact on population growth and decline on population changes and this is an argument for taking the age structure on board in the analysis.

The Gross Regional Product (GRP) is another factor that usually is suggested to be of importance both for migration and natural population changes. According to many migration models income differences are suggested to be of great importance as pull and push factors. The effects on natural population development might be more problematic to specify from a theoretical point of view as it is necessary to distinguish between levels and changes and incomes and prices. With regard to the two latter factors it can be problematic to separate the income effects from the price or substitution effects. It is also important to separate children's function as production factor—as in the agricultural society—from children as consumption factor as in the post-industrial society (see e.g. Becker 1993 about this discussion). As a consequence of data problems GRP is not integrated in the multivariate regressions but only in the bivariate ones (see the correlation matrices in Appendix).

It is also of significance to separate the levels from changes in the GRPs. It has been shown that since the middle of the 1990s and up to the middle of the 1900s the income levels between the European countries have converged but diverged within the countries (Button and Pentecost 1999; Halmai and Vásáry 2010). This is, at least partially, a catching-up effect as the start in especially the countries in Eastern

Europe stated from a low level—a 'starting from scratch phenomenon' that resulted in a fast income growth.

As the development in Europe has been of quite different character dummies for the 'old' EU-member states and the 'new' ones have been integrated in the regressions. The effect of this can be seen as with regard to the other factors in the tables below (Tables 7.9 and 7.10).

4 Ageing Europe: Geographic and Structural Patterns

Shrinking and then often rural areas are often associated with ageing areas. This is— at least partly—a consequence of out-migration of younger people from these areas to the urban ones. Despite the higher fertility rates in rural areas the out-migration of younger people has resulted in a lopsided age structure that eroded the reproduction potential (too few women in fertile ages) with slow or negative natural population result as one result. This process seems to have been reinforced today as the fertility rates have dropped even in the out-migration (rural) areas.

This is, however, not the whole truth behind the ageing process. During the past decades life expectancy has raised in Europe and the amount of elderly persons have increased and even been healthier even if there still are discrepancies between nations and regions. This means that the ageing process must be interpreted with some care with regard to both production and consumption.

One method to investigate the distribution of the EU elderly people—65 years and over—is to divide them in quartiles. Q4 has the largest share of elderly and Q1 the lowest share. In Tables 7.6 and 7.7 the population has been distributed as regards their structural types both with regard to numbers of regions and the size of the regions. It must be kept in mind that the presented shares in the quartiles are based on the ESPON Space ranking for all regions (N = 1345) in order to standardize for the various sizes between the different structural types. The distribution of the Qs within the five structural types indicates, however, the types' various position as "old" or "young" types or regions. In Table 7.8 the over- or underrepresentation is

Table 7.6 Ageing, 65 years and over

Structural types	Q1	Q2	Q3	Q4	%	N	Numbers%
0. Predominantly Urban	28.8	22.6	25.8	22.8	100.0	430	32.0
1. Agrarian	32.4	27.6	15.7	24.3	100.0	210	15.6
2. Consumption Countryside	15.3	22.0	32.2	30.5	100.0	459	34.1
3. Diversified (strong secondary sector)	38.3	35.1	13.8	12.8	100.0	94	7.0
4. Diversified (strong market services)	24.3	30.3	21.1	24.3	100.0	152	11.3
						1345	100

Numbers of regions 2008, EDORA structural types, quartiles, N = 1345
Source: Estimations based on regional population data from Eurostat

Table 7.7 Ageing, 65 years and over

Structural types	Q1	Q2	Q3	Q4	%	Size	Size %	N	Numbers %
0. Predominantly Urban	40.2	29.0	19.8	11.0	100,0	216,188,064	42.5	430	32.0
1. Agrarian	51.3	26.7	11.3	10.7	100,0	71,588,396	14.1	210	15.6
2. Consumption Countryside	26.6	23.3	27.8	22.3	100,0	119,332,748	23.5	459	34.1
3. Diversified (strong secondary sector)	50.4	33.2	8.4	7.9	100,0	33,224,744	6.5	94	7.0
4. Diversified (strong market services)	34.1	32.4	16.9	16.6	100,0	67,845,977	13.4	152	11.3
						508,179,929	100	1345	100

Size of the regions 2008, EDORA structural types, quartiles, N = 1345
Source: Estimations based on Eurostat

Table 7.8 Ageing, 65 years and over (Color figure online)

Structural Types	Q1	Q2	Q3	Q4
0. Predominantly Urban	139,5	128,4	76,6	48,3
1. Agrarian	158,3	96,8	72,2	43,9
2. Consumption Countryside	174,4	106,1	86,2	73,0
3. Diversified (strong secondary sector)	131,7	94,7	61,0	61,9
4. Diversified (strong market services)	140,1	107,1	80,2	68,2

Size/numbers: Edora/Demographic types, N = 1345. NUTS3. Over 100 = large regions overrepresented (grey), under 100 = large regions underrepresented. Source: Estimations based on Eurostat

presented according to size and numbers. The general geographic pattern at NUTS3-level is illustrated in Map 7.4.

From Table 7.8 it is obvious that structural type Predominantly Urban has the most equal distribution of elderly people—23% is localized in the oldest category (Q4) and 29% in the "youngest" category (Q1). The Agrarian type has almost one third of its population in Q1—a fact that perhaps is surprising as agrarian and rural areas often have the image of ageing regions. This can, however, been explained by the fact that most of the regions in the "new member states" can be characterized as Agrarian. These regions have still a relatively "young" population and the life expectancy is neither in level with the ones in the "old" EU-countries. This means that even if the share of children is falling the share of people in active ages is still high and the age pyramid has not yet been lop-sided like the age structure in the old EU-members such as most parts of Portugal, Spain, Italy, Greece, Germany and Sweden.

The structural type Consumption Countryside shows a quite different age structure. More than one third of the EU-regions are to be found in this type and of them the overwhelming parts are placed in Q4 and Q3. The low fertility rates during

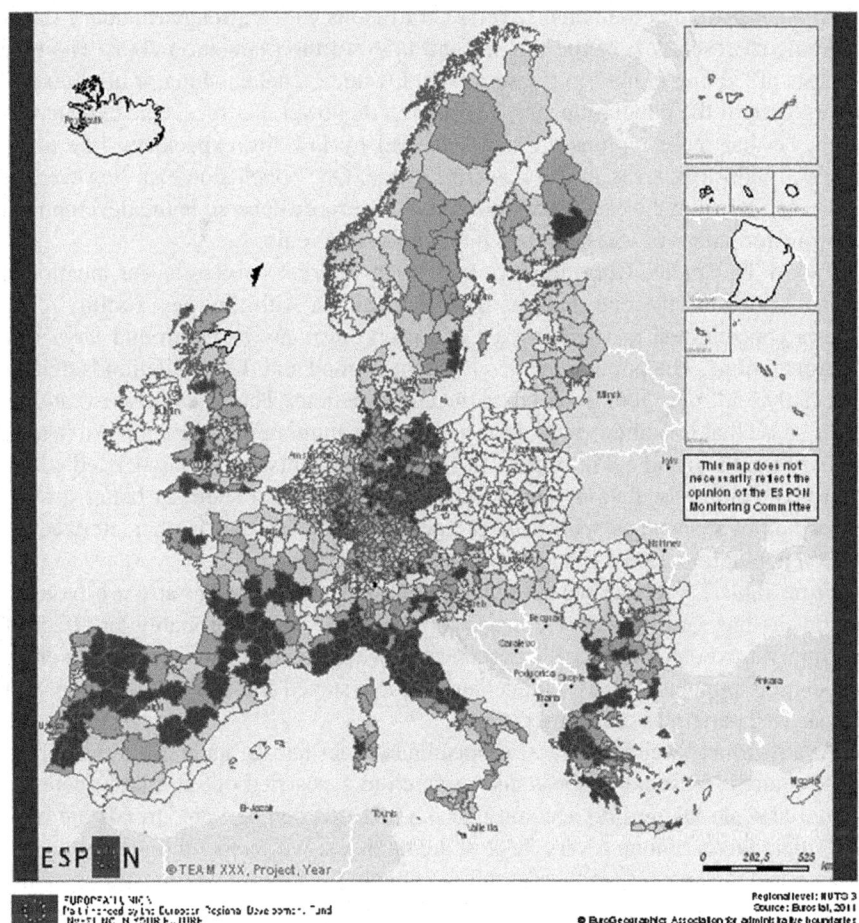

ESP N   @TEAM XXX, Project, Year   0   202,5   525

Legend			Min	Max
NUTS3_RG_20M_2006		Q1	4,1	15,6
	1	Q2	15,7	18,4
	2	Q3	18,4	20,8
	3	Q4	20,8	30,7
	4			

Map 7.4 Ageing (65 years and over) in Europe (ESPON Space), 2008. NUTS3. Quartiles. Source: Eurostat

the past decades have now resulted in high shares of elderly people in these countries and in a lot of their regions. Consumption Countryside can in many cases be seen as typical for the migratory movements' impact on ageing and eroding reproduction potential.

Another extreme type is the Diversified Regions with a strong secondary sector that only represent 7% of the regions and 6.5% of the population 2008. The type consists of "young oldies" in the sense that Q1 and Q2 take the major part; around three fourth of the population is to be found in the lower quartiles. One explanation might be that these regions are characterized by low life expectancy like many deprived industrial areas in the Eastern Europe. One conclusion can, however, be drawn and it is that the eastern regions seem to be more delayed in the development and transformation process compared to the western regions.

Type 4, Diversified Rural Regions with strong market services is—as mentioned earlier—probably the one that has most in common with the 'new rurality'. The type is concentrated to western part of Europe in many cases around large city agglomerations. The population development is good and the population is neither especially 'old' nor 'young' based on the Q-estimations. The type is also expanding in the sense that it is often characterized by both natural population increase (a high share of families) and net in-migration—two components that are associated with a relatively young population. This type will probably also result in better growth opportunities than types with a more ageing population that is characterized by natural population decrease and net out-migration.

From Table 7.8 we can see the typical pattern that large regions also are "young" regions as they are overrepresented in Q1 and Q2. This is probably an effect of migratory movements during the past decades when younger people moved to cities and densely populated areas while elderly people stayed and still stay at home with this skewed pattern as one consequence.

At a regional level, however, European narratives tell us many different stories. This requires statistical analysis and research to be carried out at a more detailed territorial scale taking into account that the fact that demographic trends are only one single factor among a very large and complex set of factors influencing socio-economic development, and—after all—probably the slowest and most predictable factor, traditionally considered to be the *outcome* rather than the *cause* of socio-economic change.

5 Data and Empirical Assessment Across European Regions

To study the influence of some of the key underlying demographic factors on population change across Europe this applies a cross-regional approach. The unit of observation is NUTS 3 regions and the dependent variable is the total change in population measured over the periods 2001–2012, 2001–2007 and 2007–2012. The degree to which demographic factors along with relevant control variables are observable at a more disaggregated level across Europe is limited and the variables that we use are attained from Eurostat at either NUTS 2 or NUTS 3 level. Variables are measured at the finest aggregation available level in Eurostat, implying that all variables are measured at the NUTS 3 level except for human capital which is measured at the NUTS 2 level. There are several problems associated with the use of these data in an empirical analysis of growth. One problem regards the high aggregation level using these regional classifications. One such problem is that some NUTS regions correspond very closely to functionally defined regions whereas others are very aggregated and therefore economically very heterogeneous. Some even contain one or more different types of metropolitan regions within them. In cases when regions correspond closely to their functional definition it is possible to study factors that may influence regional population growth. However, in cases where regions are very heterogeneous, it can be difficult to define variables that consistently affect growth. Having this in mind, the results are correlations and should be interpreted with care. The variables used in the analysis are defined in Table 7.9 and summary statistics are presented in Table 7.10.

5.1   Empirical Model and Estimations

The empirical approach is to address the influence of key demographic factors on population change across European rural regions, including a set of control variables. We set up a very simple framework and use a cross-sectional dataset to model the change in population as a function of a set of initial conditions, which could mitigate problems associated with reversed causality. The main idea is to perform case-wise estimations across growing and shrinking regions in Europe and compare the influence of demographic factors. To achieve this goal, we estimate the

Table 7.9 Variables and definitions

Dependent variables	Definition
Netmig 01–12	Percentage change in migration by NUTS 3, 2001–2012.
Netmig 01–07	Percentage change in migration by NUTS 3, 2001–2007.
Netmig 07–12	Percentage change in migration by NUTS 3, 2007–2012.
Independent variables	
Age below 15	Share of population in NUTS 3 below the age of 15
Age 16–35	Share of population in NUTS 3 between the age of 16–35.
Age above 65	Share of population in NUTS 3 above the age of 65
HC	Human capital measured as share of population aged 25–64 with tertiary education by NUTS 2, 2001.
GRP	Per capita income measured by GRP/population by NUTS 3, 2001 (in € 2011).
Density	Population density measured as inhabitants per square kilometer by NUTS 3, 2001.
Industry	Share of employment by NUTS 3 (NACE Rev. 2), 2001.
New MS	Dummy indicating countries Not included among the EU 15 member states.

Source: EUROSTAT. Independent variables are retrieved for the base year 2001 alt. closest available year when such data are missing

Table 7.10 Summary statistics

Variables	Mean	Std. Dev.	Min	Max
Netmig 01–12	0.163	0.570	−0.029	0.037
Netmig 01–07	0.254	0.625	−0.034	0.058
Netmig 07–12	0.082	0.865	−0.068	0.362
Age below 15	0.149	0.261	0.032	0.261
Age 16–35	0.567	0.321	0.366	0.653
Age above 65	0.186	0.359	0.073	0.303
HC	0.200	0.078	0.037	0.120
GRP	19,250.31	11,396.52	800	145,700
Density	448.85	1037.135	1.1	20,317.4
New MS	0.201	0.401	0	1
EDORA typology				
Predominantly urban	0.313	0.464	0	1
Agrarian	0.161	0.368	0	1
Consumption countryside	0.337	0.472	0	1
Diversified strong secondary sector	0.072	0.259	0	1
Diversified strong market services	0.115	0.319	0	1
Demographic typology				
Growing regions	0.612	0.487	0	1
Shrinking regions	0.379	0.485	0	1

following equation:

$$\Delta NM_{i,t} = \alpha_i + \beta_1 A_{it} + \beta_2 Z_{it} + \varepsilon_{it} \tag{7.2}$$

where ΔNM denote the percentage change in migration measured between the observed time periods (2001–2012, 2001–2007 and 2007–2012) and i denote the NUTS 3 regional level. Moreover, A_{it} denote the variables included to reflect age structure of region i at time t and Z_{it} denote a set of regional controls such as the initial levels of human capital, population density and per capita income, including also dummy variables to capture economic-structural factors using the EDORA typology. Population density can be seen as an indicator of agglomeration economies and serve as a size control since urbanized and densely populated areas are *ceteris paribus* more likely to attract workers and enterprises. As noted by Glaeser et al. (1992), for instance, agglomeration effects that benefit all industries may also arise from the overall size and density of a local economy (i.e., urbanisation economies). There is also other indicator of size that can be used, such as regional income per capita, which we also include in a set of robustness tests.

The results from running preliminary regressions and using a White test (of homoscedasticity) indicate that the generalized least squares (GLS) method is more appropriate than the OLS for these data. Hence, we apply the standard two-stage procedure to obtain a Feasible Generalized Least Squares (FGLS) estimator

(Kmenta 1986). This implies using the residuals estimated by OLS to build a consistent estimator.

Regression results are reported in Tables 7.11 and 7.12. In a first step, we estimate the model using the total sample of NUTS 3 regions and in two different specifications. The first specification includes the age variables and the second specification adds the additional controls. In a second step, the model is estimated across the demographic typology to examine the relative importance of explanatory variables between regions that are defined as either growing or shrinking. To strengthen the interpretation of results and control for temporal aspects the model is estimated using the three time periods: 2001–2012, 2001–2007 and 2007–2012. We use the condition number (based on the spread in eigenvalues) to assess if multicollinearity is present in the estimations.[2]

5.2 *Results*

Table 7.11 presents the results from running the regression model in Eq. (7.2) including the independent variables defined in Table 7.9. In a first step, the model is estimated using the full sample of NUTS 3 regions, thereafter controlling for regional heterogeneity by adding regional characteristics and the EDORA structural typology. In a second step, we examine the influence of the parameters using the demographic typology that divides NUTS 3 regions into shrinking and growing regions per the discussion above, these results are presented in Table 7.12.[3]

From Table 7.9 adding parameters to the model improves the explanatory power and the fit of the model. The coefficients reflecting age structure have the anticipated signs reflecting reproduction potential such that net migration is negatively related with a high initial share of senior individuals in the regional population base and positively related to a high share of young individuals.[4] Moreover, a high initial share of individuals in the cohort 16–35 is also positively associated with net migration.

Turning to the variables indicating human capital and population density, we find that human capital (measured by share of regional population that has tertiary education) is an important determinant of net migration (Funke and Strulik 2000; Badinger and Tondl 2003; Cohen and Soto 2007). The parameter reflecting human capital indicates a consistent positive and significant estimate across the two specifications and across the time periods. Although the parameter is shown to

---

[2]If the condition number is less than 100, there is no serious problem with multicollinearity, while condition numbers between 100 and 1000 reflects moderate to strong multicollinearity.

[3]The multicollinearity indicated by bivariate correlations is low and the estimates are robust with regards to their signs and magnitude.

[4]A variable that reflects fertility rate (as discussed in the theoretical section) has been included in the preliminary analyses but removed because of endogeneity issues. Nevertheless, results are robust when this variable is included.

Table 7.11 Regression results, dependent variable net migration across three different time periods

Variables	Specification A–C			Specification D–F		
	A. 2001–2012	B. 2001–2007	C. 2007–2012	D. 2001–2012	E. 2001–2007	F. 2007–2012
	Coeff. (Std. Err.)	Coeff. (Std. Err.)	(Coeff. Std. Err.)	Coeff. (Std. Err.)	Coeff. (Std. Err.)	Coeff. (Std. Err.)
Age below 15	0.087** (0.001)	0.076*** (0.002)	0.001 (0.001)	0.010*** (0.001)	0.030*** (0.001)	−0.005* (0.002)
Age 16–35	–	–	–	**0.120*** (0.002)**	**0.111*** (0.003)**	**0.101*** (0.004)**
Age above 65	−0.101*** (0.001)	−0.099*** (0.001)	−0.089*** (0.002)	−0.044*** (0.002)	−0.053***(0.002)	−0.040***(0.001)
Human capital	–	–	–	0.006** (0.000)	0.001** (0.000)	0.0004 (0.000)
Density	–	–	–	1.2e-04** (4.86e-06)	1.31e-04*** (5.14e-06)	0.00003**(6.30e-06)
New MS	–	–	–	−0.200*** (0.012)	−0.204*** (0.013)	−0.281***(0.016)
EDORA typology[a]						
Agrarian	–	–	–	−0.022*** (0.016)	−0.044*** (0.012)	−0.051 ***(0.011)
Consumption countryside	–	–	–	−0.015*** (0.004)	−0.021*** (0.001)	−0.056** (0.002)
Diversified strong secondary sector	–	–	–	0.013 (0.016)	0.005 (0.017)	−0.004 (0.003)
Diversified strong market services	–	–	–	−0.004 (0.010)	−0.010 (0.010)	−0.040** (0.010)
Constant	2.333** (0.021)	2.001 (0.046)	2.604*** (0.070)	2.668*** (0.013)	2.300*** (0.051)	2.110*** (0.011)
N	1276	1276	1276	1274	1274	1274
Adj. R square	0.443	0.456	0.391	0.453	0.498	0.532
F value	6447.46	5779.54	6362.87	3465.13	3477.06	3566.44
Condition number	26.45	20.87	39.10	30.89	46.23	46.40

***, ** and * denote significant at the 1, 5 and 10% level
[a]Predominantly urban is the omitted category

Table 7.12 Regression results across demographic typology. Net migration 2001–2012

	G. Growing regions (type 1,2 3)	H. Shrinking regions (type 4, 5, 6)
	Coeff. (Std. Err.)	Coeff. (Std. Err.)
Age below 15	0.160**(0.006)	−0.003(0.003)
Age 16–35	0.221***(0.001)	0.065***(0.003)
Age above 65	−0.117***(0.001)	−0.180***(0.002)
HC	0.010**(0.000)	−0.000(0.000)
Density	0.0055***(5.71e-05)	0.0007(0.0002)
New MS	−0.131***(0.016)	−0.457***(0.030)
Constant	2.611***(0.010)	2.202***(0.070)
N	795	493
R square	0.284	0.339
F value	1100.10	1256.37
Condition number	29.88	27.44

***, ** and * denote significant at the 1, 5 and 10% level

be significant in statistical terms its significance from an economic viewpoint is low. This may not indicate that the regional level of human capital does not have broader direct impacts on net migration since this variable is measured at the more aggregated Nuts 2 level, which may influence the results. Moreover, Beeson et al. (2001) and Backman (2013) show that the measured effect of human capital is greatly reduced when measures of educational infrastructure (e.g. presence of universities) are added to the regression, suggesting that it is not just the stock of human capital in terms of individuals that matters, but also the regions ability to produce more human capital and to replace any that it might lose through migration. Furthermore, as we proxy education or the level effect of knowledge by share of population that have tertiary education in our empirical research this may lead to biased interpretations if general intellectual achievement of school graduates' changes over time and perhaps in nonlinear ways (Beeson et al. 2001). Because of the high level of aggregation used in this empirical study we are not able to control for all these demand and supply effects since this requires data at a much more disaggregated level (Bjerke 2012; Backman 2013).

We then turn to population density, which is included to control for the size of the initial population base reflecting urbanity and agglomeration effects. The parameter is positive and significant indicating that the initial level of the type of externalities and advantages that arise because of urbanization (i.e. shared infrastructures, institutions and other benefits being associated with larger cities and densely populated urban regions) are positively associated with net migration

(Rigby and Essletzbichler 2002). However, the economic significance is very low, similarly to what was found for human capital. In line with the previous discussion, the type of externalities that are associated with larger cities and densely populated urban regions may vary widely in their geographical reach (Frenken et al. 2007; Rosenthal and Strange 2008; Andersson et al. 2016). To further assess robustness, results have been estimated using total change in population and results are robust.

5.3   Comparison Between Shrinking and Growing Regions

The discussion so far has been focused on the influence of key demographic factors on population growth in European regions. The central question addressed in this study is whether the relative importance of demographic factors on population change varies across regions defined as either shrinking or growing. In order to answer this question, we divide our sample of European NUTS 3 regions into those defined as shrinking regions and those defined as growing with regards to the different underlying components that explain population development. These results are presented below in specification G and H.

Starting with regions classified as growing, the results are shown to be in line with the estimates presented above. All the variables included in the estimations are statistically significant and have their anticipated signs. However, the results for shrinking regions show some differences. The results indicate that none of the variables Age below 15, HC or density are significantly associated with migration in these regions. One possible explanation to the insignificance of Age below 15 is that many shrinking regions tend to have a large share of children in their population base since the once that migrate tend to be in the age group 20–30/35. The coefficient of the age group 16–35 is also significant and positive indicating that migration doesn't regard the lowest age cohort, but young adults.

An insignificant estimate for human capital is also reasonable considering that shrinking regions tend to have a lower education level in general. The ones that migrate from these regions are likely to search for higher wages and improved matching in terms of job opportunities and would naturally be drawn to regions that are growing. Furthermore, since educated individuals are more mobile than educational infrastructure (e.g. institutions for higher education), regions with permanent educational infrastructure that are capable of replacing erosion also have more significant growth advantages with regards to human capital. With some exceptions, educational infrastructure especially those for higher education tend to be found in urban regions. This would suggest that shrinking (rural) regions do not have the necessary infrastructure to create neither level effects nor cumulative growth effects in human capital.

A.1   Appendix: Correlation Matrices

Variables	PC 01-12	Netmig01-12	Age +65	Age −15	TFR	HC	GRP	Density	New MS
PC 01-12	1								
Netmig 01-12	0.9101	1							
Age +65	−0.297	0.028	1						
Age −15	0.376	0.122	−0.567	1					
TFR	0.419	0.221	−0.307	0.618	1				
HC	0.153	0.094	0.030	0.116	0.354	1			
GRP	0.446	0.387	0.070	0.081	0.243	0.428	1		
Density	0.138	0.041	−0.154	−0.018	0.117	0.223	0.394	1	
New MS	−0.304	−0.349	−0.465	0.048	−0.165	−0.229	−0.391	−0.085	1

Correlations are significant at the 5% level at the maximum

Variables	PC 01-07	Netmig01-07	Age +65	Age −15	TFR	HC	GRP	Density	New MS
PC 01-07	1								
Netmig 01-07	0.8997	1							
Age +65	−0.316	0.0009	1						
Age −15	0.380	0.109	−0.567	1					
TFR	0.347	0.139	−0.307	0.618	1				
HC	0.056	−0.020	0.030	0.116	0.353	1			
GRP	0.346	0.247	0.070	0.081	0.243	0.428	1		
Density	0.060	−0.044	−0.154	−0.018	0.117	0.223	0.394	1	
New MS	−0.263	−0.268	−0.465	0.048	−0.165	−0.228	−0.391	−0.085	1

Variables	PC 07-12	Netmig07-12	Age +65	Age −15	TFR	HC	GRP	Density	New MS
PC 07-12	1								
Netmig 07-12	0.9172	1							
Age +65	−0.223	0.099	1						
Age −15	0.295	0.051	−0.567	1					
TFR	0.399	0.188	−0.309	0.621	1				
HC	0.216	0.161	0.022	0.127	0.358	1			
GRP	0.450	0.383	0.063	0.088	0.248	0.435	1		
Density	0.188	0.091	−0.157	−0.018	0.115	0.225	0.396	1	
New MS	−0.278	−0.320	−0.461	0.043	−0.169	−0.232	−0.392	−0.086	1

References

Andersson M, Klaesson J, Larsson JP (2016) How local are spatial density externalities? Neighbourhood effects in agglomeration economies. Reg Stud 50(6):1082–1095

Asheim B (1999) Interactive learning and localised knowledge in globalising learning economies. GeoJournal 49(4):345–352

Backman M (2013) Regions, human capital and new firm formation. JIBS Dissertation series. Nr. 86

Badinger H, Tondl G (2003) Trade, human capital and innovation: the engines of European regional growth in the 1990s. European regional growth. Springer, Berlin Heidelberg, pp 215–239

Barro RJ (1991) Economic growth in a cross section of countries. Q J Econ 106(2):407–443

Beeson PE, DeJong DN, Troesken W (2001) Population growth in US counties, 1840–1990. Reg Sci Urban Econ 31(6):669–699

Becker GS (1962) Investment in human capital – a theoretical analysis. J Polit Econ 70(5):9–499

Becker GS (1993) A treatise on the family. First Harvard University Press, USA

Bjerke L (2012) Knowledge flows across space and firms. JIBS Dissertation series Nr. 78

Blundell R, Dearden L, Meghir C, Sianesi B (1999) Human capital investment: the returns from education and training to the individual, the firm and the economy. Fisc Stud 20(1):1–23

Button K, Pentecost E (1999) Regional economic performance within the European Union. Edward Elgar, Cheltenham

Cohen D, Soto M (2007) Growth and human capital: good data, good results. J Econ Growth 12(1):51–76

Copus AK, Johansson M (2010) Relationships between demographic change and economic restructuring in rural Europe at the beginning of the 21st century. Paper presented at the European Population Conference, Vienna, 1–4 September 2010

Copus AK (ed) (2006) Study on employment in rural areas. A study commissioned by European Commission, Directorate General for Agriculture, SAC (Scottish Agricultural College).

Copus AK et al (2010), European Development Opportunities for Rural Areas (EDORA). www.espon.eu

ESPON 1.1.4 (2005) The spatial effects of demographic change and migration, Final report project 1.1.4. European Spatial Planning Observation Network, Luxembourg

ESPON 1.4.3 (2006) Functional urban regions. Luxembourg, ESPON. http://www.espon.eu/mmp/online/website/content/projects/259/648/index_EN.html

European Parliament (2008) Shrinking regions: a paradigm shift in demography and territorial development. Brussels, European Parliament

Frenken K, Van Oort F, Verburg T (2007) Related variety, unrelated variety and regional economic growth. Reg Stud 41(5):685–697

Friedrich J (1993) A theory of urban decline: economy, demography and political elites. Urban Studies 30:907

Funke M, Strulik H (2000) On endogenous growth with physical capital, human capital and product variety. Eur Econ Rev 44(3):491–515

Glaeser EL, Kallal HD, Scheinkman JA, Shleifer A (1992) Growth in cities. J Polit Econ 100(6):1126–1152

Haase A et al (2013) Varieties of shrinkage in Europe's cities and towns. Eur Urban Reg Stud 23:86–102

Halmai P, Vásáry V (2010) Real convergence in the new Member States of the Europena Union (shorter and longer term prospects). Eur J Comp Econ 7:229–253

Haveman RH, Wolfe BL (1984) Schooling and economic well-being: the role of nonmarket effects. J Human Resour 19(3):377–407

Hoeckfeld JJ (2012) Time-space relations and the differences between shrinking regions. Built Environ 38(2):179–195

Johansson, M. (2009) Update of the demography/migration typology map. Report to the ESPON CU 2008. Revised Version 2009. ESPON, Luxemburg. Base material for the ESPON publication *Territorial Observation No. 1, Trends in Population Developement*. Available at: www.espon.eu/territorial observations, Population Development, November 2008

Johansson M, Kupsiszwski M (2009) Demography. Thematic report to the Edora-project. In: Copus AK (ed) European development opportunities for rural areas. Available at: http://www.espon.eu

Kmenta J (1986) Elements of econometrics, 2nd edn. Macmillan, New York, p 655

McCann P (2001) Urban and regional economics. Oxford University Press, USA

Moretti E (2004) Human capital externalities in cities. In: Henderson JV, Thisse JF (eds) Handbook of regional and urban economics, vol 4. Elsevier, Amsterdam, pp 2243–2291

Myrdal G (1957) Economic theory and underdeveloped regions. Duckworth, London

Rauch JE (1993) Productivity gains from geographic concentration of human capital: evidence from the cities. J Urban Econ 34:380–400

Ravenstein EG (1885) The Laws of Migration. J R Stat Soc 48:167–227

Ravenstein EG (1889) The laws of migration. J R Stat Soc 52:214–301

Rigby DL, Essletzbichler J (2002) Agglomeration economies and productivity differences in US cities. J Econ Geogr 2(4):407–432

Romer PM (1990) Endogenous technological change. J Polit Econ 98(5 Part 2):S71–S102

Rosenthal SS, Strange WC (2008) The attenuation of human capital spillovers. J Urban Econ 64(2):373–389

Ubareviciene R, van Haam M, Burneika D (2014) Shinking regions in a shrinking country: the geography of population decline in Lithuania 2001–2011. IZA DP No. 8026

Chapter 8
More Pensioners, Less Income Inequality? The Impact of Changing Age Composition on Inequality in Big Cities and Elsewhere

Omoniyi B. Alimi, David C. Maré, and Jacques Poot

1 Introduction

This chapter examines the role of changes in age structure of the population on income inequality in New Zealand over the 27-year period from 1986 to 2013. The spatial unit of analysis is the urban area, which captures about 85% of the population. More specifically, we contrast metropolitan with non-metropolitan areas. We compare results from two popular approaches—the population decomposition by sub-group approach used in Mookherjee and Shorrocks (1982) and the density decomposition approach of DiNardo et al. (1996).

Much previous research on income inequality in New Zealand has been using survey data.[1] A disadvantage of using survey data in New Zealand is that that the number of observations in a survey is often small, leading to relatively large sampling errors at sub-national levels. This limits the extent to which survey data

---

[1] See, for example, Hyslop and Maré (2005) and Ball and Creedy (2015).

O. B. Alimi (✉)
NIDEA, University of Waikato, Hamilton, New Zealand
e-mail: niyia@waikato.ac.nz

D. C. Maré
Motu Economic and Public Policy Research, Wellington, New Zealand
e-mail: dave.mare@motu.org.nz

J. Poot
Population Economics, NIDEA, University of Waikato, Hamilton, New Zealand
e-mail: jpoot@waikato.ac.nz

© Springer International Publishing AG, part of Springer Nature 2018
U. Blien et al. (eds.), *Modelling Aging and Migration Effects on Spatial Labor Markets*, Advances in Spatial Science,
https://doi.org/10.1007/978-3-319-68563-2_8

can be used to study sub-national income inequality. This limitation of survey data is avoided in the present study by using micro-level data on individuals in urban areas from the previous six Censuses of Population and Dwellings in New Zealand between 1986 and 2013. We focus specifically on the role of changes in age structure and age-specific incomes within and between urban areas on the personal distribution of income. This is an important topic because the ageing of the population is expected to accelerate in the decades to come.

Our main finding is that, contrary to studies in some other countries, the ageing of the population in New Zealand has *slowed down* overall inequality growth.[2] We find that this effect is smaller in magnitude in metropolitan areas because these areas remain relatively more youthful. The slower ageing of the population in these large cities has made a small contribution to the faster growing inequality in metropolitan areas vis-à-vis non-metropolitan areas. However, most of the difference in inequality growth between the big cities and other urban areas is due to relatively faster growing inequality *within* specific age groups in metropolitan areas.

Inequality has risen in most of the developed world, especially over the last three decades. The literature suggests that growing inequality is *inter alia* due to: changing patterns of household formation; growing international economic integration through migration, trade and capital mobility; growing unemployment; skill-biased technical change; as well as institutional factors such as decreasing levels of unionisation and minimum wages. Most studies have found that economic factors are the biggest drivers of growing income inequality,[3] but demographic factors have played a role as well.[4]

New Zealand stands out among the developed countries as having seen the relatively fastest growth in inequality, particularly during the structural and economic reforms of the late 1980s and early 1990s.[5] Changes in income inequality in New Zealand have been well documented.[6] At the subnational level, rapid inequality growth in the two largest metropolitan areas of Auckland and Wellington stands out (Alimi et al. 2016). This is largely in line with the rest of the developed world where large metropolitan areas are often areas with high—and fast growing—dispersion of income.[7] We examine here whether ageing of the population has played a role in

---

[2]For example, studies like Deaton and Paxson (1994) and Cameron (2000) found that population ageing increases inequality.

[3]See for example Castells-Quintana et al. (2015) for a review of the literature of the trends and determinants of income inequality in Europe.

[4]See e.g. Cameron (2000), Zhong (2011) and Peichl et al. (2012).

[5]See Evans et al. (1996) for a description of these reforms.

[6]See Perry (2014, 2015), Karagedikli et al. (2000, 2003), and Alimi et al. (2016).

[7]See OECD (2016).

rising income inequality and what role spatial differences in age composition have had in this context.

In New Zealand, only few studies have examined the distributional impact of changes in the age composition of the population and these studies did so at the national level.[8] The relationship between population ageing and inequality is not clear a priori. The impact of population ageing on the income distribution is uncertain due to the possibility of opposing within-age and between-age effects (von Weizsäcker 1996). Spatially, the age structure will have effects on both intra-area and inter-area inequality, as areas often have different age profiles. Bigger areas tend to have a greater share of young people. This may mean a higher intra-area inequality, particularly when accounting for post-compulsory education and family formation. At the same time, 'prime aged' workers in the large cities have higher average incomes due to agglomeration and productivity effects. Generally, population size is positive correlated with inequality.[9] In contrast, areas that possess amenities that attract retirees may have lower intra-area inequality due to the relatively narrow dispersion of incomes among retirees. New Zealand offers a relatively generous universal pension to all citizens and most other residents aged 65 and over. Hence retirement migration from big cities to lower average income areas lowers intra-area inequality in the retirement areas and increases intra-area inequality in the big cities. Retirement migration also contributes to higher inter-area inequality. However, the nature of the relationship between age structure and income inequality is blurred by the fact that the underlying dynamics of changing age structure can be complex and dependent on the relative impacts of natural increase and migration on age composition. Additionally, the way in which migration impacts on income inequality will be strongly dependent on the type of migration.[10]

The chapter proceeds as follows: Sect. 2 reviews the literature on ageing and inequality. Section 3 discusses the two decomposition techniques that are used to analyse spatial-temporal changes in income inequality in New Zealand. Section 4 describes the data and reports the results. Section 5 concludes.

---

[8] See Hyslop and Maré (2005) and Ball and Creedy (2015).

[9] A 2016 OECD report, which examines 153 metropolitan areas in 11 countries, finds that inequality in metropolitan areas is higher than the national average in all countries apart from Canada (OECD 2016 , p. 33).

[10] Given that migrants are predominantly young, net inward migration contributes to the relative youthfulness of the big cities. However, a study of the effects of migration on the income distribution would need to take into account the differential effects of net permanent & long term migration (which is on average more skilled than the local labour force and, like student migration, disproportionally towards the metropolitan areas) and temporary migration (which is less skilled and more attracted to non-metropolitan areas). The explicit analysis of the effects of migration on income inequality is beyond the scope of the present chapter.

2 Literature Review

The patterns of ageing and income inequality in New Zealand have both been well documented at the national and sub-national levels. Jackson (2011) and Johnson (2015) provide descriptive accounts of changes in age structure at the national and sub-national levels. Perry (2014, 2015) and Easton (2013) provide evidence of the long-run upward trend in inequality at the national level. Karagedikli et al. (2000, 2003) and Alimi et al. (2016) provide a sub-national analysis of income inequality trends at the regional council level. The relationship between population ageing and the distribution of income has long been examined in the literature, alongside other socio-demographic influences on inequality.[11] However, very few studies use formal theoretical foundations to link ageing to the distribution of income. Notable exceptions are Deaton and Paxson (1994, 1995) and von Weizsäcker (1996). Deaton and Paxson (1994, 1995) use the implications of the permanent income hypothesis to show that income inequality increases as the population ages while von Weizsäcker (1996) examines the role of the public transfer system. He concludes that the effect of ageing on population is ambiguous and distinguishes several channels with opposing effects through which ageing may affect the distribution of income.

Most of the recent research on this topic has been empirically oriented. Fortin et al. (2011) provide a review of the adopted methodologies and emphasise the decomposition approaches that have become common in the literature.

Just as the theory suggests, empirical evidence on the relationship between changes in the age structure and the distribution of income has been mixed, although most studies finds that population ageing increases income inequality.[12] Nonetheless, some studies find a very small effect or no effect at all. Barrett et al. (2000) focussed on 1975–1993 consumption and income inequality in Australia and concluded that the ageing of the population had played only a minor role in growing inequality. Fritzell (1993) examined data from five countries (Canada, Germany, Sweden, UK and US) and concluded that changes in age distribution or changes in family composition cannot explain changes in inequality in these countries. Jantti (1997) came to similar conclusions when examining data from the Luxembourg Income Study on Canada, Netherlands, Sweden, UK and US.

The varied evidence from empirical studies is not surprising. As earlier identified by Lam (1997), any conflicting results on the role of age structure on income distribution can be due to variations between studies in the relative strength of between-group effects and within-group effects. The combined effect of the two depends on which effect is stronger. This may vary across populations.

---

[11] See Lam (1997) for a review of the literature that examines the role of demographic variables (including changes in age structure) on income inequality.

[12] See for example Mookherjee and Shorrocks (1982), Cameron (2000), Zhong (2011), Peichl et al. (2012) and Lin et al. (2015).

In New Zealand, few studies to date have examined the effects of age structure on income inequality. Hyslop and Maré (2005) examined the factors contributing to changes in the New Zealand distribution of income between 1983 and 1998. Using the density decomposition approach of DiNardo et al. (1996), they examined the role of household structure, national superannuation (old age pension), socio-demographic attributes (which include number, age, sex, ethnicity and education levels of adults in the household, together with the numbers of children in various age groups), employment outcomes, and economic returns' to such attributes. They found that changes in household structure and socio-demographic attributes were the major factors contributing to changes in the income distribution in New Zealand (each contributing around one-sixth of the overall increase in the Gini coefficient). Changes in household structure tended to raise the top end of the income distribution while lowering the bottom end. Changes in household socio-demographic attributes also widened the distribution of income, particularly at higher incomes.

Ball and Creedy (2015) analysed income and expenditure data from 1983 to 2007 and found that the age and gender composition of the population was important for understanding inequality. However, Aziz et al. (2015) show, using the New Zealand Treasury's microsimulation model to forecast demographic changes that are expected over the next 50 years, that population ageing and expected changes in labour force participation by themselves do not have a significant impact on aggregate income inequality.

Our present study is similar to earlier work by Hyslop and Maré (2005) but instead of taking a national approach and examining the role of several economic and socio-demographic factors using survey data, we take a sub-national approach and focus exclusively on the spatial-temporal role of the age structure on the distribution of income.

3   Decomposition Methods

We use two popular approaches in the literature—the decomposition by population subgroup approach of Mookherjee and Shorrocks (1982) and the semi-parametric density decomposition method of DiNardo et al. (1996)—to examine different ways in which changes in the age structure could affect the aggregate distribution of income at the urban area level. We use both methods to analyse the inter-temporal effect of changes in the age structure nationally as well as spatially across metropolitan and non-metropolitan areas between 1986 and 2013.[13] There are two

---

[13]Metropolitan areas defined as urban areas that make up the six largest New Zealand cities (in order of size) of Auckland, Wellington, Christchurch, Hamilton, Tauranga and Dunedin. All other urban areas are considered non-metropolitan areas.

ways in which age structure can affect the distribution of income:

- *The composition effect (or the age shares effect)*: This reveals how much of a role the population composition of an area plays in observed inequality. It is the effect on inequality of differences in the shares of different age groups for given mean incomes at various ages.
- *The age-specific income distribution effect*: This examines the effect of differences in the age-specific income distribution on observed inequality for a given age composition of the population.

For both effects, we consider changes over time and across places.

We focus on the class of Generalised Entropy (GE) measures of inequality due to their property of permitting the expression of overall inequality as a weighted sum of sub-level inequalities. Within this class, we use the Mean Log Deviation (MLD) index as our measure of inequality because the MLD weights the inequality measure for a group by the group's population share. Hence MLD provides a direct evaluation of the effect of changes in age composition. One alternative GE measure is the Theil index of inequality which weights groups by income share. In the present context of analysing the impact of changes in demographic composition, the MLD is the more natural and more easily interpretable index.

Without loss of generality, let's assume that a population of size N is grouped in A age groups indexed by $a = 1, 2, \ldots, A$. Within each age group a there are N_a individuals, with individuals indexed by $i = 1, 2, \ldots, N_a$. Hence, $N = \sum_{a=1}^{A} N_a$. Given that we have access to microdata, the income of the individuals is known and defined as y_{ia}, i.e. the income of individual i in age group a. However, in many data collections, such as the census, income is only observed in income brackets. Let there be j income brackets, $j = 1, 2, \ldots, J$. We will denote the income of individual i in age group a and in income bracket j by y_{ija}. As is done commonly, we will assume that income of each individual i in income bracket j and age group a is the same for everyone, denoted by y_j, namely the midpoint of the bracket (and a statistically estimated amount for the open-ended top bracket, see Sect. 4). We assume that there are N_{ja} individuals in income bracket j and age group a, who then each earn y_j. Hence, $N = \sum_{a=1}^{A} N_a = \sum_{a=1}^{A} \sum_{j}^{J} N_{ja} = \sum_{j=1}^{J} \sum_{a=1}^{A} N_{ja} = \sum_{j=1}^{J} N_j$. It is convenient to also introduce notation for the population fraction in each age group, $\pi_a = N_a/N$.

We can now also define various income aggregates. The aggregate income of all individuals in income bracket j in age group a is $Y_{ja} = y_j N_{ja}$. The aggregate income of all those in age group a is $Y_a = \sum_{j=1}^{J} Y_{ja} = \sum_{j=1}^{J} y_j N_{ja}$ while the aggregate income of those in income bracket j is $Y_j = \sum_{a=1}^{A} Y_{ja} = \sum_{a=1}^{A} y_j N_{ja} = y_j \sum_{a=1}^{A} N_{ja} = y_j N_j$. Total income in the economy is $Y = \sum_{a=1}^{A} Y_a = \sum_{a=1}^{A} \sum_{j=1}^{J} y_j N_{ja} = \sum_{j=1}^{J} \sum_{a=1}^{A} y_j N_{ja} = \sum_{j=1}^{J} y_j \sum_{a=1}^{A} N_{ja} = \sum_{j=1}^{J} y_j N_j = \sum_{j=1}^{J} Y_j$. Finally, we denote average income in the economy by $\mu = Y/N$, average income of those in age group a by $\mu_a = Y_a/N_a$, and relative income of those in age group a by $r_a = \mu_a/\mu$.

Given this notation, MLD can be expressed as follows (see, e.g., Mookherjee and Shorrocks 1982):

$$
MLD = \sum_{a=1}^{A} \sum_{j=1}^{J} \frac{N_{ja}}{N} \log \left(\frac{Y/N}{Y_{ja}/N_{ja}} \right) = \sum_{a=1}^{A} \sum_{j=1}^{J} \pi_{ja} \log \left(\frac{1}{r_{ja}} \right) \tag{8.1}
$$

It is useful to note that *MLD* in invariant to population scale N and the unit of measurement of income (e.g. nominal or real). It is straightforward to show that overall inequality can be decomposed into the sum of within-age-group inequality and between-age-group inequality:

$$
MLD = \sum_{a=1}^{A} \frac{N_a}{N} \left[\sum_{j=1}^{J} \frac{N_{ja}}{N_a} \log \left(\frac{Y_a/N_a}{Y_{ja}/N_{ja}} \right) \right] + \sum_{a=1}^{A} \frac{N_a}{N} \log \left(\frac{Y/N}{Y_a/N_a} \right)
$$

$$
= \sum_{a=1}^{A} \pi_a MLD_a + \sum_{a=1}^{A} \pi_a \log \left(\frac{1}{r_a} \right) \tag{8.2}
$$

in which $\sum_{a=1}^{A} \pi_a MLD_a$ is the age-group-weighted sum of within-age-group inequality and $\sum_{a=1}^{A} \pi_a \log \left(\frac{1}{r_a} \right)$ the age-group-weighted sum of the logarithm of the inverse of age-group-relative income (i.e., between-age-group inequality). It should be noted that such decompositions hold also true for any other mutually exclusive and collectively exhaustive classifications, such as gender and location. The decomposition can also be applied hierarchically, for example when overall income inequality is decomposed by age and sex.

When gauging a change in overall inequality over a given period, eq. (8.2) clearly shows that there are three contributing factors: firstly, changes in the age group shares (structural population ageing); secondly, changes in inequality within each age group; and, thirdly, changes in the age-group-relative incomes (for example due to changes in the lifecycle profile of earnings). It is easy to see that a change in the *MLD*, can be expressed exactly as follows:

$$\Delta MLD = \underbrace{\sum_{a=1}^{A} \overline{\pi_a} \Delta MLD_a}_{\substack{\text{aggregate} \\ \text{change in} \\ \text{within} - \text{age} - \text{group} \\ \text{inequality for given} \\ \text{age shares} \\ C1}} + \underbrace{\sum_{a=1}^{A} \overline{MLD_a} \Delta \pi_a}_{\substack{\text{aggregate} \\ \text{change in} \\ \text{within} - \text{age} - \text{group} \\ \text{inequality due to} \\ \text{changing age shares} \\ C2}}$$

$$+ \underbrace{\sum_{a=1}^{A} \overline{\log\left(\frac{1}{r_a}\right)} \Delta \pi_a}_{\substack{\text{aggregate} \\ \text{change in} \\ \text{between} - \text{age} - \text{group} \\ \text{inequality due to} \\ \text{changing age shares} \\ C3}} + \underbrace{\sum_{j=1}^{J} \overline{\pi_a} \Delta \log\left(\frac{1}{r_a}\right)}_{\substack{\text{aggregate} \\ \text{growth in} \\ \text{age} - \text{group relative} \\ \text{income for given} \\ \text{age shares} \\ C4}} \tag{8.3}$$

in which a bar over an expression represents the simple arithmetic average of the variable over the two periods, i.e. $\overline{x} = \frac{1}{2}(x_{t-1} + x_t)$.

Component $C4$ in eq. (8.3) above represents the aggregate impact on inequality of growth (the change in natural logarithmic values) in age-group-specific mean incomes, but *relative* to overall mean income. Mookherjee and Shorrocks (1982) argue that it is more natural to think of growth in the *levels* of age-group-specific mean incomes rather than growth in relative incomes. For this reason, they replace Eq. (8.3) by a decomposition that holds only approximately, but which explicitly includes age-specific mean income growth:[14]

---

[14]Mookherjee and Shorrocks (1982) note that this approximation appears sufficient for computational purposes (p. 897). However, experimentation with a range of changing income distributions shows that the sign of $C3$ can be sometimes different from that of $C3'$ and, similarly, the sign of $C4$ can be different from that of $C4'$. This may lead to slightly different interpretations. In this chapter we follow Mookherjee and Shorrocks (1982) and use the approximate decomposition. Results for the exact decomposition are available upon request.

$$\Delta MLD \approx \underbrace{\sum_{a=1}^{A} \overline{\pi_a} \Delta MLD_a}_{\substack{aggregate \\ change\ in \\ within-age-group \\ inequality\ for\ given \\ age\ shares \\ C1}} + \underbrace{\sum_{a=1}^{A} \overline{MLD_a} \Delta \pi_a}_{\substack{aggregate \\ change\ in \\ within-age-group \\ inequality\ due\ to \\ changing\ age\ shares \\ C2}}$$

$$+ \underbrace{\sum_{a=1}^{A} \left(\overline{r_a} - \overline{logr_a}\right) \Delta \pi_a}_{\substack{aggregate \\ change\ in \\ between-age-group \\ inequality\ due\ to \\ changing\ age\ shares \\ C3'}} + \underbrace{\sum_{a=1}^{A} \left(\overline{\pi_a r_a} - \overline{\pi_a}\right) \Delta log\mu_a}_{\substack{aggregate \\ growth\ in \\ age-group\ mean \\ income\ for\ given \\ age\ shares \\ C4'}}$$

$$(8.4)$$

In the next section we will report result by using this approximate decomposition given in Eq. (8.4).

The second decomposition method considers the income distribution as a density which may have a different shape for different age groups. Inequality is quantified by a dispersion measure applied to a given distribution of income of individuals or households. Besides the *MLD* measure of inequality described above, common alternative dispersion measures are the Gini coefficient, Theil index, the Coefficient of Variation, etc. We can quantify the effect of any change in the shape of the distribution of income by any of these inequality measures. DiNardo et al. (1996) consider it useful to decompose overall change in inequality into a contribution from *within-group* inequality change, calculated for a counterfactual income distribution in which population composition is assumed to have stayed the same, and a contribution from *between-group* change calculated for a counterfactual income distribution at which inequality within groups is assumed to remain the same.

One advantage of this approach is that it provides in our context a visual representation of the roles of the age composition effect and the age-specific distribution effect respectively. Let $f_Y(y;x) = \int f_{Y\,|\,X} dF_X$ represent the general distribution of income with respect to personal characteristic X. The integral sign is used to depict aggregate income with respect to attributes X that can be quantified by continuous variables. When X is a discrete variable, such as an age group, the corresponding expression is $f_Y(y;x) = \sum f_{Y\,|\,X}\, \varphi_X$ where $\varphi = Prob(X = x)$.

In this paper we focus exclusively on the age distribution (denoted by A as before). This distribution may be specific to a certain location, say urban area U,

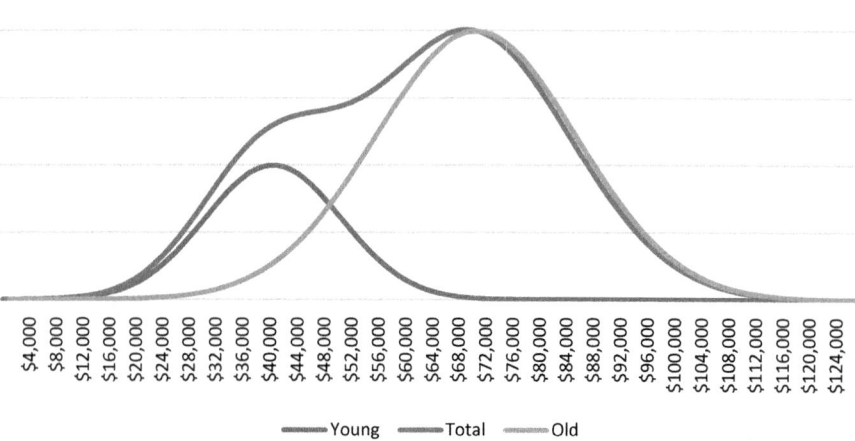

Fig. 8.1 Hypothetical income distribution in an urban area U, showing total and age-specific distributions for young and old people

and at a particular point in time. Hence the overall income distribution in urban area U is then given by

$$f_Y^U(y; a) = \underbrace{\sum f_{Y|A}^U}_{\substack{age - specific \\ conditional \\ distribution}} \quad \underbrace{Prob(A = a)}_{\substack{Compositional\ or \\ shares\ effect}} \tag{8.5}$$

To illustrate this, consider Fig. 8.1 which presents a hypothetical distribution with two broad age categories in U: younger people and older people. In this Figure older people do not only have higher incomes than younger people have but they are also more numerous.

The impact of age structure on change in the overall distribution of income in U could be through a composition effect, i.e. through changes in $Prob(A = a)$ or through changes in the age-specific conditional distribution of income $f_{Y|A}^U$. To calculate both effects, we employ a benchmarking approach. To proceed we will need to introduce some notation and keep in mind the application to New Zealand Census data from 1986 until 2013. The beginning census year of the study (1986) will be compared to the last census year (2013). We now define:

- $f_Y^{N86|N86} = \sum f_{Y|A}^{N86} \pi_a^{N86}$ represents the actual 1986 national distribution of incomes based on the 1986 conditional age-specific distributions $f_{Y|A}^{N86}$ and the 1986 shares of people in each age group π_a^{N86}. Similarly, $f_Y^{N13|N13} = \sum f_{Y|A}^{N13} \pi_a^{N13}$ represents the corresponding 2013 distribution of income;

- $\check{f}_Y^{N13|N86} = \sum f_{Y|A}^{N13} \pi_a^{N86}$ represents a 2013 counterfactual distribution, based on the 2013 age-specific conditional distribution of incomes but 1986 shares of people in each age group i.e. $\check{f}_Y^{N13|N86} = \sum f_{Y|A}^{N13} \pi_a^{N86} = \sum f_{Y|A}^{N13} \pi_a^{N13} \cdot \frac{\pi_a^{N86}}{\pi_a^{N13}}$

Changes in inequality over time can either be attributed to changes in the age composition effect or due to changes in the age-specific distribution of income. The role of changes in age composition between 1986 and 2013 can be calculated by comparing the 2013 original distribution f_Y^{N13} to the counterfactual distribution $\check{f}_Y^{N13|N86}$ which is based on 2013 age-specific conditional distribution of incomes but 1986 shares of people in each age group. i.e. the difference is $f_Y^{N13} - \check{f}_Y^{N13|N86}$. The $\check{f}_Y^{N13|N86}$ holds changes in the age-specific distribution over the period constant so any differences between the actual 2013 distribution and this counterfactual distribution are due to the changes in age composition. Since the population aged between 1986 and 2013, this will estimate the effect of the ageing of the population on the income distribution.

The effect of changes in the age-specific distribution between 1986 and 2013 will be calculated by comparing the counter factual distribution $\check{f}_Y^{N13|N86}$ to the 1986 original distribution i.e. by calculating $\check{f}_Y^{N13|N86} - f_Y^{N86}$. Since $\check{f}_Y^{N13|N86}$ is based on the 1986 age structure, any difference between this distribution and the 1986 distribution is due to the changes in the age-specific conditional distribution.

This benchmarking approach provides an alternative way of decomposing the change in inequality measured by the *MLD* index. Here we can write changes in income inequality between 1986 and 2013 as:

$$\Delta MLD_{13-86} = MLD\left(f_Y^{N13}\right) - MLD\left(f_Y^{N86}\right)$$

$$= \underbrace{\left[MLD\left(f_Y^{N13}\right) - MLD\left(\check{f}_Y^{N13|N86}\right)\right]}_{Age\ composition\ effect}$$

$$+ \underbrace{\left[MLD\left(\check{f}_Y^{N13|N86}\right) - MLD\left(f_Y^{N86}\right)\right]}_{Age-specific\ distribution\ effect}$$

(8.6)

This is a very simple way of decomposing the change in the *MLD* index into two parts: the first part shows the contribution of the changing age composition for given age-specific inequality while the second component shows how much, for a given age distribution, the change in age-specific inequality contributed to the overall change.

Finally, it should be noted that the calculation of the effect of the changing age composition on inequality can be done separately for every urban area. Of particular interest is then the extent to which the age composition effects play a greater or lesser role in explaining inequality change in certain areas and whether the sign of the age composition effect (positive or negative) is the same in all areas. Here we simply consider the distinction between metropolitan and non-metropolitan areas.

There are certain limitations to the density decomposition approach. Firstly, it follows a partial equilibrium analysis: we calculate the effect on inequality if the population composition changes but age-specific distributions remain the same, or vice versa. Hence this approach ignores the *interaction* between these two effects: changes in population composition can in general equilibrium also affect the age-specific distribution of income, and vice-versa, through migration and labour market adjustments.

Another limitation, which is a characteristic of all decomposition methods, is that such methods do not contribute to understanding the various economic mechanisms through which ageing affects inequality. Instead, decomposition provides simply an accounting framework that allows us to quantify the relative magnitude of the impact of compositional change.

4   Data and Results

4.1   Data on Personal Income

All data used are from the six New Zealand Censuses of Population and Dwelling from 1986 to 2013. The population is limited to people aged 15 and above who are earning positive incomes. Age data are available by single year of age. However, because we are interested in the broad trend of structural population ageing, we collapse all ages into four age groups: 15–24, 25–44, 45–64 and those 65 and over.

The income data represent total personal income before tax of people earning positive income in the 12 months before the census night.[15] It consists of income from all sources such as wages and salaries, self-employment income, investment income, and superannuation. It excludes social transfers in kind, such as public education or government-subsidised health care services. Instead of recording actual incomes, total personal incomes are captured in income bands in each census with the top and bottom income bands open ended. For example, the top band in the 2013

---

[15] Hence people not in paid employment and business owners reporting a loss have been excluded.

census data captures everybody earning $150,000 and over. An important issue with the open-ended upper band is the calculation of mean income in the open ended band. At the national level this is not a problem as Statistics New Zealand publishes an estimate of the midpoint of the top band for the country based on Household Economic Survey (HES) estimates. However, HES top-band mean incomes for sub-national areas are not reliable due to sampling errors. To resolve this problem, Pareto distributions have been fitted to the upper tail of the urban-area specific distributions. We use the Stata RPME command developed by von Hippel et al. (2016).

4.2   Changes in the Age Distribution of the Population

Population ageing is a key feature of the changes in the New Zealand age structure between 1986 and 2013. Jackson (2011) identified increasing longevity and declining birth rates as the main drivers of this trend. The patterns of ageing have been well described nationally and sub-nationally. Plenty of studies have examined the implications of an ageing population on the labour force, government revenues and economic growth (see Jackson 2011; Stephenson and Scobie 2002; McCulloch and Frances 2001). Spatially, attention has been given to examining the impact of accelerated aging of the rural areas and the role of rural-urban migration in driving this decline. Here we focus on differences between metropolitan and non-metropolitan areas in ageing. Table 8.1 shows the trends in population composition by age groups for metropolitan and non-metropolitan areas, and for all urban areas combined, from 1986 to 2013.

The ageing of the population between 1986 and 2013 is very clear. Nationally (all urban areas combined), the proportion of the population in the youngest age group 15–24 declined from 22% in 1986 to 14% in 2013 while for the oldest age group, 65+, the proportion increased from 15% to 18%. By 2013, the proportion of the population in the oldest age group exceeded that in the youngest age group.

Spatially, there is disparity across urban areas in the patterns of ageing. Non-metropolitan areas age more rapidly. In 1986, metro and non-metro had almost the same proportion of people in the youngest age group, 15–24, (around 22%) but by 2013 the proportion in non-metropolitan areas had fallen by about nine percentage points while in metropolitan areas it fell by only seven percentage points. The disparity is even starker when comparing the changes in the oldest age group 65+: the proportion in this group increased by about two percentage points in metropolitan areas compared to a six percentage point increase in non-metropolitan areas. It is evident that non-metropolitan areas have undergone more rapid ageing and were older on average than metropolitan areas by 2013.

Table 8.1 Structural population ageing in New Zealand from 1986 to 2013

Age group	Metropolitan areas					
	1986 (%)	1991 (%)	1996 (%)	2001 (%)	2006 (%)	2013 (%)
15–24	22	20	19	17	17	15
25–44	39	41	41	41	39	36
45–64	24	24	25	28	30	32
65–99	14	15	15	14	14	16
15–99	100	100	100	100	100	100
	Non-metropolitan areas					
15–24	21	18	17	14	14	12
25–44	37	38	38	36	33	30
45–64	25	25	26	30	32	34
65–99	17	18	19	20	20	23
15–99	100	100	100	100	100	100
	All urban areas combined					
15–24	22	19	18	16	16	14
25–44	39	40	40	40	38	35
45–64	24	24	26	29	30	33
65–99	15	16	16	16	16	18
15–99	100	100	100	100	100	100

Note: Metropolitan areas are the six largest New Zealand cities (in order of size): Auckland, Wellington, Christchurch, Hamilton, Tauranga and Dunedin. All other urban areas are considered non-metropolitan areas

4.3 Changes in the Mean Log Deviation Measure of Income Inequality

As noted in the introduction, New Zealand stands out among the developed countries as having seen the relatively fastest growth in inequality in recent decades, particularly during the 1980s and early 1990s. Across all urban areas, inequality grew by about 18% between 1986 and 2013 (see Table 8.2). It increased in all intercensal periods apart from between 1986 and 1991, and between 2001 and 2006 (see Fig. 8.2). Like the changes in age structure, the changes in income inequality are not the same everywhere. Much like what has been found in other countries, inequality increased more rapidly in metropolitan areas.[16] The metropolitan and non-metropolitan divide had been highlighted in previous New Zealand studies by Karagedikli et al. (2000, 2003) and Alimi et al. (2016). They found the highest rates of income and inequality growth in the metropolitan areas of Auckland and Wellington. Table 8.2 shows that metropolitan areas saw a 25% increase in the MLD, as compared with only 2% growth in non-metropolitan areas. It is clear that

---

[16]See OECD (2016).

Table 8.2 Metropolitan versus non-metropolitan growth rates in income inequality

	1986 (MLD)	2013 (MLD)	Growth 1986–2013 (percentages)
Metro	0.3607	0.4500	25%
Non metro	0.3563	0.3623	2%
All urban areas combined	0.3509	0.4153	18%

Note: Metropolitan areas are the six largest New Zealand cities (in order of size): Auckland, Wellington, Christchurch, Hamilton, Tauranga and Dunedin. All other urban areas are considered non-metropolitan areas. Income inequality is measured by the Mean Log Deviation (MLD) index. To calculate the MLD for all urban areas combined, the Statistics New Zealand Household Economic Survey estimates of national-level mean income in the open-ended top bracket were used, not the estimates of mean income derived from fitting Pareto distributions to the top end of the distribution. This implies that the MLD for all urban areas combined does not perfectly decompose into within-group and between-group contributions equivalent to Eq. (8.2)

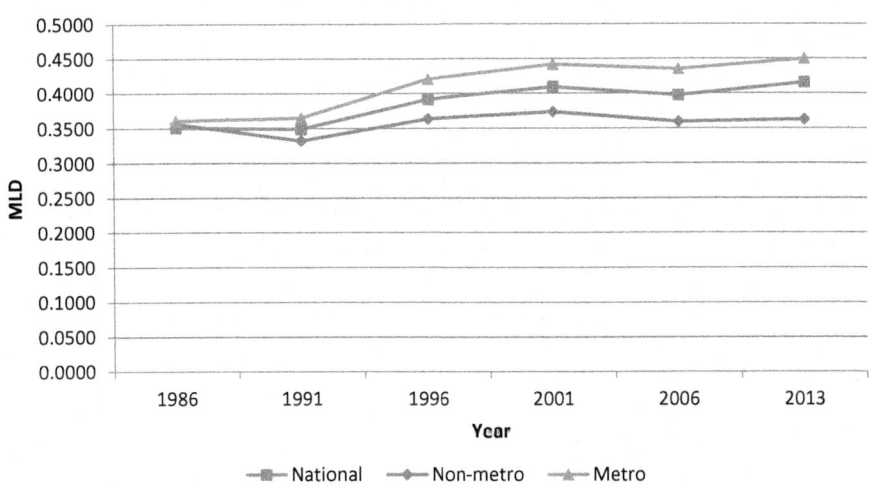

Fig. 8.2 Mean Log Deviation index of income inequality, New Zealand 1986–2013

most of the growth in inequality that happened in New Zealand between 1986 and 2013 was driven by the changes in the metropolitan areas.

The 1986–2013 change in *MLD* displayed in Fig. 8.2 is disaggregated in tabular form into changes in the inequality index for each age group in Table 8.3. Focusing on the aggregate patterns, but with the same conclusions also true for metro and non-metro areas, within-age-group inequality increased the most between 1986 and 2013 in the 65+ group, closely followed by the 15–24 age group. The within-group measure of inequality for these two groups rose across all urban areas by around 68% and 35% respectively. The 25–44 group was the only age group to experience a decline in within-group inequality, at around 10%.

One factor explaining these trends in within-group income inequality is labour force participation. Among the 15–24 group, the proportion of those attending tertiary education, and therefore only working part-time and at low wages, has been

Table 8.3 New Zealand income inequality by type of area and age group, 1986–2013

	Age group	1986	1991	1996	2001	2006	2013	Change (86–13)	Mean
	Metropolitan								
15–24	MLD	0.3708	0.3667	0.4305	0.4672	0.4879	0.5100	38%	0.4389
	r	69%	60%	50%	45%	43%	39%	−30%	51%
	π	22%	20%	19%	17%	17%	15%	−7%	18%
25–44	MLD	0.3697	0.3472	0.3463	0.3528	0.3267	0.3414	−8%	0.3473
	r	119%	121%	121%	120%	117%	113%	−5%	119%
	π	39%	41%	41%	41%	39%	36%	−3%	40%
45–64	MLD	0.3197	0.3328	0.3958	0.4030	0.3749	0.3972	24%	0.3706
	r	117%	117%	126%	124%	127%	129%	12%	123%
	π	24%	24%	25%	28%	30%	32%	8%	27%
65+	MLD	0.1638	0.1725	0.2024	0.2352	0.2743	0.2929	79%	0.2235
	R	68%	67%	60%	60%	63%	70%	2%	64%
	π	14%	15%	15%	14%	14%	16%	2%	15%
	Non-metropolitan								
15–24	MLD	0.3805	0.3500	0.4032	0.4322	0.4560	0.4881	28%	0.4183
	r	73%	64%	55%	50%	52%	49%	−24%	57%
	π	21%	18%	17%	14%	14%	12%	−9%	16%
25–44	MLD	0.3908	0.3397	0.3191	0.3158	0.2896	0.3083	−21%	0.3272
	r	118%	121%	121%	118%	116%	112%	−6%	118%
	π	37%	38%	38%	36%	33%	30%	−7%	36%
45–64	MLD	0.3166	31%	36%	36%	33%	0.3274	3%	0.3330
	r	115%	115%	123%	125%	126%	126%	11%	122%
	π	25%	25%	26%	30%	32%	34%	10%	29%
65+	MLD	0.1498	14%	16%	18%	20%	0.2152	44%	0.1760
	r	71%	73%	67%	67%	67%	73%	2%	70%
	π	17%	18%	19%	20%	20%	23%	7%	20%
	All urban areas combined								
15–24	MLD	0.3733	0.3627	0.4206	0.4554	0.4779	0.5022	35%	0.4320
	r	71%	62%	52%	47%	46%	42%	−29%	53%
	π	22%	19%	18%	16%	16%	14%	−7%	18%
25–44	MLD	0.3678	0.3398	0.3303	0.3349	0.3088	0.3309	−10%	0.3354
	r	119%	121%	122%	120%	119%	115%	−4%	119%
	π	39%	40%	40%	40%	38%	35%	−4%	39%
45–64	MLD	0.3057	0.3146	0.3617	0.3683	0.3328	0.3559	16%	0.3399
	r	116%	116%	123%	123%	124%	126%	10%	121%
	π	24%	24%	26%	29%	30%	33%	8%	28%
65+	MLD	0.1522	0.1560	0.1805	0.2069	0.2374	0.2562	68%	0.1982
	r	69%	68%	62%	62%	64%	70%	2%	66%
	π	15%	16%	16%	16%	16%	18%	3%	16%

Note: r is relative income and π is age-group share of population for given year and area

increasing. Among those aged 65+, labour force participation has been increasing, thus leading to a larger number receiving income over and above New Zealand superannuation. Both trends increase inequality. The proportion of the 65+ age group participating in the labour force in urban areas rose from 3% in 1986 to 11% in 2013. This change led to an increase in the dispersion of income between those mostly relying on superannuation (plus perhaps some income from investments or private pensions) and those still in paid work. The opposite effect happened at the other end of the scale where those in the 15–24 age group experienced a reduction in labour force participation. This is due to an increasing proportion of this group spending more time in education and formal training. The reduction in labour force participation in this group, especially the reduction in those working full time, contributed to an increase the dispersion of income within the 15–24 age group.[17]

In terms of the life course, inequality is higher within the 15–24 age group than at other ages. Apart from the high inequality in the first age group, and excluding 1986 and 1991, inequality does follow the usual life course pattern suggested in the literature, with increases in income inequality as a specific age cohort ages, until the public pension (New Zealand superannuation) becomes available at age 65.[18]

With respect to relative mean income, the 15–24 group have seen the biggest drop, irrespective of urban location. Across all urban areas, the relative income of this age group dropped by 29 percentage points, falling from 71% of average income in 1986 to around 42% of 2013 average income. In contrast, the 45–64 and 65+ groups increased their relative incomes by ten and two percentage points respectively.

Using Eq. (8.2), Table 8.4 shows how each age group contributes to income inequality measured by the MLD index: within-group inequality makes the largest contribution to total inequality (varying between 83.7% in 2006 and 91.5% in 1986. However, between-age-group inequality is becoming a bigger share of total inequality: its contribution increased from around 8.5% in 1986 to 15.7% in 2013. This is primarily due to the increased divergence in relative mean incomes across age groups.

From 1986 to 2006, the 25–44 age group made the biggest contribution to within-group inequality. The large population share of this group was responsible for this effect (see Table 8.3). By 2013 however, within-inequality of the 45–64 age group made the greatest contribution to total inequality, reflecting the combined effect of

---

[17]The labour force participation rate for those aged 15–24 declined from 76% in 1986 to 61% in 2013, with full-time employment falling by even more at 40 percentage points.

[18]New Zealand Superannuation is the public pension paid to all residents over the age of 65 (immigrants must have resided in the country for 10 years or longer). Any eligible New Zealander receives NZ Super regardless of how much they earn through paid work, savings and investments, what other assets they own or what taxes they have paid. NZ Super is indexed to the average wage. The after-tax NZ Super rate for couples (who both qualify) is based on 66% of the 'average ordinary time wage' after tax. For single people, the after-tax NZ superannuation rate is around 40% of that average wage. See https://www.workandincome.govt.nz/eligibility/seniors/superannuation/payment-rates.html

Table 8.4 Decomposition of *MLD* into between-age-group and within-age-group components: all urban areas combined

Age group	Within-group contribution to *MLD* ($\pi_j MLD_j$)					
	1986	1991	1996	2001	2006	2013
15–24	0.0816	0.0705	0.0758	0.0729	0.0775	0.0724
25–44	0.1421	0.1372	0.1328	0.1330	0.1162	0.1147
45–64	0.0744	0.0761	0.0932	0.1051	0.1010	0.1167
65+	0.0231	0.0250	0.0289	0.0326	0.0375	0.0464
Sum of within age group inequality	0.3212	0.3088	0.3307	0.3436	0.3322	0.3502
	Between-group contribution to *MLD* $\left(\pi_j \log\left(\frac{1}{r_j}\right)\right)$					
15–24	0.0749	0.0929	0.1180	0.1208	0.1244	0.1258
25–44	−0.0662	−0.0785	−0.0788	−0.0739	−0.0653	−0.0485
45–64	−0.0358	−0.0352	−0.0536	−0.0579	−0.0652	−0.0761
65+	0.0568	0.0610	0.0752	0.0765	0.0709	0.0638
Sum of between-age-group inequality	0.0297	0.0402	0.0609	0.0655	0.0649	0.0651
All urban areas combined *MLD*						
Between as a percent of total	8.5%	11.5%	15.5%	16.0%	16.3%	15.7%
Within as a percent of total	91.5%	88.5%	84.5%	84.0%	83.7%	84.3%
Total	0.3509	0.3490	0.3916	0.4091	0.3971	0.4153

population ageing and growing inequality within this group. The trends for those aged 15–24 and those aged 65+ provide an interesting contrast. In the 15–24 age group, within-inequality rose very fast but the diminishing population share of this group reduced their contribution to aggregate within-inequality over time. For the 65+ group, both within-inequality as well as population share increased, thereby increasing this group's impact on overall inequality.

The combined effect of changing age-specific relative incomes and changed age-group shares of population can be clearly seen in the middle panel of Table 8.4. Incomes in the 25–44 and 45–64 age groups are above average, thereby yielding negative between-group contributions to *MLD*. The most striking trend is the contribution of declining relative incomes of the young (see also Table 8.3) to growing overall inequality measured by the *MLD*.

4.4 Changes in the Density of the Income Distribution

We will now proceed with a visual approach to present the contribution of each age group to the overall change in the distribution of income across all urban areas between 1986 and 2013. Figure 8.3 presents the standardized 1986 and

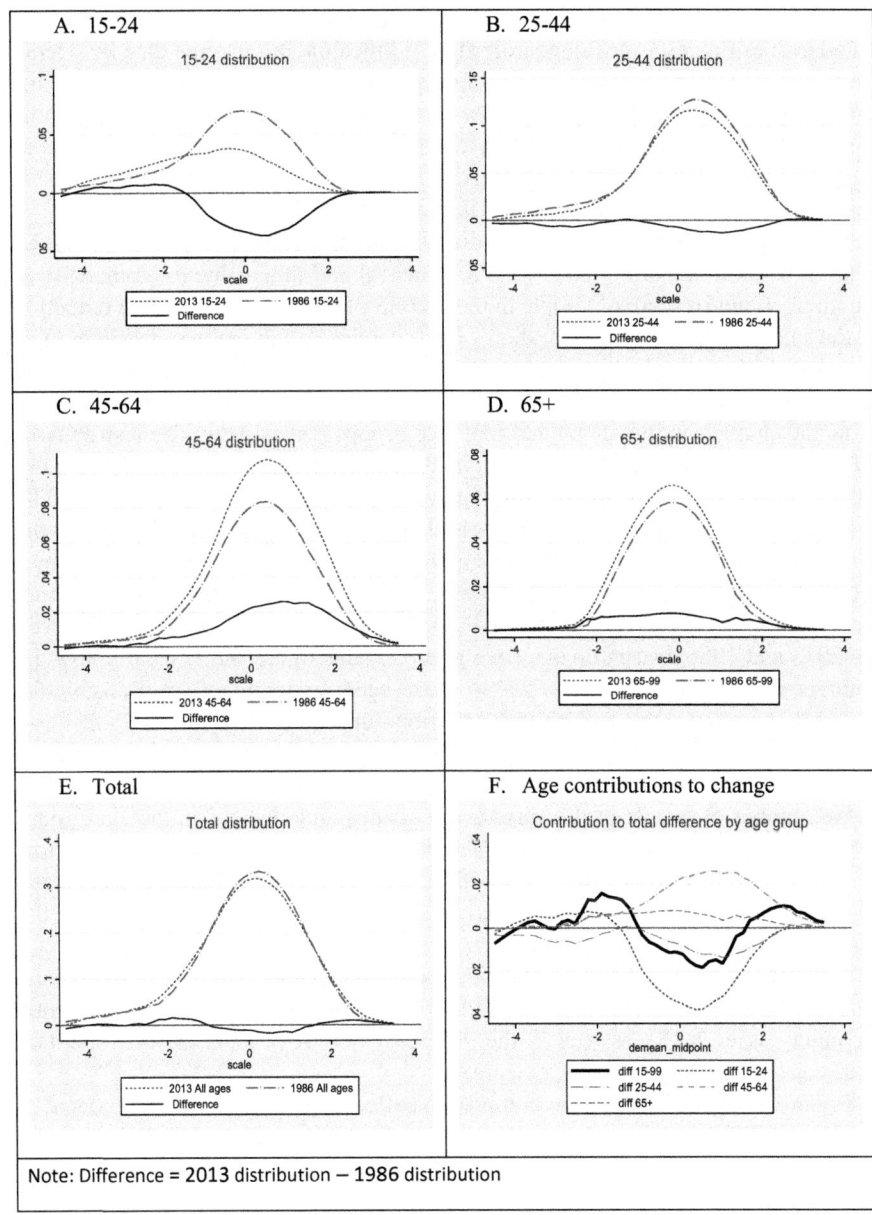

Fig. 8.3 A comparison of the 1986 and 2013 income distributions by age group: all urban areas combined

2013 log income distribution for each age group and all urban areas combined. The densities diagrams are standardized by de-meaning all income data by overall average income. The areas under the curves represent the population shares of the age groups. Hence, the overall income distribution in panel E is the sum of the densities A to D and has total density equal to one (as in the stylised example of Fig. 8.1). Overlaying the density diagrams for 1986 and 2013 provides a visual appreciation of the changes in the distribution over time.

Focusing on age groups, the 2013 distribution of the 15–24 age group is wider than the 1986 distribution (see Fig. 8.3, panel A) and this is due to an increase in the number and/or share of people in the bottom of the distribution and a reduction in the middle and top. Panel B shows that changes in the income distribution of those aged 25–44 group have been relatively minor (although they have, given the size of this group, still a major impact on the overall distribution). Panels C and D show the changes in the 45–64 and 65+ age groups respectively. The distributions for these groups are wider in 2013 than in 1986. The increase in inequality for these groups is predominantly due to an increase in the number of people in the middle and top of the distributions. Panel E pools all age groups together and shows that the overall distribution is wider in 2013 compared with 1986. This change is driven by a 'hollowing out' of the middle of the income distribution, due to more people at both the bottom and top ends of the distribution. Panel F graphs the difference between the 2013 and 1986 distributions by age group.[19] This figure shows clearly how the younger age groups (15–24 and 25–44) have been predominantly responsible for the 'hollowing out at the middle of the distribution.'[20]

Similarly to disaggregating inequality changes by the *MLD* index, changes in the aggregate income distribution density are due to the combined effect of changes in the number of people at the various age groups and changes in the age-group-specific densities. We will therefore now proceed with calculating the counterfactual densities as outlined in the previous section. Given the counterfactual densities, the change in inequality between 1986 and 2013 can be decomposed by means of the *MLD* index as given in Eq. (8.6).

Figure 8.4 presents the 2013 and 1986 original distributions, the counterfactual distribution (with age distribution fixed at the 1986 shares and within-age-group inequality as in 2013), as well as the differences between them for metropolitan, non-metropolitan and the combined areas.

Figure 8.4 shows that the age-composition effects are a very small component of the overall difference between 1986 and 2013. There are only small differences in the shape of the original distribution and the counterfactual distribution. Visually,

---

[19]The graphs in panel F are scaled. To calculate the scaled age group contribution to total difference, the density of each age group in each year is scaled by their respective income share.

[20]This hollowing out of the income distribution is not necessarily evidence of a 'vanishing middle class' phenomenon that has been reported for the USA and other developed countries (e.g., Foster and Wolfson 2010). To investigate a 'vanishing middle class' phenomenon would require a comparison of lifetime income across population groups rather than a comparison of age-specific income. This is beyond the scope of the present chapter.

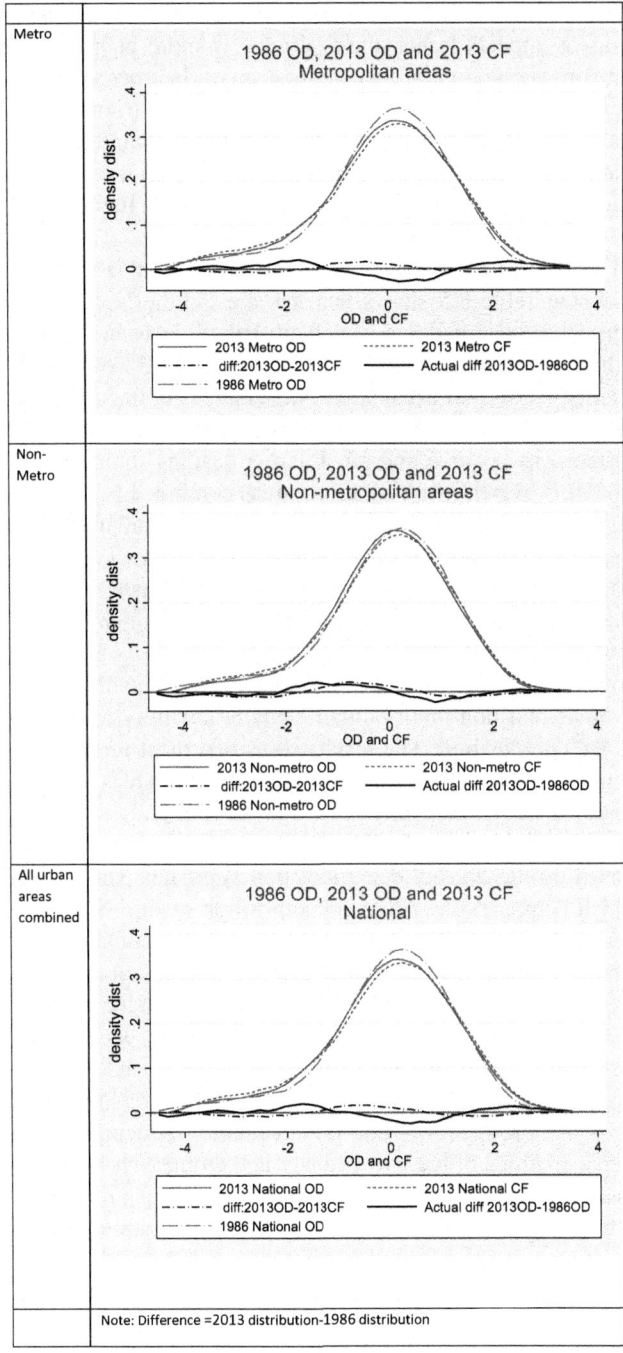

Fig. 8.4 Original and counterfactual income distributions and their differences

it is difficult to tell these distributions apart although the age composition effect in metropolitan areas appears larger and is driven by more people at the top of the distribution in comparison to non-metropolitan areas. In other words, the difference between the original distribution and the counterfactual distribution in metropolitan areas shows a bigger bump at the top of the distribution than for non-metropolitan areas. To quantify the effect of age composition, we report the *MLD* of the original and counterfactual distribution and the differences between them. Table 8.5 presents these results.

The actual *MLD*s are of course identical to those in Table 8.2. In line with the graphical evidence, Table 8.5 shows that the age-share effect has been relatively small but negative. Hence, had age-specific distributions been the same in 1986 as in 2013, the changes in the age structure from 1986 to 2013 would have led to lower income inequality. Across all urban areas, the changes in the age structure (ageing of the population) reduced the *MLD* by about 0.0295. In contrast, the age-specific distribution effect was positive and much larger, leading to an overall 1986–2013 increase in the *MLD* of 0.0939 for all urban areas combined.

While ageing has had an inequality-reducing effect overall, the magnitude of this effect varies spatially. This is not surprising giving the spatial variation in the rates of ageing. The faster ageing of the non-metropolitan areas contributed to a larger inequality-reducing age composition effect (-0.0314, compared with -0.0265 in metropolitan areas).

We see from Table 8.5 that the difference in inequality growth between metropolitan areas and non-metropolitan areas is not fully accounted for by the difference in age composition. The results show that most of the difference in the inequality trends of metropolitan and non-metropolitan areas is due to the much greater age-group-specific inequality growth in the former.

It is easy to reconcile the results based on the *MLD* decomposition approach with those based on the density decomposition approach. This can be seen from Table 8.6, which compares the *MLD* decomposition of Eq. (8.4) with the density decomposition of Eq. (8.6). Both methods show that population ageing has had income inequality-reducing effect. The effects are similar, but somewhat smaller in absolute value with the *MLD* decomposition approach. Had the age-specific income distributions remained the same, the *MLD* would have decreased by -0.0223 for all urban areas combined (the sum of effects $C2$ and $C3'$ in Table 8.6). The corresponding quantity from the density decomposition approach is -0.0295. Examination by age group shows that this inequality-reducing effect is driven by the negative contributions of the two younger age groups. The youngest age group (15–24) has seen rapidly rising within-group inequality but a reduction in the share of this group has contributed negatively to the change in within-group inequality.

The 25–44 age group experienced a narrowing of their within-group distribution as well as a reduction in their population share. Both have a negative effect on overall within-group inequality. Table 8.6 shows that the age-specific distribution effect ($C1 + C4'$ in Eq. (8.4)) and the age share effect ($C2 + C3'$) are indeed mostly negative for the 25–44 age group. Interestingly, the metropolitan areas form the exception. In these areas, growth in the mean income of this group relative to growth

Table 8.5 Estimates of age-share and age-specific distributional effects, measured by *MLD*, using the density decomposition approach

Area	2013 Distribution (OD)	2013 Counterfactual distribution (CF)	1986 Distribution (OD)	Total change = 2013OD-1986OD	Age share effect = 2013OD-2013CF	Age specific distribution effect = 2013CF-1986OD
Metro	0.4500	0.4765	0.3607	0.0893	−0.0265	0.1158
Non-metro	0.3623	0.3937	0.3563	0.0060	−0.0314	0.0374
All urban areas combined	0.4153	0.4448	0.3509	0.0644	−0.0295	0.0939

Table 8.6 Contribution to changes in Mean Log Deviation between 1986 and 2013 by age group

Age group	Components of change (see Eq. 8.4)				Total change	Age-specific distribution effect (C1 + C4')	Age share effect (C2 + C3')	Density (DFL) age share effect	Contribution to within-inequality changes (C1 + C2)	Contribution to between-inequality changes (C3' + C4')
	C1	C2	C3'	C4'						
Metropolitan areas										
15–24	0.026	−0.0309	−0.084	0.0248	−0.0641	0.0508	−0.1149		−0.0049	−0.0592
25–44	−0.0107	−0.0101	−0.0286	0.0137	−0.0357	0.0030	−0.0387		−0.0208	−0.0149
45–64	0.0219	0.0289	0.0826	0.0248	0.1583	0.0467	0.1115		0.0508	0.1074
65+	0.0198	0.0041	0.0189	−0.0146	0.0282	0.0052	0.0230		0.0239	0.0043
Sum	0.0569	−0.008	−0.0111	0.0488	0.0866	0.1057	−0.0191	−0.0265	0.0489	0.0377
Non-metropolitan areas										
15–24	0.0181	−0.0381	−0.0985	0.0123	−0.1063	0.0304	−0.1366		−0.0200	−0.0862
25–44	−0.0279	−0.0255	−0.0737	0.007	−0.1200	−0.0209	−0.0992		−0.0534	−0.0667
45–64	0.0032	0.0307	0.0973	0.0178	0.1490	0.0210	0.1280		0.0339	0.1151
65+	0.0131	0.0119	0.0684	−0.0119	0.0816	0.0012	0.0803		0.0250	0.0565
Sum	0.0065	−0.021	−0.0065	0.0252	0.0042	0.0317	−0.0275	−0.0314	−0.0145	0.0187
All urban areas combined										
15–24	0.0234	−0.0326	−0.0873	0.0209	−0.0756	0.0443	−0.1199		−0.0092	−0.0664
25–44	−0.0135	−0.0138	−0.0401	0.0134	−0.0541	−0.0001	−0.0539		−0.0273	−0.0267
45–64	0.0143	0.0279	0.0862	0.0206	0.1491	0.0349	0.1141		0.0422	0.1068
65+	0.0173	0.006	0.0313	−0.0136	0.0411	0.0037	0.0374		0.0233	0.0177
Sum	0.0415	−0.0124	−0.0098	0.0413	0.0604	0.0828	−0.0223	−0.0295	0.0291	0.0315

in overall mean income ($C4'$) more than offsets the reduction in within-age group inequality ($C1$).

The contributions of the 45–64 and 65+ groups are in the opposite direction: changes in both groups contribute to growing inequality. This is because within-group inequality, relative income, as well as population share increased for both groups between 1986 and 2013. Thus, for both age groups most components of inequality change are positive. The only exception is the negative component $C4'$ for those aged 65+, despite the growth in this group's mean income.[21]

Taking a spatial view by comparing metropolitan areas to non-metropolitan areas, Table 8.6 confirms the smaller inequality-reducing age-composition effect in metropolitan areas. This is as expected due to the less rapid rates of population ageing in the metropolitan areas. The population decomposition by subgroup approach shows that the 1986–2013 changes in the age structure in metropolitan areas reduced *MLD* by about 0.0191, compared to 0.0275 in non-metropolitan areas. As with the national results, we find that most of the growth in inequality is due to changes in the age-specific distribution effect.

Age composition only explains a negligible part of the difference between the changes in inequality between metropolitan areas and non-metropolitan areas. The increase in the age-specific distribution effect on *MLD* has been greater in metropolitan areas (0.1057, about three times the corresponding effect in non-metropolitan areas). The almost equal counteracting age-specific and age-composition effects in non-metropolitan areas explains the very small inequality growth in these areas. If the changes in the age-specific income distribution remain relatively small in non-metropolitan areas in the years to come and ageing there accelerates due to continuing net migration to metropolitan areas, then we may expect inequality to decrease or remain constant in non-metropolitan areas in the foreseeable future.

5 Conclusion

In this chapter we examined the relationship between age structure and income inequality in New Zealand using two approaches that have proven popular in the literature. We focussed on differences between metropolitan and non-metropolitan areas in the two ways in which age structure can affect inequality: an age-composition effect and an age-specific distribution effect. We found that the 1986–2013 increase in inequality has been mostly due to the changes in the age-specific income distributions. In fact, the age-composition effect has been negative. Population ageing has served to reduce inequality. However, at the same time, age-specific mean incomes diverged, at least until 2001, leading to an increasing share of between-group inequality to overall inequality.

---

[21] This is due to the approximation method. For this age group, $(\overline{\pi_a r_a} - \overline{\pi_a}) < 0$. See Eq. (8.4).

In line with previous analyses on inequality and age structure in New Zealand, we found a notable disparity between metropolitan and non-metropolitan areas in the trends in inequality and age structure. Metropolitan areas have experienced rapid growth in inequality but slower rates of ageing (mostly due to net inward migration rather than greater fertility), while non-metropolitan areas have had slow growth in inequality and faster ageing. We also found that the inequality-reducing effect of population ageing (resulting from the declining shares of younger people) varies across areas and is smaller in metropolitan areas. Notwithstanding this differential age-composition effect, our results show that most of the difference between metropolitan and non-metropolitan areas in inequality growth is due to the much larger age-specific income distribution widening in metropolitan areas.

We complemented the decomposition of changes in the *MLD* index of inequality with a visualisation of changes in density along the income distribution. This revealed a thinning of the density in the middle of the overall distribution, for which the 15–24 and 25–44 age groups were mostly responsible. At the same time, the age group 45–64 added more density to the upper end (right tail) of the distribution, while those aged 15–24 contributed to an increase in density at the lower tail. Together, these changes led to a hollowing out of the distribution.

In this research we have simplified the analysis of spatial differences in income inequality by adopting a metropolitan versus non-metropolitan dichotomy. In future work we intend to use a more refined spatial disaggregation of areas, as well as examine the role of other population composition effects on inequality, such as effects due to country of birth and migrant status, household type and education. Jointly, this may provide further in-depth insights into how population ageing impacts on mean incomes and income inequality across regions and cities.

Disclaimer Access to the data used in this study was provided by Statistics New Zealand (SNZ) under conditions designed to give effect to the security and confidentiality provisions of the Statistics Act 1975. All frequency counts using Census data were subject to base three rounding in accordance with SNZ's release policy for census data.

References

Alimi O, Maré DC, Poot J (2016) Income inequality in New Zealand regions. In: Spoonley P (ed) Rebooting the regions. Massey University Press, Auckland, pp 177–212

Aziz OA, Ball C, Creedy J, Eedrah J (2015) The distributional impact of population ageing in New Zealand. N Z Econ Pap 49(3):207–226

Ball C, Creedy J (2015) Inequality in New Zealand 1983/84 to 2013/14. Working Paper 15/06. Wellington, New Zealand Treasury

Barrett GF, Crossley TF, Worswick C (2000) Consumption and income inequality in Australia. Economic Record 76(233):116–138

Cameron LA (2000) Poverty and inequality in Java: examining the impact of the changing age, educational and industrial structure. J Dev Econ 62(1):149–180

Castells-Quintana D, Ramos R, Royuela V (2015) Income inequality in European regions: recent trends and determinants. Rev Reg Res 35(2):123–146

Deaton AS, Paxson CH (1994) Intertemporal choice and inequality. J Polit Econ *102*(3):437–467

Deaton AS, Paxson CH (1995) Saving, inequality and aging: an East Asian perspective. Asia Pac Econ Rev 1(*1*):7–19

DiNardo J, Fortin NM, Lemieux T (1996) Labor market institutions and the distribution of wages, 1973–1992: a semiparametric approach. Econometrica *64*(5):1001–1044

Easton B (2013) Income inequality in New Zealand: a user's guide. NZ Sociol *28*(3):19–66

Evans L, Grimes A, Wilkinson B, Teece D (1996) Economic reform in New Zealand 1984–95: the pursuit of efficiency. J Econ Lit *34*(4):1856–1902

Fortin, N., Lemieux, T., & Firpo, S. (2011). Decomposition methods in economics. In: O. Ashenfelter & D. Card (Eds.), Handbook of labor economics (Vol. 4, Part A, pp. 1-102): Elsevier: Amsterdam.

Foster JE, Wolfson MC (2010) Polarization and the decline of the middle class: Canada and the U.S. J Econ Inequal *8*(2):247–273

Fritzell J (1993) Income inequality trends in the 1980s: a five-country comparison. Acta Sociologica *36*(1):47–62

Hyslop DR, Maré DC (2005) Understanding New Zealand's changing income distribution, 1983–1998: a semi-parametric analysis. Economica *72*(287):469–495

Jackson N (2011) The demographic forces shaping New Zealand's future. What population ageing [really] means. Working Paper No. 1, National Institute of Demographic and Economic Analysis. Hamilton, University of Waikato

Jantti M (1997) Inequality in five countries in the 1980s: The role of demographic shifts, markets and government policies. Economica *64*(255):415–440

Johnson A (2015) Mixed fortunes. The geography of advantage and disadvantage in New Zealand. Social Policy & Parliamentary Unit, Salvation Army, Auckland

Karagedikli Ö, Maré DC, Poot J (2000) Disparities and despair: changes in regional income distributions in New Zealand 1981–96. Australas J Reg Stud *6*(3):323–347

Karagedikli Ö, Maré DC, Poot J (2003) Description and analysis of changes in New Zealand regional income distributions, 1981–1996. In: Gomez ET, Stephens R (eds) The state, economic development and ethnic co- existence in Malaysia and New Zealand. Kuala Lumpur, CEDER University of Malaya, pp 221–244

Lam D (1997) Demographic variables and income inequality. In: Rosenweig MR, Stark O (eds) Handbook of population and family economics, vol 1B. Elsevier, Amsterdam, pp 1015–1059

Lin CHA, Lahiri S, Hsu CP (2015) Population aging and regional income inequality in Taiwan: a spatial dimension. Soc Indic Res *122*(3):1–21

Mookherjee D, Shorrocks A (1982) A decomposition analysis of the trend in UK income inequality. Econ J *92*(368):886–902

McCulloch B, Frances J (2001). Financing New Zealand superannuation (Working Paper No. 01/20). Wellington: New Zealand Treasury.

OECD (2016) Making cities work for all: data and actions for inclusive growth. OECD Publishing, Paris. https://doi.org/10.1787/9789264263260-en

Peichl A, Pestel N, Schneider H (2012) Does size matter? The impact of changes in household structure on income distribution in Germany. Rev Income Wealth *58*(1):118–141

Perry B (2014) Household incomes in New Zealand: trends in Indicators of Inequality and Hardship 1982 to 2013. Ministry of Social Development, Wellington

Perry B (2015) Household incomes in New Zealand: Trends in Indicators of Inequality and Hardship 1982 to 2014. Ministry of Social Development, Wellington

Stephenson J, Scobie G (2002) The economics of population ageing (Working Paper No. 02/04). Wellington: New Zealand Treasury

von Hippel PT, Scarpino SV, Holas I (2016) Robust estimation of inequality from binned incomes. Sociol Methodol *46*(1):212–251

von Weizsäcker RK (1996) Distributive implications of an aging society. Eur Econ Rev *40*(3):729–746

Zhong H (2011) The impact of population aging on income inequality in developing countries: evidence from rural China. China Econ Rev *22*(1):98–107

Chapter 9
Investigating and Modelling Potential Demand for Retirement Housing: The Australian Context

Robert J. Stimson and Tung-Kai Shyy

1 Introduction

The ageing of the population in western countries such as Australia is set to gather pace now that the first of the post-war 'baby boomer' generation are attaining the age of 65 years. With a further twelve or so years of that cohort still to come in reaching that traditional retirement age, the scene is being set for a substantial increase over the next decade-and-a-half in the aggregate numbers of retirees. While the large majority of older person households still chose to 'age-in-place' (that is, not move out of the family home), a minority but increasing number are displaying a propensity to downsize by relocating to live in attached housing or an apartment, housing which is seen by urban planners and policy makers as being 'more suitable' for older 'empty nester' couples or 'single person' households. A relatively small but increasing proportion of older people—particularly those who are in their mid-1970s and older—are choosing alternative forms of housing that are purpose built for retirees, especially 'retirement villages' (or communities) as they are called in Australia, and but also mobile home parks.

This chapter first provides a brief discussion of ageing in Australia and the housing of older people. That is followed by an overview of the development of the retirement village industry in Australia as an alternative form of housing for older people. It then discusses what existing research tells us about older people

R. J. Stimson (✉)
School of Geography, University of Melbourne, Melbourne, VIC, Australia

School of Geography, University of Queensland, Brisbane, QLD, Australia
e-mail: rstimson@unimelb.edu.au

T.-K. Shyy
eResearch, University of Queensland, Brisbane, QLD, Australia

© Springer International Publishing AG, part of Springer Nature 2018
U. Blien et al. (eds.), *Modelling Aging and Migration Effects on Spatial Labor Markets*, Advances in Spatial Science,
https://doi.org/10.1007/978-3-319-68563-2_9

161

who have moved, or might have a high propensity to move, through downsizing, including relocating to a retirement village. The chapter then demonstrates how spatial analysis and modelling may be used to give guidance to developers of retirement villages as to where demand for new retirement village development might be distributed across space, to identify what might be optimal locations at which to develop new retirement villages, and to assess what might be the potential take-up rate of retirees from within the likely catchment area around a site that is available for the development of a new retirement village. The chapter discusses the modelling approach developed by the authors and their collaborators that has been used by retirement village industry in the Brisbane-Southeast Queensland (Brisbane-SEQ) region, the third largest metro-region in Australia.

2 The Ageing of the Population and Older Person's Housing Preferences

At the 2011 Australian census there were about 3.1 million people aged 65 years and over, representing 14% of the nation's population of 21.5 million people. Not surprisingly, the incidence of older people varies spatially, their distribution being uneven within the large metro-cities and across the regions beyond. The number of older people is set to increases substantially, particularly with the baby-boomer cohort entering retirement. Their uneven geographic distribution may be expected to continue, but the patterns of spatial concentration of the cohort could be expected to change.

The Australian Bureau of Statistics (ABS) (2013a) reports that 94% of people aged 65 years and over lived in a private dwelling, with the remaining 6% living in a non-private dwelling. But the incidence of the latter increases substantially with increasing age, increasing from 1.5% for those aged 65–74 years to 6.1% for those aged 75–84 years, and then increasing markedly to 26.2% for those aged 85 years and over as many more old-old people need to move into a supported living environment. Of the 2.7 million persons aged 65 years and over who lived in a private dwelling in 2011, 78% lived in a separate house. But that tends to decrease with increasing age, declining from 81% for those aged 65–74 years to 76% for those aged 75–84 years, and then to 70% for those aged 85 years and over. A higher proportion of men (81%) than women (76%) live in a separate house, reflecting the fact that older women are more likely to live alone and to have moved out of what would have been the family home, especially after being widowed. Around 269,000 (or 10%) of older Australians who lived in a private dwelling are in a semi-detached, row or terrace house; and 275,600 (or 10%) lived in flats, units or apartments. It is the oldest of the cohort—those aged 85 years and over—who are most likely to be living in these forms of housing (14% and 15% respectively), and more women (12%) than men (9%) lived in those forms of housing.

Home ownership among Australia's population aged 65 years over and is very high at 84%, compared with 67% for all households. Outright home ownership is by far the dominant tenure type at 74% for older person households. But, as discussed by Judd et al. (2014), there was an increase between 2001 and 2011 in the proportion of older person home owner households with a mortgage, with a doubling in what was still a relatively small incidence of such older person households. However, just 10% of older person households were home owners with a mortgage, compared with 35% for all households. And only about 17% of older person households are renting compared with almost 30% for all households.

Most older people live with a spouse or partner, but that decreases with increasing age, with women tending to be much more likely than men to be living alone, particularly with increasing age as the incidence of widowhood increases.

The large majority of older people choose to 'age-in-place', remaining in what has been the family home that is most likely to be a larger separate dwelling. The propensity of men to 'age-in-place' is a little greater than it is for women. But there is an increasing propensity of older people to move as they age. That 'ageing-in-place' has been encouraged by government policy in Australia since the 1990s in attempts to reduce the cost burden of providing aged care services and to encourage active independent living. Urban planning and housing public policies have also been promoting the diversification of housing choices for older people to encourage them to downsize into medium and higher density housing environments (see Judd et al. 2014).

Regarding the residential mobility of older people, Judd et al. (2014) note that it had, in fact, declined a little between 2001–2006 and 2006–2011, with the likelihood of moving decreasing with age except for those aged 85 years and over which is "the life stage where the most significant decline in the ability to self-care [is] most likely" (p. 2). Nonetheless, there is evidence of some *downsizing* occurring as older people move out of a separate house to live in an attached house or in a flat, unit or apartment, including moving to live in a 'retirement community'. That propensity to downsize does increase as people reach older age, particularly as they age into their 1980s. Judd et al. (2014, p. 3) profile those downsizers as being more likely to be older, female, single, one-person households; being fully retired and dependent on either superannuation or the pension, and having a lower income corresponding with the aged pension; and being resident for fewer years in the dwelling they are leaving.

High rise apartments are *not* favoured by older people who downsize, their preference being more for medium density housing types. And their preference is *not* for the inner-city areas, but rather for the suburban areas of cities (where they have been living), or for non-metropolitan locations, as demonstrated by the so-called 'sea change' retirement migration phenomenon.

The provision of special purpose housing for older people in Australia has been diversifying in recent decades, and it is dominated by what are called *retirement villages*. The ABS (2013a) estimates that, at the 2011 census, the number of persons aged 65 years and over living in a retirement village totalled 135,900, two-thirds of whom are women. But that represents only just over 5% of the population aged 65 years and over. It thus remains a niche market for retirees.

In addition, about 22,800 persons aged 65 years and over were living in a caravan, cabin or houseboat, of whom almost 60% are men, and they tended to be more at the younger end of the older age cohorts.

A crucial issue for the residential property industry in Australia is the degree to which there might be an increase in demand for the provision of housing that is oriented to the needs of older people—including the demand for retirement village living—as the population ages, especially as the 'baby boomer' generation enter and progress through their retirement years.

The sheer number of 'baby boomers' alone will drive-up demand for housing alternatives to cater for 'empty nesters' and retirees, including demand for retirement village living. This is evident from the population projections undertaken by the ABS (2013b), which estimated Australia's population will increase to between 36.8 million and 48.3 million by the year 2061, with the median age of Australia's population increasing from 37.3 years in 2012 to between 38.6 years and 40.5 years by 2031, and then to between 41.0 years and 44.5 years by 2061. That ageing effect is illustrated in the change in the projected age-sex structure for the population for the year 2061 as shown in Fig. 9.1, with the greatest magnitude of the increase being forecast to occur in the old-old age cohort. The number of persons aged 65 years and over will likely increase from 3.2 million in 2012 to between 5.7 million and

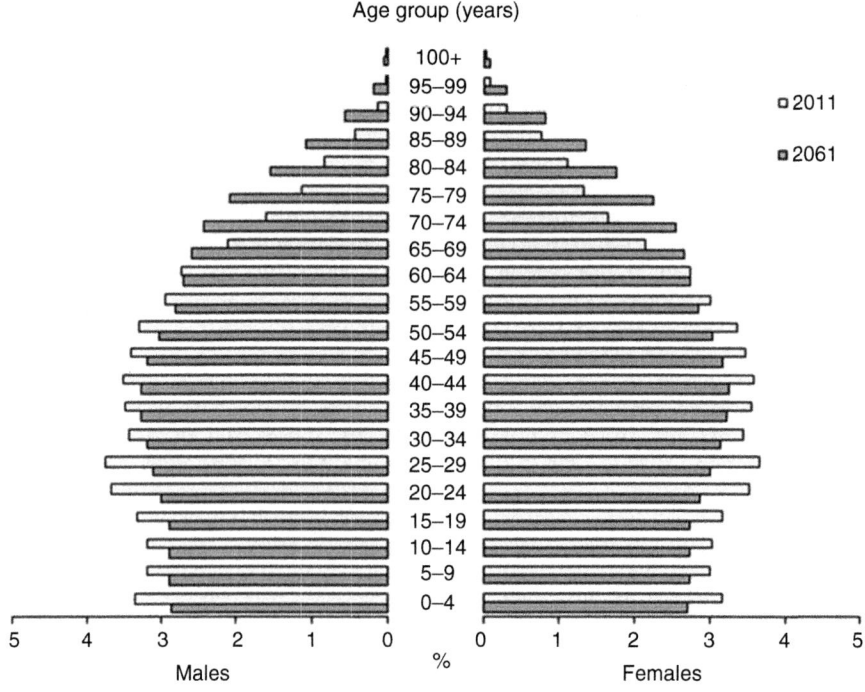

Fig. 9.1 Projected population age structure for Australia, 2011 and 2061. Source: ABS (2013b)

5.8 million by 2031, to then to between 9.0 million and 11.1 million by 2061. If one takes the ABS Series B projections, the proportion, then the proportion of the population aged 65 years and over is set to increase from 14% in 2012 to 22.4% in 2061. But it is the old-older cohort of the population that is aged 85 years and over where the most rapid growth in numbers is projected to occur, with their numbers increasing from 420,300 in 2012 to double to 842,500 by 2031, and then to double again to well over 3 million by 2061. And while men comprised just 35% of this cohort in 2012, by 2061 they are likely to comprise as high as 46% by 2061.

3 Implications for Retirement Housing

It is these forecasts of growth in the aged population that have particularly important implications for the provision of health and other services—including housing—that will need to be geared to the needs of older people in Australia. Clearly the ageing of the population and the magnitude of the projected increase particularly in the older age person cohorts will provide a substantial increase in the number of persons who might have a propensity to downsize, including relocating to a retirement village. The demography certainly provides the evidence that demand for retirement village living will increase, and there will be a need for new retirement village stock to be developed as a result of the ageing of the population, and in particular due to the ageing 'baby boomer' effect.

Over the last couple of decades there certainly has been an increase in the propensity of older people in Australia to make the decision to move into a retirement village. As documented by Stimson and McGovern (2002a), in 1996 it was estimated that just 2.7% of people aged 65 years and over were living in a retirement village, and that that increased to 4.5% for people aged 75–84 year and to 5.1% for those aged 85 years and over. While still relatively low, by 2011 that take-up rate had increased substantially to reach 5% for all people aged 65 years and over, and it continues to increase slightly with increasing age. Currently the take-up rate of those aged 75 years and over (which is around the average age of entry of older people moving into a retirement village in Australia) is estimated by to be 8% (McCrindle Baynes 2013). This is much below what is estimated to be around 10% for the 65 years and over age cohort in the United States.

However, an unknown factor is the degree to which the retirement village industry in Australia will innovate to become a more attractive/desirable housing choice alternative for retirees as they age and thus achieve increased market penetration that might be substantially above the current relatively above low take-up rate. It is reasonable to assume that there will continue to be innovation and product in the retirement village industry over the coming decades, just as there has been over the last couple of decades during which there has been significant change and innovation in the industry with a marked increase in the number and the size of villages.

4 Evolution of the Retirement Village Industry

Retirement villages in Australia are regulated under legislation enacted by State and Territory governments which permits operators to restrict entry to persons aged 55 years and over, restricts the uses to which the land can be put, and provides consumer certainty and protection. But a tiny proportion of people moving to a retirement village are between the age of 55 and 64 years, and that is likely to remain so into the future.

There is little published research on the industry and on the residential relocation decision process and choice of older people who decide to move to a retirement village. The most comprehensive research is still the edited volume by Stimson (2002).[1] Earlier studies include those by Gardner (1996), Stimson et al. (1997), and Manicaros and Stimson (1999). More recently, a project undertaken for the Australian Housing and Urban Research Institute (AHURI) investigated service integrated housing in Australia, including an analysis of the role of retirement villages (Jones et al. 2010).

In the two decades to 1996, the retirement village industry experienced "the greatest growth of any type of housing oriented to the needs of older people", emerging from being a 'cottage industry' in the late 1970s Stimson and McGovern (2002a, p. 6). As discussed by McGovern and Baltins (2002), following World War II and up to about 1974, the provision of purpose-built retirement housing was Commonwealth Government funded under the Age and Disability Persons Homes Act and the joint Commonwealth-State/Territory funding of public housing, which incorporated the provision and management of senior's housing by the State Public Housing Authorities, with qualifying church and charitable organisations also receiving public funding of capital works. Post-1974, in the absence of government funding, there was an increasing incidence of non-subsidised retirement housing, with the church and charitable organisations remaining dominant players in providing senior's housing for which residents paid an entry cost, but private developers also became involved. Both charitable and private sectors developed what became known as retirement villages developments, which incorporated the provision of communal facilities and services.

The entry of private developers and operators was made commercially viable through the retention of a proportion of the proceeds at the end of each residency period—what became known as a Deferred Management Fee (DFM)—with some development profit becoming available from a greater entry price payable for larger, better quality units in private sector villages. The private sector developers and operators saw retirement villages as another form of medium-density housing. Some were divisions of larger land and property developers, but many were small operators.

---

[1]That book reported on research undertaken in a project funded by the Australian Research Council's ARC Linkage program. That research was undertaken in collaboration with the industry peak body, which was then the Retirement Village Association (RVA).

The proliferation of forms of documentation regarding leasing ownership arrangements used by private sector development and operators, as well as the church and charitable sector, saw the emergence in the 1980s and 1990s of State and Territory Acts to regulate the industry, with an emphasis on consumer protection. The legislative definition of retirement villages in general excluded villages offering rental agreements and accommodation in mobile homes, which respectively were covered under separate Mobile Home Acts and Residential Tenancy Acts in the various Stated and Territories. Tenure arrangements in retirement villages became diverse covering Loan and Licence/Loan and Lease, leasehold, Strata Title, Company Title, Purple Title, and Trust Deed models. The DMF remains predominant whereby up to about 35% of the purchase price is retained by the village operator, and there might be a sharing of capital gain upon the sale of a unit.

From the 1990s, the industry has 'matured' with increasing corporatisation and the public listed companies, while still retaining many small operators and the continuing existence of church and charitable organisations with a diminishing market share. Substantial product differentiation has occurred catering for a wide range socio-economic groups among the older population age cohorts with their diverse needs and aspirations.

Of note is the mixed (largely bad) experiences with experimentation where the private sector has provided rental accommodation for low income households—who are trapped in the rental market who are eligible for housing assistance—through arrangements where rents are sequestered from a proportion of residents' pensions and the government rental subsidy for which they are eligible.

Jones et al. (2010, pp. 18–20) tell how it is increasingly common for retirement villages to incorporate serviced apartments and assisted living units with support and care services being available, including co-locating with a nursing home to provide 'on-going care'. The Australian Government's *Retirement Villages—Ageing in Place* initiative in 2008 encouraged this, and now the retirement village industry has become Australia's largest sector of "service-integrated housing for people in later life" (Jones et al. 2010, p. 20), which Howe (2003, p. 4) has referred to as "an outstanding example of policy by default".

Significant growth is occurring in the retirement village stock, and the industry is attracting an increasing number of retirees even though the overall penetration rate remains low. The Property Council of Australia (PwC/Property Council Census 2015) estimates there are more than 2300 retirement villages housing about 50,000 households. Its research shows the 'average' profile of a retirement village to be 23 years old with 71% of living units having two bedrooms at an entry cot of A$385,000, which is about 68% of the Australian median house price. The average monthly service fee was $435, which is the equivalent of 25% of the monthly pension for a single retiree. The average occupancy rate for retirement villages is 91%, with the average length of a vacancy being 315 days. Two-thirds of residents are women, with 50% being single women, 36% couples, and 13% single males. The average entry age to a retirement village is 74 years, and the average age of residents is 81 years. The average duration of stay is 7 years.

Over the last decade or so retirement village residents are becoming a little older, with 95% being aged 65 years and over, with 54% of recent movers into a village now being aged 75 years, and more than one-third being 80 years and over (Mc Crindle Baynes 2013).

5 Downsizing, Including Moving to a Retirement Village

5.1 Downsizing, Especially by Older People

As noted earlier, downsizing by older people is occurring, but its incidence is still relatively small as the big majority of older person households in Australia choose to continue to remain on the family home, which is typically a separate house.

Research by Judd et al. (2014, p. 4) shows that older people who have downsized, as against those who had moved without downsizing (that is, moved to a separate house), are more likely to be older, female, single and lone persons; fully retired; on a lower income; and dependent on the pension or superannuation. They identify the multi-faceted "key drivers" for older people to downsize as being a desire for a life style change (which is the most important driver), followed by an inability to maintain the home and/or garden, entering retirement, children leaving home (but only for the younger elderly), the onset of ill-health/disability (which assumes greater importance as a driver with increasing age), the death of a partner (which also assumes greater importance as a driver with increasing age, relationship breakdown (which diminishes as a driver with increasing age), financial reasons (which are a driver for relatively few elderly people). As age increases it seems that the desire for less maintenance of the home and yard, becomes particularly important, along with having a more accessible home. In contrast, the desire for life style improvement seems to decrease with increasing age. The importance of having proximity to shops, health services and public transport increases steadily with age, but it then flattens out and reduces for those aged 85 years and over. The attraction of an area as a key factor reduces in importance with age. Finally, financial considerations (reducing cost of living, discharging a mortgage and improved investment) reduces as a factor with increasing age.

Those findings largely confirm the results of earlier research by Gardner (1996), Woodbridge (2003), Stimson (2002) and Painter and Lee (2009) which had focused explicitly on movers to a retirement village.

The movement of older people to retirement village is a significant part of the downsizing phenomenon that is on the rise in Australia, now accounting for between one-quarter and one-fifth of all downsizing moves. The survey research evidence reported by Judd et al. (2014) shows that around 90% of older people who have downsized are satisfied with their move. That high level of satisfaction with the move has also been found in studies of retirement village residents (Stimson and McGovern 2002b; McCrindle Baynes 2013), with research by Gardner et al. (2005) showing that many residents reported an improved quality of life, particularly linked to the social environment of the villages.

It is evident that downsizers in general are concerned about maintaining social networks (family and friends), and that they have a strong attachment to the area with which they are familiar and wish to retain that at their new location. That is particularly significance for the retirement village industry as older people who downsize tend not to want to move too far from where they have been living so that villages will tend to draw residents from a spatially restricted catchment, hence finding sites for new retirement villages that are optimally located close proximity to where the ageing population is geographically concentrated is a key issue for the retirement village industry.

5.2 Investigating the Decision to Move to a Retirement Village

Research by Stimson, McCrea and Star (Stimson and McGovern 2002a, b) and Stimson and McCrea (2004) explicitly used the classic 'push-pull' migration model framework to model: (a) the 'push factors' (or 'stressors') underpinning the decision of retirees to leave where they have been living; and (b) the 'pull factors' (or 'attractors') leading them to move into a retirement village. A typology of movers was developed, and path analysis using structural equation modelling was used to identify the key predictors relating to characteristics of and aspirations of people that underlie those 'push factors', and the characteristics of people that underlie the 'pull factors' (or 'attractor') characteristics of villages.

Four categories of 'push' factors and their predictors were identified:

1. A change in lifestyle 'push factor', which relates to wanting more free time, wanting to spend more time with other people, and wanting to change the way they live and do things. Three predictors of equal importance in identifying retirees who move for reasons associated with lifestyle change are gender, pre-retirement occupation, (especially non-professionals), and age when moving out of the home, with those retiring at a younger age also being more likely to move for lifestyle factors.
2. A maintenance 'push factor', which relates to issues to do with difficulty and/or cost of maintaining a home and garden, wanting a smaller place, wanting more free time, and children/ family or friends having moved out of home. The most important predictors of the factor are living in a house, being single, and having worked in a non-professional occupation. The impact of relationship status is both direct and indirect, with single retirees being likely to experience the factor directly (presumably because maintaining a home and garden is more difficult when living alone), couples also being likely to experience the factor indirectly

because they are likely to be living in a house rather than in a smaller dwelling, and single retirees are who are more likely to be female or older males.

3. A *social isolation 'push factor'*, which relates to the death of a spouse, being lonely, and wanting to spend more time with people. *Predictors* of the factor are being single (which is the most important predictor), being female, and being older. Perhaps oddly, retirees moving into retirement villages at a younger age are also more likely to move because of social isolation. Age and relationship status are independent, thus younger retirees as well as older single female retirees report this factor as a reason for deciding to move. Retirees from a non-professional background are more likely than are former professional workers to report this factor, but this predictor is less important than the retiree being single.

4. A *health and mobility 'push factor'*, which relates to deteriorating health, the need for assistance, and no longer being able to drive. This factor also *relates* to the death of a spouse and the need for friendships, but those reasons are less important in defining the factor. The main *predictors* of equal importance are age when moving (with this push factor increasing with increasing age), gender (with males being more likely to experience this push factor), and dwelling type (with retirees who are living in a flat, unit or apartment being more likely to report moving for health and mobility reasons.

Three *'pull' or 'attractor' factors* and their *predictors* were identified:

1. A *built environment and affordability 'pull factor'*, which relates to a range of attributes of the retirement village, including the site, size, design and layout of the village and its independent living units, the services and facilities provided, staff and management, and the affordability of the village and unit. The main *predictors* of equal importance are age when moving (with this push factor increasing with increasing age), gender (with males being more likely to experience this push factor), and dwelling type (with retirees who are living in a flat, unit or apartment being more likely to report moving for health and mobility reasons).

2. A *location 'pull factor'*, which relates to attributes such as access to public transport, proximity to recreational facilities and places where the retiree engages in social activities, proximity to the coast or water, the climate of the area, and familiarity with and attraction to the area with the retiree having been there on holidays. The key *predictor* is the village bring close to where a retiree has been living, with those retirees being less influenced by having visited the village previously or by advertising. Single retirees are less likely to have moved over longer distance, and more likely to be attracted to a nearby retirement village that allows them to maintain their existing lifestyle and familiarity. Conversely, couples are willing to move over longer distances to a retirement village, and may have a lower need to maintain their existing lifestyle and familiarity.

3. A *maintaining existing lifestyle and familiarity 'pull factor'*, which relates to attributes such as the village being located conveniently for the retiree to maintain contact with close friends and family, being close to the services that the retiree had been using before relocating, and being familiar with the area as a result of

having lived there. The key *predictor* is the village bring close to where a retiree has been living, with those retirees being less influenced by having visited the village previously or by advertising. Single retirees are less likely to have moved over longer distance, and more likely to be attracted to a nearby retirement village that allows them to maintain their existing lifestyle and familiarity. Conversely, couples are willing to move over longer distances to a retirement village, and may have a lower need to maintain their existing lifestyle and familiarity.

6 Modelling the Spatial Patterns of Potential Future Demand for New Retirement Villages

Using small area population forecasts—disaggregated by age-sex cohorts—it is possible to employ spatial modelling to make estimates of where, and at what level of magnitude, there might be demand for provision of new retirement village stock to help guide the investment decisions and building programs of developers of retirement villages. A methodology to undertake such modelling was developed initially by Stimson and McGovern (2002b) using small area (Local Government Authorities, or LGAs) population projections over the twenty-year period 1996–2016 that were available at the time for the States of Victoria and Queensland in Australia. That was the first published example of using spatial analysis and modelling to identify where developers might focus attention to develop new retirement villages, and so far as we are aware there has not been further development of modelling tools since then until that which is reported later in this section of the paper.

6.1 Taking a Simple Approach: The Index of Concentration

A simple way to identify where there might be spatial concentrations of the age cohorts that are likely to be movers to live in a retirement village is simply to map the *Index of Concentration* of the projected age cohorts, with a focus on those aged 75 years and over as it was evident that that age cohort had the highest propensity to relocate to a retirement village. That enables s map to be produced that highlighted those areas most likely to have the highest concentrations of a specified cohort of older persons over the projection period up to 2016.[2]

---

[2]An index of 1 indicates that an LGA contains the same proportion of persons aged 75 years and over as the average proportion across the State as a whole. An index greater than 1 indicates that there is a greater proportion of persons in the LGA that are aged 75 years and over compared with that for the State as a whole. An index of less than 1 indicates that a smaller proportion of persons in the LGA are aged 75 years and over compared with that for the state as a whole.

Stimson and McGovern (2002b) produced a map for Local Government Areas (LGAs) across the State of Queensland in Australia showing the *Index of Concentration* of the projected population aged 75 years and over in 2016. The map showed that the majority of LGAs were expected to have an index exceeding 1. Those LGAs were mainly located in the suburban areas of metropolitan Brisbane south-east corner of the State, the central regions, and the north coast of Queensland. LGAs with a projected index of less than 1 are located along the central coast and in the western regions of the state.

In addition, a *rate of change* in the *Index of Concentration* over the period 1996–2016 was calculated and mapped to identify those areas where the change (increase or decrease) in the concentration of the age cohort would likely be greatest, and it was possible to identify 33 LGAs across the state where the growth in the 75 years and over age cohort was likely to be in excess of 75%. Such areas might be thought of as being key target areas to consider for finding sites for developing new retirement village stock.

6.2 More Sophisticated Modelling

A more sophisticated approach was then used by Stimson and McGovern (2002b) to better inform decisions by developers as to where the potential demand might be found to locate new retirement village developments. It used the modelling framework outlined in Fig. 9.2. Building on the work of Stimson and Qureshi (1999), optimisation modelling (employing the LINGO software) was used) to estimate retirement village demand for age cohorts based on the population projections for LGAs over four successive 5-year planning periods from the 1996 base year through to 2021. The objective was to identify the locations and the number of retirement villages of specific sizes that might need to be provided to meet a specified minimum level of potential future demand for retirement village living based on the projected future growth in the population of retirees and pre-retirees, and take-up rates for retirement village living among the various age categories of older persons (Fig. 9.2).

The modelling approach was thus a realistic assessment of growth potential in market penetration of the industry, with the projections being based on at-the-time take-up rates for the age cohorts comprising retirees. It also allowed for modest increases in market penetration which might be achieved if the industry continued to be innovative in its product diversification and marketing. Stimson and McGovern (2002b) emphasised that the modelling estimating future potential demand for new retirement village construction over successive 5-year periods from the 1996 base year to either 2016 to 2021 should be interpreted only as indicative of potential market opportunity at the States and Territory level and across LGAs within them.

The requirements for operating the model were: the specification of spatial units for analysis (that is, LGAs); population projection data for age cohorts 55 years and over for a number of sequential time periods of 5 years; estimates of different take-

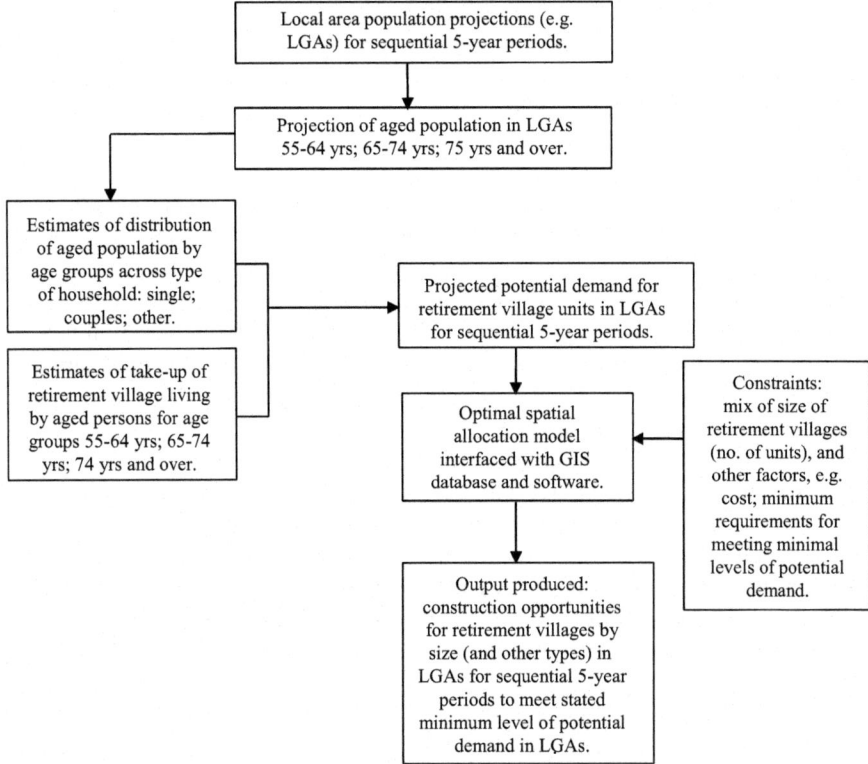

Fig. 9.2 Framework for modelling optimal spatial allocation of supply side response to meet projected demand for retirement village units. Source: Stimson and McGovern (2002a, b, p. 181)

up rates by different types of aged-person households to generate potential demand for retirement village units for age cohorts, making adjustment for the number likely to be one and two person retiree households as he household unit would represent the demand for one retirement village unit; and specification of constraints, such as the mix of retirement village sizes (from 10 to 250+ living units) and the minimum amount of potential demand that is to be met by the industry, with these being used as maximum allowable weightings (MAWs) in the mode that can be changed arbitrarily, or set my an industry user.

The model produced two outputs; optimal weightings; and the number of villages of each type in each LGA.

Three growth scenarios were modelled: (1) a *no-growth in market preference or take-up scenario* (0% p.a. change in market penetration), which assumes growth in demand will occur only through an (increase) in the numbers of aged persons in an LGA and not as a result of an increasing market preference for retirement village living; (2) a *moderate-growth scenario*, which assumes a 1% p.a. increase in market penetration or take-up rate; and (3) a *high-growth scenario*, which assumes a 3% p.a. increase in market penetration or take-up rate.

The proportion of the retiree age cohorts living in retirement villages, as estimated by the ABS at the 1996 census, were used as the basis for the above scenarios. Those were: 0.18% for 55–64 years age group; 1.43% for 65–74 years age group; and 7.51% for 75 years and over age group.

The village capacity sizes used in the initial application of the model were based on discussions with industry representatives as to the optimal number of independent living units within a retirement village, with the village capacities being set at 50, 120, 150 and 250 living units. In addition to those four retirement village capacity categories, a category of villages with a capacity of ten units was also included in the model, since some non-profit villages tend to operate smaller size villages, and in small country towns there may never be the level of demand necessary to support a minimum size village of 50 units.

This optimisation modelling approach was used to estimate levels of future demand for new retirement village units across LGAs and also for specified LGAs or groupings of LGAs to identify potential construction opportunities over successive 5-year planning period, for new villages of a particular size that might be supported by the projected forward estimates of the age cohorts of older people who would be targets for moving to a retirement village. It was applied first at the aggregate level of Australia's States and Territories, then at the disaggregated level of LGAs in the States of Queensland and Victoria.

The optimisation modelling approach developed by Stimson and Qureshi (1999) and applied by Stimson and McGovern (2002b) was thus a tool that could be used to help inform industry planning. It involved the integration of population projection methodologies and spatial optimal allocation modelling in a GIS environment:

> "... The approach has considerable potential for informing industry players. It illustrates what can be achieved through geo-demographic modelling to help guide the industry in estimating the supply needed over time to meet potential demand for retirement village housing. ... It illustrates how standard spatial modelling methods being used by regional scientists and market researchers can be applied to a specific industry such as the retirement village industry" (Stimson and McGovern 2002b, p. 190).

7 Identifying Optimal Locations for Retirement Village Development and Assessing the Market Penetration Potential for a Village Development Site

More recently the authors have developed a further modelling approach that may be used by a retirement village developer and operator to: (a) identify what areas across a metro region might be the optimal ones in which to develop new retirement villages; and (b) assess the potential of the catchment around a site that might be available for developing a retirement village to generate the level of demand that would be sufficient to support a retirement village development of a specified size.

7.1 Data Base

Such modelling requires a data base for small areas, such as suburbs (designated as SA2s in the 2011 Australian census), for which detailed population data are available from ABS census data. A data base needed to be assembled for SA2 across a metro region providing information on the older person age cohorts that are most likely to have a propensity to be attracted to live in a retirement village. Such a data base has been assembled for SA2s across the *Brisbane-Southeast Queensland metro region* for the variables listed in Table 9.1. In addition, a data base on the location of existing retirement villages and the number of living units in them is required, along with an estimate of the number of the residents, and that number needs to be discounted from the size of the target age cohort in each SA2. The data base was put into a GIS to enable mapping and spatial analysis and modelling.

As shown in Table 9.1, the data base assembled contained variables providing information on the following for all SA2s across the Brisbane-South east Queensland metro region:

- the number of older persons and older person households that are in the various age categories for the 60 years and above population, which is important given the substantial differences in their propensity to move to a retirement village;
- the number of older persons in specific age categories that are single and couple households by gender as single female older people have a higher propensity to move to live in a retirement village and are likely to have different preferences for purchasing a one, two or three bed room unit;
- the number of older person households that are home owners as being able to realise equity in a home is necessary for older people to have the financial means to afford the purchase price of buying into a retirement village;
- the number of older person single and couple households in certain income categories that match pension eligibility and are indicative of levels of financial means, including the ability to pay a specified level of on-going monthly service fee required by a retirement village operator: and
- the number of existing units in retirement villages.

Table 9.1 Variables in the data base compiled for SA2s (suburbs) across the Brisbane-Southeast Queensland metro region, derived from the 2011 census

Older persons households with home ownership
Age 60–69, owned outright households
Age 70–79, owned outright households
Age 80+ owned outright households
Older persons type of household
Age of single person households 60–69 (also split into 60–64 and 65–69)
Age of oldest person 60–69, couple with no children households also split into aged 60–64 and aged 65–69
Age of oldest person 70–79, couple with no children households
Single person households: age 60–69
Single person households: age 70–79
Single person households: age 80+
Older persons type of household and income
Age of oldest person 60–69, couple with no children households, income $600 to $1399 per week
Age of oldest person 60–69, couple with no children households, income $1400+ per week
Age of oldest person 70–79, couple with no children households, income $600 to $1399 per week
Age of oldest person 70–79, couple with no children households, income $1400+ per week
Age of oldest person 80+, couple with no children households, income $600 to $1399 per week
Age of oldest person 80+, couple with no children households, income $1400+ per week
Single person households: age 60–69, income $400 to $999 per week
Single person households: age 60–69, income $1000+ per week
Single person households: age 70–79, income $400 to $999 per week
Single person households: age 70–79, income $1000+ per week
Single person households: age 80+, income $400 to $999 per week
Single person households: age 80+, income $1000+ per week
Existing retirement villages
Number of independent living units in existing retirement villages

Source: The authors, using ABS 2011 Census data

7.2 Optimisation Modelling

For a retirement village developer and operator, it is useful to know which suburbs across a metropolitan region might be the places to develop new villages that would optimise potential access to a new village development for the older person household cohorts that are a target market for the developer. That may be done through a *spatial optimisation modelling approach* developed initially by Murray and Shyy (2000). The technique had been used to examine patterns of urban crime across the suburbs in the City of Brisbane in the Brisbane-Southeast Queensland metro region (Murray et al. 2001; Shyy et al. 2014), and it is suitable for the issue at hand here.

The approach involves using a *median clustering optimisation model* designed to address the 'bi-criterion median clustering problem' (BMCP) through a spatial optimisation procedure that is extended to a '*multi-criterion median clustering problem*' (MMCP) in which it is possible to "simultaneously integrate multiple attributes to enhance categorisation capacity" (Shyy et al. 2014, p. 265). The MMCP modelling approach is designed to "group spatial units based on spatial distance and multiple attributes" (pp. 265–266), and may be regarded as "multi-criterion decision support tool to facilitate decision-making" (p. 266).

The *MMCP optimisation model* approach is used to identify those suburbs (SA2s) across the Brisbane-southeast Queensland metro region that might be optimal areas for developing a specific number of new retirement villages in order to maximise access to the target population as defined by a selection of variables for the 60 years and over age cohorts (selected from the variables in the data base as listed in Table 9.1), and taking account of the current supply of units in existing retirement villages. In addition, maps are generated to show how SA2s (suburbs) cluster around those optimal locations that represent catchments to draw on the target older age cohorts that might be potential residents of a new retirement village that a developer might undertake. Importantly, the modelling explicitly takes account of the existing stock of retirement village units across all suburbs in the Brisbane-South east Queensland metro region.

By way of an example, if, say, a developer was interested in developing a specific number (say 2, 4, 6 or 8) of new retirement villages, then the model will identify the suburbs (SA2s) that would be optimal locations for a new village, and identify groupings of SA2s around it (across the Brisbane-South East Queensland metro region) from which the new villages located in those optimal suburbs might draw specific cohorts of persons aged 60 year and over that are the target market for the village developer (specified by the selection of variables from those listed in Table 9.1).

7.3 Assessing Potential Market Penetration for a Specific Development Site

Further spatial modelling has been developed to assess the potential of the catchment around a site that might be available to a developer for building a retirement village to generate the level of demand that would be sufficient to support a retirement village development. An example of how that is done is discussed below for a development site that was up for tender for redevelopment in a SA2 (which we refer to as 'the site in suburb X') in an inner suburban part of the Brisbane-Southeast Queensland metro region. The modelling was applied to that site.[3]

---

[3] However, the developer did not proceed with the development rights for the site in question.

Table 9.2 Target cohorts to attract to a new retirement village at 'the site in suburb X'

1. *A prime target cohort of potential clients for a village to attract*:
• Households with a person aged 70+years that are outright home owners at the 2011 census.
2. *Potential clients for the early stage of a village development who will be in their mid-1970s+ from 2016*:
• couple only households with a person aged 70+ years + single person households aged 70 years and over at the 2011 census;
• households with a person aged 70–79 years and are outright owners of their home at the 2011 census;
• couple only households with a person aged 70–79 years with a weekly income of $1,400+ at the 2011 census; and
• single person households aged 70–79 years with a weekly income above $1000 at the 2011 census.
3. *Potential clients for the mid-stage of a retirement village development who will be aged 70–74 years in 2015 and will progress to be aged 75–79 years of age from 2021*:
• couple only households with a person aged 65–69 years + single person households aged 64–69 years at the 2011 census.
4. *Potential clients for the later stage of a village development who will be aged 70+ years from 2021*:
• couple only households with someone aged 60–64 years + single person households aged 60–64 years at the 2011 at the 2011 census.

Source: The authors

As the research discussed earlier in this chapter clearly shows that older people who move into a retirement village tend to relocate to a village that is in relative close proximity to where they have been living, it was decided to identify three catchments from which is most likely a new retirement village developed at 'the site in suburb X', would draw clients, namely: a 3 km road distance primary catchment, within which there are 6 SA2s (suburbs); a catchment extended to a 6 km road distance, within which there are 27 SA2s; and a catchment further extended to a 9 km road distance—an outer catchment—within which there are 50 SA2s. As one moves from one to the next of these catchments with increasing distance from the site in question, the likelihood of attracting a retiree household to move to a new retirement village developed on 'the site in suburb X' would decline. This is a classic distance decay function.

Within those catchments, and using the data base variables listed in Table 9.1, it is possible to estimate the number of older person age cohorts that might be target clients for a new retirement village development at 'the site in suburb X'. In this case, the seven cohorts of target clients listed in Table 9.2 were used. Choropleth maps may be produced showing the pattern of distribution of these seven target cohorts. The example for the prime target cohort for the new village is shown in Fig. 9.3, with the model estimating the numbers of households with a person aged 70 years and over that are outright home owners for the SA2s (suburbs) within the three road distance catchments around 'the site in suburb X'.

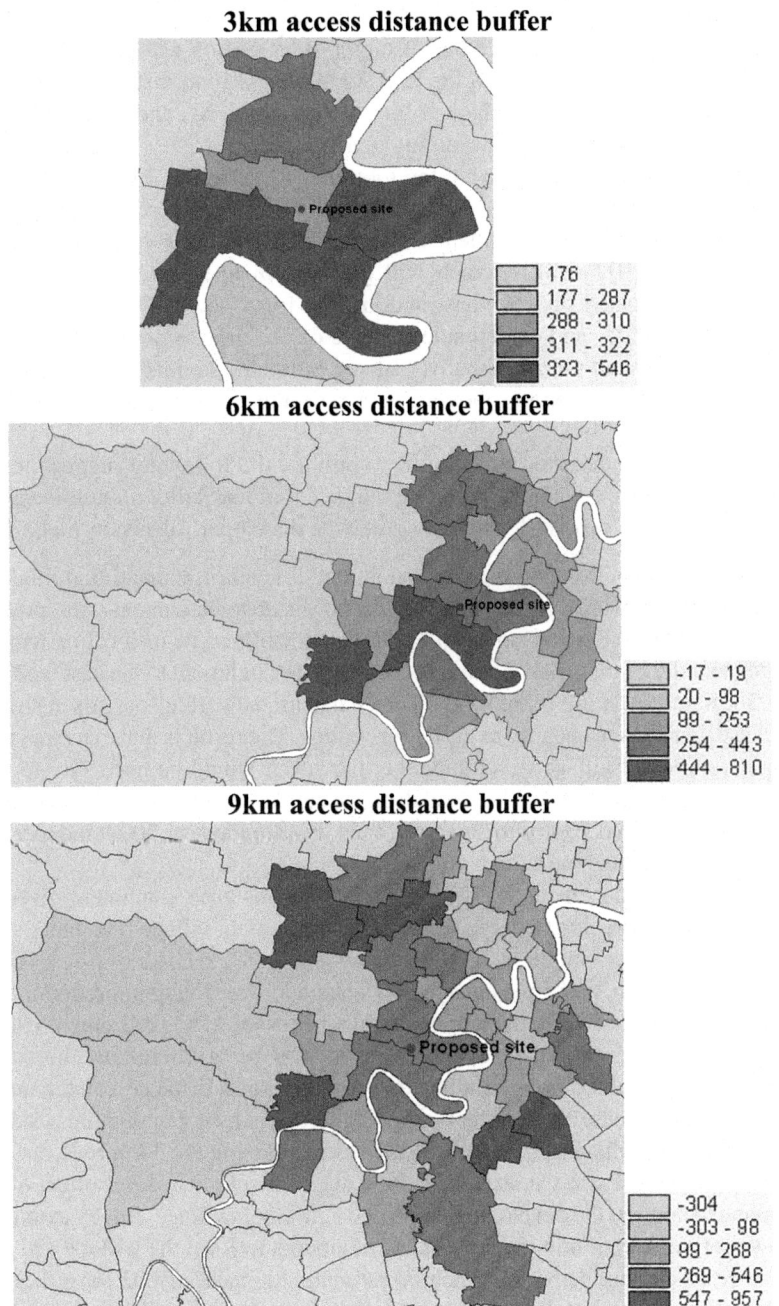

Fig. 9.3 Estimates of numbers of households with a person aged 70+years that are outright home owners within the three catchments around 'the site in suburb X'. Source: The authors

The modelling can produce tabulated output, such as that shown in Table 9.2, estimating: (a) the aggregate number of target older person age group/household cohorts living within the 3 km, 6 km and 9 km access road distance catchments around a potential retirement village at 'the site in suburb X'; and (b) the potential demand that might be generated for living in a village.

Important caveats are provided in the footnotes to Table 9.3. First, allowance is made for the number of persons/households currently living in retirement villages in each SA2. Second, an adjustment is made for mortality of the age cohorts as measured at the 2011 census which will progress in age post the 2011 census year over an estimated phased construction time for a new retirement village at 'the site in suburb X', and an estimate is made of out-movers not associated with moving to a retirement village. Finally, realistic estimates are made of the potential 'take-up' rate for age cohorts moving to a retirement village based on known rates.

The modelling undertaken can lead us to provide the following suggestions for the retirement village developer regarding the potential feasibility of building a new village at 'the site in suburb X' that may guide the developer's decision-making:

1. A prime consideration is the estimated potential level of demand that might be generated from within a confined 3 km road distance catchment—the primary catchment—of 'the site in suburb X'. A deficiency of the site its location within a large meander of the Brisbane River restricting its catchment to the east, and thus the 3 km and even the 6 km road distance catchments are a spatially restricted because there is not a nearby river road crossings. The result is that to make viable a new retirement village development at the site it would be necessary to look well beyond the restricted 3 km road distance catchment to generate the potential level of demand necessary to support a final development of 200+ independent living units in a new retirement village.

2. It is estimated that, from within the 3 km road distance catchment, over the duration of the development phases of a new retirement village (estimated to be about 8 years) there might be up to 184 *couple only households + single person households* which, had a person aged 60 years and over living in predominantly owner-occupied houses that might potentially be residents of a retirement village. Those households would be a key target market for a village at 'the site in suburb X'. Beyond that, extending into a 6 km road distance catchment, an additional 488 households in that cohort might be added as potential residents of a retirement village. Thus, the six suburbs comprising the 3 km road distance catchment for the site would *not* likely generate a sufficient level of estimated demand to support the development of a new retirement village. But by extending the target marketing into the additional 21 suburbs to form the wider 6 km road distance catchment there is a potential estimated demand of 602 for retirement village living that might be generated from the total number of households at the 2011 census that are *couple + single person households with someone aged 60 years and over*. Over the duration of the development of the proposed retirement

Table 9.3 Aggregate number of target older person age group/household cohorts living within the 3 km, 6 km and 9 km access distance catchment around a potential retirement village at 'Site X', and the estimated potential demand that may be generated for living in a village

Target population age/household cohort	From within the 3 km access distance catchment	From within the 6 km access distance catchment	From within the 9 km access distance catchment
Prime target group of clients for a retirement village			
*Households with a person aged 70 years and over that are outright home owners at the 2011 census	N = 2084	N = 5645	N = 11,423
Potential clients for early stage to mid-stage village development from			
Total households with a person aged 70–79 years and are outright owners of their home at the 2011 census	N = 1424Estimated demand = 94	N = 4901Estimated demand = 325	N = 9899Estimated demand = 658
*Couple only households with a person aged 70+ years + single person households aged 70 years and over at the 2011 census	N = 1436Estimated Demand = 95	N = 3855Estimated demand = 256	N = 7560Estimated demand = 520
*Couple only households with a person aged 70–79 years with a weekly income of $1400+ at the 2011 census	N = 193Estimated demand = 12	N = 636Estimated demand = 42	N = 1042Estimated demand = 69
*Single person households aged 70–79 years with a weekly income above $1000 at the 2011 census	N = 114Estimated demand = 7	N = 292Estimated demand = 19	N = 459Estimated demand = 30
Potential clients for the early and mid-stage village development from 2016 to 2021			
Couple only households with a person aged 65–69 years + single person households aged 65–69 years at the 2011 census	N = 766Estimated demand = 36#	N = 2868Estimated demand = 136#	N = 5439Estimated demand = 258#

(continued)

Table 9.3 (continued)

Target population age/household cohort	From within the 3 km access distance catchment	From within the 6 km access distance catchment	From within the 9 km access distance catchment
Potential clients for later stage village development from 2021			
Couple only households with a person aged 60–64 years and over + single person households aged 60–64 years at the 2011 census	N = 854*Estimated demand = 53##*	N = 3346*Estimated demand = 210##*	N = 6453*Estimated demand = 406##*

Note 1: The number cohorts identified by * are discounted by allowing for the number of households that are already residents in a retirement village

Note 2: The figures in *italics bold* indicate the estimated potential demand of a household cohort that the proposed retirement village at 'Site X' potentially might attract as residents in the early stage of the development, and are calculated on the basis that approximately 5% of the cohort will have moved or died and that of the remaining 7% of the actual number of that cohort might be likely to actually move into a retirement village

Note 3: The figures in *italics bold* and indicated by # are the estimated potential demand of a household cohort that the proposed retirement village at 'Site X' might attract during the mid-stage of the development, and are calculated on the basis that approximately 5% of the cohort at the 2011 census will have moved elsewhere or died and that of the remaining approximately 5% might choose to live in a retirement village

Note 4: The figures in italics bold and indicated by ## are the estimated potential demand of a household cohort that the proposed retirement village at 'Site X' might attract during the later stage of the development, and are calculated on the basis that approximately 10% of the cohort at the 2011 census will have moved elsewhere or died and that of the remaining approximately 7% might choose to live in a retirement village

Source: The authors

village at 'the site in suburb X', that should be sufficient to provide the level of demand necessary to fill 200+ independent living units.

3. Focusing on the population/household cohort that would be a prime target client group for marketing and pre-sales and as residents of the early stage of the development of a retirement village at 'the site in suburb X'- that is, the *couple only households with a person aged 70 years and over + single households aged 70 years and over* at the 2011 census—then within the 3 km road distance catchment, the potential level of demand for living in a retirement village is only 94. That may be sufficient to support a 1st phase of the village development of, say, 60 independent living units if a retirement village developer and operator is a successful market competitor in this part of the Brisbane-SEQ market.

4. For the 2nd phase of development with an additional 60 units, the 3 km road distance catchment is *not* likely to generate sufficient estimated demand (only 36) from the cohort that is *couple only households with a person aged 60–65 years + single person households aged 60–65 years* (at the 2011 census). It would be necessary to look beyond the primary catchment into the suburbs in the 6 km road distance catchment that might generate demand from an additional 100 of that household cohort, but it would likely not be for several years that many of that age cohort would be ready to move to a retirement village. Thus, there would be a need to penetrate beyond the 3 km road distance primary catchment to fill the 2nd phase development of 60 units.

5. For the later 3rd and 4th phases of the development of a which might occur from, four or more years down the track, there would be dependence on the cohort of *couple only households with a person aged 60–64 years + single person households aged 64–69 years* (at the 2011 census) who would start to be into their early to mid- 1970s, plus the potential 53 households from the cohort that were *couple only households with a person aged 60–64 years + single person households aged 60–64 years* (at the 2011 census), which would start to move into their early 1970s by the time of the 3rd and later phases of the development of the village. However, it is the modelling of potential estimated demand shows there might also be a need to target for the 3rd and 4th fourth phases of the village development to those two population/household cohorts living in the wider catchment beyond the 3 km road distance catchment to take account of those living in within the secondary catchment 6 km road distance catchment around the site. That might bring into play an additional 157 potential clients, but there would likely be significant competition from other existing and new retirement village alternatives.

6. There is likely to be a relatively small number of potential clients of retirement village living for the early stage of a village at 'the site in suburb X' from those cohorts at the 2011 census that were *couple only households with a person aged 70–79 with a weekly income of $1,400+* and who were *single person households aged 70–79 with a weekly income above $1000* at the 2011 census.

Within the 3 km road distance catchment there are estimated to be only 12 and 7 respectively of those important cohorts as they represent potential 'upper market' clients that are self-funded retirees or have only part pension dependence. Even within the wider 6 km road distance buffer there are potentially only 42 and 19 of those high priority clients. What that means is that both the primary and the secondary catchments around the site are characterized by relatively small number of higher income independent households (that is, not dependent on the aged person's pension). That suggests the bulk of potential estimated demand for retirement village living at the site will come predominantly from households that are pension or part-pension dependent for their income, and are thus likely to be somewhat price sensitive the payment of on-going fees when resident in the retirement village. However, the retiree households that are likely to comprise the potential estimated demand for retirement village living usually own their home outright, and thus have the equity sufficient to purchase an independent living unit in a retirement village development at the site. In view of this reality, it would be important for a retirement village at the site be developed with independent living units priced to also attract the lower income end of the retiree market from within the 6 km road distance catchment. That means there may be a need to ensure a sufficient supply of lower cost two-bedroom units as an alternative to higher cost three-bedroom units. There is no reason to expect that the potential clients for the mid-stage and later stage phases of the village development that will come from the *cohorts aged 65–69 years and 60–64 years* (at the 2011 census) will not be at least part dependence on the pension for their incomes, in spite of the fact that the suburbs within both the 3 km and 6 km distance access buffers around the site have a relatively high socio-economic status.

7. A careful approach to the business model for the development of a village at 'the site in suburb X' would be needed to: ascertain the mix of two and three bedroom units for each phase of the village development; price the units at a level that is affordable relative to the house prices in the primary and secondary catchments around the site; and to ascertain the type and standard of communal facilities that would be able to be provided and sustained at the level of on-going fees that are feasible for a relatively low household income of those retirees who are largely dependent on the pension can afford. Fortunately, the high incidence of outright home ownership among the target retiree cohorts is high in a local housing market that also has relatively high prices within the 3 km and 6 km distance catchments around the site. But it is also important to take account of the fact that households entering a retirement village have a strong preference to have a significant cash surplus following realizing the equity in their home and paying the entry price to a retirement village.

8 Conclusion

The ageing of the population in a country such as Australia will see a substantial increase in the older age cohorts (particularly in the old-old age cohorts), especially with the progression over the coming couple of decades of the 'baby boomers' through increasing old age. That has important implications for the provision of services, including housing alternatives, oriented towards the needs of older people. But the evidence so far is that a large majority of older people have a distinct preference to 'age-in-place'.

However, downsizing is certainly occurring, and a significant proportion of retirees (one-fifth to one-quarter) who are downsizers are choosing to live in a retirement village, although take-up rates are still relatively low. Downsizers, including those who have moved into a retirement village, rely primarily on family and friends for information and advice in the decision process to move, rather than on professionals, government and seniors' organisations, a finding that has been constant in research conducted over the last decade-and-a-half (Stimson 2002; Judd et al. 2014).

The survey research conducted by Judd et al. (2014, pp. 9–10) suggests policies to encourage older people in Australia to downsize might include: (1) improving dwelling and locational availability of housing alternatives, including improved age-friendly and accessible dwellings in desirable locations and in local areas familiar to older people, necessitating planning reform and encouraging greater innovation in the housing industry; (2) removing financial disincentives (such as stamp duties), including addressing housing affordability; and (3) addressing how psychological and practical barriers to moving might be overcome.

It is evident that retirement villages are playing a significant—if still relatively small—role as an alternative housing choice for older people seeking to downsize for multiple reasons, including meeting their motivation for life style change, meeting their desire avoid issues maintaining a house and a garden, meeting their wish for a secure environment, and providing a good housing solution for those suffering from deteriorating health. The research undertaken to investigating the motivations underlying the decision of older people to move into a retirement village certainly reveals that there are distinct categories of retirees that are influenced by different 'push factors', and that the propensities to move to a retirement village are differentiated by age, gender, and health status, among other variables. And it is evident that the 'pull factors' attracting older people to choose to move to live in a retirement village also vary across different older person cohorts, with a preference among many retirees who are potential movers to a retirement village to relocate over a short distance to maintain existing social and other networks and maintain familiarity with the area around where they have been living.

Jones et al. (2010, p. 109) suggest the growth of retirement villages in Australia in "all their diversity" demonstrates that retirees are "prepared to convert their housing assets into retirement village accommodation and services", with the sector providing considerable flexibility in terms of "diversity of arrangements for integrated services with housing".

This chapter has explicitly demonstrated how demographic and spatial analysis and modelling tools developed by regional scientists may be used to investigate where potential future demand for retirement village living might be spatially distributed and concentrated, including showing how optimisation modelling may be used to identify those locations across a metro region that might optimise access to the target groups that have higher propensities to be attracted to live in a retirement village. It has also shown how spatial modelling may be used to estimate the market potential of a site to attract retirees from within specified distance catchments to help inform a developer on the market potential and viability of a site for undertaking a new retirement village development. The modelling approaches discussed are being used by the retirement village industry in Australia.

References

Australian Bureau of Statistics (ABS) (2013a) Where and how do Australia's older people live, Reflecting a nation: stories from the 2011 census, 2012–13, Cat. no. 2071.0, 17 April

Australian Bureau of Statistics (ABS) (2013b) Population projections, Australia, 2012 (base) to 2101, (Cat no. 3222.1), 11 November

Gardner IL (1996) Why people move to retirement villages: home owners and non-home owners. Australas J Ageing 13:36–40

Gardner IL, Browning C, Kendig H (2005) Accommodation options in later life: retirement village or community living? Australas J Ageing 24:188–195

Howe A (2003) Housing an older Australia: more of the same or something different?, Keynote address, housing futures in an ageing Australia conference, AHURI nad the Myer Foundation, Melbourne, November

Jones A, Howe A, Tilse C, Bartlet H, Stimson R (2010) Service integrated housing for Australians in later life: final report. Australian Housing and Urban Research Institute, Melbourne, p 159

Judd B, Liu E, Easthope H, Davy L, Bridge C (2014) Downsizing amongst older Australians, AHURI Final Report No. 214, January, pp 181

Manicaros M, Stimson R (1999) Living in a retirement village: attitudes, choices and outcomes. University of Queensland Press for the Australian Housing and Urban Research Institute, Brisbane

McCrindle Baynes (2013) Retirement villages: 'the quiet achievers' – Australia's highest rated industry (McCrindle Baynes Village Census Report, 2013), The McCrindle Blog, 19 December

McGovern S, Baltins E (2002) The retirement village industry in Australia: evolution and structure. In: Stimson RJ (ed) The retirement village industry in Australia: evolution, prospects, challenges. University of Queensland Press for the Centre for Research into Sustainable Urban and Regional Futures, Brisbane, pp 23–46

Murray A, Shyy T (2000) Integrating attribute and space characteristics in choropleth display and spatial data mining. Int J Geogr Inf Sci 14:649–667

Murray AT, McGuffog I, Western JF, Mullins P (2001) Exploratory spatial data analysis techniques for examining urban crime. Br J Criminol 41:309–329

Painter G, Lee K (2009) Housing tenure transition of older households: life cycle, demographic, and familial factors. Reg Sci Urban Econ 39:749–760

PwC/Property Council (2015) 2015 PwC/Property Council Census, Property Council of Australia

Shyy T-K, Mazerolle L, Riseley K, Stimson RJ (2014) Web-bases GIS to support visualisation and analysis of community variations in crime. In: Stimson RJ (ed) Handbook of research methods and application in spatially integrated social science. Edward Elgar, Northampton, MA, pp 535–559

Stimson RJ (ed) (2002) The retirement village industry in Australia: evolution, prospects, challenges. University of Queensland Press for the Centre for Research into Sustainable Urban and Regional Futures, Brisbane, p 251

Stimson R, McCrea R (2004) A push-pull framework for modelling the relocation of retirees to a retirement village: the Australian experience. Environ Plan A 36(8):1451–1470

Stimson R, McGovern S (2002a) Retirement villages: an alternative housing lifestyle for retirees. In: Stimson RJ (ed) The retirement village industry in Australia: evolution, prospects, challenges. University of Queensland Press for the Centre for Research into Sustainable Urban and Regional Futures, Brisbane, pp 1–8

Stimson RJ, McGovern S (2002b) Future demand and construction opportunities for retirement villages. In: Stimson RJ (ed) The retirement village industry in Australia: evolution, prospects, challenges. University of Queensland Press for the Centre for Research into Sustainable Urban and Regional Futures, Brisbane, pp 173–190

Stimson RJ, Qureshi M (1999) Spatial optimisation model for allocating retirement village construction to meet potential future demand, Geodemographics of ageing in Australia Symposium, Brisbane, November/December

Stimson R, Manicaros M, Kabamba A, Murray A (1997) Ageing and housing: ageing and retirement housing in Australia. Publications and Printing Department, Queensland University of Technology for the Australian Housing and Urban Research Institute, Brisbane

Woodbridge S (2003) Coping with change: comparing the housing decisions of older people. In: Bradley R, Buys L, Lyddon J (eds) Social change in the 21st century conference proceedings. Centre for Social Change Research, Queensland university of Technology, Brisbane

Chapter 10
Demographic Transition and Firm Performance: An Empirical Analysis for Germany

Stephan Brunow and Alessandra Faggian

1 Introduction

The term demographic transition, proposed by Thompson in 1929, refers to the transition from high to low death rates accompanied, at a later stage, with a reduction of total fertility rates. The early stages of a demographic transition, when death rates drop but total fertility rates remain high, are often associated with an increase in the growth rate of a country. However, as a country progresses from the early stages to the later stages of a demographic transition, the balance between deaths and births becomes more problematic. If the total fertility rate drops below sub-replacement levels (2.1–2.2 children per woman considering the lower death rates over time), population ageing and decline occur putting pressure on the labor market due to a faster shrinking of the working age population and on the pension system due to an increase in the elderly dependency ratio.

Since the 1960s several countries have experienced a substantial decrease in total fertility rates, which are now well below replacement levels. A United Nation report

S. Brunow (✉)
Institute for Employment Research IAB, Nuremberg, Germany

University of Applied Labour Studies, Schwerin, Germany
e-mail: stephan.brunow@arbeitsagentur.de

A. Faggian
The Ohio State University, Columbus, USA

Gran Sasso Science Institute, L'Aquila, Italy
e-mail: faggian.1@osu.edu; alessandra.faggian@gssi.infn.it

© Springer International Publishing AG, part of Springer Nature 2018
U. Blien et al. (eds.), *Modelling Aging and Migration Effects on Spatial Labor Markets*, Advances in Spatial Science,
https://doi.org/10.1007/978-3-319-68563-2_10

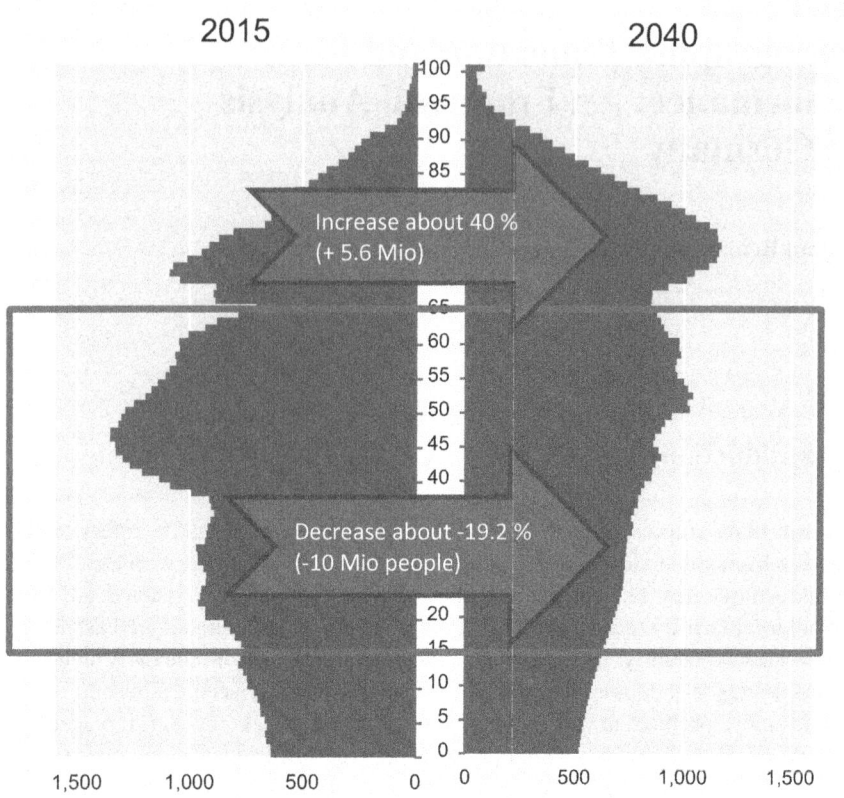

Fig. 10.1 Population trend in Germany. Note: Total fertility rate 1.4, 100,000 people net immigration. Data is taken from the Federal Statistical Office in Germany, Destatis

(2011)[1] shows that 48% of the world population in 2010 lived in countries with sub-replacement total fertility rates, including all the European countries (with the only exception of France). In Germany, the total fertility rate dropped from 2.38 in 1960 to 1.39 in 2010. This process, that followed the baby boom of the Post World War II period, will lead to an increase in people of retirement age vis-à-vis a reduction of the working-age population in the next two decades. As a result, the elderly dependency ratio is expected to increase with negative consequences on social security, the pension system and the functioning of the labor market.

Figure 10.1 shows the age profile in Germany in 2015 in the left and 2040 in the right panel. During the transition period all people born between 1950 and 1975, which are of age 40–65, will be retired in 2040. Albeit their overall group size has

---

[1] http://data.worldbank.org/indicator/SP.DYN.TFRT.IN (Accessed on August 28th 2016).

declined, there is still an increase in the total number of pensioners accompanied with a sharper decline in working age population. Therefore, the elderly dependency ratio will increase in the near future. This projection is computed assuming the average German fertility rate of 1.4 and a net-immigration of 100,000 people. Irrespective of the immigration shock due to forced migration, Germany currently experiences higher immigration rates. A computation with a net-immigration of 200,000 people mitigates the issue but still, the trend of an increase in the elderly dependency ratio remains.

To reduce the high elderly dependency ratio, several European countries started implementing—often controversial—new policies, such as holding older workers employed by rising retirement age. Other suggested measures included increasing participation of female workers or hours worked and/or rethink labor market oriented immigration policies. While there is no doubt that all these measure can indeed increase the working age population and hence reduce the dependency ratio, it is indubitable that the effects on firm productivity of the different policies might not be the same. Do firms benefit the same way from employing immigrants, older workers, and women? If they do so the negative consequences of the shrinking labor force can be compensated. However, if there is no benefit or even higher costs, productivity might decline and thus, overall welfare might be reduced. On the other hand, a more capital intensive production and technological progress of the production process can compensate the shrinking labor force. Then, not just policy effort in exploiting the labor force but also in supporting innovation and technological progress are requested.

The main aim of this chapter is to try and answer this question by investigating the consequences on firm productivity resulting from employing different types of workers in response to the demographic transition. Although this is clearly a crucial issue, with strong policy implications, it is relatively unexplored in the literature.

The structure of the paper is as follows. Section 2 introduces the theoretical framework by discussing the possible channels to reduce the dependency ratio and their implications. Section 3 presents the empirical model to test the theoretical predictions, our case study (Germany) and the data used. Section 4 discusses the main results while Sect. 5 concludes and provides some policy implications and possible avenues for further future research.

2 Policy and Theoretical Framework

2.1 Channels to Reduce the Dependency Ratio

The increase in elderly dependency ratio has become a concern in most developed countries, especially in Europe. With the fear of a shrinking working population, solutions to increase the size of the labor force have been a clear focus of policy makers around the world. To solve the problem, five main channels are often cited:

1. Increase in labor force participation of women
2. Increase in labor force participation of underrepresented minorities;
3. Increase of the retirement age;
4. Changes in immigration laws, in particular with regard to labor oriented immigration;
5. Reduce unemployment.

Although these solutions are all viable, they are very different in terms of feasibility, timing of implementation and, most of all, effects on the labor market.

The first three channels have been a priority in the European Union agenda for a while. For instance, the Europe 2020 10-year strategy proposed by the European Commission explicitly talked about a target of 75% of people aged 20–64 employed by 2020. As of 2012, while the employment rate of men was close to that target (74.2%), the female rate was still lagging behind (62.4%). The picture is even worse if part-time work is factored in. When employment is measured in full-time equivalent, the 2012 level of employment of women is equivalent to 53.5%.[2] The traditional role that women play in taking care of children and the elderly is critical here and should not be dismissed. To increase employment through an increase in female participation, two necessary (and yet not sufficient) conditions are:

a. increasing the share of part-time work offered (and hence the flexibility of the labor market);
b. providing childcare at affordable prices (i.e. well below the reservation wage of female workers). For this reason, in Germany the supply of child care has increased and all families having children above 1 year of age have the right to give their children in (public financed) child care.

The different European countries are at different level of 'maturity' in offering these conditions and the results are reflected in the gender employment gaps. As an example, the lack of flexible working arrangements is evident in countries such as Bulgaria, Slovakia and Hungary, where part-time work in 2012 accounted for less than 10%, while, at the opposite of the spectrum, in the Netherlands almost 80% of women worked part-time. In 2014 and in Germany, almost the half of the women (47%) work part-time, of which about 13% wish to work longer.[3]

From a firm perspective, while there is no conclusive evidence that part-time work has a negative effect on productivity levels, there might be higher transaction and communication costs associated with employing more employees part-time rather than fewer full-time. Moreover, flexible working might be more feasible in certain sectors (and occupations) than others. Because of the shrinking labor force, wages are expected to raise and thus, making the supply of females work capacity even more attractive. However, females might not supply their labor capacity yet

---

[2] Accessed on August 29th 2016.

[3] Statistisches Bundesamt, "Arbeitsmarkt auf einen Blick—Deutschland und Europa", 2016. https://www.destatis.de/DE/Publikationen/Thematisch/Arbeitsmarkt/Erwerbstaetige/BroeschuereArbeitsmarktBlick0010022169004.pdf (accessed on September 15th 2016).

if they only have to work full-time. If employers provide relatively more part-time vacancies, women may have higher incentives to supply their working capacity. In addition to that, firms may have two options: accepting part-time workers or having no worker at all. Therefore, part-time friendly policies may achieve an increase in the labor force participation of females.

A second solution that has been implemented by many European governments in the last decade is an increase in statutory retirement age. As a report by the European Commission points out, a large number of countries have implemented pension reforms that make the public pension systems less generous by pushing up the retirement age in a gradually phased way and restricting access to early retirement schemes and strengthening the incentives to prolong working lives (p. 79). While stimulating people to stay longer in the labor market has the benefit of reducing the elderly dependency rate of a country, it is not an uncontroversial measure. The clear difference between increasing female participation and raising the retirement age is that while the first relies on incentives to increase participation *voluntarily*, the second is *mandatory*. Although statutory retirement age is pushed up gradually, some cohorts of older workers are forced to keep on working longer than they expected. This, in turn, can create a disincentive for their productivity. Moreover, older workers are more likely to get sick and/or might have skills, which are partially obsolete. Although these negative factors can be compensated by higher levels of (at least specific) human capital due to a longer on-the-job experience, the overall effect on productivity is not clear-cut. Zwick and Göbel (2013) find that mixing older and younger workers creates synergies, which enhance the overall firm productivity. Mahlberg et al. (2013), studying the case of Austria, find that—contrary to popular belief—having a larger share of younger employees is, *ceteris paribus*, associated with lower productivity and wages than having a larger share of older employees. This confirms previous findings by Hellerstein and Neumark (1995) and Hellerstein et al. (1999) found for Israeli and US firms. Malmberg et al. (2008) call this increase in plant productivity at firm-level the 'Horndal effect'. This effect was first identified by Lundberg (1961), who observed that the increase in productivity of the Horndal steel plant in Sweden—between 1927 and 1951—was linked to a larger share of older steel workers. As was the case for part-time work, the potential positive and negative effects of employing mature workers may differ between occupations (e.g. craftsman vs. office clerk).

The fourth, and possibly most controversial, channel to increase the size of the labor force is through immigration from other countries. The effect of immigrant workers on local labor markets has been the subject of heated debate for a very long time and it basically hinges around two basic issues: (a) whether immigrants are substitutes or complement to native workers; (b) the level of skills of immigrants. The former case does not necessarily means that a complementary is given when immigrants and natives (self-) select in different occupations but it means that even within the same occupation, job and even task, immigrants positively contribute to the success. For instance, additional knowledge and distinct problem solving capacities make immigrants different from natives and thus, they might be rather complements than substitutes.

A series of studies looked at the effect of immigrants on the wages of native workers. Borjas (1995) finds that the gains from immigration for the USA are small, suggesting that immigrants are not sufficiently 'different' from native workers. Conversely, this result contradicts with the work conducted by Amuedo-Dorantes and De La Rica (2011), D'Amuri et al. (2010), Dustmann et al. (2007), Dustmann et al. (2012), Ottaviano and Peri (2012), and Peri (2007) who find a strong complementary relationship between immigrants and natives. Greenwood et al. (1996) found that recent immigrants have an adverse wage effect only on other recent immigrants but not on natives. Ottaviano and Peri (2005, 2008) go a step further by showing that overall immigration—even after categorizing immigrants according to education, experience and place of origin—generates a positive effect on the average wages of U.S.-born workers. Orrenius and Zavodny (2003), using occupation as a proxy for skills, show that the effect of immigrants is higher on low-skilled native wages than on high-skilled native wages, suggesting that immigrants are more substitutable with the former. Such result is supported by Suedekum et al. (2014) who provide evidence that immigrants and natives are rather complements as long as they do not compete in the same low-skilled jobs. Card (2005) disputes even this finding, showing that there is no convincing evidence that immigrants harm the opportunities of less educated natives. The literature provides insights into possible cost advantages for firms due to lower wages when employing immigrants. Given the rather complementary relationship between immigrants and natives the cost advantage might be minor. Immigration has the obvious advantage of being a more immediate solution than slowly increasing female participation rate or retirement age. Paserman (2013) is one of the few contributions studying specifically the relationship between firm productivity and share of immigrant workers and he finds that, for the case of Israeli firms, the immigrant share was strongly negatively correlated with productivity in low-tech industries, while it was positively correlated with productivity in high-technology industries, hinting at complementarities between technology and the skilled immigrant workforce. The effects of foreign employment on innovation at the level of firms is studied by Ozgen et al. (2013), who find that the share of employees is negatively associated with innovation but the cultural diversity among foreigners positively contributes to innovation. Brunow and Miersch (2015) and Brunow and Stockinger (2015) support that finding and show that especially cultural diversity among high-skilled foreigners positively contributes to firm innovation. However, both studies also show that the proportion of low-skilled foreigners and their diversity is negatively associated with firm innovation. The positive net-effects of cultural diversity on patenting activities at the level of region, and thus innovation, is supported by Niebuhr (2010). Parrotta et al. (2014a) focus on firm patenting activities and also find significant positive effects of cultural diversity. Taking the focus on firm productivity, Brunow and Nijkamp (2016) and Trax et al. (2015) support the existence of positive effects of cultural diversity. However, Brunow and Blien (2014) show that especially the employment of an additional foreign nationality leads to negative effects on firm productivity which can be interpreted as communication costs although the effect of diversity is positive. In addition, Parrotta et al. (2014b) find significant negative effects of ethnic diversity on productivity for Danish firms, whereas some differences between skill levels exist.

At all, at the level of firms, the effect of the employment of immigrants is unclear. There seem to be a positive effect on innovation of high-skilled workers but also negative effects are present. In principle, it could be possible to identify labor market vacancies and use immigration policies to fill them. However, in practice, it might be very difficult to implement such detailed immigration policies 'tailored' to specific labor market needs. Additionally, when the labor force shrinks, more or less all occupations will be requested during the transition period of shrinking. This makes a selection of the specific skill groups and occupations even more difficult. Moreover, not all migration is voluntary and employment-related. The recent refugee crisis in Europe is a clear example of forced migration where labor market considerations are not the main driver of the migration flows (even though they become relevant at a later stage). Large inflows of immigrants, especially if low skilled, can trigger a negative response by natives, often in the form of discrimination, with negative consequences on firm productivity. As for Germany, currently all people from within the EU are allowed to work in Germany by the free EU-wide labor market. The German law "Aufenthaltsgesetz" regulates immigration for non-EU citizens. Only people holding a university degree are allowed to enter Germany for a period up to 6 month to find an employer (Blue Card). Having a Blue Card enables family members to enter Germany as well. For potential migrants from non-EU countries with occupational training, the permission to immigrate and to work in Germany requires to have an employer in advance. For unskilled workers the contract is even limited to 6 or 9 month. For potential non-EU migrants without a university degree the Federal Employment Agency have to agree to the employment of a potential migrant. There exist some exceptions when the vacancy is in an occupational field where "shortage" of labor exists, according to a white list provided by the Federal Employment Agency. Although, such white list aims to relieve pressure on the occupational labor markets, it might be too limited to truly address the market's needs. To sum up, the current non-EU immigration policy of Germany is skill-biased towards high-skilled immigration. In Germany, employers record the nationality according to the labor market status based on citizenship. If a person from abroad is employed subject social security, she or he will be identified as foreigner with the respective citizenship as long as this person did not naturalize. Therefore, in the proceeding analysis no information on second or third generation migrants is available. Given the empirical evidence on foreign employment and cultural diversity such policy may indeed have positive net effects at the firm level.

Lastly, the fifth point records the reduction of unemployment: Of course, the workforce is relatively more exhausted the fewer people are unemployed. In February 2017 slightly more than 2.7 million people registered as unemployed and the German unemployment rate is 6.3%. Out of these, almost two third are long-term unemployed (longer than 1 year). The regional variation, however, is substantive. The better performing regions experience almost full-employment with unemployment rates about 1%. There are other regions with unemployment rates about 14%. Thus, an earlier integration of unemployed due to better conditions and matching at the labor market would increase the active workforce and thus, reduce the negative impact of the shrinkage.

The demographic transition will affect German regions quite unequally. Some regions, especially in East Germany but also West Germany, will shrink whereas other regions especially in the south with still grow in terms of population. Internal German-wide migration from growing to shrinking regions might reduce the negative consequences of the more affected regions. However, these regions are in terms of economic development behind the growth poles (mainly) of the south and therefore unattractive as a destination for internal migration. Additionally, the still growing regions experience high growth rates in labor demand and unemployment is almost negligible. Thus, although both types of regions are totally different affected by population development, they both need strategies to face the demographic transition.

2.2 Theoretical Framework and Empirical Implementation

To put the issue into a theoretical framework the link between firm productivity and the three channels described in Sect. 2.1, let us consider a simple production for the nth firm with physical capital, K, and labor, L, as inputs to produce the final output, Y. Let us also call the labor factor productivity, for the nth firm, A_n and the capital factor productivity B_n. Following the approach by Brunow and Blien (2015), and assuming a Constant Elasticity of Substitution (CES) production function with an elasticity of substitution $\sigma > 0$ between inputs, the production function can be expressed as:

$$Y_n = T_n \left[\alpha (B_n K_n)^{\frac{\sigma-1}{\sigma}} + \beta (A_n L_n)^{\frac{\sigma-1}{\sigma}} \right]^{\frac{\sigma}{\sigma-1}}. \tag{10.1}$$

Labor productivity A_n depends on a vector of firm characteristics x_n (such as legal form, plant age, foreign-owned, state of equipment and location in space), agglomeration economies z_{irt}, but also a vector of variables defining the workforce composition, $x_n^{Workforce}$ which includes factor such as gender, age and immigrant status of employees. We also include a firm, industry, region and time fixed effects (μ_n, μ_i, μ_r and μ_t, respectively) to control for unobservables.

$$A_n = \exp\left[\mu_n + \mu_i + \mu_r + \mu_t + x_n^{Workforce} + \alpha x_n + \beta z_{irt} \right], with \tag{10.2a}$$

$$
\begin{aligned}
x_n^{Workforce} &= \gamma_1 s_{n,high} + \gamma_2 s_{n,women} + \gamma_3 s_{n,foreign}^{low} + \gamma_4 DIV_{n,foreign}^{low} \\
&\quad + \gamma_5 s_{n,foreign}^{high} + \gamma_6 DIV_{n,foreign}^{high} + \gamma_7 s_{n,young} + \gamma_8 s_{n,prime-age} \\
&\quad + \gamma_9 s_{n,ft}
\end{aligned}
\tag{10.2b}
$$

where $s_{n,high}$ is the share of high-skilled employees, $s_{n,women}$ is the share of female employees, $s_{n,ft}$ is the share of fulltime employees, $s_{n,foreign}^{low}$ and $s_{n,foreign}^{high}$ are the shares of low- and high-skilled foreign workers,[4] respectively, $s_{n,young}$ and $s_{n,prime-age}$ are the shares of workers of age 15–24 and 55+, respectively and $DIV_{n,foreign}^{low}$ and $DIV_{n,foreign}^{high}$ are diversity indexes of foreign workers and related to the Fractionalization index,

$$DIV_{n,foreign}^{k} = 1 - \sum_{i,k}^{N} s_{n,i,k}^{2}, \qquad k = low, high,$$

where $s_{n,i,k}$ relates to the share of the ith foreign group of low- or high-skilled employees of the nth firm among N foreign groups employed. The Diversity measure is zero if all employees are from the same nationality and it increases with the degree of cultural diversity.

Because the data to be used do not include capital stock measure at firm level, we follow the approach by Brunow and Blien (2015) and derive an empirically testable equation for productivity of the form:

$$\frac{Y_n}{L_n} = \frac{A_n^{1-\sigma}}{\beta^{\sigma}} w^{\sigma} \left[\beta^{\sigma} \left(\frac{w_n}{A_n} \right)^{1-\sigma} + \alpha^{\sigma} \left(\frac{r_n}{B_n} \right)^{1-\sigma} \right], \qquad (10.3)$$

where w_n relates to the average wage paid and r_n to the interest rate of capital.

By substituting Eq. (10.2a) into (10.3) and taking the logs, we derive an "augmented" empirical specification (Eq. 10.4), which approximates the theoretical model in Eq. (10.3),

$$\ln \frac{Y_n}{L_n} = \mu_n + \mu_i + \mu_r + \mu_t + \delta_1 x_n^{Workforce} + \delta_2 x_n + \delta_3 z_{irt} + \sigma \ln w + \epsilon,$$

$$(10.4)$$

where the δ terms are new sets of parameters and ϵ is an error term. To avoid simultaneity between the LHS and the RHS, the RHS variables are lagged 1 year.

The final empirical model (4) can be estimated using different techniques ranging from OLS to fixed-effects (FE) panel models, to random-effects (RE) panel models. All these models have shortcomings. First, industry and region fixed effects are collinear with the firm fixed effect and therefore, can only be estimated in an OLS setting that ignores firm heterogeneity. However, firm heterogeneity

---

[4]To define high- versus low-skilled we follow the approach by Trax et al. (2015) and Brunow and Blien (2015) that assigns occupations to 'low-skilled' and 'high-skilled' on the basis of 2-digit occupations using cluster analysis. The following variables are used in the cluster analysis: The proportion of time spent in non-routine and analytical work and the share of employees holding a University degree.

and selectivity of firms in space make OLS estimation problematic. Fixed effects models (FE), such as the widely used within-transformation or first differencing, can help overcome these issues. However, such a transformation implies a loss of information, especially with regard to between-establishments variation. In fact, using first differences sometimes results in even less precise results if annual variation within plants is low. Lastly, some variables, such as the legal form, do not change much over time making identification difficult. To overcome the OLS shortcomings, a random effects (RE) model is often employed. The model requires the firm fixed-effects and the other explanatory variables to be uncorrelated. However, this assumption is likely to be violated in our case, as the firm fixed-effect partly captures the time invariant part of the term in parentheses in Eq. (10.3). This term, in fact, consists of variables, such as wages, that control for productivity and that are included also as explanatory variables. Hence, the firm specific effect is likely to be correlated with the other regressors making a random effects model mis-specified. Given the limitations of the different model specifications, we will present, compare and discuss the results of four different models, i.e. OLS, within-transformation FE, first-differencing FE and RE.

3 Data

The data used in this study comes from two datasets compiled by the Institute for Employment Research (IAB), i.e. the IAB Establishment Panel and IAB Employment Statistics datasets for the period 1995 to 2010. Thanks to the combination of the two datasets, we have firm-level information on all the variables discussed in the theoretical framework and necessary for the estimation of our empirical model.

The IAB Establishment Panel is a representative survey of German establishments conducted on an annual basis. The majority of the sample (about 85.7%) is made of one-firm-one-plant cases. However, there are cases where a firm has more than one plant and it is not possible to identify which two plants belong to the same firm. To partly correct for this, we use two dummy variables for a firm's headquarter (about 8.8%) or branch office (about 5.5%). The IAB Establishment Panel survey includes information not only on market-oriented plants but also on public sector plants, NGOs or financial institutions. Because of the different natures of these different businesses (and because we focus on productivity), we limit our analysis only to market-oriented plants whose aim is to generate revenues. The final number of observations in our sample is 100,397. Because of attrition (i.e. some plants leave while others are added to the survey), the number of observations varies by year. Table 10.3 in Appendix provides a breakdown of observations by year.

The second data source, the IAB Employment Statistics, is based on administrative data coming from the social security system. It collects information on personal characteristics of every person working and registered for social security and hence it is a very reliable source of individual data. Personal characteristics include, among others, gender, occupation and wages. The data are then used to calculate pensions and unemployment benefits. Although the data are at individual level, they include an identifier for the plant where the individual is employed, making it possible to aggregate the data at plant level (or any other more aggregate level such as industry or regional level). Table 10.1 summarizes the explanatory variables used in the empirical modeling and their source.

4 Results and Discussion

This section presents the results of our empirical analysis. Table 10.2 reports the estimation results for all four possible model specifications: OLS (Model 1), fixed-effects models both with a within-transformation (Model 2) and first-differencing (Model 3), and finally a random effects model (Model 4). Standard errors are robust against arbitrary misspecification and are clustered at the level of plants[5] in all models. In all models, the estimates are jointly significant, indicating the explanatory power of the variables included. Both an F-Test of the fixed effects model and a Breusch-Pagan test for the random effects model suggest the presence of plant heterogeneity making the results of these two models preferred over the OLS estimates. Moreover, the Hausman test provides evidence of a correlation between the plant specific effect and the explanatory variables, favoring the use of the fixed-effects models. Although we present all four models for comparison and completeness purposes, we focus more on the results of the two fixed-effects models 2 and 3, which are the preferred ones.

4.1 Channels to Reduce Dependency Ratio

We start by discussing the results on our variables of interest, i.e. the three channels to reduce the dependency ratio and increase employment.

Plants with a larger proportion of female workers are, on average, more productive, although this positive effect is only significant in the OLS and RE models and it disappears in the two FE models. Plants employing a higher share of female employees are, at worst (FE models), not different from the others and, at best (OLS and RE models), more productive.

As such, when plants have to employ relatively more women, they do not have to fear a loss of productivity. Closely related to the employment of female employees is the issue of hours worked. Although there is no information available on the hours worked in the IAB Employment Statistics, it does include information on full-time and part-time employment. As expected, a higher share of full-time workers

---

[5]As a robustness check, we also re-estimated the models clustering the errors by industry. The results are almost identical with only a slight increase in standard errors.

Table 10.1 Description of explanatory variables

Name	Description	Source
Control variables (x_n)		
Legal form	Two dummy variables if sole trader or privately owned partnership company (reference: capital limited company)	*IAB Establishment Panel*
Plant age	Dummy variables for the categories: – new: 0–4 years – young: 5–14 years – old: 15+ years (reference)	
Foreign-owned plant	Dummy if plant has a foreign owner	
Headquarter/Branch	Two dummies if the plant belongs to a firm having more than one plant: – Dummy headquarter – Dummy branch office (reference: one-plant-one-firm)	
Equipment/machinery	Dummy indicators for the state of the art of equipment and machinery employed based on survey information: – newest technology – new technology – older technology – old and out of date technology (reference)	
Location: Competition	Number of plants in the same region and 2-digit industry (in log)	*IAB Establishment Panel*
Location: Human Capital	% of employees working in complex occupations in all other plants in the same region and 2-digit industry	
Location: Diversity	Fractionalization over the plant share of the respective 2-digit industries within the region	
Region type	Assignment of NUTS3-regions to a regional type: – agglomeration region – urbanized region (reference) – rural region	*Federal Institute for Research on Building, Urban Affairs and Spatial Development (Bundesinstitut für Bau- Stadt- und Raumforschung—BBSR)*

Workforce variables ($x^{workforce}$)		*IAB Employment Statistics*
Females	% of female employees	
Full-time	% of full-time employees	
Wages	Average daily gross wages paid in the plant	
Foreigners	% of foreign employees according to citizenship and labor market status defined by the German Aufenthaltsgesetz and including EU citizens.	
Human capital	% of employees working in complex occupations (Brunow and Blien 2015)	
Low-skilled foreigners	% of foreign employees on all employees working in less complex occupations	
High-skilled foreigners	% of foreign employees on all employees working in complex occupations	
Diversity low-skilled foreigners	Fractionalization index among the foreign employees separated by nationality working in less complex occupations	
Diversity high-skilled foreigners	Fractionalization index among the foreign employees separated by nationality working in complex occupations	
Young employees	Share of employees aged 15–24	
Old employees	Share of employees aged 55+	
Plant size	Dummy for the establishment size measured in levels of employees – 1–4 employees – 5–9 employees – 10–20 employees – 20–49 employees (reference) – 50–99 employees – 100–149 employees – 150–249 employees – 250–499 employees – 500–999 employees – 1000–1999 employees – 2000+ employees	

Table 10.2 Estimation results

	Model 1	Model 2	Model 3	Model 4
	OLS	FE within-transformation	FE first-differencing	RE
Workforce variables				
1. Female participation				
Female	0.067*** (3.03)	0.019 (0.46)	0.069 (1.39)	0.077*** (3.57)
Full-time	2.420*** (128.12)	2.366*** (80.25)	2.332*** (63.57)	2.391*** (136.32)
2. Elderly participation				
Young employees (15–24)	0.078*** (2.91)	0.017 (0.60)	−0.053 (−1.54)	0.025 (1.11)
Old employees (55+)	−0.067** (−2.17)	−0.082** (−2.41)	−0.013 (−0.34)	−0.071*** (−2.62)
Human capital	0.208*** (8.29)	0.081 (1.51)	0.131** (2.11)	0.220*** (8.34)
3. Immigration				
ProportionLow-skilled foreigners	−0.041 (−0.98)	−0.123 (−1.63)	−0.130* (−1.77)	−0.103** (−2.36)
ProportionHigh-skilled foreigners	−0.208*** (−2.83)	−0.051 (−0.78)	−0.055 (−0.74)	−0.127** (−2.47)
Diversity of low-skilled foreigners	0.039* (1.76)	−0.049 (−1.64)	−0.082*** (−3.05)	0.040** (2.00)
Diversity of high-skilled foreigners	0.150*** (4.22)	−0.007 (−0.19)	−0.070* (−1.78)	0.127*** (4.48)
Other control variables				
Legal form and organization				
Sole trader	−0.147***(−10.67)	−0.013 (−0.49)	−0.020 (−0.82)	−0.164*** (−11.80)
Private partnership	0.024 (1.48)	−0.007 (−0.31)	−0.016 (−0.73)	−0.025* (−1.69)
Foreign-owned	0.128***(6.08)	0.010 (0.32)	−0.045 (−1.49)	0.112*** (5.59)
Headquarter	0.086*** (4.96)	0.032** (2.51)	0.018 (1.49)	0.062***(5.26)
Branch	0.109*** (5.60)	0.029** (2.19)	0.009 (0.73)	0.059*** (4.61)
Average wages (log)	0.696*** (39.55)	0.242*** (6.83)	0.160*** (3.51)	0.543*** (26.72)

(continued)

Table 10.2 (continued)

Plant age(*ref: 15+*)				
0–4 years	−0.096*** (−7.33)	0.013 (0.76)	0.007 (0.38)	−0.061*** (−5.17)
5–14 years	−0.011 (−1.01)	0.022** (2.25)	−0.007 (−0.73)	−0.008 (−0.96)
Equipment(*ref:old*)				
Newest	0.250*** (11.78)	0.078*** (4.07)	−0.008 (−0.43)	0.140*** (8.51)
New	0.191*** (9.53)	0.063*** (3.55)	−0.005 (−0.29)	0.112*** (7.29)
Older	0.107*** (5.44)	0.041** (2.47)	−0.001 (−0.08)	0.066*** (4.46)
Location				
Human capital	0.259*** (3.66)	0.129 (1.03)	0.142 (1.06)	0.258*** (3.78)
Competition	0.005 (1.08)	0.002 (0.09)	0.011 (0.37)	0.010** (2.01)
Diversity	3.127** (2.44)	1.320 (0.51)	−4.223 (−1.25)	3.157** (2.43)
Fixed effects				
Time	Yes	Yes	Yes	Yes
Region type	Yes	No	No	Yes
2-digit industry	Yes	No	No	Yes
Plant	Yes	Yes	Yes	Yes
Constant	−3.824*** (−3.06)	0.205 (0.08)	−0.038*** (−5.26)	−3.171** (−2.50)
R^2	0.421	0.180	0.118	0.413
No. observations	100,397	100,397	65,666	100,397
No. clusters	28,324	17,423	28,324	28,324

Notes: Cluster robust s.e. in parentheses, * significant at 10%, ** significant at 5%, *** significant at 1%

increases plant productivity. As highlighted in the theoretical section, this might be in partly linked to higher transaction and communication costs when the same amount of total worked hours is divided among more part-time employees rather than fewer full-time ones. Hence, the real issue in increasing female participation is not a different productivity of female employees, but rather the fact that they might not want to take on full-time positions.

As for increasing retirement age, the evidence points to a decrease in productivity of plants with a larger share of older (55+) employees. This effect is significant in all models (including the within-transformation FE) with the only exception of the FE with first-differences. This results seem to point at the fact that the extra human capital acquired by older employees through experience does not compensate for other issues related to older workers (such as being more expensive, having a more obsolete set of skills, more health issues or even being discouraged by being forced by the system to work longer). On the other hand, very young employees do not seem to increase productivity either. The coefficient on young workers (15–24) is only significantly positive in the OLS specification, but not in the other models. All in all, our results, confirm that the most productive workers are those in the middle age group, i.e. between 25 and 54. Policy-wise the European governments might want to take this loss of productivity due to older workers into account when increasing statutory retirement age. However, the effect on productivity is not large in magnitude. By looking at the elasticity of a marginal change of the employment on older worker, it becomes evident: the effect is economically negligible.[6]

As for the third channel to reduce dependency rate, i.e. the employment of immigrants, the evidence is mixed. The first-difference FE and the RE models point at a weakly significant negative effect on productivity of low-skilled migrants. Other work by Chiswick and Miller (2008, 2009) and Prokic-Breuer and McManus (2016) concludes that foreign employees may be forced or self-select in less productive jobs and occupations, and thus be in jobs for which they are over-educated. However, because we assign workers to the group of low-skilled and high-skilled based on their occupation and thus, their task-content, we do partially control for the issue of selectivity and the results are less biased. Moreover, the OLS and RE models point at a negative effect of productivity of even high-skilled migrants. This last result is the most surprising, although it disappears in the two preferred FE specifications. Considering at the diversity among the foreigners employed, we find a positive effect for the low-skilled and high-skilled migrants in the OLS and RE model, an insignificant result in the FE approach and a significant negative result in the FD estimation, which however suffers under less precise estimates.

One reason for the mixed evidence might be that there occurs a clustering of migrants into less productive firms which cannot effort paying higher wages. Because we control for region type, firm size and industry fixed effects, the results

---

[6]If policy makers aim is to increase the employment of prime-aged workers from 9.7 % (which is the sample mean) to 15%, for example, then the reduction of GVA per employee is approximately 0.69 € at the sample mean of GVA per employee (which is 158.69 €).

of the OLS and RE models absorb differences in immigrant employment between firms relating to these factors: the results depend on a comparison of immigrant employment of firms within the same region, industry and firm size. The firm that employs a higher share of immigrants is less productive than another one (OLS and RE). In local labor markets firms compete in employees and thus, less productive ones may fill their vacancies with immigrants (who may accept lower wages). In the FE model all between firm information is absorbed and the effect becomes insignificant. Therefore, the results indicate a selectivity of migrants into less-productive firms but the firms do not seem to be negatively affected by employing immigrants. Although more work is needed on this point, this result would not be a good news from a policy perspective because it would point at some problem related to the employment of immigrants, either in the form of discrimination by other workers, higher firm-internal communication costs and language barriers or selectivity combined with clustering into low productivity firms.

4.2   Other Control Variables

Although the other control variables are not our variables of interest, some results are worth at least mentioning. Sole traders are less productive and foreign-owned plants are found to be more productive, but both effects are not significant in the two FE models. Newer equipment and machinery is strongly positively correlated with higher productivity, which comes as no surprise. Younger plants (0–4 years) are less productive but only in the OLS and RE models. Mid-age plants (5–14 years) are found to be more productive in the preferred FE (within-transformation) model. Both branches and headquarters are found to be more productive. Finally, more productive plants also pay higher average salaries. Although the explanatory variables are lagged and conditional on region type and industry fixed effects we cannot completely exclude endogeneity or self-selection issues here. It is not surprising that salaries are higher where productivity is higher since the two are linked. However, Brunow and Blien (2015) explicitly consider the endogeneity of wages in a similar setting as in this study; their evidence shows little changes in other characteristics. We take this result and assume that at least our results are not strongly biased due to the endogeneity of wages.

5   Conclusions

Our chapter presents a first analysis of the effects of the channels to reduce dependency ratio on plant productivity in Germany. Of the three channels considered, i.e. increase female participation, increase elderly participation and immigration, the least problematic for productivity seems to be female participation, although the effect of part-time work needs to be monitored.

The results on the other two channels, especially immigration, are more mixed and require further research to look at them in more detail (e.g. by looking at specific occupations and/or industries rather than the whole economy). It is unclear, at the moment, if these insignificant and mixed results are due to a large heterogeneity among immigrant workers in terms of job and sector chosen or a selectivity of immigrants in potentially less-productive firms.

Although our work has limitations and it is just a first attempt to shed light on the links between increasing the size of the working-age population and firm productivity, it clearly shows that the three channels analyzed are not perfect substitutes and might have very different consequences for the national economy. As such, they are worth further investigation to better inform policy makers around the world, especially in countries, such as the European countries experiencing low fertility rates and the fear of a shrinking working population.

A.1   Appendix

Table 10.3 Number of observations by year

Year	No. of observations
1995	3463
1996	3647
1997	4002
1998	4334
1999	6043
2000	8683
2001	8400
2002	8455
2003	7007
2004	8248
2005	7689
2006	7631
2007	7640
2008	7597
2009	7558

References

Amuedo-Dorantes C, De La Rica S (2011) Complements or substitutes? Task specialization by gender and nativity in Spain. Labour Econ 18:697–707

Borjas GJ (1995) The internationalization of the U.S. labor market and the wage structure. Econ Policy Rev 1(1):1–6

Brunow S, Blien U (2014) Effects of cultural diversity on individual establishments. Int J Manpow 35:166–186

Brunow S, Blien U (2015) Agglomeration effects on labor productivity: an assessment with microdata. Region 2(1):33–53

Brunow S, Miersch V (2015) Innovation capacity, workforce diversity and intra-industrial externalities: a study of German establishments. In: Kourtit K, Nijkamp P, Stough RR (eds) The rise of the city. Spatial dynamics in the urban century, New Horizons in Regional Science. Elgar, London, pp 188–222

Brunow S, Nijkamp P (2016) The impact of a culturally diverse workforce on firms' revenues and productivity: an empirical investigation on Germany. Int Reg Sci Rev 41:62–85 online first, 24 pages

Brunow S, Stockinger B (2015) Establishments cultural diversity and innovation: evidence from Germany. In: Nijkamp P, Poot J, Bakens J (eds) The economics of cultural diversity. Elgar, Cheltenham, pp 235–269

Card D (2005) Is the new immigration really so bad? Econ J 115(507):F300–F323

Chiswick BR, Miller PW (2008) Why is the payoff to schooling smaller for immigrants? Labour Econ 15(6):1317–1340

Chiswick BR, Miller PW (2009) The international transferability of immigrants' human capital. Econ Educ Rev 28(2):162–169

D'Amuri F, Ottaviano GIP, Peri G (2010) The labor market impact of immigration in Western Germany in the 1990's. Eur Econ Rev 54:550–570

Dustmann C, Frattini T, Glitz A (2007) The impact of migration: a review of the economic evidence. CReAM Final Report 11/07

Dustmann C, Frattini T, Preston IP (2012) The effect of immigration along the distribution of wages. Rev Econ Stud 80:145–173

Greenwood MJ, Hunt G, Kohli U (1996) The short-run and long-run factor-market consequences of immigration to the United States. J Reg Sci 36(1):43–66

Hellerstein JK, Neumark D (1995) Are earnings profiles steeper than productivity profiles? Evidence from Israeli firm-level data. J Hum Resour 30:89–112

Hellerstein JK, Neumark D, Troske KR (1999) Wages, productivity, and worker characteristics: evidence from plant-level production functions and wage equations. J Labor Econ 17:409–446

Lundberg E (1961) Produktivitet och rdntabilitet: studier i kapitalets betydelse inom svenskt ndringsliv. Studieförb. Näringsliv o. samhälle, Stockholm

Malmberg B, Lindh T, Halvarsson M (2008) Productivity consequences of workforce aging: stagnation or Horndal effect? Popul Dev Rev 34:238–256

Mahlberg B, Freund I, Cuaresma JC, Prskawetz A (2013) Ageing, productivity and wages in Austria. Labour Econ 22:5–15

Niebuhr A (2010) Migration and innovation: does cultural diversity matter for regional R&D activity? Pap Reg Sci 89(3):563–585

Orrenius PM, Zavodny M (2003) Do amnesty programs reduce undocumented immigration? Evidence from Irca. Demography 40(3):437–450

Ottaviano GIP, Peri G (2005) Cities and cultures. J Urban Econ 58:304–337

Ottaviano GIP, Peri G (2008) Immigration and national wages: clarifying the theory and the empirics, NBER Working Papers, 14188

Ottaviano GIP, Peri G (2012) Rethinking the effect of immigration on wages. J Eur Econ Assoc 10:152–197

Ozgen C, Nijkamp P, Poot J (2013) The impact of cultural diversity on firm innovation: evidence from Dutch micro-data. IZA J Migr 2:18

Parrotta P, Pozzoli D, Pytlikova M (2014a) The nexus between labor diversity and firm's innovation. J Popul Econ 27:303–364

Parrotta P, Pozzoli D, Pytlikova M (2014b) Labor diversity and firm productivity. Eur Econ Rev 66:144–179

Paserman MD (2013) Do high-skill immigrants raise productivity? Evidence from Israeli manufacturing firms, 1990-1999. IZA J Migr 2:6

Peri G (2007) Immigrants' complementaries and native wages: evidence from California, NBER Working Papers 12956

Prokic-Breuer T, McManus PA (2016) Immigrant educational mismatch in Western Europe, apparent or real? Eur Soc Rev 32(3):411–438

Suedekum J, Wolf K, Blien U (2014) Cultural diversity and local labour markets. Reg Stud 48(1):173–191

Trax M, Brunow S, Suedekum J (2015) Cultural diversity and plant level productivity. Reg Sci Urban Econ 53:85–96

Zwick T, Göbel C (2013) Are personnel measures effective in increasing productivity of old workers? Labour Econ 22:80–93

Part III
Regional Labor Market Transitions, Aging and Migration

Chapter 11
Demographic Aging and Employment Dynamics in German Regions: Modeling Regional Heterogeneity

Thomas de Graaff, Daniel Arribas-Bel, and Ceren Ozgen

1 Introduction

Many European countries witness the persistence of high youth unemployment rates over decades despite a steady decline in the ratio of youth population to working-age population. The decrease in relative youth shares due to demographic aging did not improve the chronic unemployment of youth across Europe. Long-term unemployment rates are even more worrying, being record high after the 2008 financial crisis. The youth unemployment rate is twice as high as the overall unemployment rate in the EU where the aggregate statistics actually mask large differences between countries (e.g., Germany sees the lowest youth unemployment rate of 7% and Greece the highest with 50%).[1] These trends are contrary to the expectations that the decline in the supply of youth workers would lead to lower youth unemployment rates. Moreover, country level analysis makes mapping the relationship between demographic aging and labour market outcomes of the youth workers particularly more challenging, as there is a large variation across regions

---

[1] http://ec.europa.eu/social/main.jsp?catId=1036, Accessed on September 23rd, 2016.

T. de Graaff (✉)
Vrije Universiteit Amsterdam, Amsterdam, Netherlands
e-mail: t.de.graaff@vu.nl

D. Arribas-Bel
University of Liverpool, Liverpool, UK
e-mail: D.Arribas-Bel@liverpool.ac.uk

C. Ozgen
University of Birmingham, Birmingham, UK

IZA, Bonn, Germany

© Springer International Publishing AG, part of Springer Nature 2018
U. Blien et al. (eds.), *Modelling Aging and Migration Effects on Spatial Labor Markets*, Advances in Spatial Science,
https://doi.org/10.1007/978-3-319-68563-2_11

in the way they withstand demographic shocks. This is because a supply impact of youth population on employment and unemployment rates can be materialized in a number of ways. Youth population is typically unexperienced and lack specific information about labour markets. This not only leads to poor matching of workers with employers, but also increases on the job search due to skills mismatch of workers' qualifications with job-specific requirements. Therefore, an increase in the youth share would directly influence the employment opportunities available to others in the same age cohorts. Additionally, differently aged cohorts may impact each other to the extent of the substitutability between the workers, and between those in different skill groups (Biagi and Lucifora 2008). The magnitude of the impact would, however, depend on the degree of substitution among these groups. Labor market policies, economic downturns and business cycles, and rigidity of labour market institutions are other factors which intervene with this supply-demand adjustment.

Various studies already addressed the possible mechanisms through which the increase in youth share of total working age population may impact the employment opportunities of their own cohort while at the same time impact other age groups as well. Empirical evidence have repeatedly found cohort size to be an important determinant of (un-)employment. One of the very early studies by Bloom et al. (1988), by documenting the findings of 18 studies, launched a wide discussion on cohort size effects of the youth population on labour markets. They show that there is general agreement in the literature on the wage and employment impacts: entry of large cohorts of a certain age group adversely effected the wage and employment opportunities of the same cohort in relative terms. Korenman and Neumark (2000), in another influential work, extend the analysis of Bloom et al. (1988), by using panel data on 15 OECD countries for the period 1970–1994. They predict elasticities between youth unemployment and cohort size of around 0.5. A conflicting but influential result from the US case provided by Shimer (2001) presents much larger and *negative* impacts of large youth cohorts on both youth and adult unemployment rates. His theoretical model rationales his findings such that, assuming labour market frictions, employee's on the job search behaviour will benefit himself, but also firms as the hiring costs are lower in younger labour markets. This will then consequently lead to job creation which would also improve employment of older workers. A significant contribution to emphasise from these conflicting findings is that in different country contexts not only the impacts can vary, but also the mechanisms through which youth cohorts alter employment prospects of their own and other cohorts.

A number of studies from a European perspective produced mixed results in favour of both Shimer (2001) and Korenman and Neumark (2000). For example, by using a long panel of population and (un-)employment data with ample information on age and gender groups, Garloff et al. (2013) show that labour market entry cohort size is an important determinant of employment and unemployment rates in

Western Germany. In contrast to Shimer (2001) they find that small entry cohorts are likely to decrease the unemployment rates and small youth cohort entry increases the employment rates. Foote (2007) reports similar findings from the US labour market, while he demonstrates that the findings are sensitive to correcting for spatial correlation. The cross-sectional dependencies should be taken into account, as the regions' response to demographic shocks can be rather similar based on commuting or similarities in labour market structure of the adjacent regions. Skans (2005) points out contrasting findings from Sweden such that youth workers benefit from being in labour markets with large youth cohorts, where his findings confirms those of Shimer (2001). Biagi and Lucifora (2008) extend these analyses by introducing the role of education. In the period 1975–2002 in European countries, they disaggregate the data by education level and cohorts to analyse whether the unemployment rates are impacted differently by cohort size and education shocks simultaneously. A significant point they raise is the importance of demand in accommodating demographic and education shocks and the imperfect substitution between different skill groups. In advance economies, a demographic shock, for example a higher share of more educated workers can be accommodated better, if it coincides with a positive aggregate demand for skilled labour. They indeed show that higher educated and adult workers experience lower unemployment rates. Finally, Moffat and Roth (2013) study how the probability of being unemployed changes with the nationally and regionally defined age-cohort size. They use a more flexible (wider) definition to identify the age cohorts and utilise data from the European countries. They report that once the analysis is conducted at the regional level rather than the national level, the age-cohort size effect on the probability to become unemployed is stronger. Subsequently, the studies show a large heterogeneity in a number of dimensions from spatial scales to methods, from characteristics of the labour markets to characteristics of the youth cohorts.

A shortcoming of the literature has been its inadequacy to reconcile with variation of findings at differing level of spatial aggregation. Furthermore, though many studies are conducted at the regional level, it has still been not clear how regions' heterogeneous responses to demographic aging should be taken on board in policy making. An original contribution we make to this literature is to study regional heterogeneity, while showing regions even within the same country can be differently impacted by the same demographic shocks. In other words, the focus is on the possible variation in regions' responses to the changes in the relative share of the youth population. Theoretically, each region within a country can react uniquely to a supply shock of labour, while it is plausible to assume a certain degree of generality among sub-group of regions considering the similarity in production structure, location characteristics and demographic attributes. Our innovative methodological approach which employs a latent class analysis combined with self-organizing maps (SOM) displays a powerful segmentation and analysis of these sub-groups of homogeneous regions that show a similar pattern towards supply of youth population share in working-age workers. The next section discusses how we can model and map out regional heterogeneity, and especially how we can interpret finite mixture output using self-organizing maps. Section 3 provides an application of our proposed techniques by looking at the impact of youth shares on employment rates in Germany. The final concludes and offers suggestions for further research.

2 Modeling Regional Heterogeneity

The standard approach to model regional heterogeneity is to apply a fixed effects model where each region is modeled with its own level effect. In Sect. 2.1 we discuss this approach and argue that the standard fixed effects model can be easily extended by a model with varying slope parameters—sort of like a multilevel model—if there are repeated observations over time. Varying slope parameters are appropriate when unobserved variables interact with the independent variables. For example, the impact of regional population growth on regional GDP growth might interact with the educational level of the regional population. Such a modelling approach has two large disadvantages. First, the estimation produces inefficient and usually inconsistent parameter estimates. Namely, most fixed effects (and most slope parameters for that matter) are not statistically different from each other and it is well known that when the time period is relatively short (as is usually the case) fixed effects suffer from an inconsistency problem. Secondly, if one is interested in what drives the underlying (regional) heterogeneity, then using a fixed effects approach is not appropriate as well as the fixed effects are typically discarded from the analysis.[2] In Sect. 2.2 we deal with these disadvantages by employing a finite mixture model (henceforth as well denoted as FMM), a latent class cluster analysis that enables us to group region in clusters with similar parameter estimates. This is similar to the method of spatial regimes, although with a finite mixture estimation we are not restricted to assign regions *exogenously* into groups. One general drawback of cluster analysis, is that the resulting clusters are hard to interpret and to visualise. Therefore, we finally apply in Sect. 2.3 a self-organising map approach which allows us to display the varying multivariate regional characteristics in geographic space (see, e.g., Spielman and Folch 2015).

2.1 Regional Heterogeneity

We start by assuming that one is interested in the effect of a regional input variable x on a regional output variable y and that she has repeated observations over a set of regions. Then a straightforward and intuitive appealing model would be the

---

[2]One can apply second-stage models, where the first stage estimates the fixed effects and the second stage analyses the determinants of those fixed effects. However, note again, that this is only an analysis on the levels and not on the slopes.

following linear regression model:

$$y_{rt} = \beta_0 + \beta_1 x_{rt} + \epsilon_{rt}, \tag{11.1}$$

where r denotes the region ($r \in 1, \ldots R$), t the year ($t \in 1, \ldots T$) and ϵ an i.i.d. error term. The parameter β_0 denotes a level effect and β_1 is our parameter of interest and gives the marginal effect of x on y or $\frac{dy}{dx}$.

If there is another regional variable z that is correlated with both y and x, then our estimation of β_1 is *biased*, or $\mathbf{E}(\hat{\beta}_1) \neq \beta_1$ (see, e.g., Stock and Watson 2003). If z is known then including z in model (11.1) removes the bias. Unfortunately, z is very often not known or difficult to measure. However, by assuming that z enters the model *linearly* and does not vary over time—thus as $y_{rt} = \beta_0 + \beta_1 x_{rt} + \gamma z_r + \epsilon_{rt}$—, one can control for z by using the following fixed model:

$$y_{rt} = \beta_{0,r} + \beta_1 x_{rt} + \epsilon_{rt} \tag{11.2}$$

Here, $\beta_{0,r}$ now controls for all variables (including z) which enters the model linearly and do not vary over time.

However, the unobserved variable z might as well *interact* with the impact of x on y, so that in the most simplified version the model in fact reads as: $y_{rt} = \beta_0 + \beta_1(z_r \times x_{rt}) + \gamma z_r + \epsilon_{rt}$. Given that there are repeated regional observations the model can now be estimated as:

$$y_{rt} = \alpha_{0,r} + \beta_{1,r} x_{rt} + \epsilon_{rt}, \tag{11.3}$$

where both the level and the slope parameter is regional specific. Note that this is rather data demanding. Given that there are R regions, one need at least $2R + 1$ observations. Or the number of years should be at least three when there is a symmetric panel. Moreover, for both *consistent* level and slope parameters, the temporal dimension should be sufficiently large (say more than 40 time periods). Usually, the latter is not the case. Therefore models such as (11.3) are seldom applied, although the possibility of significant regional heterogeneity in the effect parameter $\beta_{1,r}$ is widely recognized.

One way to overcome this inefficiency is a cluster analysis in the form of multivariate mixture model, which is dealt with in the next subsection.

2.2 Regional Finite Mixture Modelling

Instead of estimating separate parameters for each region, it is far more (statistically) efficient and even consistent to estimate separate parameters for *groups* of regions. Assume that there are c more or less homogeneous groups of regions, then model (11.3) becomes:

$$y_{rt} = \beta_{0,c} + \beta_{1,c}x_{rt} + \epsilon_{rt}, \tag{11.4}$$

where the number of parameters now amount to $c \times k$, with c being the number of groups and k the number of parameters.

To do so, we adopt a finite (or multivariate) mixture modelling approach. A statistical technique which became especially popular since the 1990s in marketing (a seminal contribution is Wedel and Kamakura 2012), but since then permeated in other economic fields, although mainly applied in the econometric realm (see, e.g., Deb et al. 1997; Arcidiacono and Jones 2003; Alfo et al. 2008) and in tackling heterogeneity in discrete choice modelling (Greene and Hensher 2003).[3] The approach works as follows.

We divide our sample of regions into an, a priori unknown, number of subsamples (clusters) of regions. So we assume that our sample consists of a mixture of C clusters, with proportions $\pi_1, \ldots, \pi_C$. We can now decompose the density function of y conditional on the parameter vector β as follows:

$$f(y|\beta) = \sum_{c=1}^{C} \pi_c f(y|\beta_c)). \tag{11.5}$$

To estimate model (11.5) usually the expectation maximization (EM) procedure as introduced by Dempster et al. (1977) is applied. It starts by introducing a latent variable, u_{rc}, denoting whether region r belongs to cluster c. Thus:

$$u_{rc} = \begin{cases} 1, & \text{if region } r \text{ belongs to cluster } c \\ 0, & \text{otherwise} \end{cases} \tag{11.6}$$

We then assume the following distribution for u_{rc}:

$$f(\mathbf{u}_r|\boldsymbol{\pi}) = \prod_{r=1}^{R} \pi_r^{z_{rc}}, \tag{11.7}$$

with $\mathbf{u}_r$ a vector of (11.6) for each cluster, c. Let $\mathbf{U}$ denote the matrix of all $\mathbf{u}_r$ then the complete log-likelihood can now be written as:

$$\ln[\mathscr{L}(\beta|y, \mathbf{U})] = \sum_{r=1}^{R}\sum_{c=1}^{C} u_{rc} f(y|\beta_c) + \sum_{r=1}^{R}\sum_{c=1}^{C} u_{rc} \ln(\pi_c). \tag{11.8}$$

---

[3]Interestingly, the underlying algorithm and implementation where only the constants α_c are allowed to vary over groups is heavily applied in labour economics by, e.g., Lancaster (1992), Munch et al. (2006), and De Graaff and Van Leuvensteijn (2013), usually in a multivariate setting where the constants α_c are then argued to remove unobserved heterogeneity.

The EM algorithm now proceeds as follows:

E-step: We estimate the cluster probabilities for each region, so that the probability that region r belongs to cluster c is:

$$\hat{u}_{rc} = \frac{\pi_c \prod_{c=1}^{C} f(\ln(y_{rc}|\beta_c))}{\sum_{g=1}^{C} \pi_g \prod_{c=1}^{C} f(\ln(y_{rc}|\beta_g))}. \tag{11.9}$$

So, in this step, all $\hat{u}_{rc}$ are estimated so that they can be used in the log likelihood given by (11.8).

M-step: First, we need to derive the proportions π_c by applying the equality: $\hat{\pi}_c = \frac{1}{R} \sum_{r=1}^{R} \hat{u}_{rc}$. Using now both $\hat{u}_{rc}$ and $\hat{\pi}_c$ enables us to estimate β by using (11.5) and conventional likelihood procedures. We repeat the E- and M-step until the log likelihood (11.5) stops improving.

Although the EM algorithm is computationally cumbersome it is parsimonious as well. It results in a parameter estimation of C endogeneously and robustly formed clusters. However, cluster analyses are notoriously difficult to interpret and analyse because one not only gets a different set of regression parameters for each cluster, but a full set of probabilities of each region belonging to each cluster. To help visualize, explore, and clarify the clustering outcome we therefore propose to use a self-organising maps as a novel approach for the interpretation of the output of an FMM regression, hence facilitating the understanding of complex regional characteristics in geographic space.

2.3 Interpreting Mixture Modeling Output with Self-Organising Maps

A self-organising map (SOM, Kohonen 2001) is a kind of computational neural network that is able to simultaneously reduce the number of dimensions (*projection*) as well as observations (*quantization*) in a multidimensional data set. Although the mathematics underlying the algorithm are more intricate, the intuition is relatively straightforward. Given that, in this context, it is only required to be able to interpret its output, not necessarily the mechanism by which the algorithm reaches it, this is what we will focus on.[4] The essence of the SOM is to translate the statistical properties of the original dataset (Ω) onto a network of interconnected neurons represented by a two-dimensional grid of hexagons (H). Each of these neurons has a vector of as many dimensions as Ω whose values, after the process of *training* the network, capture the statistical variation contained in Ω. The power

---

[4]For a detailed explanation of the underlying learning mechanism and its implementation, please refer to Kohonen (2001) The analysis in this paper was carried out using the `kohonen` library in the statistical software platform R (Wehrens et al. 2007).

of the SOM resides in the fact that, once the network has been trained and its neurons have *learned* the properties of the original dataset, it is possible to map the original observations onto the network. Because H preserves information topologically, statistical similarity is turned into spatial relationships. This allows to represent multi-dimensional relationships and make intuitive comparisons through a visual display that maps the original observations to the network's neurons. In a sense, this property of the SOM is akin to other projection techniques such as Principal Component Analysis (PCA) or Multi-Dimensional Scaling (MDS), with the advantage that the output space onto which the data is projected—the network H—is limited and known. Additionally, the non-parametric and learning nature of the SOM algorithm has been shown to be more robust when it comes to capturing complex, non-gaussian relationships (Yan and Thill 2009). In the context of this paper, we use the SOM to explore the distribution of the probability that each German region belongs to each of the clusters specified by the FMM model. It is important to note that this is in essence a multi-dimensional dataset: we have several probabilities associated to every region. FMM output returns probabilities for each region to belong to each cluster (though in some cases probability for a region can be zero in well segmented distributions). For a given region r, the probability of belonging to different clusters can vary in magnitude. This makes visualizing it at once difficult simply because regions may belong to multiple clusters at the same time, while with varying probabilities. The usual approach in the literature to work around this challenge is to implicitly reduce the dimensionality to a single one, the cluster for which every region displays a highest probability of belonging. In other words, this is equivalent to "rounding up" the highest probability of each region to one, and setting all the others to zero, then focusing only on the former one. Although convenient this approach implies simplifying the FMM output greatly and it imposes an artificial degree of certainty about each region's cluster membership. In cases where the set of probabilities are not very far from this case (i.e., when there is only one cluster with a high probability and all the others are negligible), this assumption is reasonable and valid. However, in cases where the situation is less clearcut, this can be a problem, and neglecting the nuances of the distribution of probabilities can lead to incorrect interpretations. In this context, our approach is to feed the set of probabilities (a matrix of R rows and C columns) to the SOM algorithm and use its output to explore how each region r relates to others when it comes to membership to each of the clusters identified by the FMM. This is articulated through the visual display the SOM offers. By plotting in a single graph the similarity between regions based on their probabilities, *as well as* the cluster each region would have received under the traditional methodology, our approach will enable the exploration of nuances and cases where cluster membership is not a clearcut decision. This approach is novel and produces results that help the interpretation of an otherwise complex and obscure output.

3 Empirical Application: Ageing in Germany

3.1 Data

The empirical application of this paper focuses on the impact of regional youth share on employment in German regions. Furthermore, it explores the degree of variation of this impact across the regions. To this end, we have collected repeated observations of regional employment shares—the total number of the employed relative to the population aged between 18 and 64—and youth shares—the number of individuals aged between 18 and 24 relative to the population in the age group 18–64—in Germany.

The data we employ has some distinctive attractive features. First of all, it presents a geographically complete picture of employment and aging dynamics in Germany by covering both Eastern and Western regions in our empirical analysis. Secondly, we use labour market areas defined on the basis of commuting distances, meaning each region represents a self-contained labour market area. Labor market areas can be formed by one or multiple districts (kreise) which are equivalent to a NUTS 3[5] level region. The demarcation of the regions is in line with the definition provided by Kosfeld and Werner (2012). The employment data is obtained from the Institute for Employment Research (IAB), and population variables are constructed by using German Statistical Office data.

Our analysis include 141 labour market areas in the period 2000–2010. Due to a number of restrictions on data availability our sample period is confined to a decade. We control for possible sectoral demand-side shocks regions face by including a measure (the Bartik index)[6] which resorts on occupation data which is broken down on the basis of the complexity of tasks required in each occupation. Using task complexity levels rather than the standard yet very broad sector division has the advantage of properly accounting for the common nature of tasks, that cuts across the sectors and the respective demand conditions. Unfortunately, the occupation data that we use to construct the Bartik index is not available after 2011.

Figure 11.1 displays the geographical distribution of both employment rates (Fig. 11.1a) and youth shares (Fig. 11.1b) across German regions. Clearly,

---

[5]Nomenclature of Territorial Units for Statistics.

[6]The particular measure we employ reads as:

$$\hat{L}_{rt} = \sum_k \left[\frac{E_{k,t}}{E_{k,t-1}} E_{rk,t-1} \right],$$ (11.10)

where $\hat{L}$ is the weighted sum of employment across all sectors k in region r in and year $t - 1$, with the weights being given by the rate of sector-specific employment in year t and year $t - 1$ at the national level. As such, this variable represents the level of employment in region r that is predicted for the case in which employment in each sector grows at the same rate as the corresponding sector at the national level indicated by E. This variable is used as an exogenous measure for demand changes for labour.

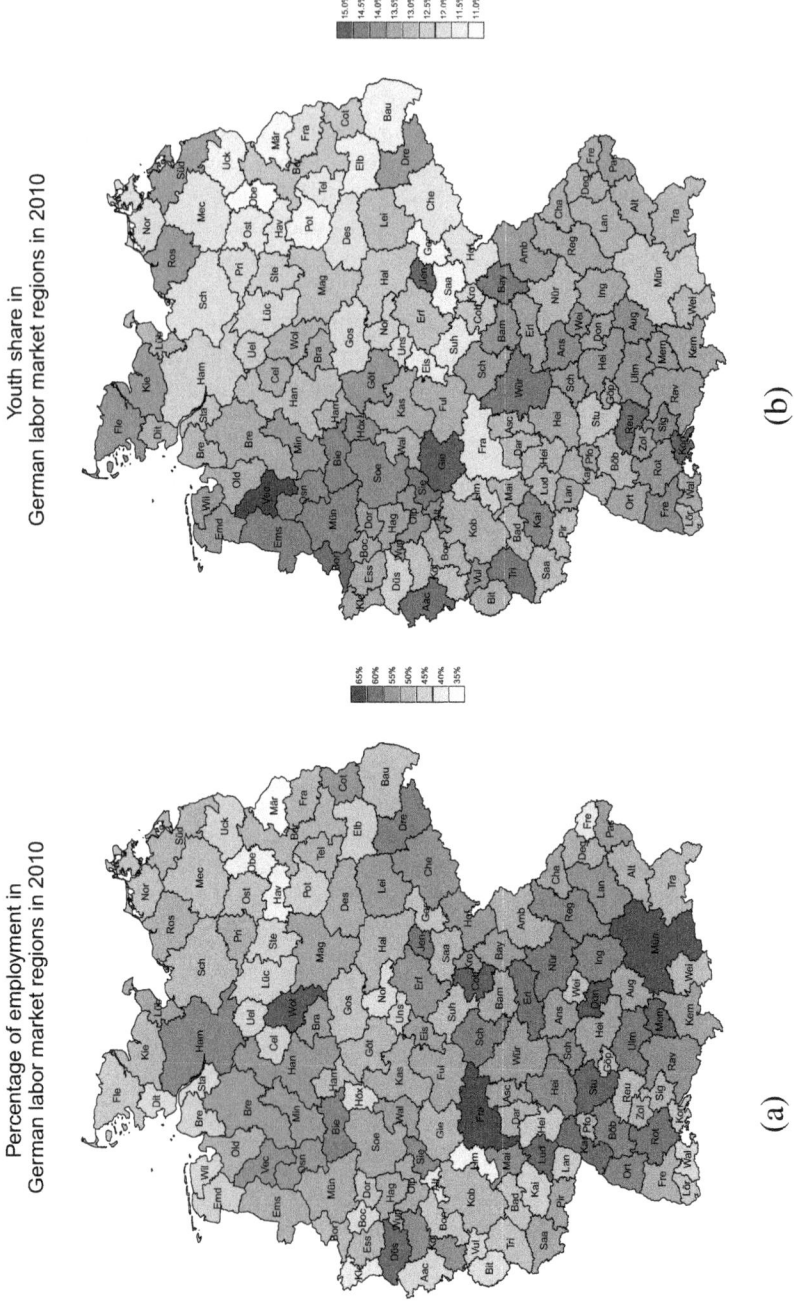

Fig. 11.1 Employment rate and youth share across German regions. (**a**) Employment rate, (**b**) Youth share

there is much variation in regional employment levels ranging from more than 60% in Frankfurt and München to less than 40% in regions as Freiburg and Oberhaven. In general, employment rates are higher in Southern Germany (with some exceptions) and lower in Eastern Germany. There is much less variation in youth shares which range from 11% to 15%. The lowest youth shares in Germany can be found in Eastern Germany (and Frankfurt) and the regions that host the highest share of youth is in Western Germany.

3.2 The Generic Impact of Youth Shares on Regional Employment Rates

We start our analysis by first applying our linear model (11.1) in natural logarithmic form as follows:

$$\ln(E_{rt}) = \beta_0 + \beta_1 \ln(YS_{rt}) + \beta_2 B_{rt} + v_t + \epsilon_{rt}, \qquad (11.11)$$

where E_{rt} defines the employment rate in region r, measured as the number of workers between 18 and 64 years old, divided by the working population between 18 and 64 years old. YS denotes the youth share in region r, and it is defined as the number of individuals between 18 and 25 years old divided by the working population between 18 and 64 years old in the same region. B is the Bartik index which controls for regional specific demand effects and v_t denotes a vector of year specific effects.

Model 1 in Table 11.1 provides the estimation results of the model (11.11). Clearly, there is a statistically significant negative impact of youth share on employment rate, where in this model the elasticity is around -0.2. Allowing

Table 11.1 Generic impact of youth share (18–64) on log(employment rate)

	log(employment)			
	OLS	First-diff	First-diff	First-diff IV
	Model 1	Model 2	Model 3	Model 4
log(Youth share)	−0.202***	−0.153***	−0.174***	−0.255***
	(0.060)	(0.018)	(0.023)	(0.004)
Bartik index	0.058***	0.634***	0.260***	0.285***
	(0.007)	(0.023)	(0.030)	(0.021)
Region first-differenced	No	Yes	Yes	Yes
Time dummies	No	No	Yes	Yes
N	1410	1269	1269	1269
R^2	0.272	0.561	0.755	0.748

*p<0.05, **p< 0.01, ***p<0.001

for regional fixed effects by estimating model (11.2) leads to Models 2 and 3 of Table 11.1.[7]

Youth shares still have a significant negative impact on regional unemployment rates, but the size of the elasticity increased slightly to around -0.15. Thus, allowing for regional heterogeneity that has a linear impact on employment rates has a moderate impact on the size of the estimate.

An important issue is the potential endogeneity that would bias the OLS estimation. Young people are likely to sort systematically to regions with better employment opportunities. We address this by instrumental variables (IV) estimation. Our identification relies on predicting the size of youth cohort that currently resides in labour market areas in our sample with the young cohort lagged by 15 years. So our instrument is the log of the number of individuals aged between 3 and 9 relative to the population in age groups 3–49, 15 years prior to the study period. It is likely that the cohort 15 years past cannot be attracted by economic opportunities of today while the size of the age groups of past is likely to strongly correlate with the size of the age groups of today. The first-stage statistics strongly confirm our expectation. Model 4 of Table 11.1 displays the IV regression. The result is in line with the impact found in OLS estimations; youth share has a negative and statistically significant impact on employment rate at 1% level. The magnitude of the predicted coefficients is fairly similar, which reduces our concerns for sorting of youth.

In addition, although we correct for demand side effects, one might be concerned with the possibility that youth cohorts are influenced by employment rates, mostly by interregional migration. Using instrumental variables, we reconfirm Garloff et al. (2013) and show that the potential endogeneity bias (where one of which underlying drives can be migration of young employees to highly prosperous areas) does not overturn our findings neither in terms of magnitude nor significance of the estimated relationship.[8]

Combining clustering and instrumental variable estimations is still however cumbersome. Therefore we do not focus on IV estimations within FMM context, given the IV-panel estimation results of above. Next, we assess whether unobserved variables might actually interact with the impact of youth share.

---

[7]Because of strong temporal autocorrelation in both the employment rates and the youth shares, we estimate model (11.2) by applying first differencing. Thus, we estimate: $\ln(E_{r,t}) - \ln(E_{r,t-1}) = \beta_1(\ln(YS_{r,t}) - \ln(YS_{r,t-1})) + (\epsilon_{r,t} - \epsilon_{r,t-1})$. Although less efficient than the usual within estimator, first differencing requires less strong identification assumptions. For the linear model, this should only affect the standard errors and indeed, both fixed effects estimation strategies lead to similar results. It matters however for the clustering analysis.

[8]Sander (2014) points out that the internal migration patterns in Germany have been predominantly within East Germany, while significant trends to urban cores from nearby suburban areas as well as metropolitan hinterlands during our study period. At the same time young adults with families out-migrated to urban agglomerations in many non-metropolitan cities. We expect that using labour market areas which includes daily commuting patterns and FMM for our analysis to some extent should tackle with potential bias internal migration patterns might cause.

3.3 Region Slope Parameters

The results of an estimation of model (11.3) are depicted in Fig. 11.2. So, every region now is associated with a value of $\beta_{1,r}$. Taken at face-value, there is an enormous regional variation in $\beta_{1,r}$, ranging from -1 to 1. Unfortunately, most of these estimates are not statistically significant and even not consistent, given that the total number of time periods T per region r is 10. So, every $\beta_{1,r}$ is based on ten observations, which is too few to comply with the usual properties of ordinary least squares.

Spatial distribution of beta coefficients across Germany

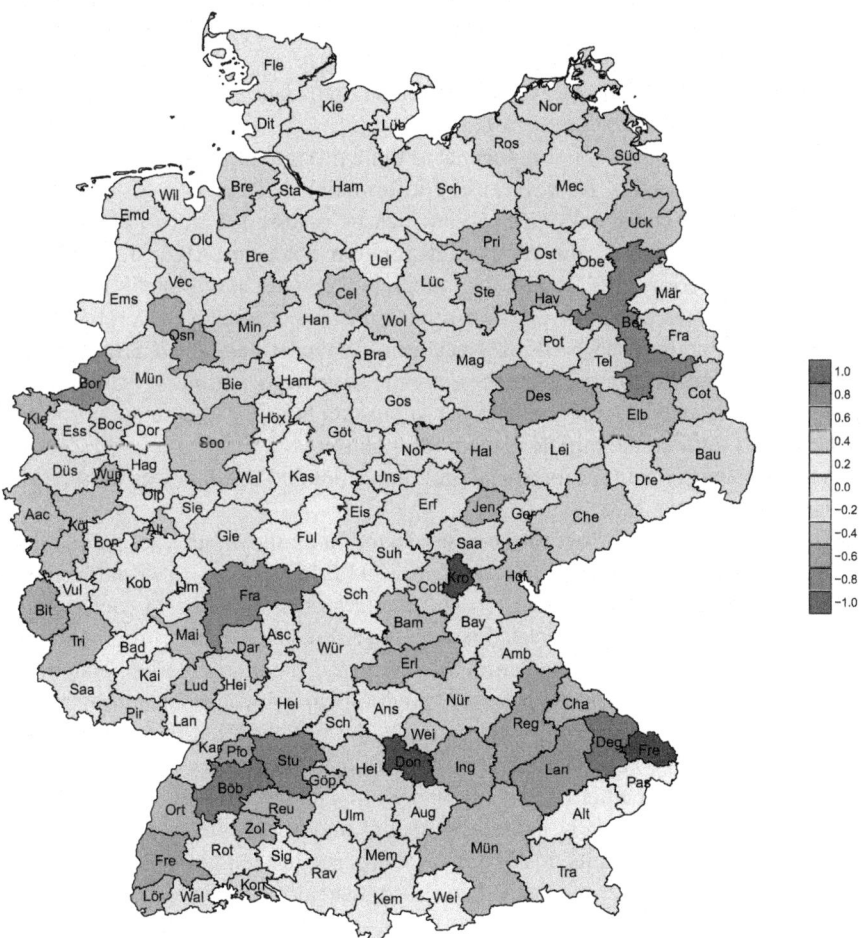

Fig. 11.2 Regional specific varying impacts of the youth share on the employment rate

Clearly, however, there is evidence that there is a large regional variation in the impact of regional youth shares on employment rates. To reveal this spatial pattern in a consistent manner, we therefore resort to estimating our clustering model of (11.4).

3.4 Finite Mixture Results

The exact model we estimate deviates slightly from (11.4) and boils down to:

$$\ln(E_{rt}) = \beta_{0,r} + \beta_{1,c} \ln(YS_{rt}) + \beta_{2,c} B_{rt} + v_{t,c} + \epsilon_{rt}, \tag{11.12}$$

where t denotes a vector of year dummies. Note that this is a very exhaustive model, where we allow for regional fixed effects with $\beta_{0,r}$ and cluster specific impact of youth share $\beta_{1,c}$, regional demand effects $\beta_{2,c}$ and year effects $v_{t,c}$. Before we estimate an FMM, we first difference our data and effectively remove the regional fixed effects.

The number of clusters or components in finite mixture modelling is determined by the researcher herself. However, using information criteria the optimal number of clusters from a statistical point of view can be assessed. Figure 11.3 provides three information criteria: the Akaike information criterion (AIC), the Bayesian information criterion (BIC), and the integrated classification likelihood (ICL) criterion. The latter two are well known to 'punish' the criterion severely for the number of parameters used. Strikingly, according to the BIC and the ICL the optimal number of clusters is 2 (in our case, these are the largest city regions versus the rest). According to the AIC the optimal number of clusters is 8. For illustration purposes, we choose to settle in the middle and opt for 4 clusters.

When allowing for four clusters we get the estimation results of model (11.12) as displayed in Table 11.2.

As we focus on the impact of the youth share on employment rate, we see that the impact differs from -0.33 (cluster 2) to -0.06 (cluster 3). To visualise these clusters, Fig. 11.4 displays the cluster with the largest probability for each region. Clearly, there is spatial autocorrelation except for cluster 2. This cluster contains the largest and most important cities of Germany, including Berlin, Hamburg, Munich and Frankfurt. Cluster 1 is formed predominantly by clusters in the northern and western part of the cluster (and some in the periphery). Cluster 3 displays mostly regions in Eastern Germany and some in the periphery and cluster 4 is a very distinctively southern Germany and Ruhr area phenomenon. This spatial autocorrelation is most likely caused by spatial unobserved heterogeneity where variables as local institutions, history and sector structure might play an important role. Note that the impact of youth shares is statistically similar for these clusters 1 and 4. The difference is formed by the Bartik index, where cluster 4 seems to be more affected by regional demand effects.

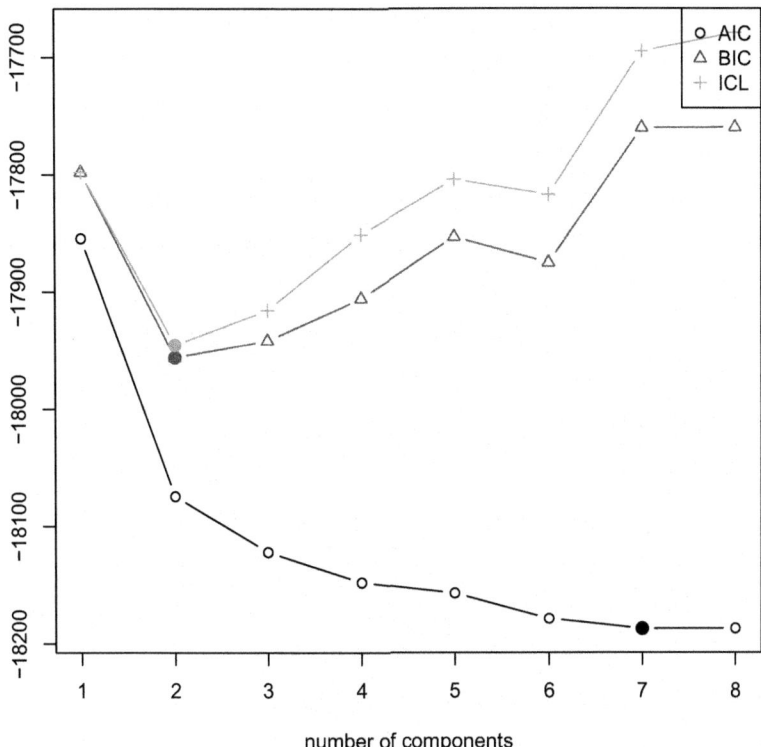

Fig. 11.3 Number of clusters and information criteria

Table 11.2 Finite mixture estimation results (dependent variable: ln(Employment rate))

	Cluster			
	1	2	3	4
ln(Youth share)	−0.206***	−0.329**	−0.056*	−0.258***
	(0.033)	(0.108)	(0.026)	(0.033)
Bartik index	0.184***	0.272**	0.277***	0.336***
	(0.060)	(0.085)	(0.042)	(0.040)
Region fixed effects	Yes	Yes	Yes	Yes
Year fixed effects	Yes	Yes	Yes	Yes
N	1269	1269	1269	1269

*p<0.05, **p<0.01, ***p<0.001

As FMM works each region received a probability to 'belong' to a cluster. Typically, these probabilities are close to 0 or 1 (about 65% of the regions have a dominant probability larger than 0.8). However, some regions are more difficult to classify and have significant probabilities for two clusters or more (in this case, usually for cluster 1 and 4). To visualise these probabilities, the next subsection applies a SOM analysis.

Spatial distribution of clusters across Germany

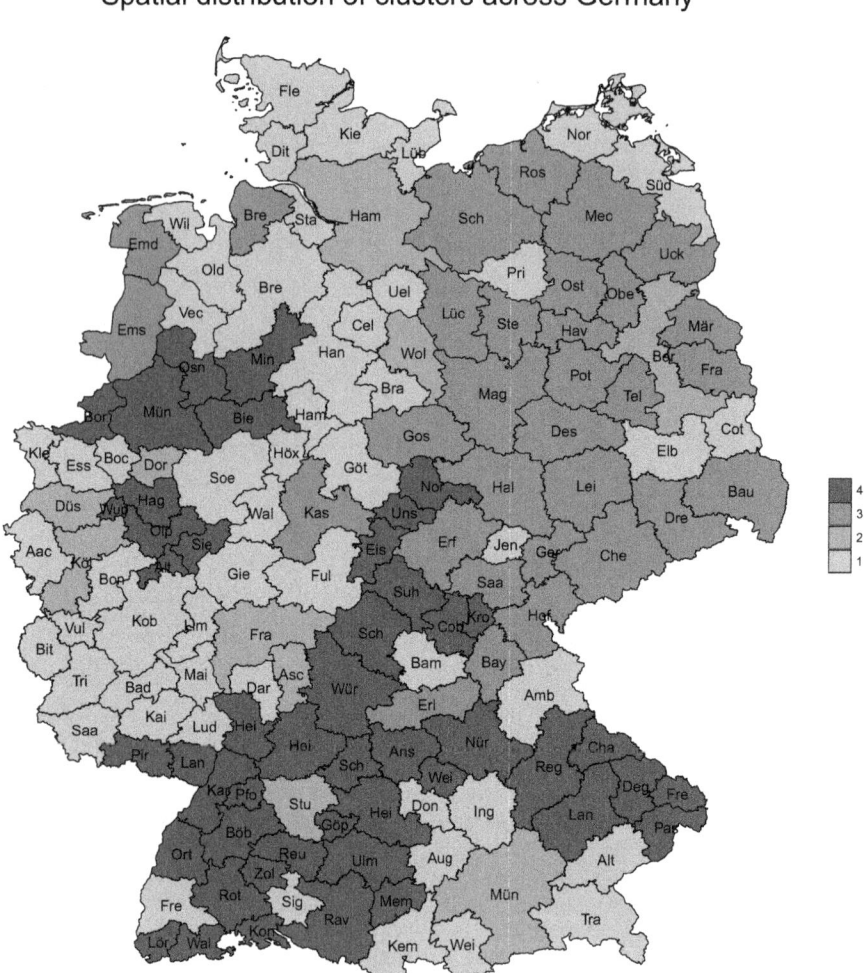

Fig. 11.4 Clusters in Germany of the impact on employment rates

3.5 A Self-Organising Map of Ageing Regions in Germany

Figure 11.5a displays the SOM output. We use 900 neurons laid out as a 30 by 30 grid in order to allow the 141 regions to spread freely within the output space. The figure presents the location where the region has been assigned in the network although, for visibility regions, we slightly alter their location randomly. As explained above, the properties of the SOM algorithm imply that the location of each observation in the network is representative of its statistical attributes. Thus, being similar in the attribute space translates into being located nearby in the SOM

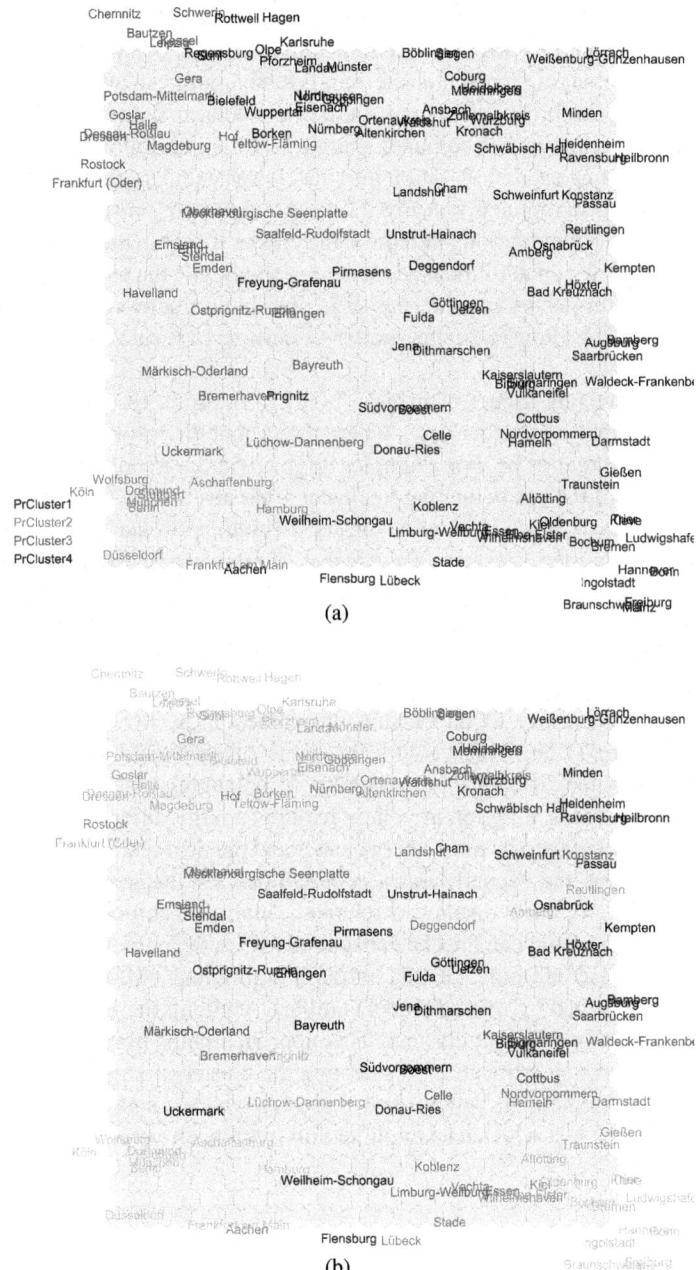

Fig. 11.5 SOM of probabilities. (**a**) Cluster memberships, (**b**) Stability of membership

space. This means that, for instance, Chemnitz and Bautzen, both regions located in the top-left corner of the SOM can be assumed to have a very similar distribution of probabilities of belonging to each clustering. Equally, both can also be assumed to have a rather different profile than Ingolstadt, in the bottom-right corner.

The name of each region is coloured using a scheme that follows the traditional approach of assigning each observation into the cluster with largest probability (and that is displayed geographically in Fig. 11.4). As expected, most regions that the traditional approach would group into the same cluster locate in the same part of the SOM. This allows for an additional advantage of the SOM: the clusters themselves can be explored further by considering their distribution across the network. For example, cluster 2 (yellow) is more similar to cluster 4 (purple) than to cluster 3 (green).

The most interesting aspect of using a SOM to interpret results from a FMM model comes when we consider cases where the probability profile is not as clear-cut as we would like it to be. For example, Prignitz (in the middle of the network) has a probability of 0.48 of belonging to cluster 1 but also one of 0.46 of belonging to cluster 3. As such, it is coloured as cluster 1 (blue), but located close to many others labeled as cluster 3 (green). This degree of nuance and detail is completely eliminated when we adopt the traditional approach, as we would only observe the region is assigned into cluster 1. However, the SOM is capable of representing it in an intuitive and useful way, allowing the researcher to explore the FMM output much more richly.

A complementary way to understand the value of the SOM in this context is provided in Fig. 11.5b, which colors the name of each region on a yellow to purple gradient by the difference in probability of belonging to the two most likely clusters. In other words, a region in yellow features a large difference between the probability of belonging to its most likely cluster and the next one (i.e. the difference between the largest and second largest probabilities for that region is large). In contrast, a region in purple displays a relatively high probability of belonging to more than one cluster and can thus be considered as "on the border". On-the-border regions, which we could only identify through combining FMM with SOM, are those that are impacted by a youth shock similarly while in the FMM output they appear in completely different clusters. This approach helps highlight regions for which the traditional simplification of selecting the cluster of largest probability is a valid approach (regions in yellow) and those for which a significant amount of information may be lost with such simplification (regions in purple).

4 In Conclusion

Demographic aging is a significant concern for many developed countries. In order to correctly address the associated problems, it is crucial to properly identify the needs of the labour markets. In this paper we focus on the impact of youth on regional employment rates in 141 German labour market areas. We show that fixed effects models with varying β coefficients are not adequate to reflect and handle the heterogeneity. By employing an innovative methodology that is combining a latent class analysis with self-organising maps, this research depicts a great deal of variation of how ageing impacts employment opportunities of the working age population at the regional level. Although our OLS and IV estimations are in line with previous research on German local labour markets (e.g., with Garloff et al. (2013))—although contradicts with the work of Shimer (2001), we offer further explanations for a number of issues not yet addressed in the literature.

First, although the OLS predicts an aggregate elasticity for the youth impact on employment rate around -0.2, we find that the elasticities actually vary in the order of -0.06 to -0.33 in 4 types of regions in Germany. FMM analysis partitions Germany into four unique clusters of broader regions, namely metropolitan areas, Southern Germany, West Germany with industrial core and finally Eastern Germany (excluding Berlin). Second, we show that the labour market areas with highest employment rates are hurt the most by a demographic shock of youth share. These are large metro regions like Munich, Frankfurt, Düsseldorf, Stuttgart, Hamburg and Berlin. In contrast, eastern German labour markets which experience significantly large internal migration within, are those which are affected the least from increasing youth population. Note that however, as a result of FMM estimation, typically some regions receive probabilities that allow them to be assigned in more than one of these clusters. SOM helps visually mapping the distribution of these probabilities across all the regions in the analysis. Therefore, this extension allows us to interpret the FMM output in further detail and to identify regions for which a single cluster membership might not reflect the output of the model. Through this approach we are able to exactly pinpoint which regions better embody the characteristics of the cluster and which ones are found to be "on the border" between two clusters. Finally, our results also show that regions exhibit different levels of resilience to regional demand shocks.

Our results imply that policy challenges for demographic ageing require to look beyond a country as a whole. Given the extension in longevity does not meet increase in active labour period, an economic perspective taking regional labour market heterogeneity into account is crucial. Our results are suggestive for policymakers to consider the possible impacts of aging on employment opportunities in varying regional economic contexts both for adults and also for the youth. As shown in our analysis local resources, region's sector structure and characteristics of the local youth workforce are important factors to influence employment rate.As shown in our analysis local resources, region's sector structure and characteristics of the local youth workforce are important factors to influence employment rate. We hope that our methodological application sheds some light on the contrasting empirical findings in the literature and opens new avenues for research to analyse further the determinants behind the differing impacts found, possibly based on the economic character of the labour markets. On the methodological side, this application can be useful for studies trying to uncover a range of issues where there is significant underlying heterogeneity in a number of dimensions of locations, workers, firms and regions.

Acknowledgements Daniel Arribas-Bel and Ceren Ozgen gratefully acknowledge research funding by "Population Ageing and Regional Labour Market Development" project. An edited version of the paper will appear in Modelling Aging and Migration Effects on Spatial Labor Markets book by Springer-Verlag.

References

Alfo M, Trovato G, Waldmann RJ (2008) Testing for country heterogeneity in growth models using a finite mixture approach. J Appl Econ 23(4):487–514

Arcidiacono P, Jones JB (2003) Finite mixture distributions, sequential likelihood and the em algorithm. Econometrica 71(3):933–946

Biagi F, Lucifora C (2008) Demographic and education effects on unemployment in europe. Labour Econ 15(5):1076–1101

Bloom DE, Freeman RB, Korenman SD (1988) The labour-market consequences of generational crowding. Eur J Popul 3(2):131–176

De Graaff T, Van Leuvensteijn M (2013) A european cross-country comparison of the impact of homeownership and transaction costs on job tenure. Reg Stud 47(9):1443–1461

Deb P, Trivedi PK et al (1997) Demand for medical care by the elderly: a finite mixture approach. J Appl Econ 12(3):313–336

Dempster AP, Laird NM, Rubin DB (1977) Maximum likelihood from incomplete data via the em algorithm. J R Stat Soc Ser B Methodol 39:1–38

Foote CL (2007) Space and time in macroeconomic panel data: young workers and state-level unemployment revisited

Garloff A, Pohl C, Schanne N (2013) Do small labor market entry cohorts reduce unemployment? Demogr Res 29:379

Greene WH, Hensher DA (2003) A latent class model for discrete choice analysis: contrasts with mixed logit. Transp Res B Methodol 37(8):681–698

Kohonen T (2001) Self-organizing maps. Springer series in information sciences, vol 30. Springer, Berlin

Korenman S, Neumark D (2000) Cohort crowding and youth labor markets: a cross-national analysis, number January, University of Chicago Press, Chicago

Kosfeld R, Werner D-ÖA (2012), Deutsche arbeitsmarktregionen–neuabgrenzung nach den kreisgebietsreformen 2007–2011. Raumforsch Raumordn 70(1):49–64

Lancaster T (1992) The econometric analysis of transition data, vol 17. Cambridge university press, Cambridge

Moffat J, Roth D (2013) The cohort size-wage relationship in europe, technical report. Philipps-Universität Marburg, Faculty of Business Administration and Economics, Department of Economics (Volkswirtschaftliche Abteilung)

Munch JR, Rosholm M, Svarer M (2006) Are homeowners really more unemployed? Econ J 116(514):991–1013

Sander N (2014) Internal migration in germany, 1995–2010: new insights into east-west migration and re-urbanisation. Comp Popul Stud 39(2):217–246

Shimer R (2001) The impact of young workers on the aggregate labor market. Q J Econ 116:969–1007

Skans ON (2005) Age effects in Swedish local labor markets. Econ Lett 86:419–426

Spielman S, Folch DC (2015) Chapter 9. Social area analysis and self-organizing maps. In: Brunsdon C, Singleton A (eds) Geocomputation: a practical primer. Sage, Los Angeles, pp 152–168

Stock JH, Watson MW (2003) Introduction to econometrics, vol 104. Addison Wesley, Boston

Wedel M, Kamakura WA (2012) Market segmentation: conceptual and methodological foundations, vol 8. Springer Science & Business Media, New York

Wehrens R, Buydens LM et al (2007) Self-and super-organizing maps in r: the kohonen package. J Stat Softw 21(5):1–19

Yan J, Thill J-C (2009) Visual data mining in spatial interaction analysis with self-organizing maps. Environ Plann B Plann Des 36(3):466–486

Chapter 12
What Is the Effect of Population Ageing in Regional Labour Market Fluctuations of Germany? A SVAR with Zero-Sign Restrictions Approach

Vicente Rios and Roberto Patuelli

1 Introduction

There is the widespread belief among social scientists and policy-makers that the acceleration of demographic ageing is likely to be one of the key factors shaping the development of societies along the twenty-first century (Bloom et al. 2007a; Borsch-Supan 2003). In Germany, the share of population above 65 years old has been gradually rising, with an average annual growth rate of the 1.39% during the period 1970–2014. However, a look at the data reveals that this process has not been constant over time. Fast ageing began in the 1970s and experienced a slowdown during the 1990s. During the period 2000–2014 the share of population above 65 years increased by 1.72% per year. The baseline scenario in Germany projected by the United Nations and the World Bank plotted in Fig. 12.1 shows that this process will continue during the first half of the twenty-first century. It will slow down during 2020–2030 and it will speed up again during 2030–2050, when annual growth rates are expected to be around 2%. For the 2050–2060 decade, however, the forecast suggests an important stabilization. Overall, these figures imply that the share of population above 65 years old will increase from a 19% level in 2015 to 32.3% by 2060. Therefore, the projected scenario means that Germany is not going to be an exception in the long-run demographic trend and a better understanding of

V. Rios (✉)
Department of Economics, Universidad Pública de Navarra, Pamplona, Spain
e-mail: vicente.rios@unavarra.es

R. Patuelli
Department of Economics, Universitá di Bologna, Bologna, Italy
e-mail: roberto.patuelli@unibo.it

© Springer International Publishing AG, part of Springer Nature 2018
U. Blien et al. (eds.), *Modelling Aging and Migration Effects on Spatial Labor Markets*, Advances in Spatial Science,
https://doi.org/10.1007/978-3-319-68563-2_12

233

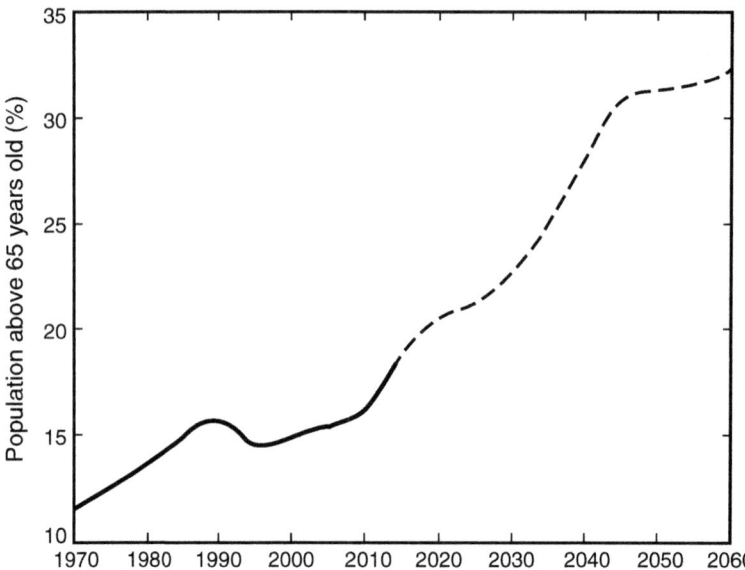

Fig. 12.1 Ageing in Germany 2013–2050. Sources: Author's own elaboration with United Nations and World Bank data

the economic aspects of population ageing will be needed so that policy-makers can provide adequate responses the challenges of the magnitude implied by this process.

In this regard, previous analyses stress that ageing might have important negative consequences for the functioning of the economy as it may: (1) decrease the sustainability of pension, health and long-term care insurance systems, (2) increase the risk of deflation in land, capital and financial market assets (Poterba 2001; Poterba 2004; Bullard et al. 2012; Anderson et al. 2014; Fujita and Fujiwara 2014), (3) foster political economy conflicts given that older groups will try to influence policy decisions to obtain low inflation and higher return for their savings, (4) decrease innovation and labour productivity (Lovasz and Rigo 2013; Romeu-Gordo and Skirbekk 2013; Maestas et al. 2016) and (5) decrease growth rates because of higher savings for pensions may reduce productive capital investment (Acemoglu and Johnson 2007; Bloom et al. 2007b, 2010; Aksoy et al. 2015).

Nevertheless, the study of the possible relationship between ageing and regional labour market performance has received hardly any attention in this context. Indeed, the overall understanding of the role of population ageing on regional labour market dynamics is still limited and to the best of our knowledge, there are only few analyses of ageing and labour market dynamics focusing separately on the relationship between ageing and (1) participation rates, (2) unemployment rates, and (3) wages. As it can be seen in Table 12.1, previous studies point to a negative link between ageing and unemployment while the effects on participation rates and wages are less clear.

Table 12.1 The effects of population ageing in labour market outcomes

Authors (year)	Sample and period	Methodology	Relationship
Participation			
Aaronson et al. (2014)	US, T = 1980–2014	Three way fixed effects panel data	Positive in 1970–1990
			Negative 1990–2014
Unemployment			
Biagi and Lucifora (2008)	N = 10 European countries T = 1980–2000	Panel data	Negative
Garloff et al. (2013)	N = 108 West German regions T = 1991–2009 T = 1996–2012	Spatial panel	Negative
Fuchs and Weyh (2014)	N = 77 East German regions	Spatial panel	Negative own estimate Positive neighbor's estimate
Fuchs (2016)	N = 77 East German regions T = 1994–2014	Spatial panel data	Negative
Wages			
Dostie (2011)	N = 17,516 firms and 103,391 workers (Canada) T = 1999–2005	Panel data	Positive
Mahlberg et al. (2013)	N = 1963 firms and 1.9 million workers (Austria) T = 2002–2005	Panel data	Not significant
Van Ours and Soteldraijer (2011)	N = 2944 firms and 61,562 workers (Netherlands) T = 2000–2005	Panel data	Not significant

Sources: Author's own elaboration
Notes: The US studies of Aaronson et al. (2014) is not performed at the regional scale but at the national level using individual level data considering age, sex and cohort effects

A common problem of the studies in Table 12.1 analysing the relationship between population ageing and labour market outcomes is that they are based either on cross-section or panel data analysis, which does not take into account the fact that there might be highly relevant endogenous feedback effects among the variables explaining the behavior of most of labour market time series. For instance, if population ageing affects negatively the level of wages and these affect the level of unemployment, which could also increase or reduce wages after some time, empirical studies that only model the first channel of causality will be miss-specified and might suffer from the omitted variable bias when estimating the effect of population ageing on wages. For this reason, in this research, we model the effects of ageing in the labor market by means of a multivariate dynamic representation of the labour market and estimate a Structural Vector AutoRegressive (SVAR) which allows us to capture such interactions.

In this regard, there are some applications of SVAR modeling in the field of regional labour market analysis focusing mainly on the interaction between migration, labour demand and participation rates. However, to the best of our knowledge, there are no SVAR studies analysing population ageing and its effects on these variables. The only studies analysing the effect of demographic change employing the VAR modeling framework are Kim and Lee (2008) and Aksoy et al. (2015). However, these analyses did not pay attention to labour market outcomes. On the other hand, as it is shown in Table 12.2, most of the SVAR analyses in the field of regional science have employed either zero or long run restrictions (Carlino and DeFina 1998; Fredriksson 1999; Carlino et al. 2001; Partridge and Rickman 2003, 2006, 2009) while others carried out the analysis by means of non-structural impulse responses, also known as Wald-impulse-response (Blanchard and Katz 1992; Decressin and Fatas 1994; Jimeno and Bentolila 1995; Maki-Arvela 2003; Alecke et al. 2010; Vega and Elhorst 2014).

In relation to the identification of structural shocks using zeros restrictions, some comments are necessary at this point. Zero Restrictions are set on variables that are not affected by the shock of interest for a certain period of time. Traditionally, zero restrictions have been imposed on the estimated variance-covariance matrix by means of the Cholesky decomposition, which in turn, implies a recursive structure in the dynamic system in order to identify structural shocks. Relying on a recursive ordering of the shocks limits the reliability of this methodology to few applications where the causal relationships among variables are very clear. Additionally, in most of the cases, the number of zero restrictions that are necessary to identify the model are often hard to justify. That is to say, most of regional labour market studies employed highly restrictive structural shock identification schemes which are difficult to justify from a theoretical point of view or did not identify structural shocks at all.

In view of the observed limitations of previous studies, within the context of a SVAR model, we implement a novel structural shock identification procedure that allows to combine zero and sign restrictions in both the short and the long run. Until recently, the standard methodologies used for imposing those restrictions were difficult to implement simultaneously. Examples of early attempts to implement jointly zeros and sign restrictions are Mountford and Uhlig (2009), Baumeister and Benati (2013), Benati (2013) and Binning (2013). Nevertheless, unlike previous methods of combining sign and zero restrictions, the algorithm by Rubio-Ramirez et al. (2014) has been proven to draw from the correct posterior of the structural parameters. Note that zero and sign restrictions impose different type of information on the model. While zero restrictions specify that some variables are not affected by a shock, sign restrictions incorporate information on how some macroeconomic indicators are expected to react to a structural disturbance. While it is difficult to

Table 12.2 SVAR analyses on regional labour markets

Authors (year)	Sample and period	VAR variables	Structural identification
Blanchard and Katz (1992)	N = 51 US states T = 1978–1992	$Y = [e, u, par, mig]$	No identification
Decressin and Fatas (1994)	N = 51 European regions T = 1975–1987	$Y = [e, u, par]$	No identification
Jimeno and Bentolila (1995)	N = 17 Spanish regions T = 1976–1994	$Y = [e, u, par, mig]$	No identification
Carlino and DeFina (1998)	N = US states T = 1958–1992	$Y = [\Delta y, p, m]$	Zeros short run
Fredriksson (1999)	N = Sweden T = 1966–1993	$Y = [e, er, w, par, m]$	Zeros short run
Carlino et al. (2001)	N = 35 US MSAs T = 1951–1998	$Y = [e_s, tbills, y/e]$	Zeros short run
Maki-Arvela (2003)	N = 11 Finland provinces T = 1976–1996	$Y = [e, u, par, mig, y]$	No identification
Partridge and Rickman (2003)	N = 48 US states T = 1969–1998	$Y = [\Delta w, mig \Delta e]$	Zeros long run
Partridge and Rickman (2006)	N = 48 US states T = 1970–1998	$Y = [\Delta w, mig \Delta e]$	Zeros long run
Partridge and Rickman (2009)	N = 10 Canada provinces T = 1976–2003	$Y = [\Delta w, mig \Delta e]$	Zeros long run
Alecke et al. (2010)	N = 16 German regions T = 1991–2006	$Y = [mig, u, w, p]$	Zeros short run
Vega and Elhorst (2014)	N = 112 NUTS-2 T = 1980–2011	$Y =$ $[e, u, par, We, Wu, Wpar]$	No identification

Sources: Author's own elaboration

Notes: Y is a vector of endogenous variables, e denotes employment, er denotes employment rate, e_s employment in industry s, $tbills$ denote 3-month treasury bill rate, m is the monetary supply, mig denotes migration, p is price, par stands for participation, u is the unemployment/unemployment rate, w are the wages, y denotes income and W denotes the spatial lag of the corresponding variable

impose sign restrictions directly in the parameter matrix of the VAR model, it is easy to impose them ex-post on a set of orthogonalized impulse response functions. An important advantage of the use of sign restrictions to perform structural shock identification in this context is that it allows us to incorporate the expected co-movements of some variables following a shock while at the same time we can remain agnostic on the effect of ageing shocks letting the data speak, by leaving its impulse-response function almost totally unrestricted. Therefore, the main contribution of this study when compared to previous studies of regional labour markets and population ageing is methodological given that: (1) we develop our own identification scheme to identify structural ageing shocks and disentangle them from other sources of variation such as labor demand, supply and wage bargaining shocks and (2) we apply the recently developed algorithm of Rubio-Ramirez et al. (2014) to that aim.

This paper is organized as follows. Section 2, which follows this introduction, provides an exploratory analysis of regional German labour market data. Section 3 presents the econometric modeling methodology used to analyse the effect of ageing in labour market dynamics. The empirical findings are presented in Sect. 4, while Sect. 5 concludes.

2 Data and Preliminary Evidence

2.1 Data

We employ official data for the former West Germany, aggregated at both the national (NUTS-0) and Länder (NUTS-1) level. All data come from the German Federal Statistical Office and the Institute for Employment Research (IAB) and kindly provided by the latter. The Länder of Berlin, which formally used to be part of West Germany, is excluded from our analysis because of the effects of the German reunification of 1989. East German data, instead, are not used in this paper, since the related time series are significantly shorter. The variables considered here are: (1) mean nominal wage per employee; (2) unemployment rates; (3) participation rates; and (4) the share of population older than 65.[1] All variables are available on an annual basis, from the year 1970 until 2014. Descriptive statistics are provided in Table 12.3.

---

[1]Notice that an important difference with respect other regional labor market studies is that we do not include the net migration in the model. This is because of data was not available. The potential negative effects on the quality and reliability of the estimates implied by the omission of this variable are discussed in Sect. 3.2.

Table 12.3 Descriptive statistics

	Wages	Unemployment rate	Labour force participation rate	Share of population above 65 years
Mean	18,837.5	7.009	76.108	15.293
Std. deviation	6624.2	2.750	6.089	2.195
Min	6644.8	0.845	69.147	12.120
Max	29,319.70	11.000	87.586	19.372

Sources: Author's own elaboration with the German Federal Statistical Office and the Institute for Employment Research (IAB)

2.2   Demographic and Labour Market Trends, 1970–2014

In Fig. 12.2, we plot the normalized the evolution of our selected labour market and demographic variables (where 100 denotes the original value in 1970). With regard to the share of older (65+) population, in Fig. 12.2a we observe a continuous increase over time which is typical of developed countries. Most of the regions experienced an increase, ranging between the 50–70%. However, there is some heterogeneity in the cross-section of regions given that for some regions such as Saarland—a South-West region bordering with France-, the share of older population doubled during the sample period while for others such as Hamburg the share of old population has remained fairly constant, with a 45-year increase of less than 20%. As it is observed, nominal wages grew considerably over time. However, wages (Fig. 12.2d) appear as the most homogeneous variable, where all German Lander follow a clear trend, and where only Bavaria can be noticed as growing significantly faster in the last 20 years. In terms of participation rates, Germany evolved similarly to many developed economies towards increasingly higher rates, moving from about 70% in 1970 to more than 87% in 2014. Figure 12.2b, shows that all regions appear to follow a common trend, as noted above, with some heterogeneity in the cumulated result. Unemployment rates (Fig. 12.2c) show the most diverse behavior, which is partly explained by the extremely low starting rates of 1970 observed for some regions. In particular, the unemployment rate, which was lower than 1% (nationally) in 1970 soon stabilized around the mean and current value of about 7%, with 11% being the highest in 2005. Across space, more heterogeneity was present in recent times but still much less than we would have observed for East Germany. Common business cycles are clearly recognizable, and rather stable relative positions can be observed since the 1980s. Hamburg and Baden-Württemberg appear as the regions with most variation.

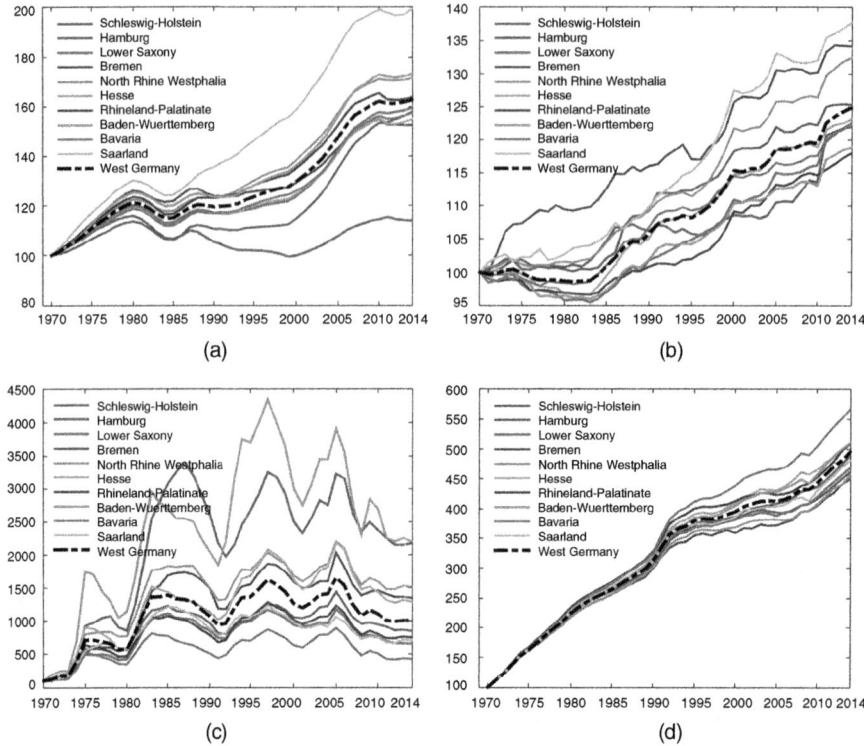

Fig. 12.2 Normalized labour market indicators, 1970–2014. (**a**) Population above 65 years, (**b**) Labour force participation rate, (**c**) Unemployment rate, (**d**) Wages. Sources: Author's own elaboration with the German Federal Statistical Office and the Institute for Employment Research (IAB)

3   Econometric Methodology

3.1   The Model

The standard reduced-form VAR representation of lag length P can be written as:

$$y_t = c + \sum_{i=0}^{P} B_i\, y_{t-i} + u_t \qquad (12.1)$$

where y_t is a $N \times 1$ vector of endogenous variables [(1) Population above 65 years old (%), (2) Unemployment rate (%), (3) Labour force participation rate (%), (4) Ln Wages], c is a $N \times 1$ vector of constants, B_i for $i = 1, \ldots, P$ are $N \times N$ matrices of coefficients and $u_t \sim N\,(0, \Sigma)$ where Σ is the $N \times N$ covariance matrix. To perform the Bayesian estimation we rewrite Eq. (12.1) compactly as:

$$y_t = X_{t-1} B + u_t \tag{12.2}$$

where $X_{t-1} = (1, y_{it-1}, y_{it-2}, \ldots, y_{it-p})$, B is of dimension $(1 + N \times P) \times N$ and $u_t | y_{t-1}, y_{t-2}, \ldots, y_1 1 \sim N(0, \Sigma)$. Defining $b = vec(B)$, we assume a normal prior for the VAR coefficients:

$$p(b) \sim N\left(\tilde{b}_0, \tilde{V}_0\right) \tag{12.3}$$

and an inverse Whishart distribution as the prior for Σ:

$$p(\Sigma) \sim IW\left(v_0, \bar{S}\right) \tag{12.4}$$

where v_0 are the degrees of freedom and $\bar{S}$ is the prior scale matrix.[2] The conditional posterior distribution for the VAR coefficients is given by:

$$p(b | \Sigma, y_t) \sim N\left(M^*, V^*\right) \tag{12.5}$$

where $M^* = \left(\tilde{V}_0^{-1} + \Sigma^{-1} \otimes X'_{t-1} X_{t-1}\right)^{-1} \left(\tilde{V}_0^{-1} \tilde{b}_0 + \Sigma^{-1} \otimes X'_{t-1} X_{t-1} \hat{b}_{ols}\right)$ and $V^* = \left(\tilde{V}_0^{-1} + \Sigma^{-1} \otimes X'_{t-1} X_{t-1}\right)^{-1}$. Finally, the posterior distribution for the variance-covariance matrix conditional to the parameters and the data is given by:

$$p(\Sigma | b, \mathbf{y}_t) \sim IW\left(v_0 + T, \bar{\Sigma}\right) \tag{12.6}$$

where $\bar{\Sigma} = \bar{S} + (y_t - X_{t-1} B)' (y_t - X_{t-1} B)$. Inference is performed based on $n = 1000$ draws from the conditional posterior distributions for b and Σ with a burn in sample of $n_1 = 500$ draws.

3.2 Structural Identification

Importantly, the reduced form VAR in Eq. (12.1) does not serve as a basis for structural analysis because the cross-correlations between the reduced form errors

---

[2]Often, Bayesian analysis tries to avoid situations where the conclusions depend heavily on subjective prior information by relying on diffuse or non-informative prior distributions. As parameters governing the prior distributions such as the prior variance increase, the prior distributions become more vague or diffuse. Non-informative priors are obtained in this context by setting $\tilde{V}_0^{-1} = 0.001$, $v_0 = 0.001$ and $\bar{S} = 0.001$. Note that given the diffuse prior specification employed, the reduced-form estimates obtained are very close to those that one would derived if the model was estimated by ordinary least squares or maximum likelihood procedures.

imply that the interpretation of a change in variable h on variable k when the other variables are hold constant $\partial y_t^h / \partial y_t^{-k} = 0$ is no longer valid. From the Bayesian estimates of the model in Eq. (12.1) an interpretation is provided by means of a SVAR:

$$A_0 y_t = A_0 \alpha + \sum_{i=0}^{P} A_0 B_i y_{t-i} + \epsilon_t \tag{12.7}$$

where ϵ_t are shocks that have zero mean, no serial correlation, constant variances and no correlation between the individual shocks (i.e, $E[\epsilon_{it}, \epsilon_{jt}] = 0$). Comparison of Eqs. (12.1) and (12.7) reveals that (1) $u_t = A_0^{-1} \epsilon_t$ and (2) $E\left[u_t', u_t\right] = \Sigma = \left(A_0' A_0\right)^{-1}$. Therefore, the matrix A_0 allows us to find the structural shocks we seek to measure. Under the perspective that dynamic economic models can be viewed as restrictions on stochastic processes, an economic theory is a mapping between a vector of structural economic shocks ϵ_t and y_t of the form $y_t = \mathbf{C}\epsilon_t$, where ϵ_t represents the whole history of shocks up to period t. The construction of the mapping $\mathbf{C}(\cdot)$ is the sense in which economic theory tightly relates shocks and observables (Villaverde et al. 2014). Also, the mapping $\mathbf{C}(\cdot)$ can be interpreted as the structural impulse response of the model to an economic shock:

$$y_t = C_0 \epsilon_t + C_1 \epsilon_{t-1} + \ldots+ \tag{12.8}$$

where C_j denotes the jth impulse response of y_{t+j} to ϵ_t so that $C_j = D_j A_0^{-1} = D_j C_0$ as $C_0 = A_0^{-1}$ and D_j is the jth period impulse response of y_{t+j} to a unit change in u_t ($D_0 = I_n$).

As explained in Sect. 1, relying solely on zero restrictions to identify a model is not a good idea given that in many cases the identifying restrictions are too hard to believe. On the other hand, sign restrictions provide a very appealing way of recovering the structural shocks from an economic point of view. The key idea behind sign restrictions is to characterize a shock through placing restrictions on the responses of some variables, but being agnostic about others. However, several papers have pointed out a number of shortcomings of sign restrictions. The main concern is that although in principle it is possible to identify all shocks of the model, doing so by just using sign restrictions is inherently difficult. As shown by Fry and Pagan (2011) there are many cases in the literature, where researchers aim to identify all shocks in the model but failed at doing so. One reason for this is that the different structural shocks we aim to identify in the model might be characterized by the same set of restrictions. Therefore, in order to give an economic interpretation to the equations of our labour market model we will proceed to isolate exogenous shocks by imposing zero and sign restrictions on the decomposition of Σ in order to obtain shocks that generate responses that are sufficiently different from each other.

Using the notation developed by Rubio-Ramirez et al. (2010, 2014), the restrictions on short-run and long-run impact matrices can be written as:

$$
f(A_0, B) = \begin{bmatrix} A_0 \\ A_\infty \end{bmatrix} = \begin{matrix} v_1 \\ \vdots \\ v_n \\ v_1 \\ \vdots \\ v_n \end{matrix} \begin{bmatrix} s_1 & s_2 & \ldots & s_k \\ 0 & x & \ldots & x \\ \vdots & \ddots & \ldots & x \\ x & x & \ldots & x \\ \hline x & x & \ldots & x \\ x & x & \ldots & x \\ x & x & \ldots & x \end{bmatrix}
$$

where A_0 is the *nvar* $\times$ *nshocks* short run impact matrix and A_∞ is the long run impact matrix such that $A_\infty = (I - B)^{-1} A_0$.

The rows denote the variables v while the columns represent the structural shocks s. Zeros are placed in the $f(A_0, B)$ matrix in order for the shock to have no contemporaneous effect on a variable and/or no long-run effect on a variable. However, the zeros can not be placed anywhere, and depending on their position, the system will be over-identified, exactly identified or under-identified (see Rubio-Ramirez et al. (2010); Binning (2013) for details). Forming linear combinations of structural innovations that satisfy theoretically well-grounded zero and sign restrictions following the algorithm developed by Rubio-Ramirez et al. (2014) is one of the key contributions of this study.

This algorithm can be summarized as follows[3]:

Step 1.   Draw B and Σ from the posterior distribution of the reduced-form parameters.

Step 2.   Draw an orthogonal rotation matrix Q such that the structural parameters satisfy the zero restrictions.

Step 3.   Keep the draw if the sign restrictions are also met. Otherwise go back to Step 1 and take a new draw of the reduced-form parameters and of Q.

Step 4.   Return to Step 1 until sufficient draws from the posterior distribution conditional on the sign and zero restrictions have been collected.

There are two important elements about the scheme of identification employed to disentangle labor market shocks and ageing shocks from each other that deserve some comments. The first one is that the number of zeros and sign restrictions implemented is sufficiently numerous to fully identify the structural shocks in the model. This is due to the fact that taking together the restrictions of zeros and signs in both the short and the long run, each shock generates a sufficiently diverse

---

[3]Notice that the combination of zero and sign restrictions is not straightforward given that multiplying A_0 by a randomly drawn Q violates might violate the zero restrictions embodied in A_0. Thus, the main contribution of this algorithm is a method for drawing Q matrices without violating the zero restrictions we aim to impose. For details see pp 23–24 of Rubio-Ramirez et al. (2014).

response function among the variables, so that it is possible to isolate it from the other shocks. However, in order to achieve this set of sufficiently diverse shocks, we have used as few restrictions as possible, given that the more restrictions are placed in the short-run and long-run matrices of multipliers the more difficult they become to justify from a theoretical basis and the more difficult they become to find computationally. Therefore, we have used the minimal but crucial assumption that the share of population is not affected immediately by changes in demand and labor supply or by changes in wage bargaining. At the practical level this implies zero restrictions on the response of the population over 65 years old. The second key assumption is that an ageing shock that affects the demographic structure will have immediate effects on the share of old population. We prefer this approach over the alternative of imposing the zero restrictions on the matrix of long-run multipliers as the former approach is less restrictive. To see this clearly, note that zero restrictions in the long run are less realistic and much more difficult to believe for a variety of reasons. First, changes in the supply and demand of labor, after some periods, could affect the level of production and income of the economy which is likely to affect key variables that also affect the share of population over 65 years old. An example of this is the case of health expenditure, life expectancy, etc. Similarly, changes in wage bargaining may affect the level of incomes, well being and other variables related the ageing phenomenon, thus, making the zero assumption in the long run too severe. Table 12.4 summarizes the identification conditions employed to carry out inference by means of zero and sign restrictions.

First, *Ageing shocks* are the only ones that are assumed to increase the share of population above 65 years old, while the effect on the other variables in the short and the long run is left unrestricted so that the impulse-response functions are completely determined by the data. This assumption relies on the insights stemming from Aksoy et al. (2015) who consider ageing as a low-frequency phenomenon

Table 12.4 Zero and sign restrictions labour market VAR

		Structural labour market shocks			
	Variables	Labour supply	Labour demand	Wage bargaining	Demographic ageing
Short run	Wages	−	+	+	x
	Unemployment	+	−	+	x
	Participation	+	+	+	x
	Population > 65	0	0	0	+
Long run	Wages	x	x	x	x
	Unemployment	x	x	x	x
	Participation	x	x	x	x
	Population > 65	x	x	x	x

Sources: Author's own elaboration
Notes: The sign "+" denotes a positive response of the variable to the shock, while "−" denotes a negative response of the variable to the shock. Also note that a 0 denotes a zero response of the variable to the shock. Finally, "x" means the response of the variable is left unrestricted

and specify this variable as the most exogenous one. Importantly, while most of the shocks are identified using information on the sign of expected responses, the effect of ageing shocks in the different variables is not specified beforehand, which allows to remain agnostic with respect to the effects of our key variable of interest following the spirit of Uhlig (2005).

Labour demand shocks are assumed to increase wages, decrease unemployment and move up participation rates. This is because, ceteris paribus, a higher labour demand, in order to attract workers, will increase wages. Additionally, a positive labour demand shock is expected to increase participation rates as higher wages can encourage more people to enter the labour market. Given that more jobs will be created, labour demand shocks are expected to decrease unemployment rates. This identification scheme is consistent with previous work of Blanchard and Katz (1992) and the literature survey of Elhorst (2003).

Labour supply shocks are identified as those shocks displaying a negative effect on wages, a positive effect on unemployment rates and also in participation rates. An increase in the number of job seekers makes it easier to firms to fill vacancies and decrease hiring costs which leads to a decrease in wages as in Peersman and Straub (2009) and Foroni et al. (2015), who derive a set of sign restrictions from a New Keynesian Dynamic Stochastic General Equilibrium (DSGE) model. In this context, a positive labour supply shock leads to an increase in the size of the labour force and because wages do not adjust immediately to an increase in unemployment. Notice the key distinct feature employed to disentangle labour supply from labour demand shocks is that both are assumed to increase labour force participation rates while at the same time they generate the reverse effects on unemployment, wages and prices.

Wage Bargaining Shocks are interpreted as those that favor the position of workers with respect firms or employers. Hence, this shock has a direct positive effect on wages. This contributes to higher marginal costs and prices. Because firms now capture a lower share of the surplus associated with employment relationships, they decrease vacancies and employment, which decreases overall output. In spite of the lower job finding rate, the increase in wages tends to increase participation as it becomes more attractive to stay in the labour market. The combined effect of decreasing vacancies and higher participation rates is deemed to increase unemployment rates. As explained in Foroni et al. (2015) the restrictions employed here to identify the pro-worker wage-bargaining shock are also consistent with two other labour market shocks, a negative matching efficiency shock and a positive unemployment benefit shock.

3.3 Empirical Specification

In order to carry out inference in the context of multivariate time-series analysis a number of issues need to be considered. In a first step, we analyse the optimal lag length. Second, we determine the stationarity of the system. Note that instead of

Table 12.5 Optimal lag
length

Regional VAR	AIC	BIC
West Germany	1	1
Schleswig-Holstein	1	1
Hamburg	2	1
Saxony	1	1
Bremen	1	1
North Rhine Westphalia	1	1
Hesse	1	1
Rhineland-Palatinate	1	1
Baden-Wuerttemberg	4	1
Bavaria	1	1
Saarland	1	1
Berlin	2	1

Sources: Author's own elaboration

using the data in levels we work with Hodrick Prescott filtered data which implies our analysis focus on business-cycle properties of the labour market.[4]

a) **Lag Length** We carry out an exercise aiming at the determination of the optimal lag length by means of the AIC-BIC criteria in a VAR model with the de-trended data. As it is shown in Table 12.5 the two different criteria point out to parsimonious model structures with a typical lag length of 1. This is always the case when using the BIC, while when using the AIC, only for Hamburg, Baden Wuerttemberg and Berlin the optimal number of lags changes. In view of these results, we adopt a VAR(1) model structure to perform inference.

b) **Stationarity** In order to check for the stationarity of the model we apply a battery of Augmented Dickey Fuller tests. We first run the Dickey Fuller Autoregressive Test (dfARTest). This test takes as the null model the integrated AR (P+1) process $y_t = y_{t-1} + \sum_{k=1}^{P} \psi_k \Delta y_{t-k} + \epsilon_t$ being the alternative $y_t = \phi y_{t-1} + \sum_{k=1}^{P} \psi_k \Delta y_{t-k} + \epsilon_t$ for some $\phi < 1$. As an alternative, we also check for the stationarity by means of Dickey Fuller Autoregressive Test with drift $y_t = c + \phi y_{t-1} + \sum_{k=1}^{P} \psi_k \Delta y_{t-k} + \epsilon_t$. The results obtained are shown in Table 12.6 below. As observed, for all the variables and for almost all of the lag-lengths considered, we can reject the null hypothesis of a unit root, which prevents us from spurious regression problems.[5]

---

[4]The HP filter finds the series μ_t that minimizes: $\sum_{t=1}^{T} (y_t - \mu_t)^2 + \lambda \sum_{t=2}^{T-1} [(\mu_{t+1} - \mu_t) - (\mu_t - \mu_{t-1})]^2$ where $\lambda = 100$ is the corresponding optimal annual smoothing parameter value. We use this filter instead of other possible alternatives such as the Bo as it is the most common filter employed in the macroeconomics literature.

[5]For the shake of brevity, we only report the p-values of these tests for West Germany. However, the results for regions under consideration provide strong evidence for the VAR time-series system in cyclical-fluctuations to be stationary.

Table 12.6 Stationarity tests

	Unemployment		Wages		Labour force		Pop > 65 years	
Lags	ADF-test AR	ADF-test ARD	ADF-test AR	ADF-test ARD	ADF-test AR	ADF-test ARD	ADF-test AR	ADF-test ARD
1	0.001	0.001	0.002	0.021	0.001	0.005	0.001	0.001
2	0.001	0.003	0.001	0.010	0.001	0.007	0.001	0.009
3	0.001	0.001	0.001	0.010	0.001	0.008	0.001	0.008
4	0.001	0.001	0.006	0.066	0.003	0.030	0.005	0.052
5	0.001	0.009	0.003	0.030	0.008	0.087	0.001	0.019
6	0.001	0.005	0.004	0.048	0.001	0.004	0.002	0.027
7	0.002	0.021	0.008	0.083	0.001	0.005	0.013	0.128
8	0.002	0.021	0.005	0.055	0.001	0.004	0.006	0.071
9	0.008	0.078	0.003	0.037	0.001	0.001	0.014	0.133
10	0.027	0.195	0.004	0.047	0.050	0.313	0.031	0.237

Sources: Author's own elaboration
Notes: P-values below 0.05 indicate the tests rejection of the null of a unit root $\phi = 1$. AR denotes the autoregressive version of the test while ARD stands for the autoregressive version with a drift parameter

4   Results

This sections presents the results and discusses the main findings of this study. We begin by documenting the impulse-response patterns of West-Germany. We also analyse how heterogeneous are these patterns at the regional level. Finally, we estimate the relative importance of the various structural shocks by means of a forecast variance-decomposition exercise. Importantly, it should be noted that the impulse-response and variance decompositions results reported in this section are the median responses reported across models draws from the posterior distribution and do not reflect sampling uncertainty. Similarly, in each model draw, the variance decomposition shares add up to 1, but when using sign restrictions we do no use a single model, rather we use all the model draws selected satisfying the restrictions.[6]

4.1   Ageing Shocks

As shown in Fig. 12.3, a 1% shock to the percentage of old population exerts a positive effect on the share of old population, on the unemployment rate and on the participation rate. On the contrary, it has a depressive effect on the log of nominal wages. The response pattern described by unemployment rates shows that,

---

[6]See Fry and Pagan (2011) for a detailed discussion on the specifities of interpreting sign-restrictions analyses.

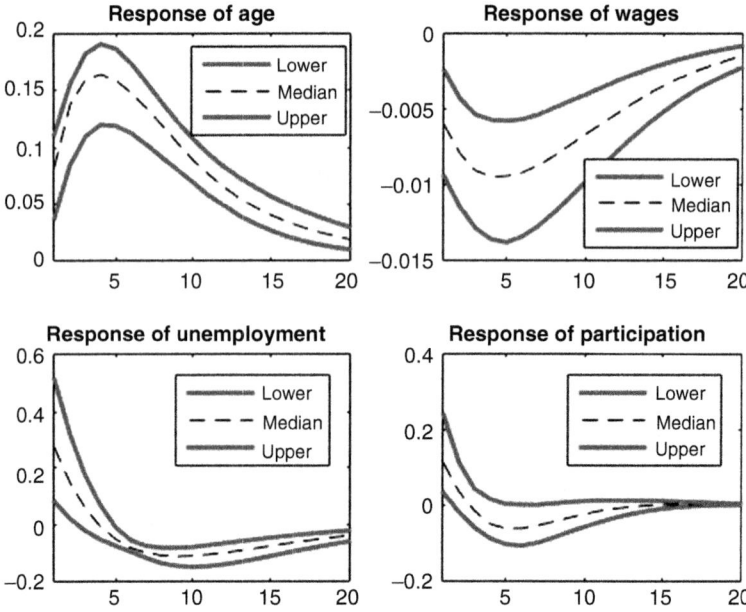

Fig. 12.3 Ageing shocks

while during the first years after the impact, ageing increases unemployment, after some periods its effect becomes negative. This finding supports previous empirical findings of Biagi and Lucifora (2008), Garloff et al. (2013) and Fuchs (2016), who find an overall negative link between population ageing and unemployment. Labour force participation displays a similar pattern. During the first periods after the shock takes place, the effect of ageing appears to be positive, while in the long−run it becomes negative and converges slowly towards the equilibrium. The intuition behind this pattern is that over time, as population ages, an increasing share of the labour force moves to groups with lower participation rates which yields a negative effect. On the other hand, ageing shocks decrease wages after the shock takes place, but converges fastly to zero after the fifth period after the shock was originated.

This finding goes against the body of literature reviewed above, employing firm-worker matching, which finds that ageing has no relevant effects on wages. These findings, although of complex interpretation, appear to be generally consistent, in the short run, with a loss of competitivity of labour markets and of the economy as a result of population (e.g. because of the increased constraints to geographical and job mobility of an older population). Such effect is possibly balanced, over the medium run, by the entrance of new resources in the labour market. This speculation could be tested in an augmented model where migration (or other means of generating new competencies, e.g. through professional education policies) should be considered.

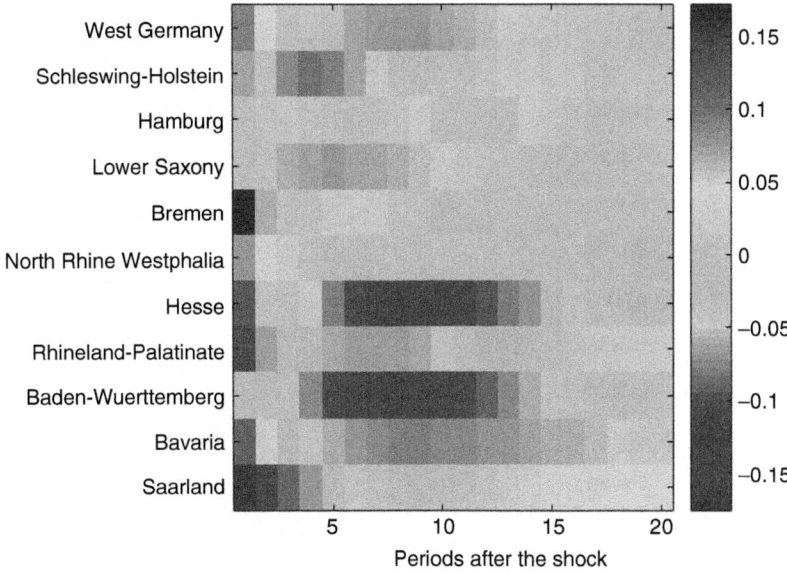

Fig. 12.4 Regional unemployment response to population ageing

Figure 12.4 plots *the response of the unemployment rate after a shock in population ageing* by region. Although the overall impulse response pattern is similar to the one seen for the whole of West Germany, there is clear evidence of regional heterogeneity. It can be seen that there are regions where population ageing has a positive effect on impact which subsequently becomes negative, (as in the case of Schleswig-Holstein, Bremen, Hesse or Bavaria), while in regions such as Saarland and Rhineland-Palatinate, the effect of the shock at the period of impact is negative and becomes positive over time. To provide an overall assessment of impulse-response pattern dissimilarity, we compute Euclidean distances between the various regions and West Germany. We find that the regions that display the most similar response to that of West Germany are Bavaria ($ED = 1.50\%$) and North-Rhine Westphalia ($ED = 2.05\%$), while the most dissimilar response pattern is seen for Saarland with $ED = 7.1\%$. Being the former two regions among the richest and most developed ones in the country, it is reasonable to find that they are most similar in behaviour to the macro-level.

The regional *response of wages to population ageing shocks* are summarized in Fig. 12.5, which also shows a distinct pattern by region. While Bremen, Hamburg, North-Rhine Westphalia, Bavaria and Hesse show a negative response in the period of impact, Saarland and Rhineland display a positive response in both the impact period and during the next twenty periods. However, after the shock takes place, the group of regions that react negatively on impact can be further subdivided into two groups depending on the persistence of the shock. While in Bremen, North-Rhine Westphalia, Hesse and Bavaria the persistence of the negative effect on wages is very

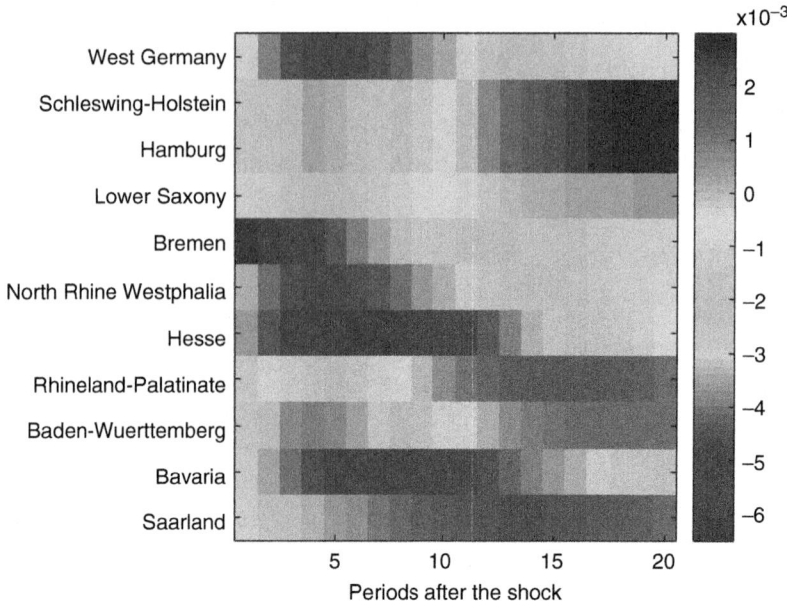

Fig. 12.5 Regional wages response to population ageing

high, in Schlesweig-Holstein, Hamburg, Lower Saxony and Baden-Wuerttemberg the shock is absorbed within 10 years and during the subsequent decade, the effect on wages becomes positive. Regarding the degree of similarity we find that North-Rhine Westphalia is the region that matches more closely the West German mean ($ED = 0.016\%$), while the highest level of dissimilarity with respect to West-Germany's average response is once again found for Saarland $ED = 0.04\%$. In general, it appears that all regions show a U-shaped effect of population ageing on wages, although with heterogeneous intensity and speed of adjustment.

Regarding *the response of the labour force participation to ageing shocks* at the regional level, we find that the pattern is less heterogeneous than the case of unemployment, but more diverse than for wages. However, overall dissimilarity is mainly due to the very distinct behavior experienced by Hamburg. All regions except the latter show a U-shaped pattern. At first, the effect of population shock starts as mildly positive, it quickly turns negative within 10 or 15 years, to eventually get back to equilibrium (Fig. 12.6).

Overall, the previous analysis shows that the observed degree of heterogeneity supports the preliminary evidence of Sect. 2.1. However, ageing shocks have complex effects on labour market variables that vary largely in both sign and strength depending on the period and region considered. The regions that how more remarkable differences with respect to West Germany are Saarland in the case of wage and unemployment dynamics, and Hamburg in the case of labour force participation.

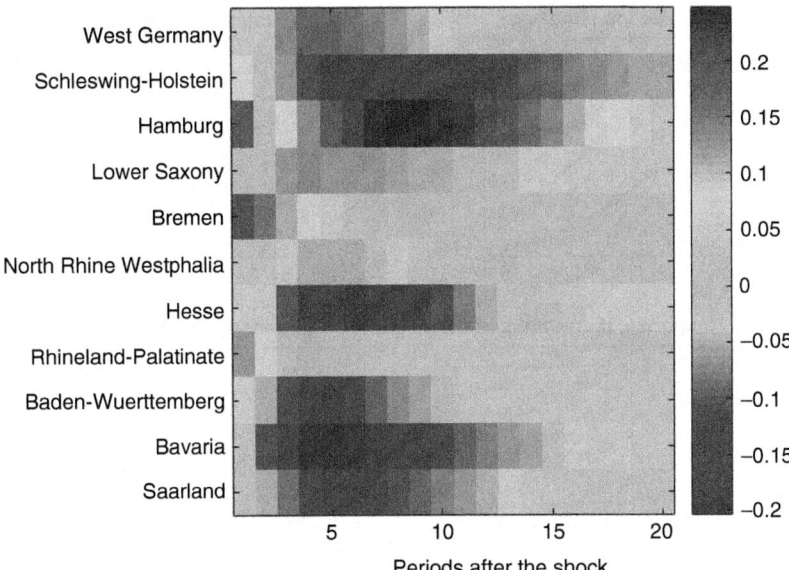

Fig. 12.6 Regional labour force participation response to population ageing

4.2 Other Labour Market Shocks

As shown in Fig. 12.7, a 1% positive shock to the workers bargaining position, at impact, increases wages by a 0.04%, unemployment rates by 0.2%, participation rates by 0.18% and, given our zero-restriction, has no effect on ageing. Generally, all effects have a peak between 5 and 10 years, and are reabsorbed towards the previous equilibrium by year 20. However, the dynamic responses of the variables are quite different from each other. While the one for the share of older population describes a positive hump-shape pattern, the response of wages and participation rates is the opposite (negative hump), becoming negative the first periods from the shock. On the other hand, consistently with theory, the effect of increasing bargaining power is always positive on the evolution of unemployment rates. Moreover, as it can be observed, its persistence is quite strong, given that the unemployment rate does not go back to its equilibrium before ten periods.

Figure 12.8 shows that, on impact, the effect of a positive 1% labour supply shock increases by 0.35% the unemployment rate, by 0.17% the labour force participation rate, and decreases (the log of nominal) wages by −0.008%. The dynamic response patterns after a positive labour supply shock are similar to those implied by wage bargaining shocks. The effect on the share of old population is higher during the first periods after the shock, and subsequently decreases smoothly (while remaining positive). On the contrary, the response of unemployment rates and participation rates displays a smooth decay towards zero that is achieved after ten periods. Finally,

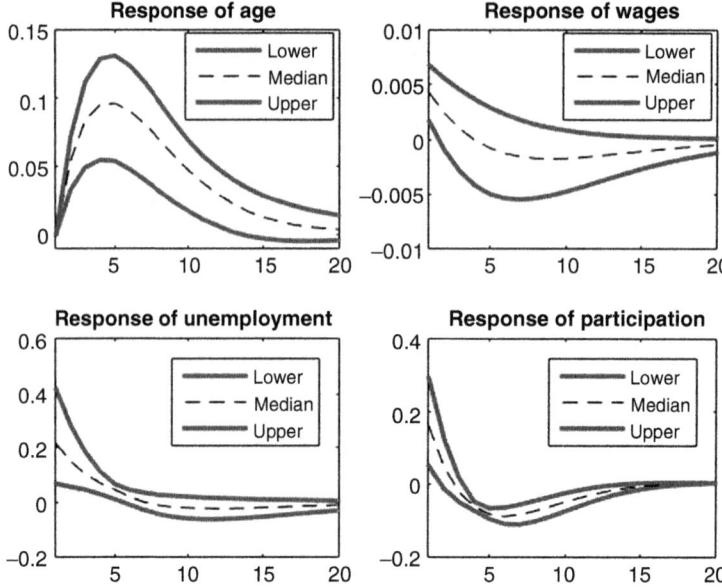

Fig. 12.7 Wage bargaining shocks

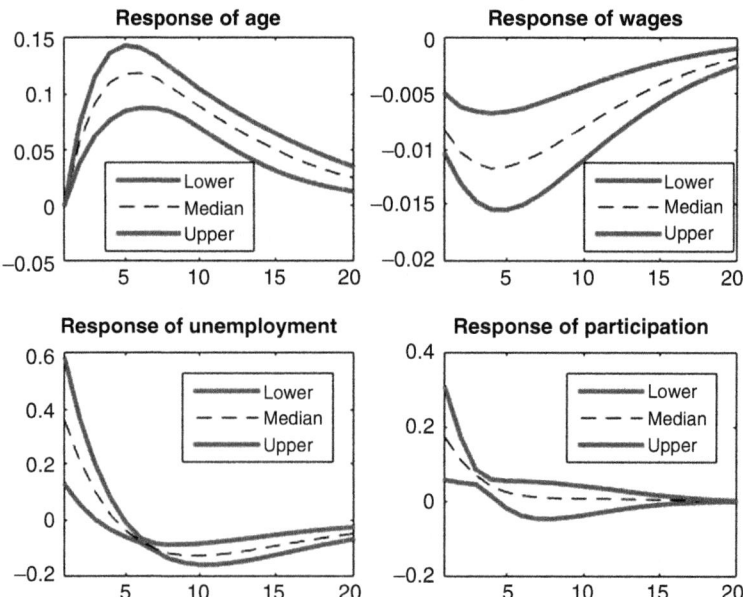

Fig. 12.8 Labour supply shocks

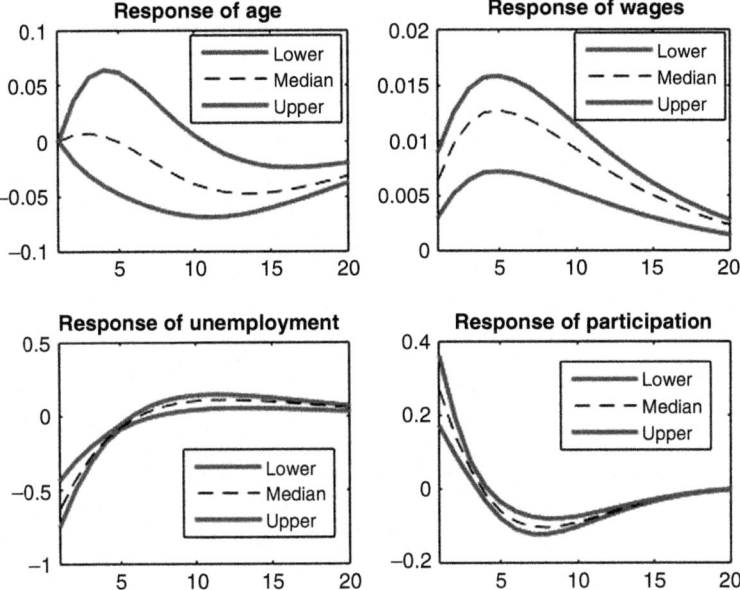

Fig. 12.9 Labour demand shocks

we find that the effect of an increase in the labour supply on wages is always negative and highly persistent, although the economic significance of the effect is small.

Figure 12.9 shows that on impact, the effect of a positive 1% labour demand shock decreases by 0.53% the unemployment rate, increases the labour force participation rate by a 0.25%, and the log of nominal wages by 0.007%, and has no impact on the share of old population (from the zero-restriction). Interestingly, the response patterns to demand shocks are different from the previous ones. With regard to the effect on population age, we cannot find a statistically significant finding, based on the observation of the computed confidence intervals. Secondly, we observe that the effect on unemployment is negative for seven periods after the shock and then converges towards zero. Given the strength of the response during the periods immediately following the shock, its net contribution is clearly negative. Additionally, we find that labour demand shocks have a positive effect on participation rates that is even stronger than that of labour supply shocks. Finally, we find that the response of wages is positive during all the years following the shock, actually describes a hump-shape pattern, and vanishing slowly. More generally, our findings pertaining to labour demand are again consistent with economic theory, as demand stimulates wages and participation, bringing down unemployment rates.

4.3   Variance Decompositions

We now proceed to examine the empirical relevance of the shocks with respect to labour market fluctuations, by analysing the median forecast error variance decomposition across models. Figure 12.10 shows that the main determinant of the variability in the unemployment rates is labour demand shocks, which account for approximately 56% of variance. Secondly, we find that labour supply shocks explain 36% of the variability in unemployment. At a lower level of importance, we find the shocks to wage bargaining and ageing population. In subsequent periods, we observe a considerable change in the relevance of labour demand and supply shocks. While the relevance of labour demand shocks falls to 10%, the importance of supply shocks increase to stand at a level close to 60%. Similarly, both shocks to the bargaining position of workers and the ones to the level of ageing population increases their relevance to stand at slightly below 10%. Although this result emerges from a different methodological approach from that of Blanchard and Quah (1989), our results tend to confirm previous findings, suggesting that in the long run, the most relevant determinant of unemployment is labour supply, while labour demand is what matters in the short run.

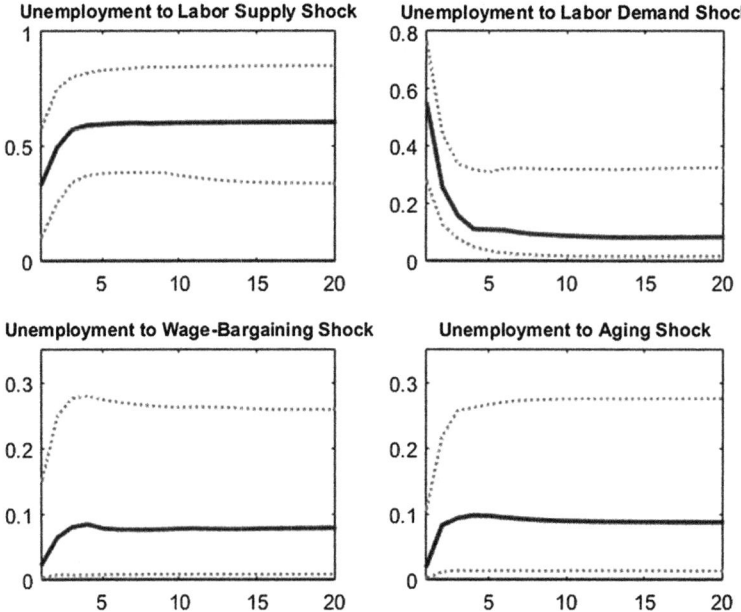

Fig. 12.10 The determinants of unemployment fluctuations

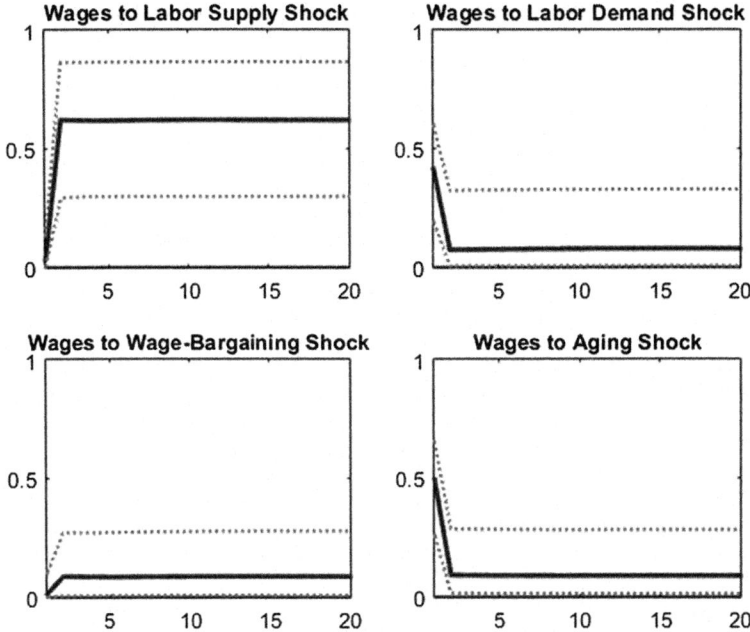

Fig. 12.11 The determinants of wage fluctuations

Figure 12.11 shows the decomposition of the forecast error variance of wages. With regard to their fluctuations, we find that labour supply shocks account for more than 50% of forecast errors variance in the long run, while in the short term, the main determinants of wage fluctuations are shocks to labour demand and population ageing. Finally, we find that changes in the bargaining power of workers do not appear to significantly affect (the uncertainty in) the trajectory of wages. Such findings appear to be consistent with the ones described above for unemployment rates.

Finally, Fig. 12.12 shows the forecast error variance decomposition of participation rates. The main short-term drivers are, in descending order, shocks to labour demand, wages and ageing population. However, already from a relatively short time horizon (not exceeding 5 years), the relative contribution of different factors stabilize, showing that labour supply is again the main variable responsible for the variability in the long run. Again, this finding tends to support the intuition that, in the long run, what matters is the supply side, while in the short run the demand side dominates other sources of dynamics.

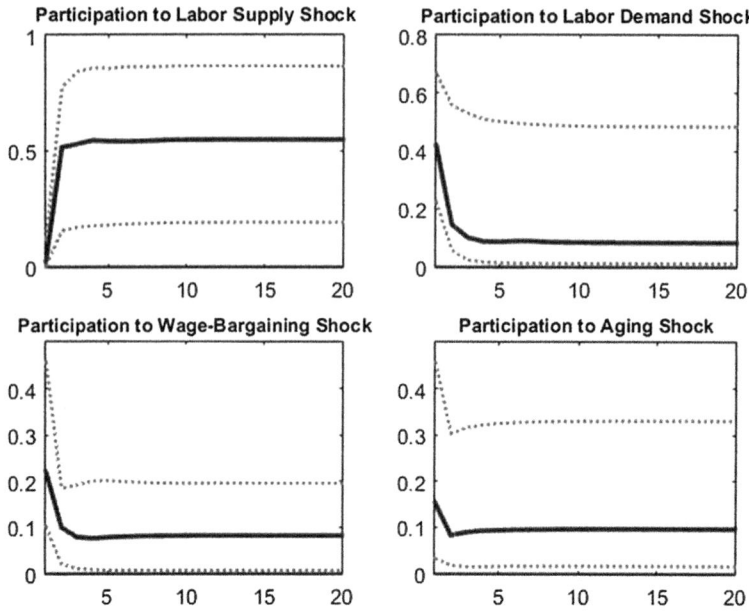

Fig. 12.12 The determinants of labour force participation

5   Conclusions

This study analyses the effect of shocks to population ageing in the evolution of the labour market outcomes in West Germany during the period 1970–2014. To this end, we estimate an SVAR model using Bayesian techniques and we implement the algorithm developed by Rubio-Ramirez et al. (2014) to implement zero and sign restrictions for the identification of structural shocks of demand, supply, wages and demographic ageing. We find that shocks to the latter increase participation and unemployment rates while decreasing wages.

However, this response is heterogeneous at the regional level, depending on the time horizon considered and most likely on pre-existing conditions and other factors not considered here, such as migration. While the negative effect of ageing on wages is quite persistent, the positive effect on the unemployment rate becomes negative after a few periods, and the negative effect on the participation rate is reabsorbed relatively quickly. On the other hand, we find that the greatest differences in the pattern of impulse response from the average of West Germany are observed in Saarland and Rhineland-Palatinate for both wages and unemployment, and in the Hamburg region in the case of participation to the labour market. Finally, through an exercise of variance decomposition of forecast errors, we find that the role played by population ageing is not relevant in determining either unemployment rates or participation rates. In contrast, ageing population appears to be a determining factor in the evolution of wages.

These results, taken together, have obvious and relevant policy implications. They clearly suggest that the result of the macro-trend of population ageing predicted by different international organizations for the first half of the twenty-first century will be that of promoting wage deflation. In this sense, our results conform to the evidence from other studies that have shown that ageing has a deflationary effect on the economy. In response to this, policymakers may implement expansionary demand policies to counter the effects caused by falling wages. However, given the current funding constraints of the public sector in many countries, this option does not seem to be viable in the upcoming years. Alternatively, policies that reduce barriers to immigration can be beneficial, because they can facilitate the entrance of younger workers in the labour force. Migration itself should be one of the factors considered in possible extensions of this empirical exercise, as its role in shaping the new (future) demographic profile of countries and of high-demand regions cannot be ignored.

Acknowledgements The research presented in this chapter is part of the project "Population Ageing and Regional Labour Market Development", funded by the Institute for Employment Research (IAB), Germany, which the authors gratefully acknowledge. The research has also benefited from the financial support of the Spanish Ministry of Economy and Competitiveness (Project ECO2016-76681-R) and the Excellence Grants Program of the Fundación Bancaria Caja Navarra.

References

Aaronson S, Cajner T, Fallick B, Galbis-Reig F, Smith C, Wascher W (Fall 2014) Labour force participation: recent developments and future prospects. Brooking Papers on Economic Activity, pp 197–275

Acemoglu D, Johnson S (2007) Disease and development: the effect of life expectancy on economic growth. J Polit Econ 115(6):925–985

Aksoy Y, Basso HS, Grasl T, Smith R (2015) Demographic structure and macroeconomic trends, Birkbeck working papers in economics and finance, no 1501

Alecke B, Mitze T, Untiedt G (2010) Internal migration, regional labour market dynamics and implications for German east-west disparities: results from a panel VAR. Jahrb Reg 30:159–189

Anderson D, Botman D, Hunt B (2014) Is Japan's population aging deflationary? IMF working paper WP/14/139

Baumeister C, Benati L (2013) Unconventional monetary policy and the great recession: estimating the macroeconomic effects of a spread compression at the zero lower bound. Int J Cent Bank 9(2):165–212

Benati L (2013) Why are recessions associated with financial crises different? Working paper university of bern

Biagi F, Lucifora C (2008) Demographic and education effects on unemployment in Europe. Labour Econ 15(5):1076–1101

Binning A (2013) Underidentified SVAR models: a framework for combining short and long-run restrictions with sign-restrictions. Norges bank working paper, no 14/2013

Blanchard OJ, Katz LF (1992) Regional evolutions. Brook Pap Econ Act 1:1–75

Blanchard O, Quah D (1989) The dynamic effects of aggregate demand and supply disturbances. Am Econ Rev 79:655–673

Bloom DE, Canninga D, Mansfield RK, Moore M (2007) Demographic change, social security systems, and savings. J Monet Econ 54(1):92–114

Bloom D, Canning D, Fink G, Finlay J (2007) Does age structure forecast economic growth? Int J Forecast 23(4):569–585

Bloom D, Canning D, Fink G (2010) Implications of population ageing for economic growth. Oxf Rev Econ Policy 26(4):583–612

Borsch-Supan A (2003) Labour market effects of population aging. Labour Rev Labour Econ Ind Rel 17(1):5–44

Bullard J, Garriga C, Waller CJ (2012) Demographics, redistribution, and optimal inflation. Institute for Monetary and Economic Studies (IMES), Discussion paper series 2012-E-13

Carlino G, DeFina R (1998) The differential regional effects of monetary policy. Rev Econ Stat 80:572–587

Carlino G, DeFina R, Sill K (2001) Sectoral shocks and metropolitan employment growth. J Urban Econ 50(3):396–417

Decressin J, Fatas A (1994) Regional labour market dynamics in Europe. Discussion paper no. 1085, Centre for Economic Policy Research, London

Dostie B (2011) Wages, productivity and aging. De Economist 159(2):139–158

Elhorst JP (2003) The mystery of regional unemployment differentials: theoretical and empirical explanations. J Econ Surv 17(5):709–748

Fernandez-Villaverde J, Rubio-Ramirez JF, Sargent TJ, Watson MW (2007) ABCs (and Ds) of understanding VARs. Am Econ Rev 97:1021–1026

Foroni C, Furlanetto F, Lepetit A (2015) Labour supply factors and economic fluctuations. Norges bank research working paper

Fredriksson P (1999) The dynamics of regional labour markets and active labour market policy: swedish evidence. Oxf Econ Pap 51(4):623–648

Fry R, Pagan A (2011) Sign restrictions in structural vector autoregressions: a critical review. J Econ Lit 49(4):938–960

Fuchs M (2016) Unemployment decline in East Germany: the role of demography. Rev Reg Res 36(2):145–168

Fuchs M, Weyh A (2014) Demography and unemployment in East Germany. How close are the ties? IAB discussion paper 26/2014

Fujita S, Fujiwara I (2014): Aging and deflation: japanese experience. Unpublished manuscript

Garloff A, Pohl C, Schanne N (2013) Do small labour market entry cohorts reduce unemployment? Demogr Res 29(15):379–406

Gordo LR, Skirbekk V (2013) Skill demand and the comparative advantage of age: Jobs tasks and earnings from the 1980s to the 2000s in Germany. Labour Econ 22:61–69

Jimeno JF, Bentolila S (1995) Regional unemployment persistence (Spain 1976–1994), Documento de Trabajo, FEDEA

Kim S, Lee JW (2008) Demographic changes, saving, and current account: an analysis based on a panel VAR model. Jpn World Econ 20:236–256

Lovasz A, Rigo M (2013) Vintage effects, ageing and productivity. Labour Econ 22:47–60.

Maki-Arvela P (2003) Regional evolutions in Finland: panel data results of a VAR approach to labour market dynamics. Reg Stud 37(5):423–443

Maestas N, Mullen JK, Powell D (2016) The effect of population aging on economic growth, the labour force and productivity. NBER working paper, no 22452

Mahlberg B, Freund I, Crespo-Cuaresma J, Prskawetzc A (2013) Ageing, productivity and wages in Austria. Labour Econ 22:5–15

Mountford A, Uhlig H (2009) What are the effects of fiscal policy shocks? J Appl Econ 24(6):960–992

Partridge MD, Rickman DS (2003) The waxing and waning of regional economies: the chickenegg question of jobs vs. people. J Urban Econ 53:76–97

Partridge MD, Rickman DS (2006) An SVAR model of fluctuations in U.S. migration flows and state labour market dynamics. South Econ J 72(4):958–980

Partridge MD, Rickman DS (2009) Canadian regional labour market evolutions: a long-run restrictions SVAR analysis. Appl Econ 41(13–15):1855–1871

Peersmand G, Straub R (2009) Technology shocks and robust sign restrictions in a euro area SVAR. Int Econ Rev 50(3):727–750

Poterba JM (2001) Demographic structure and asset returns. Rev Econ Stat 83(4):565–584

Poterba JM (2004) The impact of population aging on financial markets. NBER working paper, no 10851

Rubio-Ramirez JF, Waggoner DF, Zha T (2010) Structural vector autoregressions: theory of identification and algorithms for inference. Rev Econ Stud 77(2):665–696

Rubio-Ramirez JF, Arias JE, Waggoner DF (2014) Inference based on SVARs identified with sign and zero restrictions: theory and applications. International finance discussion papers, no 1100

Uhlig H (2005) What are the effects of monetary policy on output? Results from an agnostic identification procedure. J Monet Econ 52:381–419

Van Ours JC, Stoeldraijer L (2011) Age,wage and productivity in dutch manufacturing. De Economist 159:113–137

Vega SH, Elhorst P (2014) Modelling regional labour market dynamics in space and time. Pap Reg Sci 93(4):819–841

Chapter 13
Regional Population Structure and Young Workers' Wages

Alfred Garloff and Duncan Roth

1 Introduction

Germany is in the middle of a demographic transition. The size of its population was on the decline between 2003—when positive net immigration started falling short of the natural population decrease—and 2010 and is projected to continue shrinking over the coming decades, falling by 11% between 2010 and 2040 (Statistisches Bundesamt 2009).[1] However, this transition also has a second dimension: during the second half of the twentieth century fertility rates declined permanently and eventually fell below replacement level. Coupled with increases in life expectancy, these processes are having a substantial effect on the age structure of Germany's population as evidenced by the ongoing increases in the size of older age groups at the expense of younger ones.

Between 1990 and 2010 the ratio of the working-age to the total population fell by over three percentage points, a downward trend that is expected to be exacerbated by the entry into retirement of the large post-World War II birth

---

[1]To ensure comparability with the empirical analysis of this paper, the reported numbers refer to Western Germany (excluding West Berlin). With the availability of the 2011 census, the basis for estimating population variables has changed. As the population measures in this paper are based on pre-census data, we also use the population projections that are derived from this data rather than the recently released projections that make use of the 2011 census.

A. Garloff
Institute for Employment Research (IAB), Frankfurt am Main, Germany

D. Roth (✉)
Institute for Employment Research (IAB), Düsseldorf, Germany
e-mail: duncan.roth@iab.de

© Springer International Publishing AG, part of Springer Nature 2018   261
U. Blien et al. (eds.), *Modelling Aging and Migration Effects on Spatial Labor Markets*, Advances in Spatial Science,
https://doi.org/10.1007/978-3-319-68563-2_13

cohorts. Moreover, demographic change has affected the age composition of the working-age population: while the share of individuals aged 15–24 in the working-age population increased between 2000 and 2010, this development is expected to reverse in the near future with the youth share projected to fall by 2.5 percentage points between 2010 and 2025. The implications of these changes—the combination of a shrinking and ageing population—for the future standard of living constitutes a widely discussed area of research (see Börsch-Supan 2013). In this context, the question of how labour productivity will be affected by the changes in the population-age structure will be of prime importance (see Bloom and Sousa-Poza 2013). Likewise, the sustainability of health care and public pension systems in light of demographic pressure has received considerable attention (see Arnds and Bonin 2002; Jimeno et al. 2008).

The objective of this paper is to empirically analyse the impact of changes in the size of the youth population within regional labour markets on the wages of young workers. In the light of the projected population developments, this type of analysis is relevant as it provides a basis for evaluating how demographic processes can be expected to affect the wages of future cohorts of young workers. Given its focus, this paper belongs to a larger body of literature that analyses the effects of changes in the age structure on labour-market outcomes. In addition to wage adjustments, a considerable amount of research has addressed the impact on age-specific (un-)employment (Zimmermann 1991; Korenman and Neumark 2000; Shimer 2001; Skans 2005; Biagi and Lucifora 2008; Ochsen 2009; Garloff et al. 2013; Moffat and Roth 2017) and educational attainment (Connelly 1986; Stapleton and Young 1988; Fertig et al. 2009).

While wage differences and wage trends between different cohorts in Western Germany are documented in Fitzenberger (1999), his analysis does not focus on the consequences of changes in the age structure, which is the concern of this paper. In a world with a single type of labour input, an increase in the size of the labour force will lead to an outward shift of the labour supply curve. If the labour market works in a way that the wage rate adjusts so as to equate the demand for and the supply of labour and diminishing marginal productivity implies a downward-sloping labour demand curve, the effect of an increase in the labour force will be a lower equilibrium wage rate. If instead labour inputs are not homogenous but rather only imperfectly substitutable across age groups, the effects of a change in age-specific labour supply will—depending on the degree of substitutability—be concentrated on the members of that age group. Within such a framework, an increase in the share of young individuals should be accompanied by a decrease in their wages.

This paper contributes to the existing literature on cohort-size effects by addressing the question through which channels changes in the size of the youth population affect the wages of young workers. Specifically, we focus on the issue of occupational up- or downgrading. Gertler and Trigari (2009) argue that individuals have a better chance of moving into higher-paying industries, firms or jobs during boom periods than during recessions. Since increased competition—as a result of belonging to a large age group—may lead individuals in larger age groups to take up positions in lower-paying industries or occupations than they would have done as part of a smaller cohort, we compare the estimated wage effect of the youth share from models that exclude or include detailed information about an individual's industrial and occupational affiliation.

We find that the youth share has a statistically significant negative effect on the wages of young workers. Specifically, an increase by one percentage point is predicted to decrease wages by approximately 3% in our baseline model. However, once controlling for an individual's industry and, particularly, occupation reduces the estimated wage decrease to about 2%, which suggests that a substantial part of the negative effect of age-group size is the result of individuals in larger age groups being more likely to be employed in lower-paying occupations. According to these results, future generations of young workers can expect to benefit from demographic developments. Specifically, a decrease in the youth share by 2.5 percentage points, as projected to occur between 2010 and 2025, would be predicted to lead to an increase in young workers' wages of about 5%, ceteris paribus.

The remainder of the paper is structured as follows. Section 2 addresses the relationship between age structure and wage outcomes and reviews the relevant theoretical and empirical literature. Section 3 provides descriptive statistics on the youth population in Germany. The empirical analysis is the topic of Sect. 4, while Sect. 5 discusses the regression results. Section 6 presents the conclusion.

2 Population Structure and Wages

Differently aged workers are not perfectly substitutable. Age can be expected to be correlated with a worker's set of skills, which in turn affects his suitability for different tasks. First, age is a good predictor for work experience, and, ceteris paribus, more experienced workers will usually have more firm-specific, occupation-specific, industry-specific or general human capital. If this type of knowledge is relevant for on-the-job performance, differently aged workers can be expected to be only imperfectly substitutable. Indeed, Welch's (1979) career-phase model can be interpreted as an example of a model in which imperfect substitutability arises from differences in firm-specific human capital. Second, jobs vary with respect to the tasks that they contain and therefore also concerning the abilities that workers are required to have in order to perform these tasks. Older workers may be less easily substitutable for younger workers in occupations requiring physical or certain types of cognitive skills (Mazzonna and Peracchi 2012). As a consequence of imperfect substitutability a change in the relative size of an age group will mainly affect the labour-market outcomes of the members of that group.

As a starting point to analysing the effects of a change in the size of a specific age group on the wages of its members, it is useful to assume a production function with differently aged workers as distinct factors of production (see Card and Lemieux 2001; Fitzenberger and Kohn 2006). In the benchmark case of a perfectly competitive labour market, in which each factor of production is paid the monetary value of his marginal product, a change in the supply of a specific production factor will cause the wage to adjust in a way that the market is again cleared. In the case of each factor of production exhibiting diminishing marginal productivity, an increase in the size of an age group will reduce the wages paid to its members. Labour markets, however, do not necessarily clear. The existence of minimum or efficiency wages as well as collective wage bargaining are possible sources that can prevent the wage rate from fully adjusting in response to a change in labour supply, while the coexistence of unemployment and vacancies provides evidence against the existence of a market-clearing equilibrium as predicted by the benchmark model of a competitive labour market. Existing theoretical models, however, suggest that even in the absence of clearing labour markets, changes in the relative supply of an age group will have an effect on age-specific wages (Michaelis and Debus 2011).

The extant empirical literature, though differing with respect to the time periods and countries (or regions) under study, the model specification and identification strategy, provides evidence that increases in the size of an age group are associated with depressed wage outcomes for the members of that group.[2] Early studies using US data estimate a negative relationship between the relative size of an age group and the average wages that are earned by individuals within that group for different levels of educational qualification (Welch 1979; Berger 1985). Alternatively, Freeman (1979) finds a negative effect of the young-to-old population ratio on the average wages of young workers relative to those of old workers. The existence of a negative effect of age-group size is also supported by evidence from Sapozhnikov and Triest (2007). Most recently, Morin (2015) exploits an exogenous shock to the supply of high-school graduates in Canada due to a reform of the secondary schooling system and finds negative cohort-size effects on wages. Empirical evidence from Europe is scarcer but also supports the hypothesis that wages earned in larger age groups are depressed compared to those of smaller age groups (see Wright 1991, for the UK and Brunello 2010, and Moffat and Roth 2016, for a sample of European countries).

It should be noted that changes in the age structure of the population do not necessarily imply changes in age-specific labour supply as participation rates as well as the number of hours worked could in principle adjust in a way as to completely counteract changes in age-group size. However, such a reaction seems unlikely as empirical evidence suggests that male labour supply is inelastic—at

---

[2]Notable exceptions can be found in the migration literature where many studies conclude that natives' wages are not negatively affected by age-specific immigration (Ottaviano and Peri 2012). A possible explanation for this finding is that migrants are complements rather than substitutes for native labour.

the extensive and the intensive margin—to changes in the wage rate (Blundell and MaCurdy 1999). More specifically, Garloff et al. (2013) show that a counteracting development in participation rates has not taken place in Germany in response to changes in the age structure at the national level in recent years.

3   Youth-Population Structure in Western Germany

This section provides information about the development of the working-age (15–64) and the youth population (15–24) in Western Germany at the national level and at the level of the labour-market region. Figure 13.1 shows the absolute size of both populations at 5-year intervals between 1995 and 2040. While the actual values are shown up to the year 2010[3], subsequent developments represent projections based on the variant *Untergrenze der mittleren Bevölkerung*, which assumes an annual net immigration of 100,000 individuals and a fertility rate of 1.4 and which represents the lower bound of corridor within which population development is expected to take place (Statistisches Bundesamt 2010).[4]

Except for a small increase between 1995 and 2000, the working-age population has been shrinking steadily and is projected to continue decreasing in size over the coming decades. By 2040 it will have fallen by almost 25% compared to its 2010 value, which reflects the effect of the large post-World War II birth cohorts reaching retirement age. In contrast, the number of young individuals grew by half a million between the years 2000 and 2010[5], but this development is expected to reverse in the near future with the size of the age group 15–24 projected to fall continuously until 2040. Reflecting changes in these two populations' relative rate of growth, the youth share, i.e. the size of the population aged 15–24 relative to the working-age population, displays a cyclical development: from 2000 to 2010 the share of young individuals expanded by approximately one percentage point (equivalently, 7%). However, as the youth population is expected to decrease at a faster rate than the working-age population, its share is projected to fall by 2.5 percentage points (equivalently, 15%) between 2010 and 2025. At the national level, the increase in the youth share during most of the sample period therefore contrasts with its projected development in the immediate future, which implies that changing demographics may contribute positively towards the development of young workers' wages in the coming years.

---

[3]Data comes from the Federal Statistical Office and has been obtained through the following link: https://www-genesis.destatis.de/genesis/online/link/tabellen/12411*.

[4]The upper bound of this corridor (*Obergrenze der mittleren Bevölkerung*) differs by assuming that annual net immigration will increase steadily to 200,000 in the year 2020 before plateauing at that level. Despite this difference the projection for the youth share is very similar (the largest difference between both projections amounts to 0.25 percentage points in the year 2040).

[5]These age groups are the children of the large post-World War II birth cohorts. This increase therefore reflects the large size of the parental generation.

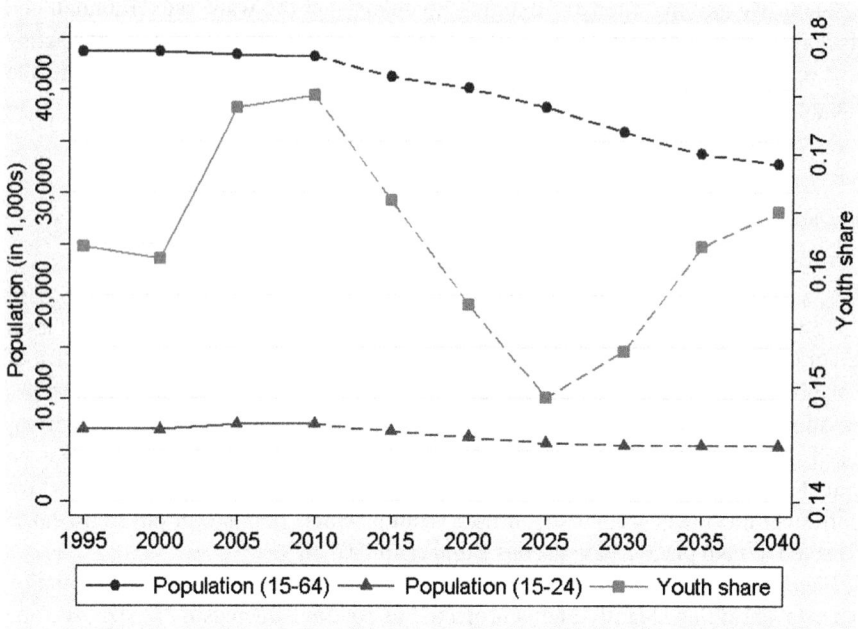

Fig. 13.1 Development of the population and the youth share at the national level. Source: Federal Statistical Office

Figure 13.2 illustrates the existing regional heterogeneity in the share of individuals aged between 15 and 24 in the working-age population by reporting the value of this variable for the West-German regional labour markets. The extent of cross-sectional variation in the youth-share variable is revealed for the year 1995 in the top left map, in which the labour-market regions are grouped into quartiles based on the size of the youth share. Compared to a value of about 16% at the national level, the regional youth share varies between 14% and 21%. The other maps show the cross-sectional variation in the youth-share variable for the years 2000, 2005 and 2010, respectively. Moreover, they reveal the within-region variation in this variable, i.e. its development over time (to allow for a comparison of the different years, the same intervals are chosen as for the year 1995). Reflecting the drop in the national youth share in the year 2000, the share has also generally fallen at the regional level as illustrated by a number of regions that were in the fourth or third quartile in 1995 now being in the third or second quartile, respectively. Likewise, an increasing number of regions are registered in higher quartiles in the years 2005 and 2010, reflecting the increase in the youth share at the national level.

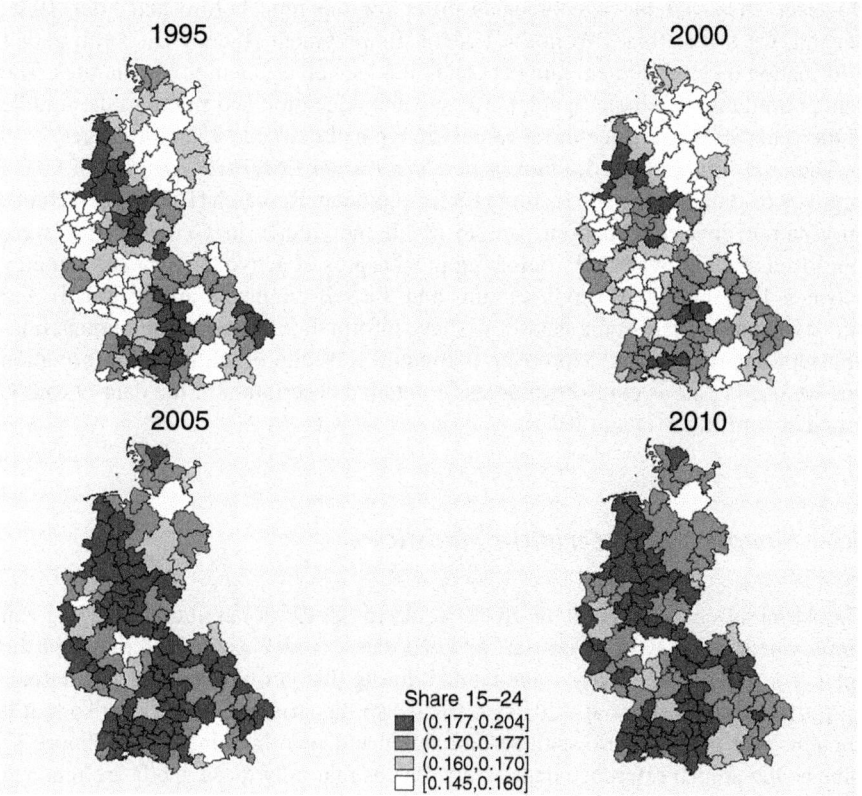

Fig. 13.2 Variation in the youth share (15–24) at the regional level. Source: Federal Statistical Office (population data) and Federal Institute for Research on Building, Urban Affairs and Spatial Development (geodata)

4   Empirical Analysis

4.1   Data

Three data sources are used for the empirical analysis. The first source is population data for Germany on the regional level according to age groups which is used to construct the relative size of the youth population within a regional labour market. The information reported by the statistical offices refers to the end of the year (31 December). There is no information beyond age and sex in these data. Particularly, there is no information available on the educational composition. Corrections have to be made to account for changes in the delineations of municipalities and districts which results in a dataset that is spatially consistent over time back until 1978.

However, the available age brackets differ for the time before and after 1985. Second, we use statistics from the Federal Employment Agency (FEA) to gather information on employment numbers and rates as well as unemployment rates. The data is available by single-age cohorts, sex and education and refers to the middle of the year (30 June), since those values are typically close to yearly averages.

The final source is the *Stichprobe der Integrierten Erwerbsbiografien* (SIAB), a large micro-dataset from the Institute for Employment Research (IAB), that includes information on a 2% random sample of all individuals in Germany that were employed, unemployed or participating in measures of active labour-market policy between 1975 and 2010 (civil servants and the self-employed are excluded). For employed individuals in the dataset we have information on their employment relationship on a daily basis. Moreover, it contains a wealth of additional information that we use in part as control variables. A detailed description of the dataset can be found in vom Berge et al. (2013).

4.2 Sample and Descriptive Statistics

The observations contained in SIAB refer to spells of an individual (e.g. an employment spell) with given start and end dates as well as characteristics of the spell (e.g. the average daily wage earned during this period). We use the setting-up routines by Eberle et al. (2013) to transform the structure of the data so that it contains data from a single spell per individual and year. In doing so, we choose 15 June as the annual reference date, which means that only those spells are retained that include the reference date in a given year. As employers are required to report the wages of their employees once a year and this is typically done on 31 December, the longest spells run from 1 January to 31 December in a given year. Using 15 June as the reference date implies that spells starting and ending before (or after) 15 June within a given year are not being considered. This specific reference date is chosen because June values of employment figures are usually close to annual averages, while the middle of the month is used to avoid any end-of-calendar-month effects. However, the results are robust to using 31 December as the reference date.[6]

The sample covers the period 1999–2010 and consists of regularly employed (*sozialversicherungspflichtig Beschäftigte*) males who are between 15 and 24 years old. Individuals in vocational training are excluded because the mechanisms determining their remuneration are considered to be different from the rest of the labour market. As there is no information about the number of hours worked in the data, the sample is further restricted to full-time employees. While 95% of the observations have one full-time job, some observations hold other jobs in addition to being full-time employed, e.g. 3% of observations are also in minor employment

---

[6]The results of this and all other robustness checks can be found in the Appendix to this paper.

(*geringfügige Beschäftigung*). In such a case only information about the first full-time job is retained.[7]

The model's dependent variable is an individual's inflation-adjusted daily wage including social security contributions and taxes.[8] The reported wage is censored at the value of the corresponding year's upper social security threshold; but given that our sample is restricted to individuals aged between 15 and 24 only a small fraction of observations will have wages above the threshold, and since imputation procedures (see Gartner 2005) suggest that in such a case the true wage values are close to the censoring value, we use the censored wage for these observations. At the other end of the spectrum, we also observe unrealistically low daily wages. To remove these observations we truncate the wage distribution at twice the value of the minor-employment threshold (*Geringfügigkeitsgrenze*)—an approach that has also been taken by other authors working with the same data source (e.g. Gürtzgen 2016). This implies that observations with wages of less than 650 Euro per month (21.26 Euro per day or, alternatively, 2.57 Euro per hour, assuming an 8-h working day) between 1999 and 2002 or less than 800 Euro per month (26.28 Euro per day or 3.29 Euro per hour) between 2003 and 2010 are dropped.

The main variable of interest is the youth share, which measures the number of individuals aged between 15 and 24 relative to the number of working-age individuals (ages 15–64) within a regional labour market as defined by Eckey et al. (2006). The labour-market region refers to an individual's place of employment.[9] Due to limitations pertaining to the availability of population data preceding re-unification, our empirical analysis is restricted to the 108 labour-market regions of Western Germany. This restriction is unfortunate: the demographic processes that have seen the youth share in Eastern Germany fall from 19% in 2004 to 14% in 2012 (Fuchs and Weyh 2014) certainly warrant an analysis of the corresponding wage effects.

Using a sub-national variable allows us to identify the effect of the youth share on young workers' wages while also controlling for macroeconomic shocks at the national level in a flexible way. A range of control variables are included in the model. At the individual level, SIAB contains information on age and labour-market experience as well as on an employee's level of education and his nationality. At the firm level, we use the size of the establishment and, in an extension to the baseline model, we also include two-digit indicators for an individual's occupation

---

[7]For individuals holding more than one job at the same time it would in principle be possible to use total earnings from all jobs rather than just the wage earned in one job as the relevant dependent variable. We abstain from doing so as our focus is on how the supply of young workers affects the wages earned in a particular job. Similar results to those shown in Table 13.1 are obtained when observations with more than a full-time job are removed from the sample.

[8]Inflation-adjustment is done using the consumer price index (base year: 2010). The data comes from the Federal Statistical Office and has been obtained through the following link: https://www.destatis.de/DE/ZahlenFakten/GesamtwirtschaftUmwelt/Preise/Verbraucherpreisindizes/Tabellen_/VerbraucherpreiseKategorien.html?cms_gtp=145110_slot%253D2&https=1.

[9]Comparable results are obtained when an individual's place of residence is used instead.

Table 13.1 2SLS regression results

Dependent variable: log real daily earnings	Baseline	+Industry	+Occupation	+Industry +Occupation
Youth share	−2.89 (1.22)*	−2.77 (1.06)**	−1.96 (1.08)†	−2.11 (1.01)*
Age	0.21 (0.02)***	0.15 (0.02)***	0.16 (0.02)***	0.13 (0.02)***
Age^2	−0.00 (0.00)***	−0.00 (0.00)***	−0.00 (0.00)***	−0.00 (0.00)***
Experience	0.05 (0.01)***	0.05 (0.00)***	0.05 (0.00)***	0.05 (0.00)***
Experience^2	−0.00 (0.00)***	−0.00 (0.00)***	−0.00 (0.00)***	−0.00 (0.00)***
Education				
Lower secondary (with apprenticeship)	0.22 (0.01)***	0.16 (0.00)***	0.14 (0.00)***	0.12 (0.00)***
Upper secondary (without apprenticeship)	0.04 (0.02)**	0.00 (0.01)	0.01 (0.01)	−0.02 (0.01)
Upper secondary (with apprenticeship)	0.30 (0.01)***	0.21 (0.01)***	0.20 (0.01)***	0.16 (0.01)***
Tertiary (University of Applied Sciences)	0.31 (0.02)***	0.25 (0.02)***	0.22 (0.02)***	0.18 (0.02)***
Tertiary (University)	0.46 (0.03)***	0.42 (0.03)***	0.34 (0.03)***	0.32 (0.03)***
Nationality				
Turkey	0.01 (0.01)	−0.00 (0.00)	0.01 (0.01)	0.00 (0.01)
Switzerland/Austria	−0.02 (0.04)	0.06 (0.04)	0.02 (0.05)	0.05 (0.03)
Western Europe	−0.03 (0.03)	0.02 (0.02)	0.01 (0.02)	0.02 (0.02)
Northern Europe	−0.07 (0.07)	−0.00 (0.04)	0.04 (0.04)	0.05 (0.03)
Central Europe	−0.03 (0.02)*	−0.01 (0.01)	−0.00 (0.01)	−0.00 (0.01)
Eastern Europe	−0.08 (0.03)***	−0.02 (0.03)	−0.04 (0.03)	−0.01 (0.02)
South-East Europe	−0.02 (0.01)†	−0.01 (0.01)	−0.01 (0.01)	−0.01 (0.01)
Southern Europe	−0.07 (0.01)***	−0.05 (0.01)***	−0.05 (0.01)***	−0.04 (0.01)***
Africa	−0.11 (0.02)***	−0.06 (0.02)***	−0.06 (0.02)***	−0.05 (0.02)***
Asia	−0.12 (0.02)***	−0.04 (0.01)***	−0.04 (0.02)**	−0.04 (0.01)*
America/Oceania	−0.08 (0.06)	0.09 (0.04)**	0.11 (0.05)*	0.10 (0.03)***
Firm size (in 1000s)	0.21 (0.03)***	0.00 (0.00)***	0.00 (0.00)***	0.00 (0.00)***

Unemployment rate	0.00 (0.00)	0.00 (0.00)	0.00 (0.00)	0.00 (0.00)
Youth unemployment rate	−0.00 (0.00)	−0.00 (0.00)	−0.00 (0.00)	−0.00 (0.00)
Constant	2.02 (0.32)***	2.53 (0.26)***	2.28 (0.30)***	2.52 (0.26)***
Dummies				
Year	Yes	Yes	Yes	Yes
Labour-market region	Yes	Yes	Yes	Yes
Industry	No	Yes	No	Yes
Occupation	No	No	Yes	Yes
First-stage regression				
Instrument	0.46 (0.00)***	0.46 (0.00)***	0.46 (0.00)***	0.46 (0.00)***
First-stage test statistics				
F-statistic	131.80***	132.31***	132.33***	132.67***
Shea's partial R²	0.32	0.32	0.32	0.32
Observations				
Individuals	107,351	107,351	107,351	107,351
Labour-market region-year cells	1296	1296	1296	1296
Labour-market regions (clusters)	108	108	108	108
R²	0.24	0.46	0.41	0.51
ME(stdev)	−3.67%*	−3.52%**	−2.49%†	−2.68%*

Cluster-robust standard errors in parentheses (clustered at the level of the labour-market region). ***/**/*/† indicate significance at the 0.005/0.01/0.05/0.10 level, respectively. *Instrument* shows the coefficient of the instrument in the first-stage regression. *ME(stdev)* gives the percentage change in daily earnings given an increase in the youth share by one standard deviation

and industry which allows us to address the issue of industrial and occupational up- and downgrading (see Gertler and Trigari 2009). In order to control for local macroeconomic effects we use the region-specific (district-specific) unemployment rate and, as the corresponding youth-unemployment rate is not available, the share of unemployed young individuals in the population. Descriptive statistics of the variables included in the baseline model are shown in Table 13.2 in the Appendix.

The average log real daily wage earnings are equal to 4.28 (approximately 72.24 Euro). The share of individuals aged between 15 and 24 in the working-age population is 17%. Since only employed individuals are included in the sample and individuals in vocational training are not considered, over 95% of observations are 20 years or older and a similar share has acquired up to four years of work experience. In terms of educational qualification the sample is rather homogenous as more than nine out of ten observations have lower secondary education and about three quarters of the cases also have a completed apprenticeship. The average firm size is slightly below 1000 employees, while the regional unemployment rate has a mean value of about 8%, which is slightly higher than the share of unemployed youths in the population.

4.3   Empirical Model and Identification

In order to estimate the relationship between the wages of young workers and their relative supply, we specify an enhanced Mincer equation (Mincer 1958) and regress the natural logarithm of an individual's inflation-adjusted daily wage earnings w_{irt} on the youth share y_{rt} and a set of control variables x_{irt} as formulated in Equation (13.1).[10] The indexes i, r and t denote individuals, labour-market regions and years, respectively. The variables δ_r and μ_t represent dummies for the labour-market region an individual is employed in and for the sample year, respectively. Due to the inclusion of the region dummies it is only the within-region variation from which the coefficient of the youth share is identified. The error term ε_{irt} captures stochastic shocks as well as the effects of all other variables that are not explicitly controlled for:[11]

$$\log(w_{irt}) = \alpha + \beta y_{rt} + x'_{irt}\gamma + \delta_r + \mu_t + \varepsilon_{irt} \tag{13.1}$$

---

[10]The specification of Eq. 13.1 can also be interpreted as a special case of the model provided by Card and Lemieux (2001) in as far as our analysis also assumes imperfect substitutability across age groups but considers only the age group 15–24 in the empirical analysis.

[11]We abstain from estimating a model that includes fixed effects at the individual level. Since 44% of observations come from individuals that are included in the sample only once, estimation of such a model suffers from an insufficient degree of within-variation. Notice that for consistent estimation of the youth share's marginal effect, a fixed effects approach would only be required in the presence of unobserved, time-invariant heterogeneity at the individual level that is correlated with the youth share.

Consistent estimation of the effect that the youth share has on the wages of young workers by pooled ordinary least squares (OLS) requires that the regressor y_{rt} be conditionally uncorrelated with the error term. We argue that this requirement is unlikely to hold because individuals are able to self-select into regions where they can expect to earn higher wages, ceteris paribus, thereby turning the youth share into an endogenous variable. To address this issue we employ an IV identification strategy. Our instrument is the variable that has also been used by Skans (2005), Garloff et al. (2013) and Moffat and Roth (2016, 2017). This variable is defined as the relative size of the group of individuals who are 15 years younger than the age group on which the youth-share variable is based and who are observed 15 years earlier, i.e. we instrument the current share of those aged 15–24 (relative to the age group 15–64) with the share of those aged 0–9 (relative to the age group 0–49) 15 years earlier.

The strength of the instrument derives from the fact that in the absence of migration and natural population changes the instrument and the youth-share variable would be based on the same group of individuals and both variables would actually be identical. We argue that migration and natural changes do not purge the association between the instrument and the endogenous regressor, meaning that if an age group in a given labour-market region was comparatively large (relative to the size of the same age group in other labour-market regions and years), the group of individuals in the same region who are 15 years older will still be relatively large in the present. This argument is supported by the results of the first-stage statistics, which show the instrument to have a high degree of explanatory power.

The identifying assumption is that individuals in the age group 0–9 do not choose where to reside based on the anticipation of their earnings 15 years in the future. If this condition is satisfied, the causal effect of the relative supply of young individuals in a given labour-market region on young workers' earnings can be identified by using a two-stage least squares (2SLS) estimator with the time-lagged and age-lagged population variable as an instrument. An argument that can be brought forward against the validity of the instrument is that the relative size of the age group 0–9 will depend on the locational choices of their parents. If parents, and thus their children, self-selected into high-wage areas and their wages were correlated with the wages of their children 15 years in the future, this would lead the proposed identification strategy to fail. Notice, however, that if the parental generation's choice of location and the correlation between their own and their children's wages are due to time-invariant factors, these will be accounted for by the region dummies of Eq. (13.1).

Finally, a feature of the model in Eq. (13.1) is that the explanatory variable of interest, y_{rt}, is defined at a higher level of aggregation than the dependent variable, which also varies across individuals.[12] To account for this feature we cluster at the level of the labour-market region in order to avoid biased standard errors (see Moulton 1990).

---

[12]Comparable results are obtained when all variables are averaged across the individuals in a region-year cell and the regression is weighted by the number of observations per cell (see Angrist and Pischke 2009).

5 Results

Table 13.1 contains the 2SLS coefficients of the youth-share variable for four
different specifications of Eq. (13.1). The baseline specification, shown in the first
column, includes only those control variables that were discussed in the previous
section. In order to asses to what extent the effect of changes in the size of the youth
population can be ascribed to selection into industries or occupations, the remaining
columns estimate an extended model that also contains dummy variables to control
for an individual's industrial and/or occupational affiliation.

The results from the first-stage regressions indicate that the 2SLS estimates are
not affected by the presence of weak instruments as the F-statistics are well in
excess of the threshold value of 10 (Staiger and Stock 1997) in each specification.
Furthermore, the instrument is found to be positively related to the endogenous
youth-share variable, indicating, as expected, that an age group that was especially
large in the past continues to be so in the present. However, there is no one-to-one
relationship between both variables which suggests that natural population change
as well as migration can lead to changes in the relative size of an age group over
time.

As hypothesised, the estimated youth-share coefficients turn out to be negative.
It can be shown that the corresponding OLS estimates are also negative, but smaller
than their 2SLS counterparts and statistically insignificant. This difference is in line
with the hypothesis that contemporaneous increases in the wages that can be earned
by young workers induces youths to move into such regions. In the baseline model
an increase in the size of the youth share by one percentage point is associated with
a decrease in a young worker's wages of almost 3%, ceteris paribus, with the effect
being significant at the 5% level. Moreover, the bottom row of Table 13.1 shows the
marginal effect for a change in the youth share by one standard deviation which is
estimated to lead to a wage decrease of about 3.7%.

The results displayed in the second column show that controlling for the industry
of the firm that an individual is working for does not materially change the
estimated wage effect of the youth-share variable. In contrast, if dummy variables
for an individual's occupation (column three) or the combination of industry
and occupation dummies (column four) are added to the model, the estimated
coefficient of the youth share decreases in magnitude by about one third and
one quarter, respectively, compared to the baseline specification. These findings
provide evidence that a substantial portion of the negative wage effect associated
with belonging to a large age group can be ascribed to occupational selection.
Specifically, it appears that members of larger youth cohorts have a higher likelihood
of being employed in lower-paying occupations.

This result is also relevant in light of recent results pertaining to the wage effects
of labour-market conditions. Kahn (2010) and Brunner and Kuhn (2014) find that
adverse labour-market conditions (measured by the unemployment rate at the time
of labour-market entry) depress wages and increase the probability of employment
in lower-quality occupations. Morin (2015) studies the wage effects of the increase

in labour supply due to the double cohort of high-school graduates in Ontario and provides evidence that part of the negative wage effect is due to selection into lower-paying occupations. Alternatively, higher-quality jobs may require a specific type of qualification. If the supply of training positions does not adjust to the supply of young individuals, the number of individuals barred from entering higher-paying occupations will increase in larger age groups.

Qualitatively, the finding that, ceteris paribus, an increase in the relative size of an age group depresses the wages of its members is in line with the results of other empirical analyses in this literature (Brunello 2010; Moffat and Roth 2016). In terms of the magnitude of the effect, Moffat and Roth (2016), using a similar identification strategy, find that an increase in cohort size by one standard deviation decreases wages by 10% for individuals who have completed secondary education, whereas the effect for individuals with lower secondary education is statistically insignificant. Those results are, however, not directly comparable with the findings of this paper, primarily because the cohort-size variable that is used in that paper is also education-specific.

In terms of the control variables, wages are predicted to increase at a decreasing rate in age and experience—the latter being suggestive of the widely documented concave experience-earnings profile (Polachek 2008).[13] Higher levels of schooling and professional qualification are associated with higher earnings. Nationals from Eastern European, South-East and Southern European countries are predicted to earn significantly less than Germans, while the largest difference is found for Africans and Asians with earnings lower by more than 10%. Individuals who are employed in firms with larger workforces are found to have higher earnings, which is in line with evidence by Lehmer and Möller (2010). Finally, the estimated effects of the unemployment rate and the share of young unemployed individuals are small. The youth-unemployment variable draws a negative coefficient estimate, but in contrast to findings by Baltagi and Blien (1998) its effect is not statistically significant.

6 Conclusion

This paper empirically analyses how changes in the size of the youth population affect the wages of young male workers. Under the assumption that differently aged individuals are only imperfectly substitutable because of differences in firm-specific, occupation-specific, industry-specific or general human capital, economic theory predicts that an increase in the size of an age group reduces the earnings of the members of that group. This hypothesis is tested using a sample of young male employees from Western Germany. The demographic forces that are currently changing the age-structure of the German population illustrate the relevance of this analysis. Specifically, the share of young individuals is projected to fall by

---

[13]We have also estimated Eq. 13.1 using mutually exclusive sets of age and experience dummies. Changing the specification in this way has no effect on the estimated youth-share coefficients.

2.5 percentage points (equivalently, by 15%) at the national level over the period 2010–2025.

To avoid confounding of the estimated coefficients due to selected labour-market participation, females are excluded from the sample (though they are included in the youth-share variable). The downside of this approach is that the results of the empirical analysis are only informative about the relationship between wages and the age structure on regional labour markets for male workers. Whether and to what extent the wages of young females are responsive to changes in the youth share remains a subject for future research. Moreover, the results of this analysis raise the question whether the youth share, through its impact on wages, exerts an indirect effect on the participation decision of females.

In addition to providing an analysis of this relationship based on recent administrative data, the question is addressed through which channels variation in the size of an age group affects its members' wages. Using an IV approach to deal with the possibility of the youth share being endogenous as a result of migration into high-wage regions, we find that an increase in the youth share by one percentage point is predicted to decrease the wages of young worker's by approximately 3%, ceteris paribus. However, since the size of the youth cohort may have an effect on the industry or occupation an individual is employed in, we proceed by adding corresponding indicator variables to the model. While controlling for the industry of the firm that a young worker is employed in does not change the results, the inclusion of occupational dummies leads to a reduction of the estimated youth-share effect by approximately one third. This finding suggests that parts of the negative wage effect of belonging to a larger youth age group are the result of a higher probability of working in a lower-paying occupation. These result therefore provide indirect evidence that there is occupational downgrading for members of larger age groups.

What are the implications of these findings for the wages of young workers in the future in light of Western Germany's changing demographics? As the youth share is projected to decrease over the coming years, demographic processes appear to be favourable to the development of the wages of young workers, at least for the group of male, full-time employees with relatively little work experience that form the basis of this analysis. Furthermore, to the extent that a negative relationship between wages and population structure also applies to older age groups the results of this paper suggest that demographic processes exert upward pressure on the wages of younger age groups, while putting downward pressure on the wages of older age groups, which might lead to a flattening of future age-earnings profiles.

Acknowledgements The authors would like to thank Stefan Fuchs, Bernd Hayo, John Moffat, Norbert Schanne and two anonymous referees for their advice and are grateful for comments from the participants of IAB's regional research network meeting in Aalen, the 54th Conference of the European Regional Science Association (ERSA), the 5th ifo Workshop Arbeitsmarkt und Sozialpolitik, the joint IAB Regional Science Academy workshop in Amsterdam and the 28th Conference of the European Association of Labour Economists (EALE). The Federal Institute for Research on Building, Urban Affairs and Spatial Development kindly provided the shapefile of the German labour-market regions. Our thanks also go to Annie Roth for proof-reading an earlier version of this paper.

Appendix

Table 13.2 Descriptive statistics

Variable	Mean	Standard deviation	Minimum	Maximum
Log daily earnings	4.28	0.31	3.18	6.21
Youth share				
Labour market region				
Population-based (place of residence)	0.17	0.01	0.14	0.21
Population-based (place of employment)	0.17	0.01	0.14	0.21
District				
Population-based (place of residence)	0.17	0.01	0.13	0.23
Population-based (place of employment)	0.17	0.01	0.13	0.23
Instrument				
Labour market region				
Population-based (place of residence)	0.16	0.02	0.12	0.20
Population-based (place of employment)	0.16	0.02	0.12	0.20
District				
Population-based (place of residence)	0.16	0.02	0.10	0.21
Population-based (place of employment)	0.16	0.02	0.10	0.21
Age	22.33	1.46	15	24
15	0.00	0.01	0	1
16	0.00	0.01	0	1
17	0.00	0.03	0	1
18	0.00	0.07	0	1
19	0.03	0.17	0	1
20	0.09	0.29	0	1
21	0.16	0.37	0	1
22	0.20	0.40	0	1
23	0.24	0.43	0	1
24	0.28	0.45	0	1
Experience	2.04	1.48	0	10
0	0.14	0.35	0	1
1	0.27	0.44	0	1
2	0.24	0.43	0	1
3	0.18	0.38	0	1
4	0.11	0.31	0	1
5	0.04	0.20	0	1
6	0.01	0.11	0	1
7	0.00	0.06	0	1

(continued)

Table 13.2 (continued)

Variable	Mean	Standard deviation	Minimum	Maximum
8	0.00	0.04	0	1
9	0.00	0.02	0	1
10	0.00	0.01	0	1
Education				
Lower secondary (without apprenticeship)[a]	0.19	0.39	0	1
Lower secondary (with apprenticeship)	0.76	0.42	0	1
Upper secondary (without apprenticeship)	0.01	0.12	0	1
Upper secondary (with apprenticeship)	0.03	0.17	0	1
Tertiary (University of Applied Sciences)	0.01	0.08	0	1
Tertiary (University)	0.00	0.05	0	1
Nationality				
Germany[a]	0.90	0.30	0	1
Turkey	0.04	0.20	0	1
Switzerland/Austria	0.00	0.03	0	1
Western Europe	0.00	0.04	0	1
Northern Europe	0.00	0.02	0	1
Central Europe	0.01	0.09	0	1
Eastern Europe	0.00	0.04	0	1
South-East Europe	0.02	0.14	0	1
Southern Europe	0.02	0.13	0	1
Africa	0.00	0.05	0	1
Asia	0.01	0.08	0	1
America/Oceania	0.00	0.02	0	1
Firm size	970.47	3897.56	1	42,626
Unemployment rate				
Labour-market region (place of residence)	8.16	2.53	2.60	18.04
Labour-market region (place of employment)	8.13	2.51	2.60	18.04
District (place of residence)	8.01	2.94	1.90	25.59
District (place of employment)	8.28	3.01	1.90	25.59
Youth unemployment share				
Labour-market region (place of residence)	7.26	2.65	1.90	24.38
Labour-market region (place of employment)	7.23	2.63	1.90	24.38
District (place of residence)	7.20	2.95	1.70	24.92
District (place of employment)	7.36	2.99	1.70	24.92
Observations	107,351			

[a]Base category in the regression analysis

Table 13.3 Use of 31 December as the reference date

Dependent variable: log real daily earnings	Baseline	+Industry	+Occupation	+Industry +Occupation
Youth share (2SLS)	−3.26 (1.16)**	−3.07 (1.06)***	−2.51 (1.06)*	−2.49 (1.01)*
Youth share (OLS)	−0.75 (0.74)	−0.90 (0.61)	−0.51 (0.66)	−0.60 (0.60)
Dummies				
Year	Yes	Yes	Yes	Yes
Labour-market region	Yes	Yes	Yes	Yes
Industry	No	Yes	No	Yes
Occupation	No	No	Yes	Yes
Control variables	Yes	Yes	Yes	Yes
First-stage regression				
Instrument	0.46 (0.00)	0.46 (0.00)***	0.46 (0.00)***	0.46 (0.00)
First-stage test statistics				
F-statistic	130.83***	131.28***	131.35***	131.57***
Shea's partial R^2	0.32	0.32	0.32	0.32
Observations				
Individuals	113,784	113,784	113,784	113,784
Labour-market region-year cells	1296	1296	1296	1296
Labour-market regions (clusters)	108	108	108	108
R^2 (2SLS)	0.30	0.49	0.44	0.53
R^2 (OLS)	0.30	0.49	0.44	0.53
ME(stdev, 2SLS)	−0.04**	−0.04***	−0.03*	−0.03*
ME(stdev, OLS)	−0.01	−0.01	−0.01	−0.01

Cluster-robust standard errors in parentheses (clustered at the level of the labour-market region). ***/**/*/† indicate significance at the 0.005/0.01/0.05/0.10 level, respectively. *Instrument* shows the coefficient of the instrument in the first-stage regression. *ME(stdev)* gives the percentage change in daily earnings given an increase in the youth share by one standard deviation

Table 13.4 Exclusion of observations with more than a full-time job

Dependent variable: log real daily earnings	Baseline	+Industry	+Occupation	+Industry +Occupation
Youth share (2SLS)	−2.90 (1.22)*	−2.83 (1.08)**	−2.08 (1.07)†	−2.21 (1.01)*
Youth share (OLS)	−0.81 (0.77)	−0.81 (0.64)	−0.48 (0.69)	−0.55 (0.59)
Dummies				
Year	Yes	Yes	Yes	Yes
Labour-market region	Yes	Yes	Yes	Yes
Industry	No	Yes	No	Yes
Occupation	No	No	Yes	Yes
Control variables	Yes	Yes	Yes	Yes
First-stage regression				
Instrument	0.46 (0.00)***	0.46 (0.00)***	0.46 (0.00)***	0.46 (0.00)***
First-stage test statistics				
F-statistic	131.05***	131.54***	131.51***	131.84***
Shea's partial R^2	0.32	0.32	0.32	0.32
Observations				
Individuals	102,387	102,387	102,387	102,387
Labour-market region-year cells	1296	1296	1296	1296
Labour-market regions (clusters)	108	108	108	108
R^2 (2SLS)	0.24	0.46	0.41	0.51
R^2 (OLS)	0.24	0.46	0.41	0.51
ME(stdev, 2SLS)	−0.04*	−0.04**	−0.03†	−0.03*
ME(stdev, OLS)	−0.01	−0.01	−0.01	−0.01

Cluster-robust standard errors in parentheses (clustered at the level of the labour-market region). ***/**/*/† indicate significance at the 0.005/0.01/0.05/0.10 level, respectively. *Instrument* shows the coefficient of the instrument in the first-stage regression. *ME(stdev)* gives the percentage change in daily earnings given an increase in the youth share by one standard deviation

Table 13.5 Use of an individual's place of residence

Dependent variable: log real daily earnings	Baseline	+Industry	+Occupation	+Industry +Occupation
Youth share (2SLS)	−3.22 (0.97)***	−2.81 (0.92)***	−1.88 (0.91)*	−1.89 (0.86)*
Youth share (OLS)	−1.46 (0.63)*	−1.36 (0.57)*	−0.90 (0.60)	−0.97 (0.53)†
Dummies				
Year	Yes	Yes	Yes	Yes
Labour-market region	Yes	Yes	Yes	Yes
Industry	No	Yes	No	Yes
Occupation	No	No	Yes	Yes
Control variables	Yes	Yes	Yes	Yes
First-stage regression				
Instrument	0.46 (0.00)***	0.46 (0.00)***	0.46 (0.00)***	0.46 (0.00)***
First-stage test statistics				
F-statistic	136.60***	137.17***	137.32***	137.70***
Shea's partial R^2	0.32	0.32	0.32	0.32
Observations				
Individuals	107,351	107,351	107,351	107,351
Labour-market region-year cells	1296	1296	1296	1296
Labour-market regions (clusters)	108	108	108	108
R^2 (2SLS)	0.24	0.46	0.40	0.51
R^2 (OLS)	0.24	0.46	0.40	0.51
ME(stdev, 2SLS)	−4.05%***	−3.54%***	−2.36%*	−2.39%*
ME(stdev, OLS)	−1.84%*	−1.71%*	−1.14%	−1.22%†

Cluster-robust standard errors in parentheses (clustered at the level of the labour-market region). ***/**/*/† indicate significance at the 0.005/0.01/0.05/0.10 level, respectively. *Instrument* shows the coefficient of the instrument in the first-stage regression. *ME(stdev)* gives the percentage change in daily earnings given an increase in the youth share by one standard deviation

References

Angrist J, Pischke J-S (2009) Mostly harmless econometrics: an empiricist's companian. Princeton University Press, Princeton

Arnds P, Bonin H (2002) Arbeitsmarkteffekte und finanzpolitische Folgen der demographischen Alterung in Deutschland, IZA Discussion Paper No. 667, Institute of Labor Economics, Bonn

Baltagi BH, Blien U (1998) The German wage curve: evidence from the IAB employment sample. Econ Lett 61:135–142

Berger MC (1985) The effect of cohort size on earnings growth: a reexamination of the evidence. J Political Econ 93:561–573

Biagi F, Lucifora C (2008) Demographic and education effects on unemployment in Europe. Labour Econ 15:1076–1101

Bloom DE, Sousa-Poza A (2013) Aging and productivity: introduction. Labour Econ 22:1–4.0

Blundell R, MaCurdy T (1999) Labour supply: a review of alternative approaches. In: Ashenfelter O, Card D (eds) Handbook of labor economics, vol 3. North-Holland, Amsterdam

Börsch-Supan A (2013) Myths, scientific evidence and economic policy in an aging world. J Econ Ageing 1-2:3–15

Brunello G (2010) The effects of cohort size on European earnings. J Popul Econ 23:273–290

Brunner B, Kuhn A (2014) The impact of labor market entry conditions on initial job assignments and wages. J Popul Econ 27:705–738

Card D, Lemieux T (2001) Can falling supply explain the rising return to college for younger men? A cohort-based analysis. Q J Econ 116:705–746

Connelly R (1986) A framework for analyzing the impact of cohort size on education and labor earning. J Hum Resour 21:543–562

Eberle J, Schmucker A and Seth S (2013) Programmierbeispiele zur Datenaufbereitung der Stichprobe der Integrierten Arbeitsmarktbiografien (SIAB) in Stata. Generierung von Querschnittsdaten und biografischen Daten, FDZ Methodenreport No. 04/2013, Institute for Employment Research, Nuremberg

Eckey H-F, Kosfeld R, Türck M (2006) Abgrenzung deutscher Arbeitsmarktregionen. Raumforschung und Raumordnung 64:299–309

Fertig M, Schmidt C, Sinning M (2009) The impact of demographic change on human capital accumulation. Labour Econ 16:659–668

Fitzenberger B (1999) Wages and employment across skill groups: an analysis for West Germany. Physica-Verlag, Heidelberg

Fitzenberger B, Kohn K (2006) Skill wage premia, employment, and cohort effects: are workers in Germany all of the same type?, IZA Discussion Paper No. 2185, Institute of Labor Economics, Bonn

Freeman RB (1979) The effect of demographic factors on age-earnings profiles. J Hum Resour 14:289–318

Fuchs M, Weyh A (2014) Demography and unemployment in East Germany. How close are the ties?, IAB Discussion Paper No. 26/2014, Institute for Employment Research, Nuremberg

Garloff A, Pohl C, Schanne N (2013) Do small labor market entry cohorts reduce unemployment? Demogr Res 29:379–406

Gartner H (2005) The imputation of wages above the contribution limit with the German IAB employment sample, FDZ Methodenreport No. 02/2005, Institute for Employment Research, Nuremberg

Gertler M, Trigari A (2009) Unemployment fluctuations with staggered nash wage bargaining. J Political Econ 117:38–86

Gürtzgen N (2016) Estimating the wage premium of collective wage contracts – evidence from longitudinal linked employer-employee data. Ind Relat 55:294–322

Jimeno JF, Rojas JA, Puente S (2008) Modelling the impact of aging on social security expenditures. Econ Model 25:201–224

Kahn LB (2010) The long-term labor market consequences of graduating from college in a bad economy. Labour Econ 17:303–316

Korenman S, Neumark D (2000) Cohort crowding and youth labor markets: a cross-national analysis. In: Blanchflower DG, Freeman RB (eds) Youth employment and joblessness in advanced countries. University of Chicago Press, Chicago

Lehmer F, Möller J (2010) Interrelations between the urban wage premium and firm-size wage differentials: a microdata cohort analysis for Germany. Ann Reg Sci 45:31–53

Mazzonna F, Peracchi F (2012) Ageing, cognitive abilities and retirement. Eur Econ Rev 56:691–710

Michaelis J, Debus M (2011) Wage and (un-)employment effects of an ageing workforce. J Popul Econ 24:1493–1511

Mincer J (1958) Investment in human capital and the personal income distribution. J Political Econ 66:281–302

Moffat J, Roth D (2016) The cohort size-wage relationship in Europe. Labour 30:415–432

Moffat J, Roth D (2017) Cohort size and labour-market outcomes in Europe. Econ Bull 37:2735–2740

Morin L-P (2015) Cohort size and youth earnings: evidence from a quasi-experiment. Labour Econ 32:99–111

Moulton BR (1990) An illustration of a pitfall in estimating the effects of aggregate variables on micro units. Rev Econ Stat 72:334–338

Ochsen C (2009) Regional labor markets and aging in Germany, Thünen-Series of Applied Economic Theory Working Paper No. 102, Department of Economics, Faculty of Economics and Social Sciences, University of Rostock, Rostock

Ottaviano G, Peri G (2012) Rethinking the effect of immigration on wages. J Eur Econ Assoc 10:152–197

Polachek SW (2008) Earnings over the life cycle: the Mincer earnings function and its applications. Found Trends Microecon 4:165–272

Sapozhnikov M, Triest RK (2007) Population aging, labor demand, and the structure of wages, Research Department Working Paper 07-8, Federal Reserve Bank of Boston, Boston

Shimer R (2001) The impact of young workers on the aggregate labor market. Q J Econ 116:969–1007

Skans ON (2005) Age effects in Swedish local labor markets. Econ Lett 86:419–426

Staiger D, Stock JH (1997) Instrumental variables regression with weak instruments. Econometrica 65:557–586

Stapleton DC, Young DJ (1988) Educational attainment and cohort size. J Labor Econ 6:330–361

Statistisches Bundesamt (2009) Bevölkerung Deutschlands bis 2060: 12. koordinierte Bevölkerungsvorausberechnung. Statistisches Bundesamt, Wiesbaden

Statistisches Bundesamt (2010) Bevölkerung und Erwerbstätigkeit: Bevölkerung in den Bundesländern, dem früheren Bundesgebiet und den neuen Ländern bis 2060: Ergebnisse der 12. koordinierten Bevölkerungsvorausberechnung. Statistisches Bundesamt, Wiesbaden

vom Berge P, König M, Seth S (2013) Sample of integrated labour market biographies (SIAB) 1975–2010, FDZ Datenreport No. 01/2013, Institute for Employment Research, Nuremberg

Welch F (1979) Effects of cohort size on earnings: the baby boom babies' financial bust. J Political Econ 87:S65–S97

Wright RE (1991) Cohort size and earnings in Great Britain. J Popul Econ 4:295–305

Zimmermann K (1991) Ageing and the labour market. Age structure, cohort size and unemployment. J Popul Econ 4:177–200

Chapter 14
Ageing and Labour Market Development: Testing Gibrat's and Zipf's Law for Germany

Marco Modica, Aura Reggiani, Nicola De Vivo, and Peter Nijkamp

1 Introduction

Gibrat's law and Zipf's law represent two well-known empirical regularities, which are currently much debated among scholars in the spatial sciences. Very briefly, Gibrat's (1931) law states that the growth rate of an entity (i.e. firm, city) is independent of its size, meaning that there is no automatic relationship between its growth rate and its size. In the field of city-size distribution, this implies that, although cities can grow at different rates, it is not possible to state that larger cities grow faster than smaller ones, or vice versa.

Zipf's law (1949), instead, states that the city-size distribution could be closely approximated by a power-law distribution, at least in its upper tail. A rough way of clarifying Zipf's law is what is called the 'rank size rule', which states that the size of a city in a country is proportional to its rank in the urban hierarchy. This means that, for example, the largest city of a country is twice the size of the second largest city, three times that of the third largest, and so on. In fact, Zipf's law (following this

M. Modica (✉)
CNR –IRCrES, Research Institute on Sustainable Economic Growth, L'Aquila, Italy

Gran Sasso Science Institute, L'Aquila, Italy
e-mail: marco.modica@gssi.it

A. Reggiani
Department of Economics, University of Bologna, Bologna, Italy

N. De Vivo
IMT Lucca – School for Advanced Studies, Lucca, Italy

P. Nijkamp
Adam Mickiewicz University, Poznań, Poland

JADS (Jheronimus Academy of Data Science), 's-Hertogenbosch, The Netherlands

© Springer International Publishing AG, part of Springer Nature 2018   285
U. Blien et al. (eds.), *Modelling Aging and Migration Effects on Spatial Labor Markets*, Advances in Spatial Science,
https://doi.org/10.1007/978-3-319-68563-2_14

rank-size rule) is able to measure how unequal the city distribution is. According to Gabaix (1999), Zipf's law is directly linked to Gibrat's law, because it is an outcome of Gibrat's law, at least in the upper tail.

Many studies have focused on the analysis of these two regularities, driven by the idea that an accurate description of the distribution of people in geographical space is important for policy-relevant issues and also for specifying more appropriate theoretical models. These issues can range from a better understanding of firms' and peoples' localisation choices to the implementation of national and regional policies, for instance, in terms of growth incentives and transport infrastructures (Fazio and Modica 2015; Modica et al. 2013). Indeed, Gabaix (1999) provides a theoretical model leading to a population growth process that follows Gibrat's law (i.e. a random growth process described by a common mean and variance) driven by migration which, in turn, *forces utility-adjusted wages to equate at the margin* (Berry and Okulicz-Kozaryn 2011 p. S18). At the same time, Eeckhout (2004), when providing empirical evidence about the validity of Gibrat's and Zipf's law, models a city growth process characterised by two main driving forces: a random productivity process of local economies and a perfect mobility of workers.

Both these models (the literature provides other similar models; see for instance, Cordoba 2008) underline that local labour market characteristics and migration are important factors that contribute to the 'materialisation' of both Gibrat's and Zipf's law. Indeed, if we consider a situation where no migration is allowed, the proportionate city growth might be also interpreted as a constant city growth rate, regardless of the city size and *ceteris paribus* (e.g. fertility rate across municipalities). However, there might also be idiosyncratic reasons why individuals decide to locate in a given city (or to choose to move between cities) that typically are not considered in this literature that depends on ageing and that can lead to distortion of the proportionate growth rate. For instance, Peri (2001) shows that young educated workers prefer working in larger cities. Hunt (2006) provides evidence of different localisation behaviour between old and young people, finding that young German people are more mobile and show more sensitivity to regional wages and a relative insensitivity to regional unemployment, in comparison with their elders. Moreover, the migration of young people is seen as labour-force related in densely populated urban areas (Bures 1998; Frey and Speare 1988, Longino et al. 1984), while elderly migrants prefer less densely populated and amenity-rich areas (Bures 1998; Longino et al. 1984; Scott and Storper 2003). Furthermore, many countries—and especially those in Europe—will become ageing societies in the decades to come. Indeed, as revealed by Eurostat, over the years, the age pyramid has changed from the usual triangular shape (that is associated with a growing population) into a trapezoid shape due to a smaller proportion of young people and an increasing share of the elderly (European Union 2015).

This shift in the old-age dependency ratio will predictably have a massive impact on many socio-economic phenomena, such as the housing market, the labour market, the demand for goods and services, and so forth. Consequently, ageing has become an important source of serious research and policy concern. However, it should be noted that the multitude of ageing effects will not show a uniform pattern across and within countries. Most likely, the spatial (urban and regional) variations will be significant, as a result of different local circumstances, region-specific labour market participation, differences in regional in- and outmigration patterns, etc (Marin and Modica 2017).

The above-mentioned demographic developments will certainly have major consequences for the functioning and evolution of local and regional labour markets. They will most likely exhibit varying developmental profiles, in terms of labour force participation, exit rates, productivity impacts, and the like; ageing is not a neutral generic phenomenon, but may create significant socio-economic disparities across cities and regions in the same country, especially over a longer time horizon. A country like Germany, for example—with a rapidly rising ageing profile—will most likely witness a unprecedented dynamics on its regional labour markets.

The aim of the present chapter is therefore to provide an accurate description of the distribution of people in space, taking into account the demographic differences between people.[1] To provide this analysis, we focus on both population (in terms of place of residence) and employment (in terms of place of work) data: we use annual observations regarding population and employment for all German towns and cities in the period 2001–2011. So, the questions we want to answer are the following: does the growth rate of employment/population depend on the size of the cohort? What is the level of employment and population concentration/deconcentration? Are there any differences between these two variables? Are there any differences if we differentiate for age cohorts?

In answering all these questions, we will first show the results of the analysis of Zipf's law and then those of the analysis of Gibrat's law. The main idea is to verify whether the size of a city (measured by population and employment) and its growth rate are independent for 5-year age groups. To the best of our knowledge, this is the first study which attempts to introduce demographic characteristics (and, in particular, age structure) into an analysis of Zipf's and Gibrat's law. The novelty introduced by the present study is therefore: the introduction of demographic characteristics in the use of different measures for city size other than population for place of residence (e.g. number of employees for place of work). Furthermore, our study will provide new information for modelling the city growth process more in line with reality, by incorporating idiosyncratic factors of the population and the different localisation preferences of the young and the old. Moreover, it will provide a better picture of the local and regional labour markets able to support the implementation of national and regional employment and urban policies.

The chapter is structured as follows. In Sect. 2, we provide the readers with a brief reminder of the theory underlying Zipf's law and Gibrat's law and the literature dealing with these two empirical regularities. In Sect. 3, we describe the data used

---

[1]A first attempt trying to add age into Gibrat/Zipf's literature has been proposed by Giesen and Suedekum (2014). Even though this approach has not considered the age structure of the population/labour force but the age of the city, it might be considered as one of the first works that goes beyond the simple city size spatial distribution.

to perform our analysis. In Sect. 4, we show the methods that we used to obtain our results and the results themselves. Then, in Sect. 5, we draw some general conclusions.

2   Gibrat's Law and Zipf's Law: A Reminder

Gibrat's law, also known as the proportionate growth process (Gibrat 1931), may explain in stochastic terms the systematically skewed pattern of the distribution of city size (Santarelli et al. 2004). Indeed, since the study which first introduced Gibrat's law (1931), it has been observed that the size distribution of firms (in the first instance) and of cities are well approximated by a log-normal distribution (even though, at least for cities, there is no general consensus on which distributions should be used; see for example, Giesen et al. 2010). The main reason why this happens is always related to the initial arguments provided by Kapteyn (1903), which state that, if a variable is generated by a stochastic growth process that is proportionate, it gives rise to an asymptotically lognormal distribution. This process thus states that if '*the change in the variate at any step of the process is a random proportion of the previous value of the variate*' (Chesher 1979, p. 403), then '*the probability of a given proportionate change in size during a specified period is the same for all firms—regardless of their size at the beginning of the period*' (Mansfield 1962, p. 1031).

Although much effort has been devoted to the theoretical implications of Gibrat's law and to the mechanisms that can lead to the fulfilment of the law, only recently economic interpretations of the law have been explored. For instance, according to the city-size distribution literature, several authors have suggested a fair number of economic interpretations, but they differ only to a small degree. In our opinion, two studies are relevant for the aim of this chapter (readers interested in a more complete description should consult Modica et al. (2017a, b)). In the short run, Black and Henderson (2003) state that a shock affects big and small entities in the same way (or to put it another way, has the same relative effect on their growth rates, independently of the initial size of the entity). In the long run, Brakman et al. (2004) state that a large temporary shock can have a permanent impact. This means that a shock can change the growth path towards another size equilibrium.

According to Gabaix (1999), Gibrat's law explains well what is known as Zipf's law. This law can be formalised as a Pareto distribution with defined parameters so that that the probability density function of the population size, P, is given by:

$$Prob\,(P_i > P) = \frac{K}{P^q}, \tag{14.1}$$

where K is a positive constant and $q = 1$ for all the cities i of the distribution. That is, the size (P) of a city (i) times the percentage of cities with a larger size equals a constant. As explained earlier, there is also a rough and popular way of stating Zipf's law: the rank-size rule. This is a deterministic rule that follows from the definition: the second largest city is roughly half the size of the largest, the third largest city is roughly a third the size of the largest, etc. That is, if we rank cities from largest (rank 1) to smallest (rank n) and denote their population $P_1 \geq P_2 \geq P_3 \geq \ldots \geq P_n$, respectively, the rank R_i for a city of population P_i is proportional to the proportion of cities greater than i. Therefore, we can rewrite the previous equation in the following way:

$$P_i = K R_i^{-q} \tag{14.2}$$

Equation (14.2) is also known as the 'rank-size rule' and is usually expressed in logarithmic form, as follows:

$$\log(P)_i = \log(K) - q \log(R_i) \tag{14.3}$$

where P_i is the population of city i; R_i is the rank of the ith city; and K is a constant. Zipf's law holds precisely when the coefficient q is equal to one.

In recent years, several economic interpretations have also been proposed for Zipf's law (see, e.g. Gabaix and Ioannides 2004). Roughly speaking, the Zipf coefficient, q, can be seen as a proxy for the hierarchical degree of a system of cities (e.g. if q is exactly equal to 0, all the cities are of the same size; on the contrary, if q tends to infinity the city system is composed of one enormous city, where all the population is concentrated). Another interesting interpretation is the one proposed by Reggiani and Nijkamp (2015), who consider the urban structure as a network. In this way, they are able to compare Zipf's law with the connectivity degree distribution as in Barabási and Oltvai (2004), meaning that the smaller the value of the connectivity degree, the higher the number of the connections of the hubs.

In the field of spatial economics, these two regularities have given rise to an increasing number of empirical and theoretical studies. Empirical studies have tried, in different ways, to test the (non)validity of both these laws, singularly or in combination; the following partial list covers the most recent works: Black and Henderson (2003); Glaeser, et al. (2014); Gonzalez-Val (2012); Guerin-Pace (1995); Modica (2014); Rosen and Resnick (1980); Soo (2005); and Storper (2010). In most studies, Zipf's law and Gibrat's law are generally accepted; we mention among others: Black and Henderson (2003); Eeckhout (2004); Gabaix and Ioannides (2004); Giesen and Suedekum (2011); Gonzalez-Val (2012); Gonzalez-Val et al. (2013) and Ioannides and Overman (2003).

Typically, all the above-mentioned studies differentiate cities by their population size, without taking into account any demographic difference (for example, in age structure) and without considering any regularities in the employment size. However, it might be useful to build a more realistic random population growth model, to delineate more relevant policy implications in terms of population ageing, and to consider appropriate labour market polices, taking into consideration the demographic characteristics of the population and of the employment size at a municipal level. Therefore, in contrast to the relevant existing literature, this chapter aims to identify trends in the geographic concentration of employment across municipalities with a particular focus on the demographic characteristics of the population.

3 Data

The data set for this study has been provided by the German Institute for Employment Research (IAB). It contains the number of inhabitants and the number of employees for all German cities, even very small towns, covering the time period from 2001 to 2011. Data cover not only the totals for employment and population, but are also available also for cohorts of 5 years (i.e. 20–24, 25–29, and so on), for both employment and population, giving us the possibility to analyse in depth the two above-mentioned empirical regularities, also for the age structure of the country. Descriptive statistics for the data are summarised in Table 14.1. We have been provided with a sample of annual observations in the period 2001–2011 for more than 11,000 towns and cities. It is interesting to observe that the average growth rate of employment and population in the period taken into consideration shows different patterns, both the aggregate and the cohort level. The total employment shows an average growth rate of 9.1%, while the total population, instead, decreases by 3.5%. We can observe the same pattern in the youngest cohorts: the employment of young cohorts (for example, 20–29 years) shows a positive trend (an increase of about 7%), while the population of the same cohorts decreases (by almost 2%). This decrease in the population of the younger cohorts can also be seen as a first sign of population ageing. This ageing process is even more underlined by the huge increases we can observe in the population of the older cohorts that is also reflected by the increase in employment for those cohorts.[2] The only cohort in which this pattern breaks down is the cohort 60–64, in which we can observe decreasing population growth, even though we can observe a huge increase in employment.

However, the correlation between population and employment (either on a global level or on a cohort level) is high (ranging from 0.94 to 0.98, as can be seen in Table 14.2), indicating a fair comparability between the results.

---

[2]Note that the huge increase in employment in the older cohorts can also be due to the reform of the labour market that took place in Germany between 2003 and 2005, also known as the Hartz package (Hartz I–IV). In brief, the first three stages of the reforms sought to improve job search efficiency and employment flexibility. They included deregulation of the temporary work sector to give individual employers more flexibility to vary employment levels without incurring hiring or firing costs, as well as a restructuring of the federal labour agency in order to improve the training and matching efficiency of job searchers. The final set of reforms entailed a major restructuring of the unemployment and social assistance system that considerably reduced the size and duration of the unemployment benefits and made them conditional on tighter rules for job search and acceptance.

Table 14.1 Descriptive statistics, 2011

Variable	Observations	Mean	Standard deviation	Min	Max	Average growth rate 2011–2001 (%)
Total employment	10,975	2585.947	19,800.52	0	1,151,344	9.1
Employment 20–24	9690	257.3647	1709.776	0	92,707	7.3
Employment 25–29	9809	305.4488	2491.825	0	140,546	7.4
Employment 30–34	9848	309.5874	2610.989	0	142,905	−21.6
Employment 35–39	9854	298.1878	2344.959	0	122,459	−30.5
Employment 40–45	10,127	391.4582	2859.821	0	154,350	5.3
Employment 45–49	10,182	428.0003	3053.741	0	176,104	40.8
Employment 50–54	10,088	362.3459	2441.646	0	138,754	52.8
Employment 55–59	9819	284.677	1907.361	0	110,110	78.4
Employment 60–64	8845	144.3618	1001.869	0	54,978	120.6
Total population	11,209	7252.436	47,194.49	29	3,501,872	−3.5
Population 20–24	11,209	439.5144	3158.614	1	231,178	0.1
Population 25–29	11,209	442.2332	3772.009	1	284,687	−1.9
Population 30–34	11,209	438.0074	3706.798	1	276,989	−29.2
Population 35–39	11,209	424.0293	3185.058	1	232,551	−37.6
Population 40–44	11,209	563.8595	3691.971	1	270,099	−4.9
Population 45–49	11,209	632.4886	4019.146	1	307,041	26.6
Population 50–54	11,209	569.1584	3352.405	1	253,595	37.3
Population 55–59	11,209	491.8081	2854.181	1	215,153	58.7
Population 60–64	11,209	434.0488	2639.211	1	200,495	−7.8

Table 14.2 Correlation between variables

	Total Empl.	Empl. 20–24	Empl. 25–29	Empl. 30–34	Empl. 35–39	Empl. 40–45	Empl. 45–49	Empl. 50–54	Empl. 55–59	Empl. 60–64
Total population	0.97	0.9712	0.9689	0.9608	0.9556	0.961	0.9742	0.9744	0.9774	0.979
Population 20–24	0.9677	0.9722	0.9682	0.9578	0.9514	0.9567	0.9705	0.9724	0.9771	0.9777
Population 25–29	0.9704	0.9702	0.9741	0.9662	0.9582	0.9601	0.972	0.9709	0.9749	0.9787
Population 30–34	0.9735	0.9707	0.9774	0.9719	0.9643	0.9649	0.9747	0.9719	0.9743	0.9801
Population 35–39	0.9765	0.9737	0.9783	0.9733	0.9678	0.9697	0.9785	0.9758	0.9761	0.9825
Population 40–44	0.9731	0.9722	0.9727	0.9663	0.9615	0.9657	0.9766	0.9752	0.9761	0.9805
Population 45–49	0.9631	0.9635	0.9621	0.9536	0.9479	0.9539	0.9685	0.9681	0.9706	0.9728
Population 50–54	0.9618	0.9639	0.9589	0.9496	0.9448	0.9523	0.9679	0.969	0.9722	0.9717
Population 55–59	0.9587	0.9617	0.955	0.9453	0.9404	0.9483	0.965	0.967	0.972	0.9693
Population 60–64	0.9601	0.962	0.9573	0.9483	0.943	0.9499	0.9658	0.967	0.9716	0.9709

4 Methods and Results

In some studies, especially in the first reappraisal of Gibrat's and Zipf's law, the interest in small towns and cities was very low (Giesen and Suedekum 2011; Ioannides and Overman 2003; Soo 2005). This is because Zipf's law holds only in the upper tail of the distribution, and it deviates in a substantial way when it comes to the body of the city-size distribution; for this reason, the studies exploring Zipf's law focus mainly on the upper tail of the distribution. However, more recently, the interest in the distribution of all types of cities has increased. This is due to the seminal works of Gabaix (1999) and Eeckhout (2004) which focus respectively on the theoretical relation between Zipf's and Gibrat's law and the empirical implications that may lead to misspecification and wrong results (for instance, Eeckhout (2004) shows that the estimated OLS coefficient of the rank-size rule varies depending on the truncation point in the city-size distribution). This has also led to a greater interest in the robustness of the statistical methods which provide tools for the truncation of the sample (see Fazio and Modica 2015, for a comparison of the methods).

For our purposes, we retain all the data when exploring Gibrat's law, while we truncate the sample for Zipf's law, using the method proposed by Ioannides and Skouras (2013). They provide an approach that estimates the truncation point as a parameter of a Pareto-lognormal distribution, $h()$, by means of maximum likelihood estimation:

$$\max_{\mu,\sigma,\tau,q} \sum_{i=1}^{N} \ln h\left(P; \mu, \sigma, \tau, q\right),$$

$$s.t. \quad \tau > \exp\left(\mu\right) \tag{14.4}$$

where the Pareto-lognormal distribution has a density:

$$h\left(P; \mu, \sigma, \tau, q\right) = \left\{ \begin{array}{ll} b\left(\mu, \sigma, \tau, q\right) f\left(P; \mu, \sigma\right), & \tau > P > 0 \\ a\left(\mu, \sigma, \tau, q\right) b\left(\mu, \sigma, \tau, q\right) g\left(P; q, \tau\right), & P \geq \tau \end{array} \right\}. \tag{14.5}$$

Here, μ and σ are the parameters of the lognormal density function $f(.)$, while q and τ are the parameters of the Pareto density function with τ as the truncation parameter. Finally, $a(\cdot)$ is a continuity condition for $h(\cdot)$, and $b(\cdot)$ represent conditions that ensure that $h(\cdot)$ is a density (see Ioannides and Skouras 2013 for more details).

In our analysis, depending on whether we use population data or employment data, we get different results. The first different result is that the employment sample is truncated after 300 cities, while the population sample is truncated after 125 cities, even though we apply exactly the same method. To summarize the results we define average values of employment and population over the period 2001–2011 and we then apply Eq. (14.3) (also known as the rank-size rule, expressed in logarithmic terms) but we use a slight modification of this equation: we estimate the

q-coefficients in the rank-size rule by means of a modification proposed by Gabaix and Ibragimov (2011)[3] that is expressed as follows:

$$\log{(P_i)} = \log(K) - q \log{(R_i - 0.5)}, \qquad (14.6)$$

where P_i is the population of city i; R_i is the rank of the ith city; and K is a constant: Zipf's law is said to hold precisely when the coefficient q is equal to one.

The results are shown in Tables 14.3 and 14.4. According to Soo (2005), the estimated Zipf coefficient might be interpreted as a measure of inequality; this is because, if we assume that $q = -\infty$, it is then plausible that all the population will be agglomerated in only one city. On the other hand, if we assume that $q = 0$, then all cities will have same size. According to that assumption, our results show that the total employment results are much more concentrated with respect to total population for all samples used. Moreover, these results hold if we direct our attention to the different cohorts: the employment results are always much more concentrated with respect to population for every cohort. However, we do not find any substantial differences between the concentration of employment of young people and that of older ones (the estimated rank-size coefficient for cohort 25–29, *viz.* 0.880, is, for example, almost the same as it is for the cohort 60–64, *viz.* 0.887)[4]. On the contrary, if we look at the estimated results for population, young people tend to concentrate more than the older people (if we take into consideration the same cohorts that we took before, we can see that the estimated rank size coefficient is 0.828 in the cohort 25–29, while it is 0.760 in cohort 60–64). These first results show that agglomeration is higher when we look at employment; this result was quite as was expected, because places of work are not spread uniformly across all cities and tend to agglomerate in some cities more than in others. On the population side, instead, we observe that young people (in the cohorts ranging from 20 to 34 years old) show a higher concentration in larger cities than the older cohorts: that is, young people prefer living in larger cities, while elderly people are more spread across cities. This could be explained, for example, by the fact that larger cities usually have a wider range of leisure activities and amenities (for example, more gyms, a wider range of restaurants, concerts, theatres, and so on), which are usually more used by younger people than by the older ones.

If instead we zoom in on Gibrat's law, we make use of a non-parametric analysis, closely following Ioannides and Overman (2003). We use the normalised growth rate: namely, the difference between a city's growth rate and the mean city growth rate, all divided by the standard deviation of the growth rate. The strength of this non-parametric estimation is that we do not impose any relationship between the dependent and the independent variables. According to Cameron and Trivedi (2005,

---

[3]In that paper, the authors show that the estimator obtained by means of the usual regression is biased. They also show that this bias could be minimised if we subtract 0.5 from the rank value.

[4]Even the test of the equality of the two estimated parameters is not significant. Pairwise tests are available upon request.

Table 14.3 Zipf's coefficient (and its standard error) for total employment and employment age cohorts

Cohort	Tot	20–24	25–29	30–34	35–39	40–44	45–49	50–54	55–59	60–64
q	−0.837***	−0.830***	−0.880***	−0.867***	−0.844***	−0.827***	−0.823***	−0.835***	−0.859***	−0.887***
	(0.00501)	(0.00615)	(0.00546)	(0.00506)	(0.00471)	(0.00480)	(0.00548)	(0.00647)	(0.00706)	(0.00764)
Cons	14.29***	11.85***	12.20***	12.26***	12.33***	12.36***	12.26***	12.12***	11.90***	11.04***
	(0.0241)	(0.0295)	(0.0262)	(0.0243)	(0.0227)	(0.0231)	(0.0264)	(0.0311)	(0.0339)	(0.0367)
r2	0.989	0.984	0.989	0.990	0.991	0.990	0.987	0.982	0.980	0.978
F	27,832.4	18,226.3	25,987.5	29,311.3	32,041.0	29,772.8	22,529.4	16,690.6	14,830.3	13,464.8
N	300	300	300	300	300	300	300	300	300	300

$*p < 0.1$, $**p < 0.05$, $***p < 0.01$

Table 14.4 Zipf's coefficient (and its standard error) for total population and population age cohorts

Cohort	Tot	20-24	25-29	30-34	35-39	40-44	45-49	50-54	55-59	60-64
q	-0.754***	-0.772***	-0.828***	-0.821***	-0.787***	-0.761***	-0.745***	-0.742***	-0.753***	-0.760***
	(0.00806)	(0.0117)	(0.0111)	(0.00833)	(0.00716)	(0.00712)	(0.00772)	(0.00816)	(0.00826)	(0.00909)
Cons	14.84***	12.19***	12.41***	12.38***	12.37***	12.36***	12.24***	12.10***	12.02***	12.03***
	(0.0319)	(0.0463)	(0.0439)	(0.0329)	(0.0283)	(0.0282)	(0.0305)	(0.0323)	(0.0327)	(0.0359)
r2	0.986	0.973	0.978	0.987	0.990	0.989	0.987	0.985	0.985	0.983
F	8748.5	4358.2	5569.0	9707.6	12,088.2	11,440.4	9315.4	8248.8	8299.9	6994.7
N	125	125	125	125	125	125	125	125	125	125

*$p < 0.1$, **$p < 0.05$, ***$p < 0.01$

p. 294), we: '*let the data show the shape of the relationship*'; this is an especially convenient approach when we do not know *a priori* the correct distribution of the data. In our analysis, we use the Nadaraya-Watson (NW) method (Nadaraya 1964; Watson 1964), where the bandwidths are calculated with an optimal rule of thumb.[5]

If Gibrat's law holds, the non-parametric estimation of the conditional mean and variance should be stable across different population sizes. Furthermore, because of normalisation, we expect the conditional mean growth to be equal to zero, and the conditional variance of growth to be equal to one. It should be noted that, while the standard parametric regression methods provide only an aggregate relationship between growth and size, which is constrained to hold over the entire distribution of city sizes, the non-parametric estimates allow the growth to vary with size over the distribution.

In Fig. 14.1, we show the NW estimator for conditional mean growth (upper panel) and variance (lower panel) for the entire city-size distribution. Again, we differentiate for employment and population. Following Cordoba (2003), the independence of the expected conditional growth rate always has to be satisfied, while the variance can be affected by the city size.[6] In general, smaller cities are experiencing faster growth than larger ones. However, very quickly (in most cases), the conditional mean appears to become stable. This evidence is consistent with the model proposed by Gabaix (1999), where a truncation concerning the small cities is necessary in order to have stationarity.

Considering the entire sample, without differentiating for cohorts, we find that Gibrat's law behaves differently according to the choice of the analysed variable. For instance, for employment, Gibrat's law holds true: namely, the growth rate of employment of a city is independent of its initial size, when we consider the entire sample (Fig. 14.1a), while, looking at the population, we can conclude that larger cities grow more than smaller ones (Fig. 14.4a). This evidence points at the possibility of a break-down in the choice of where to live in relation to the availability of work (i.e. a person chooses to live in a large city close to the city where he/she works, because a larger city can offer more amenities in terms of leisure activities, as said earlier).

This result is corroborated by the different behaviour of Gibrat's law when we differentiate for age cohorts. The young cohorts (20–29) show a different relationship between employment and population: Gibrat's law is verified for cohorts 20–24 and 25–29 in terms of employment, but it is not verified with respect to population (see Figs. 14.1b, c, 14.4b, c); in particular, we can see that the growth rate increases significantly, as the city size increases. Cohorts in the range 30–49 (see Figs. 14.2, 14.3a, 14.5 and 14.6a) instead show the same results, for both employment and population; we can clearly see that the growth rate of employment and population depends on the initial size. More in detail, larger cities show a higher

---

[5]We refer readers to their papers for a more detailed description.

[6]Gibrat's law might also be considered in terms of economic vulnerability, for more details see Modica et al. (2017b), Modica and Reggiani (2014), Modica and Zoboli (2016).

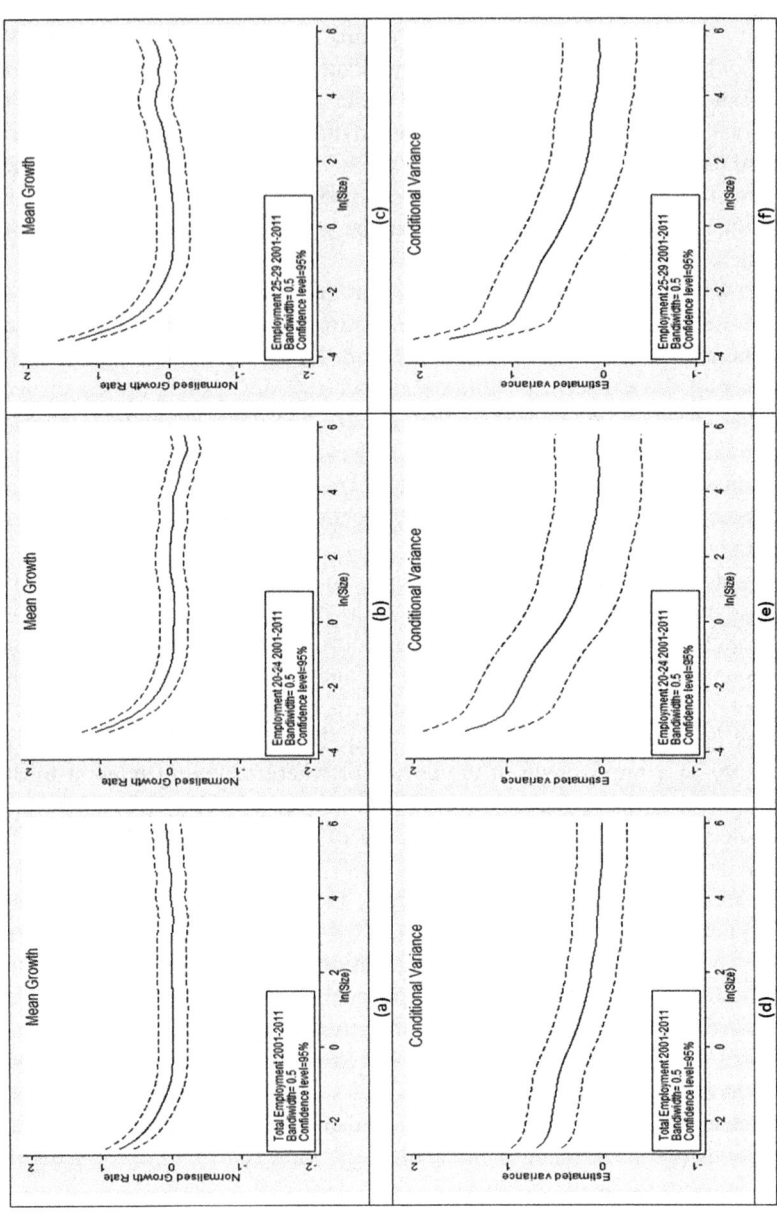

Fig. 14.1 Conditional mean (upper panels) and conditional variance (lower panels) for total employment (**a**) (**d**), 20–24 cohort (**b**) (**e**) and 25–29 cohort (**c**) (**f**)

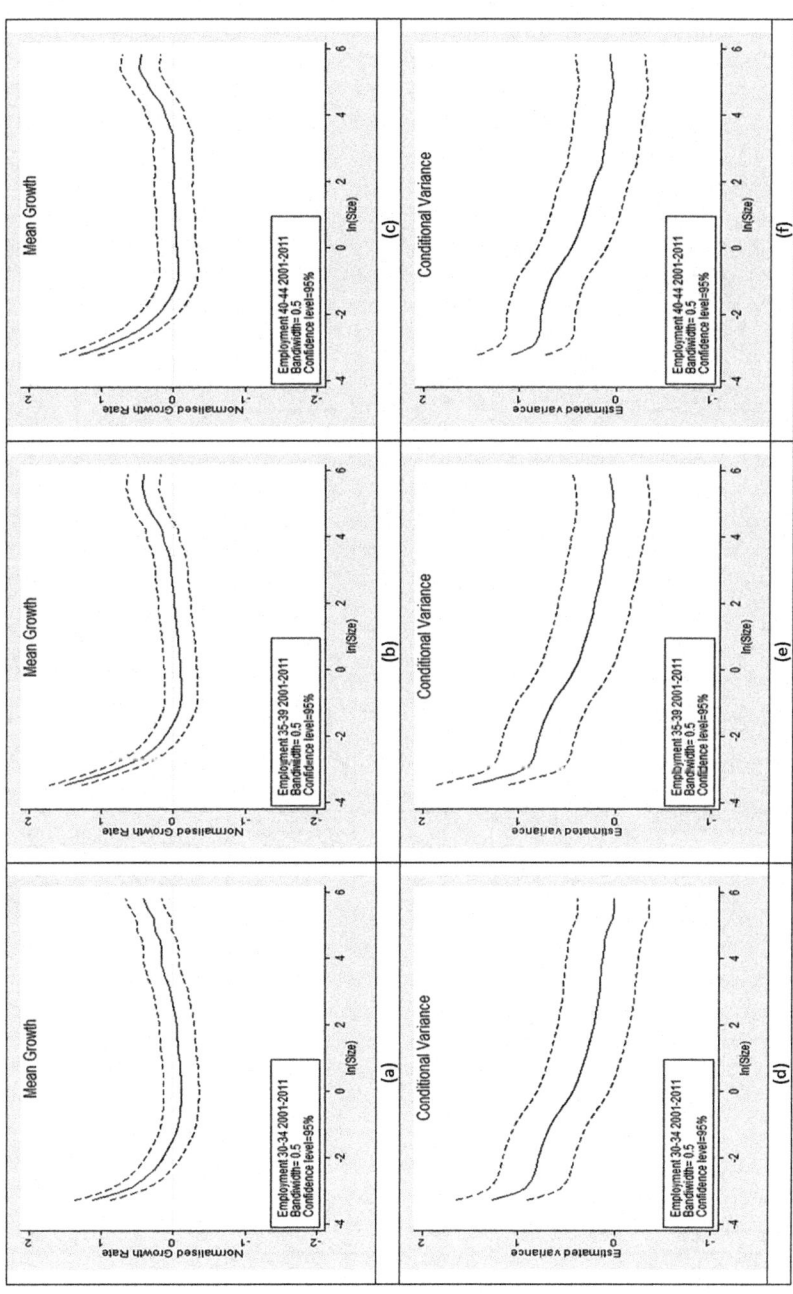

Fig. 14.2 Conditional mean (upper panels) and conditional variance (lower panels) for employment of cohorts 30–34 (**a**) (**d**), 35–39 (**b**) (**e**) and 40–44 (**c**) (**f**)

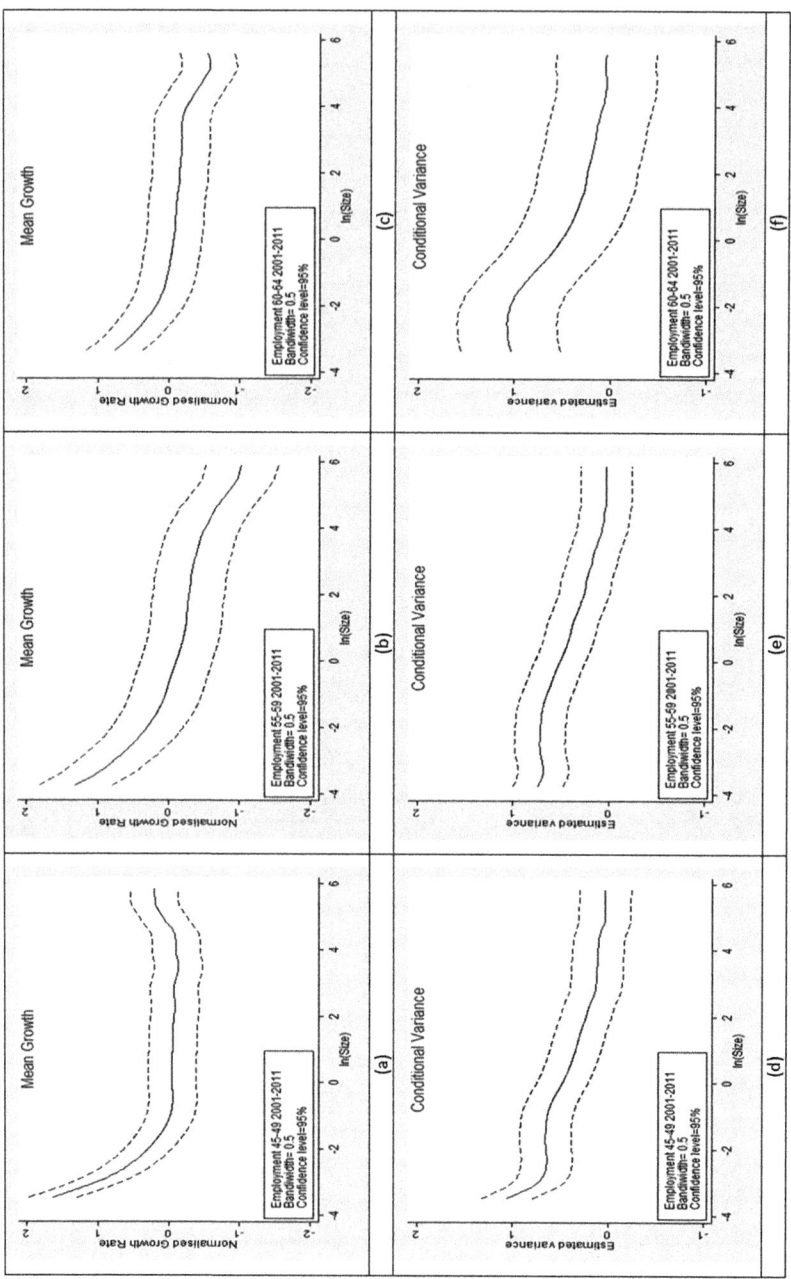

Fig. 14.3 Conditional mean (upper panels) and conditional variance (lower panels) for employment of cohorts 45–49 (**a**) (**d**), 55–59 (**b**) (**e**) and 60–64 (**c**) (**f**)

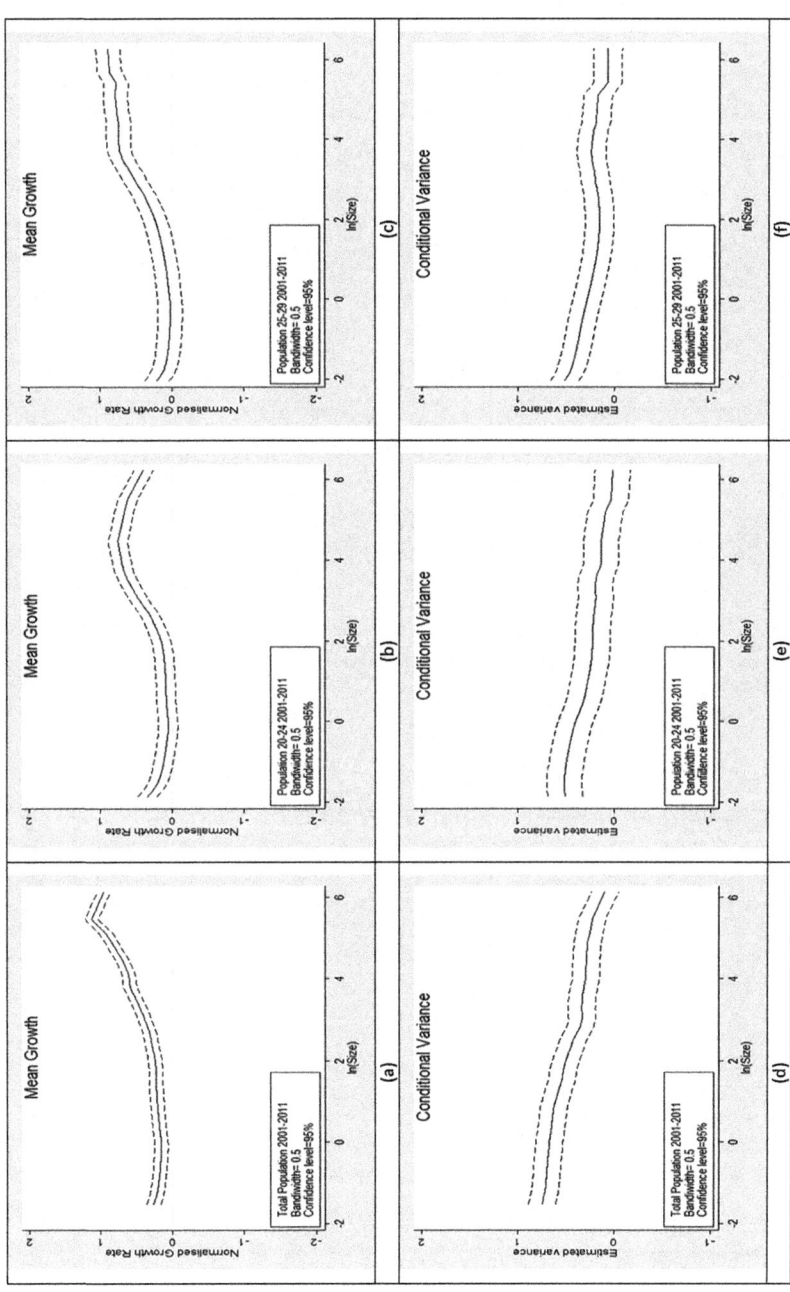

Fig. 14.4 Conditional mean (upper panels) and conditional variance (lower panels) for total population (**a**) (**d**), 20–24 cohort (**b**) (**e**) and 25–29 cohort (**c**) (**f**)

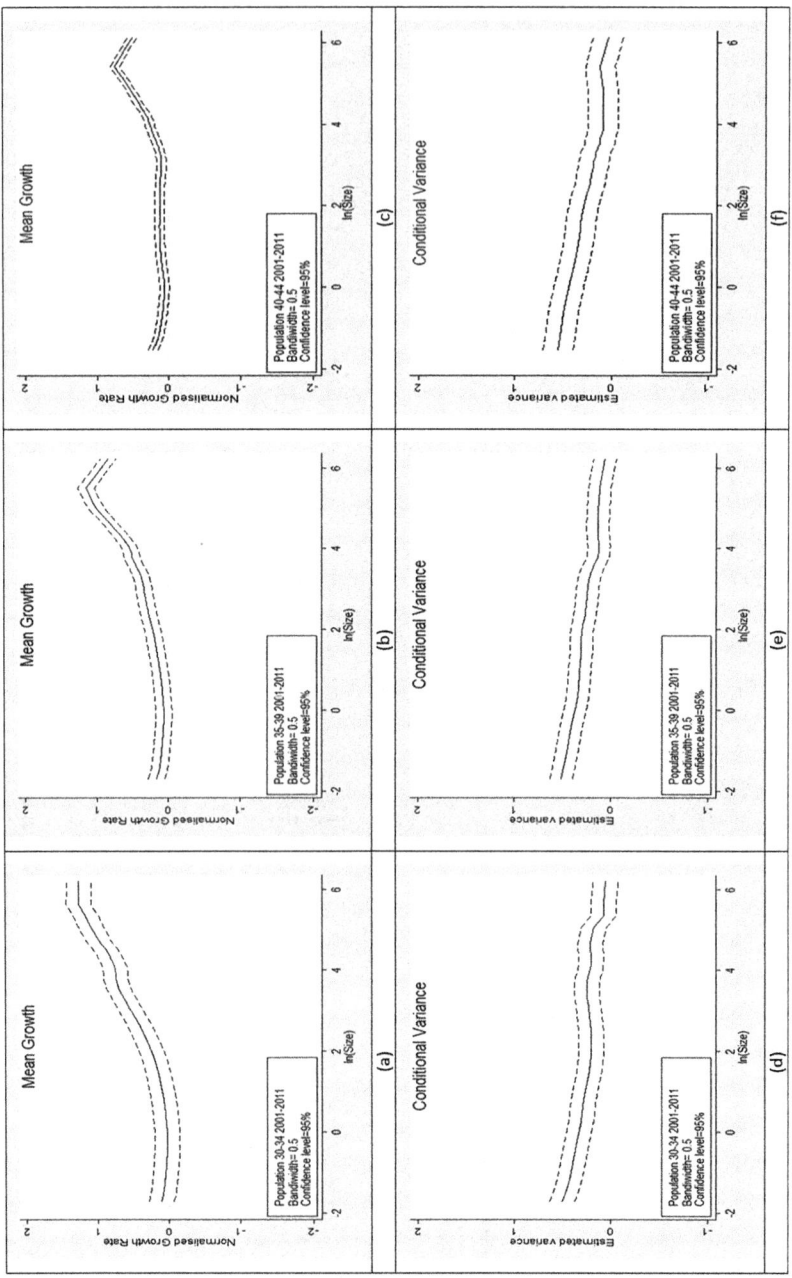

Fig. 14.5 Conditional mean (upper panels) and conditional variance (lower panels) for population of cohorts 30–34 (**a**) (**d**), 35–39 (**b**) (**e**) and 40–44 (**c**) (**f**)

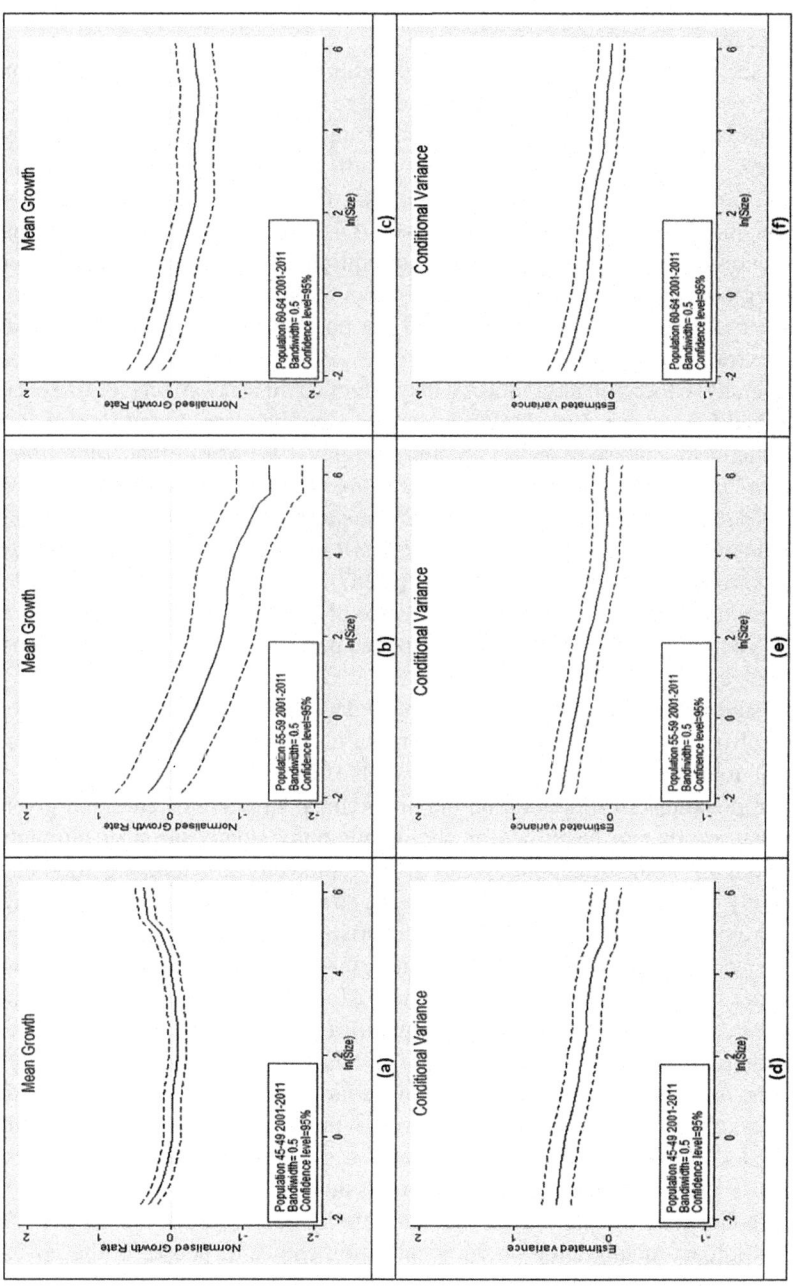

Fig. 14.6 Conditional mean (upper panels) and conditional variance (lower panels) for population of cohorts 45–49 (**a**) (**d**), 55–59 (**b**) (**e**) and 60–64 (**c**) (**f**)

growth rate. For the older cohorts (50–65) we obtain opposite results (see Figs. 14.3b–c and 14.6b–c); indeed, larger cities show a lower growth rate in terms of both population and employment, indicating a situation where older people tend to concentrate in smaller cities.

In this section we have provided initial insights on the different agglomeration patterns of people and workers in small and large cities. Even though the aim of the analysis is mainly descriptive without inferring any socio-economic or policy implications, we are aware that these first results might underline several other issues. For instance, it is possible to argue that the rank or the growth rate of population and employment (Tables 14.3 and 14.4) might change when migration and/or economic wellbeing are considered as additional explanatory variables other than the regional age patterns. Unfortunately, due to data constraints we could not explore in a detailed way these issues and we postpone more precise empirical analyses to further works.

However, if we focus on migration we may infer that this may affect city size even distinguished for age structure. Unfortunately, the link between migration and city size is difficult to analyse (e.g. Keyfitz and Philipov 1981 affirm that '[*migration and natural increase in the growth of cities*] *are problems too difficult to solve analytically and may often be dealt with by simulation. But simulation will not always provide a solution; a problem too difficult for a closed form solution may also suffer from some inherent ambiguity*' p. 287). Migration is indeed linked to the age structure and the economic performance of a region, because migrants are relatively young and they are looking for better performing regions (Greenwood 1985).

As we said before, however, we do not have data on migrants at a municipality level that also consider the demographic structure of migrants. However, data on number of total foreign employees are available. In order to partially consider possible implications of migration on the hierarchical structure of cites and given the fact that we do not have data on the demographic composition of migrants (even though this could affect the overall demographic city structure, e.g. migrants are relatively young), we propose the following strategy: (1) we subtract the same ratio of foreign employees for all selected cohorts; (2) we test different ratios (e.g. 50%, 40% and so on). This means for instance, that if we adopt the ratio 30%, we will subtract from the employees in the cohort 25–29 the 30% of the total foreign employees in the sample; (3) we run again equation (14.6) throughout all age cohorts and we compare the estimated coefficients. In this way we are able to 'roughly' measure the impact of potential migration on the hierarchical city structure. Indeed, if there is no change in the estimated coefficients, this can be interpreted as a result of similar localization behaviour of people of a given age cohort, regardless of migration (or put in a different way, the migrants then have the same behaviour as a given age cohort). If the estimated coefficients are instead different, this underlines a potential impact of migration on the localization choice of people in that given cohort. The results are summarised in Table 14.5, where we use as a measure of city size the difference between employees in a given age cohort minus the 30% of the foreign employees.

Table 14.5 Zipf's coefficient (and its standard error) for total employment with no non-native workers and age cohorts

Cohort	Tot	20–24	25–29	30–34	35–39	40–44	45–49	50–54	55–59	60–64
q	−0.835***	−0.827***	−0.876***	−0.859***	−0.834***	−0.817***	−0.814***	−0.830***	−0.866***	−0.987***
	(0.00501)	(0.00976)	(0.00616)	(0.00534)	(0.00495)	(0.00521)	(0.00659)	(0.00866)	(0.0122)	(0.0321)
Cons	14.26***	11.60***	11.99***	12.06***	12.15***	12.19***	12.08***	11.92***	11.68***	10.58***
	(0.0241)	(0.0469)	(0.0296)	(0.0257)	(0.0238)	(0.0251)	(0.0317)	(0.0417)	(0.0586)	(0.151)
r2	0.989	0.960	0.985	0.989	0.990	0.988	0.981	0.969	0.944	0.779
F	27,742.3	7187.1	20,225.9	25,891.9	28,403.7	24,567.6	15,260.1	9179.5	5043.9	943.9
N	300	300	300	300	300	300	300	300	300	300

$*p < 0.1$, $**p < 0.05$, $***p < 0.01$

The comparison between these results and those presented in Table 14.3 do not provide evidence of a significant impact of migration on the city size hierarchy, especially so for young cohorts (e.g. the estimated coefficient for cohort 20–24 is 0.830 in Table 14.3, while if we subtract the 30% of foreign workers in that cohort the estimated coefficient is not significantly different, 0.827). Clearly, considering the cohort 60–64, the difference is relevant (e.g. 0.887 in the baseline and 0.987 in the case we subtract the 30% of foreign workers).

This first and preliminary evidence underlines two main things. First, very likely migrants are relatively young and they are looking for better performing regions. Similar considerations may be inferred for young people: their localization choices are similar to those of the migrants. Demographic characteristics appear to be more important when looking at the spatial distribution of young people. At the same time, older people behave differently than young people and migrants. Indeed, if we would suppose that most migrants are in the eldest cohort, this would lead to a dramatic change in the estimated coefficients. Second, these overall results provide evidence that when considering the city size distribution, the results will be different if we add to the analysis the demographic structure of the society. Localization choices might be indeed different for people of younger age who prefer to settle in large cities (e.g. hot-spots) and older people that are more spread over the territory. Studies on urban growth and city size distribution, should therefore incorporate demographic characteristics in their models.

Our analysis is able to provide interesting policy implications for the localisation choices of people of different ages. Indeed, this analysis shows interesting evidence of the relationship between employment growth rates, ageing and size of municipalities in terms of employment. In more detail, we find evidence that large municipalities attract more young people, while small municipalities experience a considerable increase in the employment of older people. One possible explanation is that large municipalities (in terms of employment) are the most innovative ones attracting especially young people, while medium-sized and smaller municipalities, with maybe lower levels of innovation and job opportunities, are not able to attract many young people.

Another important relevant issue for policy implications is the link between the analysis of Gibrat's law and the vulnerability of the economic system. Previous studies have shown the need of a dedicated operational method to assess the vulnerability to economic shocks of selected cohorts based on the Gibat's law literature (for a review, see Modica and Reggiani 2014). Indeed, Gibrat's law implies a non-stationary growth process, meaning that any external shock to the growth process will last forever (because of the lack of mean reversion) (Gibrat 1931; Lalanne and Zumpe 2015). In this case, the system will experience an increase in the vulnerability because of the reduction in the ability to return to the existing pre-shock conditions. Clearly, Figs. 14.1b, c show that in Germany in the period 2000–2011, the cohorts 20–24 and 25–29 face a higher vulnerability to financial crises. Policy makers may then put in operation adequate measures to improve the ability of young people to face economic shocks and to enhance spatial mobility of young people.

5 Conclusion

Understanding the actual distribution of people in cities (including migrants) and the dynamics leading to this spatial pattern is of critical importance, both for policy-relevant issues and for developing more satisfactory theoretical models. When one analyses these topics, it is necessary to employ the two most recognised empirical regularities: Zipf's law and Gibrat's law. Roughly put, the first of these laws states that the city size in a country is proportional to its rank, while the second states that the growth rate of an entity (cities, for example, but it can also be applied to firms) is independent of its size. Scholars have dedicated many studies to the analysis of these two empirical regularities, both in supporting them and in criticizing them, but, as yet, no universal consensus has been reached. For our purposes, it is noteworthy that the existing literature provides an analysis of Gibrat's law and Zipf's law without taking demographic characteristics into account.

In this chapter, we have focused on population (and its age structure) and employment (and its age structure) by using a unique data set with annual observations of these two variables for all German cities and towns. What we have shown is that a differentiation among age cohorts and a use of different dependent variables may lead to differences in empirical results. In particular, on an aggregate level, we found that employment is much more concentrated compared to residential population (and this seems to be plausible, as places of work are usually not spread across all cities). All these results can be explained by the different amenities and housing needs that people of different ages can have. For example, larger cities offer usually a wider range of leisure activities that are often more appreciated by younger people than by older people. These new results should be taken into consideration, both in developing new theoretical models of urban growth that need to be more accurate and in structuring new policies that need to be more effective.

References

Barabási AL, Oltvai ZN (2004) Network biology: understanding the cell's functional organization. Nat Rev Genet 5:101–113

Berry BJL, Okulicz-Kozaryn A (2011) An urban-rural happiness gradient. Urban Geogr 32:871–883

Black D, Henderson V (2003) Urban evolution in the USA. J Econ Geogr 3:343–372

Brakman S, Garretsen H, Schramm M (2004) The strategic bombing of German cities during WW II and its Impact on city growth. J Econ Geogr 4:201–218

Bures RM (1998) Migration and the life course: is there a retirement transition? Int J Popul Geogr 3:109–119

Cameron C, Trivedi PK (2005) Microenometrics: methods and applications. Cambridge University Press, New York

Chesher A (1979) Testing the law of proportionate effect. J Ind Econ 27:403–411

Cordoba JC (2003) On the distribution of city sizes. J Urban Econ 63:177–197

Cordoba JC (2008) A generalized Gibrat's law. Int Econ Rev 49:1463–1468

Eeckhout J (2004) Gibrat's law for (All) cities. Am Econ Rev 94:1429–1451

European Union (2015) Being young in Europe today – demographic trends, EuroStat – statistics explained. Publications Office of the European Union, Luxembourg

Fazio G, Modica M (2015) Pareto or log-normal? Best fit and truncation in the distribution of all cities. J Reg Sci 55:736–756

Frey WH, Speare A Jr (1988) Regional and metropolitan growth and decline in the United States: a 1980 census monograph. Russell Sage Foundation, New York

Gabaix X (1999) Zipf's law for cities: an explanation. Q J Econ 114:739–767

Gabaix X, Ibragimov R (2011) Rank-1/2: a simple way to improve the OLS estimation of tail exponents. J Bus Econ Stat 29:24–39

Gabaix X, Ioannides Y (2004) The evolution of city size distribution. In: Henderson JV, Nijkamp P, Mills ES, Cheshire PC, Thisse JF (eds) Handbook of regional and urban economics, vol 4. Elsevier, North-Holland, pp 2341–2378

Gibrat R (1931) Les Inégalités économiques; Applications: aux Inégalités des Richesses, à la Concentration des Enterprises, aux Popolations des Villes, aux Statistiques des Familles, d'une loi Nuvelle, la Loi d'Effet Proportionnel. Librairie du Recueil Sirey, Paris

Giesen K, Suedekum J (2014) City age and city size. Eur Econ Rev 71:193–208

Giesen K, Suedekum J (2011) Zipf's law for cities in the regions and the country. J Econ Geogr 11:667–686

Giesen K, Zimmerman A, Suedekum J (2010) The size distribution across all cities – double pareto log normal strikes. J Urban Econ 68:129–137

Glaeser EL, Ponzetto GAM, Tobio K (2014) Cities, skills and regional change. Reg Stud 48:7–43

Gonzalez-Val R (2012) A nonparametric estimation of the local Zipf exponent for all US cities. Environ Plann B Plann Des 39:1119–1130

Gonzalez-Val R, Lanaspa L, Sanz F (2013) Gibrat's law for cities, growth regression and sample size. Econ Lett 118:367–369

Greenwood MJ (1985) Human migration: theory, models, and empirical studies. J Reg Sci 25(4):521–544

Guerin-Pace F (1995) Rank-size distribution and the process of urban growth. Urban Stud 32:551–562

Hunt GL (2006) Population-employment models: stationarity, cointegration and dynamic adjustment. J Reg Sci 46:205–244

Ioannides YM, Overman HG (2003) Zipf's law for cities: an empirical examination. Reg Sci Urban Econ 32:127–137

Ioannides YM, Skouras S (2013) US city size distribution: Robustly Pareto, but only in the tail. J Urban Econ 73:18–29

Kapteyn JC (1903) Skew frequency curves in biology and statistics. Noordhoff, Astronomical Laboratory, Groningen

Keyfitz N, Philipov D (1981) Migration and natural increase in the growth of cities. Geogr Anal 13(4):287–299

Lalanne A, Zumpe M (2015) Zipf's law, Gibrat's law and cointegration (No. 2015-27). Groupe de Recherche en Economie Théorique et Appliquée

Longino CF Jr, Biggar JC, Flynn CB, Wiseman RF (1984) The retirement migration project (Final report to the National Institute on Aging). University of Miami, Center for Social Research on Aging, Coral Gables, FL

Mansfield E (1962) Entry, Gibrat's law, innovation, and the growth of firms. Am Econ Rev 52:1023–1051

Marin G, Modica M (2017) Socio-economic exposure to natural disasters. Environ Impact Assess Rev 64:57–66

Modica M (2014) Does the EU have a homogeneous urban structure area? The role of agglomeration and the impact of shocks on urban structure In: ERSA conference papers (No. ersa14p229). European Regional Science Association

Modica M, Reggiani A (2014) An alternative interpretation of regional resilience: evidence from Italy. In: ERSA conference papers (No. ersa14p369). European Regional Science Association

Modica M, Zoboli R (2016) Vulnerability, resilience, hazard, risk, damage, and loss: a socio-ecological framework for natural disaster analysis. Web Ecol 16(1):59–62

Modica M, Reggiani A, Nijkamp P (2013) Methodological advances in Gibrat's and Zipf's laws: a comparative empirical study on the evolution of urban systems. Research memorandum 2013–35. Faculty of Economics and Business Administration

Modica M, Reggiani A, Nijkamp P (2017a) Are Gibrat and Zipf monozygotic or heterozygotic twins? A comparative analysis of means and variances in complex urban systems. In: Socioeconomic environmental policies and evaluations in regional science. Springer, Singapore, pp 37–59

Modica M, Reggiani A, Nijkamp P (2017b) Vulnerability, resilience and exposure: methodological aspects (forthcoming)

Nadaraya EA (1964) On estimating regression. Theory Probab Appl 10:186–190

Peri G (2001) Young people, skills and cities, CESifo working papers, 610, CESifo Group Munich

Reggiani A, Nijkamp P (2015) Did Zipf anticipate spatial connectivity structures? Environ Plann B Plann Des 42:468–489

Rosen KT, Resnick M (1980) The size distribution of cities: an examination of the Pareto law and primacy. J Urban Econ 8:165–186

Santarelli E, Audretsch DB, Klomp L, Thurik RA (2004) Gibrat's law: are the services different? Rev Ind Organ 24:301–324

Scott AJ, Storper M (2003) Regions, globalization, development. Reg Stud 37:579–593

Soo KT (2005) Zipf's law for cities: a cross-country investigation. Reg Sci Urban Econ 35:239–263

Storper M (2010) Agglomeration, trade, and spatial development: bringing dynamics back in. J Reg Sci 50:313–342

Watson GS (1964) Smooth regression analysis. Sankhya A 26:359–372

Zipf GK (1949) Human behavior and the principle of least effort. Addison-Wesley, Cambridge, MA

Chapter 15
Career Moves: Migration Histories of Selected Regional Workforces in Bendigo, Australia

Fiona McKenzie and Jonathan Corcoran

1 Introduction

Human capital is essential for growth and development. Regional science scholars have consistently revealed that labour migration from rural to urban areas is a growing phenomenon (OECD 2007; Partridge et al. 2008) and that rural communities increasingly battle to both attract and retain highly educated people. The issue is particularly prominent in Australia, a nation with one of the highest degrees of spatial population concentration globally (OECD 2007). More particularly, out-migration from rural areas in Australia has been a persistent feature of its population dynamics for more than half a century (see for example, McKenzie 1994; Rowland 1979), offset only by counter-urban movements to high amenity coastal regions (Bell and Hugo 2000).

The long-standing trend of Australian young adults leaving non-metropolitan areas to seek out educational and employment opportunities in capital cities has raised a number of policy concerns (McKenzie 2010). Scholarship highlights the critical importance of young adults both to the economy in terms of their accrued skills and knowledge (Schultz 1961) and demographically, since this age group is most likely to bear and raise children. These stages of the lifecourse that encapsulate

F. McKenzie (✉)
Department of Environment, Land Water and Planning, Melbourne, VIC, Australia
e-mail: fiona.mckenzie@delwp.vic.gov.au

J. Corcoran
Queensland Centre for Population Research, School of Earth and Environmental Sciences,
The University of Queensland, Brisbane, QLD, Australia
e-mail: jj.corcoran@uq.edu.au

© Springer International Publishing AG, part of Springer Nature 2018   311
U. Blien et al. (eds.), *Modelling Aging and Migration Effects on Spatial Labor Markets*, Advances in Spatial Science,
https://doi.org/10.1007/978-3-319-68563-2_15

commencing higher education, entry into the labour market and early career development are significant economically given that they represent a key period of human capital accumulation for individuals. As such, the destinations chosen by young adults at these lifecourse stages have important economic consequences both for individuals as well as the regions in which they reside.

The net gain and loss of human capital have long been recognised as key ingredients in regional economic growth and development and productivity (Romer 1986, 1994; Lucas 1988; Barro 1992). The spatial outcomes of population flows can lead to gains and losses for different regions which, in turn can affect levels of economic and population growth (Mathur 1999; Wilson and Briscoe 2004; Stimson et al. 2011). Increasingly, large cities have been recognised as locations where human capital is attracted and concentrates (Glaeser and Saiz 2004; Glaeser and Resseger 2010).

Net population flows from rural and remote communities to Australia's metropolitan areas reinforces the concentration of economic activity along with a relatively young labour force. At the same time, it has led to a gradual ageing of the population structure and an erosion of the local stock of human capital in many rural communities, placing constraints on local development (Tonts 2005; Hogan and Young 2013). To enhance their social fabric and economic performance, rural communities often seek to develop policies for improving the attraction and retention rates of young and educated population (Corcoran et al. 2010). A comprehensive understanding of the complex blend of forces underpinning the migration patterns of young adults and their changes over time is therefore a critical component for regional policy development.

The importance of both stemming the outflows of highly educated people along with promoting return migration of young adults have been signalled as important components for successful rural development (Sher and Sher 1994). Yet despite the importance of return migration to redress rural decline, little is known about its dynamics. In particular, the spatial patterns and reasons underpinning return migration are yet to be full understood. More specifically, scholarship is still to reveal the extent to which individuals from regional areas are more likely to return to a regional area at a later date, a deficit underpinned by a lack of suitable data that record such population mobility. Furthermore, the motivations that underpin these return moves remain under-researched. For regional policy makers, these uncertainties make it difficult to develop effective attraction and retention strategies. To redress this gap, the aim of this paper is to reveal the characteristics and motivations of professional workers' migration histories for those living and working in a large regional centre in Australia (Bendigo, Victoria).

The remainder of the paper is structured as follows: We begin with reviewing sources of longitudinal data necessary to study return migration in Australia before introducing our regional case study context, Bendigo. We next present and discuss the results of our survey of professional workers for three major employers in the region: (1) the Bendigo Bank; (2) Bendigo Health; and, (3) the Greater Bendigo City Council drawing insights on the characteristics and motivation of workers' migration histories with a particular emphasis on return migration.

2 Longitudinal Data Sources and Their Limitations

In 2012, the Australian Research Council (ARC) funded a Linkage Grant for a 3-year project entitled *Attraction and Retention: The role of mobility in educational pathways and human capital development.* This project involved the University of Queensland, several Victorian government agencies, Graduate Careers Australia and Latrobe University Bendigo. The research proposal arose from earlier work undertaken by McKenzie (2010) and Corcoran et al. (2010) that examined the spatial implications of educational and employment pathways chosen by young adults.

For the Victorian government, the research was attractive given the high priority to the retention and attraction of people to non-metropolitan areas. The research team used the Longitudinal Survey of Australian Youth (LSAY) to undertake pathway analysis. A cohort of 847 Victorians was available for analysis. Mobility sequences were followed as this group aged from 15 to 24 with the spatial outcomes shown in Fig. 15.1.

It can be seen that the regional students are much more mobile than Melbourne students in the years covering school, tertiary education and labour force entry. There is an ongoing flow from regional Victoria to Melbourne for ages 16–23 years, which covers the period of higher education and entry into the workplace. This confirms earlier findings indicating that many regional students who undertake tertiary studies in the regions will still move to Melbourne for employment afterwards (McKenzie 2010, p. 12). The lack of movement from Melbourne to regions is notable.

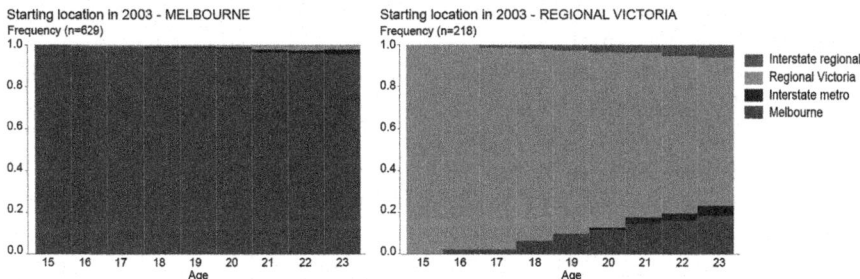

Fig. 15.1 Spatial patterns of longitudinal migration pathways, 2003–2011. Source: ARC Linkage Project analysis of LSAY data

3   Using LSAY Data to Examine Return Migration

Drawing on data from the 2003 LSAY, some insights can be gained in relation to return migration, although the fact that the LSAY stops at age 23 limits the findings that may be drawn. Nevertheless, by using the national, rather than Victorian, dataset from LSAY Wave 1, researchers were able to extract a large enough sample (1037 persons) for some basic analysis of early return migration among those who recorded a regional location at the start of the period.[1] Around half of these (532 persons) moved to metropolitan areas after leaving school. Of those who moved to a metropolitan area, 29% (153 persons) had made a return move to a regional area by age 23.

Most returning school leavers appear to remain in metropolitan areas for between 1 to 4 years, which would presumably represent the length of most university degrees. Nearly half (48%) of those returning did so at ages 22 and 23. While this return movement brings enhanced human capital to the regions, the fact that many stay in metropolitan areas adds to human capital concentration there. So, over time, net losses of human capital may be assumed to occur in regional areas. While flows of young adults may favour the cities, there are counter flows involving people later in their career or at early retirement ages. This group is likely to have the advantage of lifelong learning and work experience. The degree to which this group might counteract the flow of young adults is unclear although two factors may limit the equivalence of their human capital:

1. Generational differences may mean that an older group, while experienced, may not have the currency of skills for emerging industry sectors;
2. As highlighted by Stockdale (2006), they may bring a wealth of skills and experience, but this does not necessarily create the type of entrepreneurial development which subsequently creates jobs for an area.

As stated above, the major limitation of the LSAY data is that it stops when respondents are 23 years old. Census data indicate that metropolitan to regional migration is more likely when people are in their mid to late 20s than in their late teens or early 20s (Fig. 15.2).

Earlier work by McKenzie (2010) used qualitative data collected by Sweeney Research Ltd to examine the motivations behind moves between regional Victoria and Melbourne for university. The findings of this research are relevant to the question of whether the return migration shown in the LSAY data is likely to continue in subsequent age groups. The qualitative research included interviews with university students as well as recent alumni (up to 5-years after graduation). The students (mostly aged between 18 and 22) who had grown up in regional

---

[1]Regional youth are defined as young people who reported their place of residence in a non-metropolitan Statistical Area Level 4 at the age of 15, i.e. at the first wave of the 2003 LSAY cohort.

Number of persons

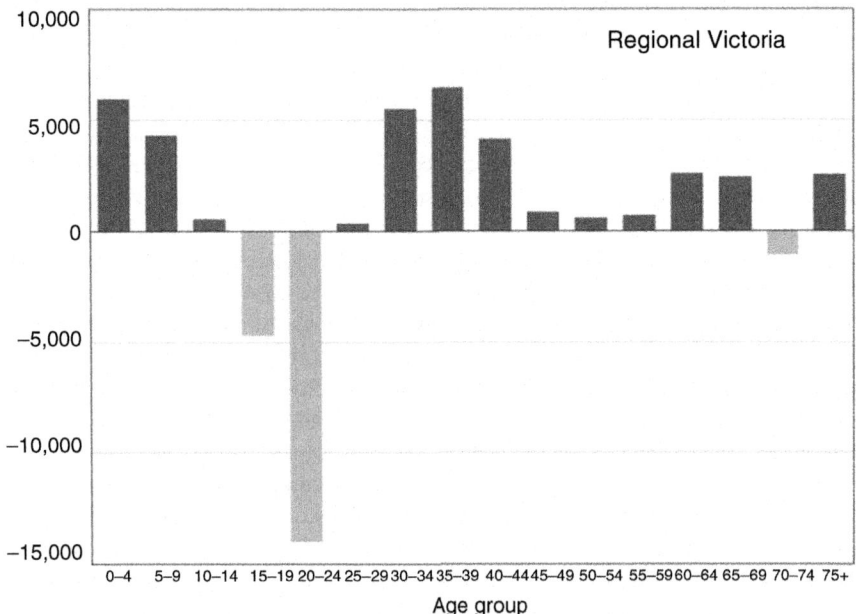

Number of persons

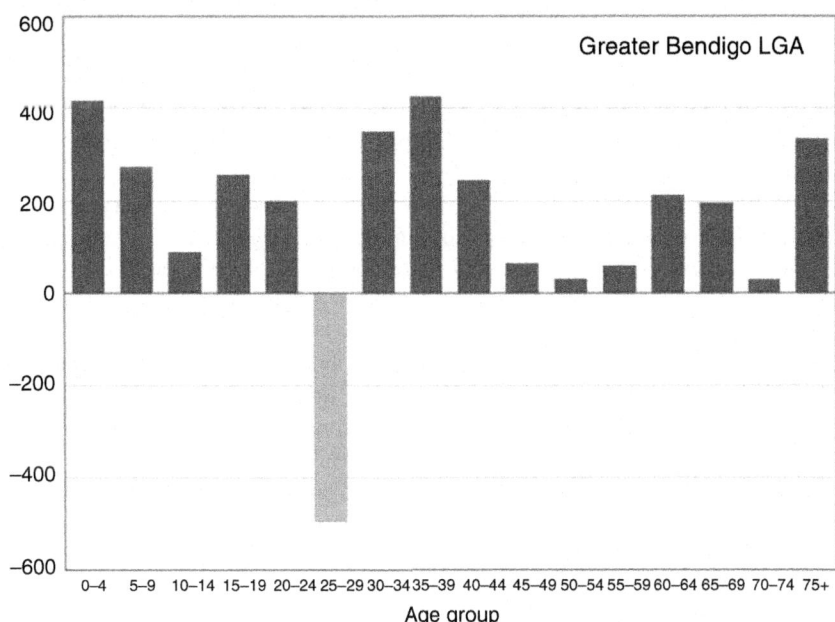

Fig. 15.2 Implied net migration by age, selected regions, 2006–2011. Source: DELWP unpublished data

Victoria indicated that, once they reached their thirties, they would settle down in regional Victoria to raise their children. However, the alumni group (mostly in their mid to late 20s) suggested that such early intentions had been complicated by the pathways that their metropolitan stay had created. These were affected by career opportunities arising in Melbourne and/or relationships developing with people who had grown up in Melbourne. Both factors created an anchor that could increase in strength the longer people stayed. On the whole, students from regional backgrounds who had undertaken a professional degree were more willing to live in the city than vocational students, despite personal preferences to reside regionally. They recognise that the city is where the majority of job and career opportunities are located and they are willing to move to where the jobs are. While retirement was a very long way off for those in the study, there was agreement among alumni who had grown up in the country that retirement was a life-stage best spent in the country. Almost all pictured an idyllic seaside lifestyle—far enough away from the hustle and bustle yet still within easy reach of the medical facilities of Geelong or Melbourne. Surprisingly, only a handful suggested that they would consider retiring to their regional hometown, suggesting that return migration may still lead to areas of regional depopulation in more remote areas, while the redistribution of population would favour areas near Melbourne and the major regional centres. Analysis of Bendigo survey data presented in this paper supports this pattern of return migration to a regional centre rather than regional place of birth.

Comparing the qualitative and quantitative data presents the question: who are the people contributing to the net gain in population in regional Victoria in the age groups 25–40? After a great deal of research effort has been expended, this is the data gap that remains. We might assume that the intentions voiced in the qualitative work—returning to regional Victoria to raise children—are in fact being played out; the quantitative picture shows net gains in late 20s and early 30s. Alternatively, the net gain may be due to people from Melbourne moving to regional areas (i.e. not regional returners).

The quantitative data in Fig. 15.3 show another element of the story: a regional city like Bendigo actually has a net loss in the 25–29 age group, something noted in the qualitative study as potentially representing the 'staging post' role of some regional cities with people staying there for tertiary education but then subsequently completing their studies or gaining employment in Melbourne. Again, the data do not reveal whether such people would be more or less likely to return to regional Victoria than other groups. Despite the net loss in this age group, Bendigo shows net gains in the subsequent cohorts, suggesting a balance between losses and gains of the working age population. In regional Victoria overall there is a deeper net loss of young working age people that is not balanced by gains in subsequent age groups until near-retirement ages.

% of respondents

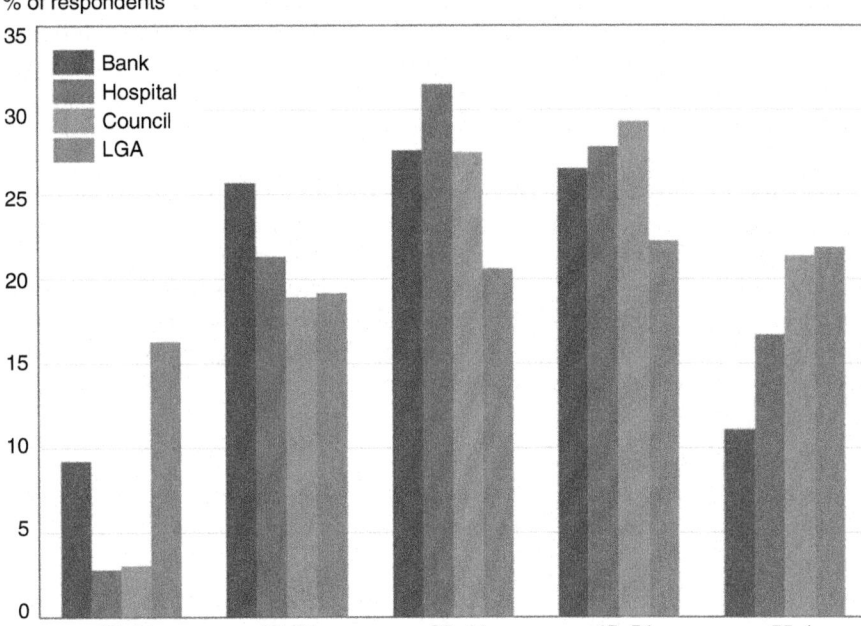

Data for the LGA of Greater Bendigo is for those aged 55–65

Fig. 15.3 Age profile of respondents from Bank, Hospital and Council samples 2015 and for the Local Government Area of Bendigo 2011. Sources: Bendigo Bank Survey 2015; Bendigo Health Survey 2015; City of Greater Bendigo Council survey 2015; ABS Census 2011 using TableBuilder

4   Insights on Return Migration Using Regional Workforce Samples

Faced with this problematic data gap to uncover the characteristics and dynamics of return migration, the research team undertook a survey of a regional workforce to map migration histories. This retrospective approach was regarded as the best way in which the pathways of those living and working in regional areas can be tracked over time. The significance of capital cities in the context of human capital development for a regional workforce can then be more fully examined.

4.1   Research Methods

A sample of professional workers in a regional location was sought. As Latrobe University Bendigo was represented on the ARC Linkage Research team, Bendigo was chosen as the case study location and three organisations—Bendigo Bank,

Bendigo Hospital (Bendigo Health) and the City of Greater Bendigo Council—were identified as sources for participant recruitment. Bendigo is a city of around 100,000 persons, located 150 km northwest of Victoria's state capital city, Melbourne (population 4.5 million). Each of the chosen organisations is a major employer in Bendigo and each represents an important industry sector within the local economy: financial services; health services and public administration.

The survey targeted the collection of information about the spatial histories of individuals currently working in these regional organisations to reveal their educational and employment pathways and the role played by spatial mobility. The part played by Melbourne is these pathways was hypothesised to be important in higher education given its much larger size and more diverse educational opportunities. The web-based survey was conducted at Bendigo Bank in February 2015 and concurrently at the hospital and council in November 2015. Key questions included:

- *Did workers originate from the local area?*
- *Did they train in the local area or did they train elsewhere and return?*
- *What have been the motivations for various migration decisions?*

4.2 General Characteristics of the Sample

A total of 734 respondents participated in the combined surveys: 440 from Bendigo Bank; 119 from Bendigo Health (Hospital) and 175 from the City of Greater Bendigo (Council). In all three samples, female respondents outnumbered male. The highest proportion of females was in the Hospital sample (76%) and the lowest in the Bank sample (57%). Sixty-three percent of the Council respondents were female. The age profile of the three samples is shown in Fig. 15.3 below. Compared to the wider working age population of Bendigo, the sample has fewer workers aged 55 plus and fewer younger than 25. The Bank sample has a younger age profile than the Hospital or Council samples.

4.3 Locational Backgrounds of the Respondents

Around a third of the total survey sample were Bendigo-born (32.5%), while another third (32%) had originated in other parts of regional Victoria. A smaller proportion had been born in Melbourne (19%) or overseas (8%). Under 5% of the sample were from other capital cities or from interstate regional areas. All regional categories (Bendigo, regional Victoria and Interstate regional) amounted to 69% of the combined sample.

The dominance of the Bendigo-born cohort is most noticeable at the Bank where 39% of respondents had been born locally. This compares to 26% at the Council and only 19% at the Hospital. The Bendigo Bank was established locally and maintains a high profile in the local economy. It offers training opportunities via the local university as well as entry-level opportunities via internships and this probably contributed to a strong local profile in its workforce. The Hospital has a larger share of Melbourne-born staff (30%), however, it also has the highest proportion for those born in regional Victoria (38% compared to 31% at both the Bank and the Council).

Another line of investigation was determining whether senior positions in the three organisations were more likely to be held by those coming from metropolitan backgrounds. The reason for this expectation was that metropolitan areas offer a much wider range of specialist education opportunities. Thus senior managers and executives might be more likely to have trained in capital cities where a greater range of specialist training opportunities were available. The Australian settlement pattern, which is dominated by large state capital cities and few medium-sized cities, makes such an assumption more plausible. However, when stratified by role in each organisation, the dominance of regional or Bendigo-born people can be seen—most notably in the bank sample where 72% of senior staff had been born in Bendigo or other regional locations.

Senior roles at the Bank are dominated by people with regional backgrounds (Fig. 15.4). The hospital has strong representation from regional backgrounds in both management and officer level. The assumption that more senior roles require higher levels of education and experience may hold, but the degree to which these skills need to be acquired in metropolitan areas is challenged by the findings.

The Council seems to be the only organisation surveyed where metropolitan birthplaces are dominant, particularly for management roles. The Council also shows a higher proportion of staff born overseas compared to the Bank and Hospital.

4.4 Locational Histories of Respondents

Apart from birthplace location, the survey asked respondents to indicate where they had lived at three additional points in their lives:

- Up until the age of 15
- During their period of secondary schooling
- During their period of post-school education and training.

Figure 15.5 shows the location of respondents at four key points: birth; childhood; secondary school and higher education. At each stage, Bendigo is more highly represented and regional Victoria becomes less prominent—a pattern that accords with our understanding of movements of young people from rural areas to regional cities to access educational opportunities. This pattern holds for each of the organisations although the bank, as stated previously, starts with a higher base of Bendigo-born respondents and maintains a higher proportion of people who lived locally at each of the subsequent life stages. While 'overseas' does appear in the birthplace data, it remains in the minority at each of the three organisations.

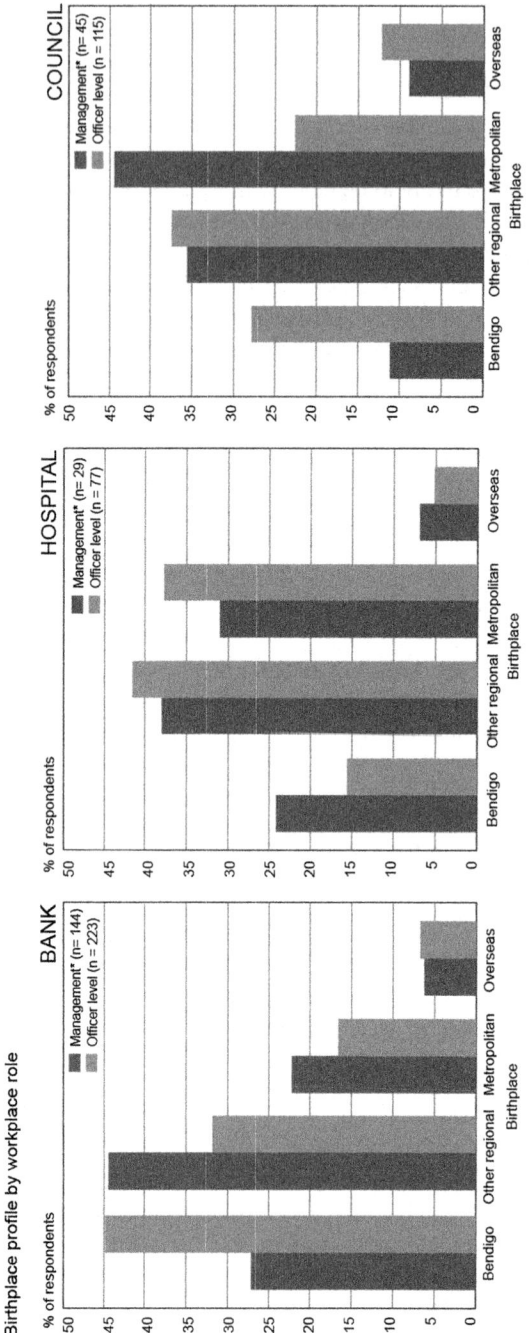

Fig. 15.4 Birthplace profile by workplace role, Bank, Hospital and Council samples. Sources: Bendigo Bank Survey 2015; Bendigo Health Survey 2015; City of Greater Bendigo Council survey 2015

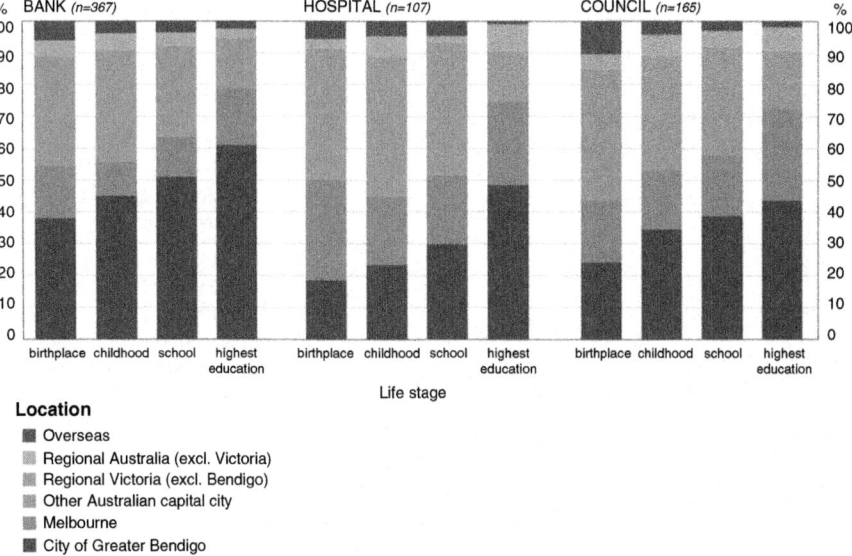

Fig. 15.5 Locations of respondents at key life stages, Bank, Hospital and Council samples. Sources: Bendigo Bank Survey 2015; Bendigo Health Survey 2015; City of Greater Bendigo Council survey 2015

The expectation that Melbourne would be more important as a location during the attainment of higher qualifications is only partly evident in the findings. In fact, it is not of greater prominence than Bendigo in any of the organisations, suggesting that the local education and training sectors are playing an important role in delivering services to local businesses.

As well as this aggregate picture at each life-stage, the data were analysed longitudinally. Where respondents answered all locational questions unambiguously, a migration history could be ascertained. The sample of 734 yielded 639 useable responses. A simplified location categorisation was developed: Bendigo (B); other regional (R); metropolitan (M) and overseas (O). These were then combined according to the respondent's location at each of the life-stages indicated earlier. Hence, someone who had been born and spent their childhood in a rural location, then had moved to Bendigo for secondary school and Melbourne for higher education would have the coded migration history "RRBM", keeping in mind that such respondents subsequently moved to their existing location in Bendigo. A pattern of MMMM would describe a respondent who had spent all of these points of time in Melbourne and was now in Bendigo. Using this summary approach, 65 migration combinations were identified, of which the most common are shown in Fig. 15.6. These nine migration patterns represent 71% of the total sample of 639 useable responses.

The most common migration history pattern is, in fact, a non-migration pattern: 22.5% of the combined sample consists of those who have spent each of their

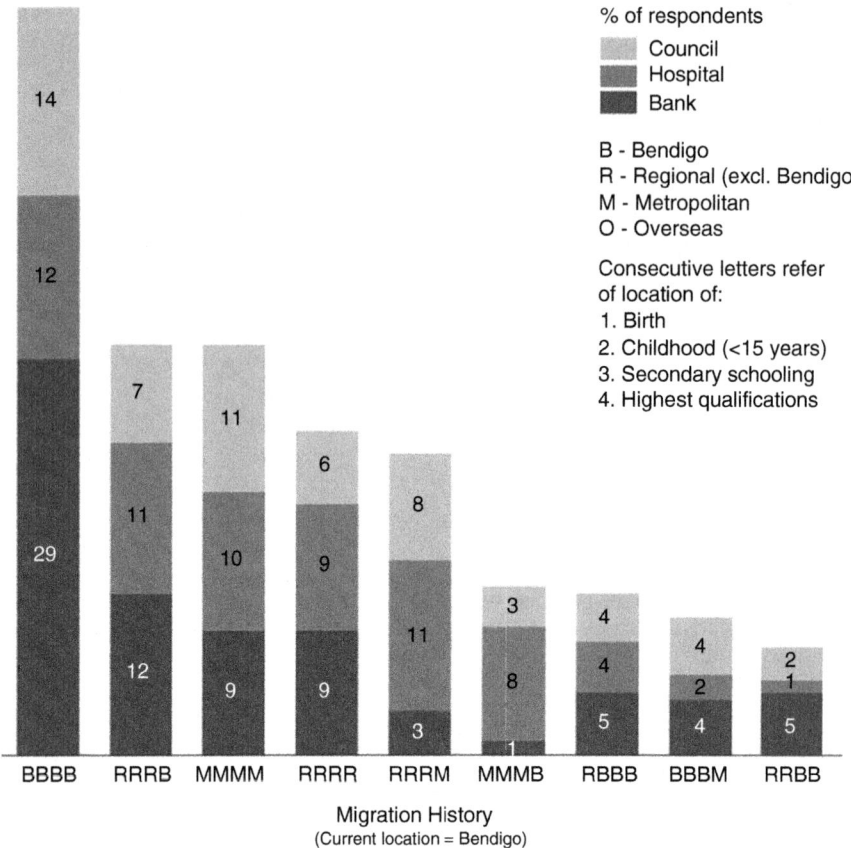

Fig. 15.6 Simplified migration histories, Bank, Hospital and Council samples. Sources: Bendigo
Bank Survey 2015; Bendigo Health Survey 2015; City of Greater Bendigo Council survey 2015

life-stages locally. This was more common for the Bank sample where 29% had
the "BBBB" pattern. Several categories accounted for 10–14% of the sample in
each of the three organisations. RRRB was relatively common across the three
organisations accounting for 11% of the total sample. This suggests that Bendigo
is drawing from rural areas and other regional centres, mostly within Victoria.
The appearance of MMMM and RRRR, which accounted for 10 and 8% of the
combined sample respectively, shows again that non-migration is a common pattern.
The importance of family and friendship networks is likely to be a reason for this
population 'inertia'.

Patterns of return migration can be seen in the codes that include a metropolitan
component, for example the patterns of BBBM and RRRM in Fig. 15.7. The latter

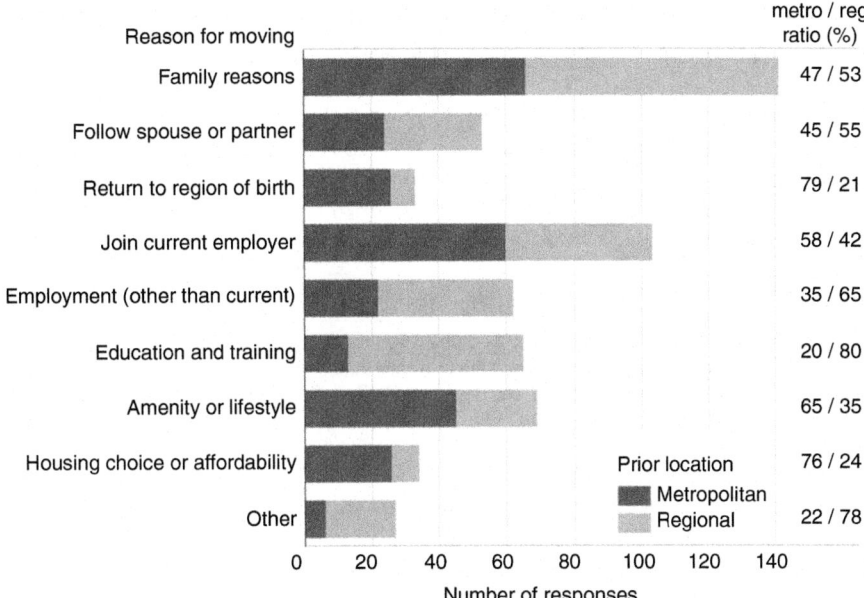

Fig. 15.7   Reasons for moving to Bendigo by prior location, combined sample. Sources: Bendigo Bank Survey 2015; Bendigo Health Survey 2015; City of Greater Bendigo Council survey 2015

shows a migration pattern in which the return is to a regional city rather than a return to the regional area of origin.

There is one caveat to the data on these returnees. Survey questions asked respondents to state where they had attained their highest level of qualification. The 24 respondents showing the BBBM pattern had attained their highest qualification in Melbourne, however cross tabulation of their response with an earlier question "After the age of 15, have you lived outside the City of Greater Bendigo?" reveals eight respondents who had not lived outside Bendigo after age 15 but had a post-school qualification from Melbourne, presumably through distance education or commuting.

4.5   Reasons for Moving to Bendigo

Respondents who had moved to Bendigo at some point in their lives were asked about the reasons for their move. This group of respondents included people born outside Bendigo as well as those who had been born in Bendigo, moved away, and then returned. This group was given a list of eight options with respondents able to select up to three reasons. Table 15.1 reveals the dominance of family and employment reasons, which account for 39 and 31% of responses in the combined

Table 15.1 Reasons for moving to Bendigo-Bank, Hospital, Council and combined samples

Reason for moving	Bank		Hospital		Council		Total	
	No.	%	No.	%	No.	%	No.	%
Family related*	103	44	42	34	60	35	205	39
Employment related**	74	32	37	30	52	30	163	31
Education/training	37	16	10	8	14	8	61	12
Amenity/lifestyle reasons	9	4	20	16	22	13	51	10
Housing choice/afford ability	1	<1	10	8	15	9	26	5
Other	9	4	4	3	8	5	21	4
TOTAL	233	100	123	100	171	100	527	100

*Includes: Family reasons; Follow spouse or partner. Return to region of birth
*Includes: Join current organisation; Employment (other than current)
Sources: Bendigo Bank Survey 2015; Bendigo Health Survey 2015; City of Greater Bendigo Council survey 2015

sample. The reasons of "education and training" and "amenity" account for a much smaller proportion of responses—12 and 10% respectively. "Housing choice and affordability" accounts for only 5% of all responses.

In terms of particular organisations, the results presented in Table 15.1 show that amenities were a much more important factor for those at the Hospital and Council compared to the Bank sample; education and training was of greater importance to those in the Bank sample. Housing choice and affordability accounted for less than 10% of responses in each location although it was noticeably higher for the Hospital and Council sample than for the Bank sample.

While housing choice and affordability appear to have little significance as drivers of migration, subsequent survey questions shows that they were listed by many as advantages of being in Bendigo. This highlights an important point for regional policy makers—drivers of migration are not the same as a locational advantage or asset. Just because a place has a key advantage (like affordable housing), it may not act as a driver to attract in-migration. In fact, affordable house prices are a very poor indicator of migration potential as some of the most expensive cities still attract in-migration.

By considering the location prior to moving, analysis of the reasons for moving can be further enhanced, showing whether metropolitan and regional in-migrants reported different reasons for moving. In Fig. 15.7, the prior location of "Metropolitan" includes Melbourne and other capital cities while "Regional" includes regional Victoria and other areas of regional Australia. Due to small numbers, respondents who moved from overseas have been excluded.

As highlighted earlier, "family reasons" is the main reason for moving and this is the case irrespective of prior locational background. While many of those moving from regional areas had come to Bendigo seeking general employment opportunities, those from metropolitan areas were more likely to have moved for specific job opportunities. This highlights the important role that a city like Bendigo has in being able to offer a range of employment opportunities to people from smaller towns or rural areas. It also shows that, for those coming from employment-rich capital cities like Melbourne, the specific job opportunity is important. Other reasons for moving that were more important to metropolitan rather than regional in-migrants include: "return to region of birth", "amenity/lifestyle" and "housing choice and affordability".

4.6 Reported Advantages and Disadvantages of Living in Bendigo

Respondents were asked about the advantages and disadvantages of living in Bendigo. An open-ended question was presented for each of these and respondents were able to record up to three items. Their responses were subsequently grouped thematically for ease of analysis.

Table 15.2 shows the types of advantages reported across the combined sample. Lifestyle and the size of the city rank highly in the proportion of responses, each accounting for more than 10%. Affordability, accessibility and quality of services also rank highly. Whereas key drivers were found to be family and employment, these appear less often in the list of advantages, highlighting the differences between why people move and why people like a particular location when they get there. There was general consistency of responses across the three organisations with most categories showing little variation.

In terms of disadvantages, there were five categories that each accounted for more than 10% of responses (Table 15.3). Infrastructure was often referred to, with the major issues being lack of car parking and lack of public transport. Presumably, the lack of public services means that there is a greater reliance on cars and this heightens the demand for parking.

Jobs and income were also important. While respondents were themselves employed, issues around career progression were referred to, with alternative opportunities in their field of expertise often being limited. Income levels were also mentioned and, as with career opportunities, Melbourne was often the point of comparison. This highlights the problem for any regional centre that is inevitably more limited in labour market choices simply because of its smaller size.

It is of interest to note the prominence of environmental factors in people's lists of disadvantages. These factors are largely immutable, yet climatic and landscape factors were often mentioned, particularly in relation to the hot environment and the lack of a beach or other water bodies.

There is more variation between organisations regarding disadvantages compared to advantages. Infrastructure is more commonly listed as an issue by Bank employees than the other two organisations; environmental factors are more commonly listed by Council respondents (Fig. 15.8). The higher response to issues of "culture" in the Hospital and Council sample may reflect the timing of those surveys (November 2015) compared to the Bank (June 2015). In late 2015, a local

Table 15.2 Advantages of living in Bendigo, as reported by respondents, combined sample

Advantages	Examples	No. of responses	%
Lifestyle	*Relaxed atmosphere; slower lifestyle.*	229	14.1
Less congestion/Good size	*Size of city makes it easy to commute; lack of traffic congestion compared to capital cities.*	174	10.7
Quality services/facilities	*High quality facilities—health care; education; sporting venues; arts; shops.*	153	9.5
Accessibility/Ease of travel	*Short drive to almost anything; ease of getting around; short distance between home and work.*	151	9.3
Affordability	*Cheaper housing costs; affordable acreage; cheaper cost of living.*	139	8.6
Close to family/friends	*Family here; close to my family/extended family.*	126	7.8
Access to Melbourne	*Accessible to Melbourne.*	116	7.2
Friendly community	*Community focus; community spirit.*	103	6.4
Employment	*Big enough city to provide good employment opportunities; Bank provides career opportunities.*	95	5.9
Access to services/activities	*Access to medical, sporting, education facilities.*	85	5.3
Location (not further defined)	*Central location in Victoria; central to Melbourne or the Murray River; central to most things.*	69	4.3
Natural amenity	*Pleasant place to live; bush; climate; landscape.*	63	3.9
Good place to raise family	*Comfortable safe place to live and raise a family.*	60	3.7
Other		35	2.2
Built form	*Heritage buildings; parks and gardens.*	21	1.3
TOTAL*		1619	100

*Up to three responses were allowed hence the number of responses is higher than the number of participants. Sources: Bendigo Bank Survey 2015; Bendigo Health Survey 2015; City of Greater Bendigo Council survey 2015

mosque development and the associated protests and counter-protests received much media attention in the city. While the mosque was not specifically mentioned by survey respondents, various comments were suggestive, for example, "negative discriminatory attitudes" and "recent political climate means there is a lot of unrest". Other responses did mention multiculturalism—either the lack of it being seen as a disadvantage or in a few cases, its existence being viewed as a problem. Further comments about intolerance and community conflict are also suggestive of the public controversy over the mosque.

Table 15.3 Disadvantages of living in Bendigo, as reported by respondents, combined sample

Theme	Examples	No. of responses	%
Infrastructure	*Lack of car parking; public transport.*	212	17.7
Jobs/Income	*Can be difficult to find work; limited employment opportunities for young adults; lower salaries; lack of senior professional roles.*	194	16.2
Environment	*No beach; no river/lake; too hot/dry.*	136	11.3
Services	*Limited choice of schools; lack of medical specialists; childcare expensive and hard to find.*	121	10.1
Location/Distance	*Distance to Melbourne.*	120	10.0
Culture	*Old boys clubs; small town mentality; anti-multicultural attitude.*	101	8.4
Lack of activity	*Lack of shopping; don't get big events; boredom.*	98	8.2
Council	*Hard to obtaining approvals; rates too high; lack of funding for sport.*	62	5.2
Social issues	*Growing drug culture; crime.*	43	3.6
Cost of living	*Cost of living too high/rising.*	36	3.0
Congestion	*Traffic.*	32	2.7
None	*No disadvantages.*	27	2.2
Other		18	1.5
TOTAL*		1200	100.0

* Up to three responses were allowed hence the number of responses is higher than the number of participants. Sources: Bendigo Bank Survey 2015; Bendigo Health Survey 2015; City of Greater Bendigo Council survey 2015

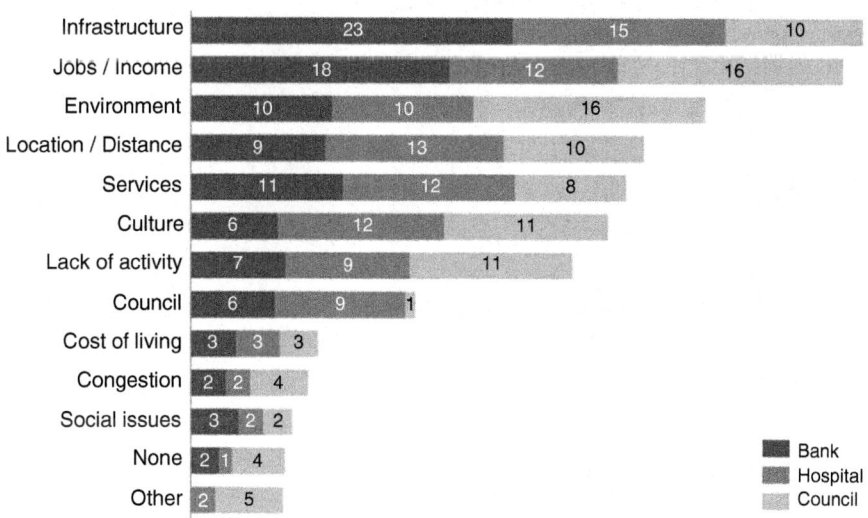

Fig. 15.8 Disadvantages of living in Bendigo, responses as a proportion of total Bank, Hospital and Council samples. Sources: Bendigo Bank Survey 2015; Bendigo Health Survey 2015; City of Greater Bendigo Council survey 2015

5 Future Migration Intentions

Most respondents (86%) had no intention of moving away from Bendigo in the near future. The Hospital had the highest proportion intending to leave within two years (20%) and Council had the lowest proportion (10%) (Table 15.4).

When analysed by age, the results show that younger adults are more likely to move away from Bendigo than older age groups (Fig. 15.9). Given that young adults are, on average, the most mobile age group in the population, this result is not surprising.

Melbourne was the most likely destination for those intending to leave (33%), followed by regional Victoria (26%). Interstate locations accounted for 9% (capital city) and 7% (regional) respectively while overseas accounted for 9% of respondent's intended destinations. Seventeen percent were unsure about their potential destination.

Table 15.4 Intention to leave Bendigo in next two years, Bank, Hospital and Council samples

	Bank		Hospital		Council		Total sample	
	No	%	No.	%	No.	%	No.	%
Intend to leave	53	14.3	21	19.6	16	9.8	90	14.1
Don't intend to leave	316	85.2	86	80.4	148	90.2	550	85.9
Total	369	100	107	100	164	100	640	100

Sources: Bendigo Bank Survey 2015; Bendigo Health Survey 2015; City of Greater Bendigo Council survey 2015

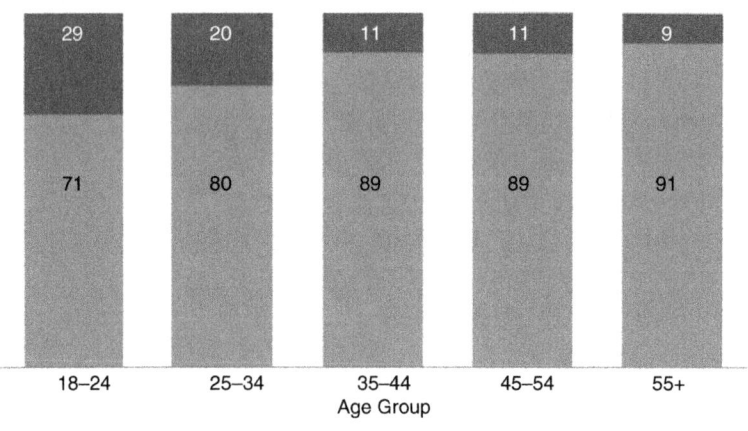

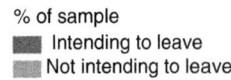

% of sample
◼ Intending to leave
◼ Not intending to leave

Fig. 15.9 Intention to leave Bendigo in next two years by age group, combined sample. Sources: Bendigo Bank Survey 2015; Bendigo Health Survey 2015; City of Greater Bendigo Council survey 2015

6   Discussion and Conclusion

Young adults gain skills and experience through school and post-school education and from entry into the workforce. The locational choices made by these young adults as they progress through their lifecourse accumulating human capital can differ. With a long-standing pattern of net loss of young adults from regional areas, the concern held by many policy makers is that areas of net loss of young people (such as regional Victoria) may lead to a net loss of the human capital needed to sustain and grow regional economies. The aim of this paper was to shed new light onto the characteristics and motivations of professional workers' migration histories for those living and working in Bendigo. To this end, a number of important findings were revealed.

Our research findings confirmed that there was indeed a continuing net loss of young adults from regional Victoria although this loss does appear to take place at slightly older ages than in the past (DELWP 2016, p. 7). A possible reason for this shift in the age of the migrant might be attributed to the way in which young adults in regional areas need to spend time in the workforce to afford the costs of moving away from home for education (Klatt and Polesel 2013). By the age of 23, it was shown that around a third of those who had left regional areas for education return to a regional location. This presents a positive story for regions in terms of human capital accumulation as skills learnt and developed in Melbourne can be transferred to regional areas. There is also likely to be additional return migration after the age of 23 although existing longitudinal data is unable to provide evidence of these pathway patterns.

In terms of human capital accumulation, survey results for the Bendigo Bank show that a relatively high proportion of senior bank employees had originated from regional backgrounds. This suggests that, even for sectors like financial services, a metropolitan education was not essential. It should be noted that, in the case of Bendigo Bank, the organisation itself plays an important role in the human capital development of their staff. Scholarships, internships and partnerships with local education providers forms an important part of the company's culture. This benefits the bank, in terms of overcoming skills shortages, but it also benefits employees (through sponsorship of their education locally) and local service providers (through the purchase of education and training services within the regional city).

The Bendigo survey also highlighted the role of family factors in peoples' migration decisions. Among the various components of this category, people were found to be moving closer to parents or other relatives and people were returning to the region of their birth after leaving Bendigo at an earlier age. The significance of this for regional policy makers is that having a connection with a place (e.g. through family) makes moving there more likely. Given that social networks usually act as an anchor on migration, it is likely to be much more difficult for people who have lived their lives in a major city to consider living in a regional location. For policy makers interested in attracting people to a regional location, targeting people who grew up in such areas may be a more effective promotional strategy.

As regional scientists and demographers continue to augment their understandings of the complex drivers and dynamics of migration, the results presented in this paper offer some advance in this space. While our findings are empirical in orientation, we recognise the value of building on these results through the adoption of a more formal modelling approach. Here, future work could model the determinants of regional attraction and retention and isolate the key characteristics shaping the decision to remain, move to, or move back to a regional area. The results of such a modelling exercise offer the potential to further contribute to better designed and targeted regional development policy.

In summary, unveiling the characteristics and dynamics of migration histories is an important academic endeavour and one where scholarship remains in its infancy. In this paper we have sought to draw on existing longitudinal survey data in addition to a primary survey of regional employees to reveal the migration histories of professional workers in Bendigo, Australia. We go some way to unpacking the complex sets of spatial mobility and their associated motivations that collectively have important consequences for the social and economic futures of both individuals and regional communities.

Acknowledgements This survey forms part of a wider project funded by the Australian Research Council (ARC), University of Queensland and Victorian Government namely, ARC Linkage Project LP120100212: Attraction and Retention: The Role of Mobility in Educational Pathways and Human Capital Development. Researchers on that project have provided data and feedback for this paper, notably, Martin Bell, Jonathan Corcoran and Francisco Rowe Gonzalez from the University of Queensland and Trevor Budge, La Trobe University. Support from Joshua Pell on behalf of Bendigo Bank and survey assistance from Melissa Kennedy at Latrobe University Bendigo is also acknowledged. Quantitative estimates of age specific migration were developed from ABS census data by the Forward Policy & Research Branch of DELWP in Melbourne, Victoria.

Disclaimer The views expressed in this paper are those of the authors and should not be regarded as representing the views of Bendigo City Council, Bendigo Bank, Bendigo Health or the Victorian Department of Environment, Land, Water and Planning.

References

Barro R (1992) Human capital and economic growth. In: Policies for long-run economic growth, a symposium sponsored by the Federal Reserve Bank of Kansas City, Kansas

Bell M, Hugo G (2000) Internal migration in Australia 1991–96: Overview and the overseas-born. Department of Immigration and Multicultural Affairs, Canberra

Corcoran J, Faggian A, McCann P (2010) Human capital in remote and rural Australia: the role of graduate migration. Growth Change 41(2):192–220

DELWP (Department of Environment, Land, Water and Planning) (2016) Attraction and retention. Education and labour force pathways of metropolitan and regional school leavers in Victoria. Forward Policy and Research Branch, Victorian Government, Melbourne

Glaeser E, Resseger M (2010) The complementarity between cities and skills. J Reg Sci 50(1):221–244

Glaeser E, Saiz A (2004) The rise of the skilled city. Brookings Wharton Pap Urban Aff 5:47–94

Hogan A, Young M (2013) Visioning a future for rural and regional Australia. Reg Econ Soc 6(2):319–330

Klatt M, Polesel J (2013) Deferring a University Offer in Victoria 2009 year 12 graduates – three years out. Youth Affairs Council of Victoria (YACVic), Melbourne, Australia

Lucas R (1988) On the mechanics of economic development. J Monet Econ 22:3–42

Mathur V (1999) Human capital-based strategy for regional economic development. Econ Dev Q 13(3):203–216

McKenzie F (1994) Population decline in non-metropolitan Australia: impacts and policy implications. Urban Policy Res 12(4):253–263

McKenzie F (2010) The influence of tertiary institutions on regional youth migration in Victoria, In: Dalziel P (ed) Innovation and regions: theory, practice and policy. Refereed Proceedings of the 34th Annual Conference of the Australia and New Zealand Regional Science Association International, 7–10 December 2010, Melbourne. Published by AERU Research Unit, Lincoln University, New Zealand, pp 144–160

OECD (2007) OECD regions at a glance, organisation for economic cooperation and development, Paris

Partridge M, Rickman D, Ali K, Olfert M (2008) Lost in space: population dynamics in the American Hinterlands and small cities. J Econ Geogr 8(6):727–757

Romer P (1986) Increasing returns and long-run growth. J Polit Econ 94(5):1002–1037

Romer P (1994) The origins of endogenous growth. J Econ Perspect 8(1):3–22

Rowland D (1979) Internal migration in Australia, Census Monograph Series. ABS, Canberra

Schultz TW (1961) Investment in human capital. Am Econ Rev 51:1–17

Sher J, Sher K (1994) Beyond the conventional wisdom: rural development as if Australia's rural people and communities really mattered. J Res Rural Educ 10(1):2–43

Stimson R, Robson A, Shyy T (2011) Modelling endogenous regional employment performance in non-metropolitan Australia: what is the role of human capital, social capital and creative capital? In: Kourtit K, Nijkamp P, Stough R (eds) Drivers of innovation, entrepreneurship and regional dynamics. Springer, Berlin, pp 179–204

Stockdale A (2006) Migration: pre-requisite for rural economic regeneration? J Rural Stud 22(3):354–366

Tonts M (2005) Internal migration and Australia's agricultural regions. Dialogue 24(2):53–65 Academy of Social Sciences in Australia

Wilson R, Briscoe G (2004) The impact of human capital on economic growth: a review. In: Descy P, Tessaring M (eds) Impact of Education and Training Third Report on Vocational Training Research in Europe: Background Report, Cedefop Reference series, vol 54. Office for Official Publications of the European Communities, Luxembourg

Chapter 16
Compensation or Substitution? Labour Market Effects of Technological and Structural Change

Uwe Blien and Oliver Ludewig

1 Introduction

Some of the dominating approaches of macroeconomics explain unemployment primarily by the institutional regulations of the labour market (Layard et al. 2005, cf. the review by Blanchard 2007). In the following, however, it is argued that this is at least not the complete story: differences in regional unemployment cannot be explained by institutional regulations, since these are mostly constant within a country. And regions differ in terms of their unemployment nearly as much as do nations (Südekum 2005).

An alternative explanation of unemployment relates the emergence and disappearance of jobs to the elasticity of demand on product markets and the effects of technical change (see Appelbaum and Schettkat 1999; Cingano and Schivardi 2004; Combes et al. 2004). The argumentation is underpinned by appropriate formal models. The central point of such models is that technical change has a contradictory effect on employment and unemployment. In the case of elastic demand for goods,

U. Blien (✉) · O. Ludewig
Institute for Employment Research (IAB), Nuremberg, Germany

Otto-Friedrich-University of Bamberg, Bamberg, Germany
e-mail: uwe.blien@iab.de

© Springer International Publishing AG, part of Springer Nature 2018
U. Blien et al. (eds.), *Modelling Aging and Migration Effects on Spatial Labor Markets*, Advances in Spatial Science,
https://doi.org/10.1007/978-3-319-68563-2_16

increases in productivity result in employment growth, whereas in the case of inelastic demand employment is reduced.

In this paper we intend to present some basic theoretical arguments concerning the relationships between product markets, labour markets and technical progress (which we regard as represented by productivity growth). Our intention is to show that there are substitution and compensating effects of productivity increases. We also present some preliminary empirical results.

The basic argument for the connection between technical progress, elasticity of product demand and employment is already found in an essay by Neisser (1942). There, however, it is not formalized because it is presumed to be self-evident. Several simple but ingeniously constructed models on the theme were presented in some papers by Ronald Schettkat. He co-operated with Eileen Appelbaum (Appelbaum and Schettkat 1999; see Schettkat 1997) in developing a special approach.

In recent times there has been a renewed interest in the labour market effects of technological progress. However, so far there is no complete explanation of the employment effects by technological changes. Most papers can be classified into two categories:

- The first one is the "Task Approach" developed by David Autor and co-authors (see Autor et al. 2003; Autor and Dorn 2013). In this approach the effects of technical changes on the distribution of occupations is regarded. A global effect on employment is excluded in most papers, since they assume full utilization of the factor labour. For the US and for other countries (see Rendall and Weiss 2016) a polarization of employment is diagnosed: Well and poorly paid jobs grow, whereas the middle of the distribution loses.
- The second approach could be addressed as the 'technical theory of labour demand'. Frey and Osborne (2017) and Brynjolfsson and McAfee (2011, 2014) look at single occupations and formulate expectations about the substitutability by technology within one or two decades.

Both approaches do not give answers to the question about the development of a possible "technological unemployment" (Keynes, see Piva and Vivarelli 2017). With the exception of some counter-examples (Gregory et al. 2016) the task approach regards the employment level as given. The second approach ignores possible feedbacks between productivity increases, price decreases and employment changes. The many interacting economic and social variables are not regarded.

Our paper is included in a volume about demographic changes, since it shows one of the important general conditions the ageing process of the developed countries is taking place.

2 Theory

To illustrate the argument put forward originally by Neisser, we consider a very simple numerical example, which uses the demand elasticity. The relevance of the elasticity can be seen in the context of price changes and sales. If demand is elastic, a price reduction results in an increase of turnover. On the other hand, inelastic demand leads to a fall in turnover. This property follows directly from the definition of the price elasticity of demand.

The demand elasticity also conveys the effects of technical progress on employment with profit oriented firms. Technological progress leads initially to the reduction of the demand for labour. Since the same product can be produced with fewer workers, this consequence could be called the substitution effect of technical progress. Workers are substituted by new technical equipment. However, in addition, there is a counteracting effect: Cost reduction as a result of technical progress also results in a price reduction. This, in turn, increases the demand for the product and therefore also the demand for labour which is needed for production. Therefore, a compensation effect occurs (see the discussion of the effects and of much literature on it in Piva and Vivarelli 2017). How strong both effects are, whether the second effect is even "overcompensating" is an empirical question.

Table 16.1 summarizes the effects of a productivity increase through technical progress. It is assumed that the productivity advantage is passed on to consumers. Productivity gains and price declines are therefore of the same magnitude. The price reduction results in a change in the quantity sold. In the elastic case, this gain will be greater than the price change. In the inelastic case, the change in volume will be comparatively smaller. This means that the net effect on turnover is positive in the case of elastic demand but negative in the case of inelastic demand. The content of the theorem of Neisser and of Appelbaum/Schettkat is that employment reacts in the same direction as does turnover.

The context given in the table can be formalized. In the following, a basic model is presented, which is a variant of a version that is found in Möller (2001, based on Appelbaum and Schettkat 1999) and in Partridge et al. (2016). This model (see also the very simple model of Combes et al. 2004) begins with a definition equation for

Table 16.1 Relationship between consumer demand and employment development in the approach of Appelbaum and Schettkat (1999), presented as a fictional numerical example

	Elastic product demand (%)	Inelastic product demand (%)
Productivity gains through technical progress	20	20
Price change	−20	−20
Products sold	30	10
Change in turnover	4	−12
Employment change	4	−12
Dominating effect	Compensating effect	Substitution effect

productivity π in a firm j. To this end, the quantity of the product Q is set in relation to the employment N.

$$\pi_j = \frac{Q_j}{N_j} \qquad (16.1)$$

The second equation is a pricing function based on mark-up calculation. The price P_j includes the cost of wages and a mark-up factor z_j, which also covers capital expenditure:

$$P_j = \frac{z_j W_j}{\pi_j} \qquad (16.2)$$

Finally, there is a function that describes demand and falls with the price of the product and rises with the level of income y:

$$Q_j = f\left(P_j, y\right), \quad \text{mit:} \quad dQ_j/dP_j < 0, \quad dQ_j/dy > 0 \qquad (16.3)$$

From these comparatively general static equations, expressions for the growth rates of the various variables can be derived. If $\varepsilon_j = -\frac{dQ_j}{dP_j} \cdot \frac{P_j}{Q_J}$ is the price elasticity of demand and η_j is the income elasticity, the following equations can be given:

$$\widehat{N}_j = \widehat{Q}_j - \widehat{\pi}_j \qquad (16.4)$$

$$\widehat{P}_j = \widehat{z}_j + \widehat{W}_j - \widehat{\pi}_j \qquad (16.5)$$

$$\widehat{Q}_j = \eta_j \cdot \widehat{y} - \varepsilon_j \cdot \widehat{P}_j \qquad (16.6)$$

Assuming that the growth rate of the mark-up z is equal to zero, the following Eq. (16.7) results for employment:

$$\widehat{N}_j = \eta_j \widehat{y} + \left(\varepsilon_j - 1\right) \widehat{\pi}_j - \varepsilon_j \widehat{W}_j \qquad (16.7)$$

All these equations were developed for individual firms. But the Eq. (16.7) can easily be aggregated to all firms in a region or country, assuming that all firms of a region or nation are identical, thus resulting in a regional or collective employment function. However, we want to limit this assumption to the companies of a specific industry i and to make the aggregation accordingly. In this way, we are able to distinguish between different industries of a region r. Let us assume that regions r represent our aggregates. All developed statements can be easily transferred to nations.

$$\widehat{N}_{ir} = \eta_{ir} \widehat{y} + (\varepsilon_{ir} - 1) \widehat{\pi}_{ir} - \varepsilon_{ir} \widehat{W}_{ir} \qquad (16.8)$$

In this aggregation, however, we have to take into account that the price elasticity of demand at the level of firms differs from those at the level of sectors. A "multi-level problem" must therefore be considered. If a company increases its price, a very strong demand reaction can be the consequence, because the buyers perceive the unchanged price of the other companies and accept their offers. If, on the other hand, all firms change their price in the same way, only a relatively modest change in demand will follow. In the following, we will discuss price variations that are similar for all firms in an industry. A firm that is not a monopolist or oligopolist will consider the behaviour of all other firms as given. The situation of a monopolist is clearly distinguishable from the one described here, since a profit-maximizing monopolist will only offer his products in the elastic part of the demand curve. In the present case, a larger number of firms are present in each industry, and the demand may be elastic or inelastic.

The model describes productivity gains as Hicks-neutral technical progress, which implies that the ratio of the production factors remains constant. Then it can be seen immediately from (Eq. 16.8) that when productivity increases, the number of workers is reduced when demand is inelastic, that is, if $\varepsilon_{ir} < 1$. If demand is elastic ($\varepsilon_{ir} > 1$), employment will grow. This means that the basic theorem of the employment effects of technical change can be derived directly from this simple model: Technical progress increases employment in industries with elastic demand for goods, but lowers employment when demand is inelastic.

The model also has some other general features that need to be considered. Income inequality is also important. If demand rises with higher income, the negative effects of technological progress may be offset. This explains why it is not easy to separate the effect of the different variables, and may help to pay little attention to the role of demand elasticity in conventional economic theory. Certainly, the lack of attention has also contributed to the construction of standard models. Often, isoelastic functions are used in which the elasticities are not variable at all.

Blien and Sanner (2014) and Blien and Ludewig (2016) are interested in developing a micro-foundation of the above model. Blien and Sanner (2014) also offer a generalization to the case of many products. This shows that not only the own demand elasticity of a product is to be considered, but also the cross-price elasticities with other products. If goods are manufactured that are close substitutes for consumers, it may be that employment falls as a result of technical progress, although the direct price elasticity of demand is larger than one.

Blien and Ludewig (2016) achieve a surprising result: They derive a labour demand function on the basis of a standard micro-economic approach with a Cobb-Douglas production function. A transformation into growth rates results in an equation which is very similar to Eq. (16.8). A main difference is, that the coefficient of the wage variable is of a more complicated nature.

3 Structural Change and the Product Cycle

It has already been pointed out that demand elasticities are not constant. This applies both to the cross-sectional comparison of the products as well as to the temporal development of the markets. Once again, a formal model can be offered for the product cycle, in which three products play a role (see Blien and Sanner 2006). One represents an unspecified bundle of products, which contains all products which are not of specific interest. In addition there are two products of different quality, which are competing with one another for the consumer's budget. These products can, for example, be imagined as cars of different quality, of which the higher quality is more expensive.

On the basis of very general assumptions about consumer preferences and a steady rate of technical progress, the market launch of the more favourable one of the two "cars" can be described as a function of the technical progress with elastic demand. On the basis of very general assumption about preferences, this shifts into the inelastic range in the case of further productivity increases. The process is accelerated when the better quality of the two "cars" is available to consumers which decreases the prices of the two products. Ultimately, the qualitatively better but more expensive product completely replaces the less favourable one.

The consequences for employment are both obvious and are indicated by the above-mentioned theorem or by its generalization in the case of many goods. The empirical implications are also obvious: If a nation or a region specializes in a specific product, it gets into a crisis when it reaches the end of its "product cycle". This does not necessarily mean the disappearance of the product, it is sufficient that demand becomes less price-responsive, e.g. because everyone already has the product and only its replacement plays a role. In the case of inelastic demand for products, however, technical progress already leads to the loss of workers. Consequently, it is important for an economy to produce as many innovative products as possible which are subject to elastic demand. An economy will only have a high employment level as long as its "young" industries are dominant, which ideally show a rapid productivity improvement. An "old-industrial" mix, on the other hand, leads to crises even if the sectors concerned are internationally competitive, since in this case productivity gains are linked to job cuts.

The idea that products are going through a particular cycle goes back to Schumpeter. It is based on empirical regularities with respect to important variables. Like the gramophone was replaced by the record player, this in turn was replaced by the CD player and the MP3 player, many products have a finite "lifetime". As an empirical example of a product cycle, consider the development of CD audio technology, whose launch was primarily run by the developer and manufacturer companies Sony and Phillips. When the first CD players came on the market in October 1982, they cost just under 2000 DM in Germany. The single CD was not cheap with about 40 DM. At this time, CD players were sold mainly to specialists who could afford the high prices, especially to connoisseurs of classical music, for whom the product innovation improved the quality of the music. Since the product was initially very expensive, sales initially only reached a low level. When, after a short time, the price halved, the purchase of a CD player was interesting for a wider customer group and the sales of the devices and CDs grew rapidly.

The first CD with over one million copies was "Brothers in Arms" by Dire Straits, which was released in 1985. The following year, more than 60 million CDs were sold worldwide. The price elasticity of demand in this phase was certainly much greater 1, i.e. the demand was in the elastic range. Later the market slowed down and further price reductions did not have the same effect as in the initial phase. After the turn of the millennium, the market was already largely saturated, with sales primarily having the effect that replacement procurement was preferred. Now competing products arrived at the market, the MP3 player displaced some of the demand, while the mini-disk did not reach a breakthrough. The product cycle of the CD player has not yet been completed, there are still players and CDs sold. However, it can be assumed that advances in production technology will go at the expense of jobs in this industry.

It is above all the workforce, which is burdened by the consequences of the processes described. In many cases the profit outlook for the firms may be excellent. Nevertheless, the mechanism described can lead to unemployment in the labour market.

4 Empirical Approaches

Stylized facts are not yet a hard empirical test. After all, there was such an empirical test carried out in a seminal study by J. Möller (2001), who set the pace for later research. He used state-space models with time varying parameters to estimate the price elasticity of demand and the income elasticity for a number of industries of three countries (USA, UK, Germany). He observed a general shift in demand in the direction of the inelastic range, which took place in the transition from the sixties to the seventies. As a result, unemployment increased significantly during this time period.

Blien and Ludewig (2016) present results on the labour market of western Germany which are achieved in two steps. In the first step data from industry statistics are used to calculate demand and income elasticities. In the second step employment development is analysed with data from the employment statistics provided by the Institute for Employment Research (IAB).

In the first step Marshallian demand functions are estimated for industries in IV regressions which produce estimates for the demand and for income elasticities. These are used in the second step carried out at the regional level (326 districts) with yearly employment growth (1975–2004) as the response variable. It is assumed that industries are homogenous between regions. The analysis is closely oriented towards Eq. (16.8). As indicated there the elasticities are included as interactions with productivity growth. The equation suggests to take the interaction of the

Table 16.2 Employment growth per region & industry (pooled regression—OLS)

	(1)	(2)	(3)	(4)
Interaction (Demand elasticity−1) *	−9.45***	−9.49***	−6.92***	−6.95***
Productivity growth	(−3.15)	(−3.21)	(−2.68)	(−2.70)
Interaction income		−1.10	−0.534	−0.681
Elasticity/Produc. Gr.		(−0.27)	(−0.13)	(−0.17)
Wage growth			−0.158***	−0.158***
			(−3.35)	(−3.35)
Emploment density				−0.168***
				(−9.14)
Accessibility				−0.00774***
				(−2.69)
Constant	2.476***	2.570***	3.308***	3.765***
	(5.68)	(4.88)	(5.93)	(6.80)
N	367,693	367,693	367,693	367,693
adj. R^2	0.045	0.045	0.050	0.052
F	59.94	66.20	67.75	64.13

t statistics in parentheses $^{*}p < 0.1$, $^{**}p < 0.05$, $^{***}p < 0.01$, data from the employment statistics

income elasticity with productivity growth as an additional variable into account. Also wage growth is relevant.

Some basic results obtained in a pooled regression are shown in Table 16.2. The coefficients are given as percentages for the elasticities. In the table, the coefficient of the interaction between the demand elasticity and productivity growth has the expected sign, whereas the corresponding coefficient for the income elasticity has the "wrong" sign. However, the models of Table 16.2 might be plagued by reverse causality and by unobserved regional variables. To take care of these problems, the models of Table 16.3 use lagged values of the demand elasticities as instruments and regional fixed effects.

The results of Table 16.3 confirm the hypothesis about the connection between the price elasticity of demand and the effects of productivity growth on employment: The more elastic demand is, the more favourable is the employment effect of productivity growth. Regions characterised by a concentration of industries with elastic demand show—ceteris paribus—an employment growth. Regions with mainly inelastic demand are shrinking. There are some variables which have additionally to be taken into account. Especially the income elasticity is important. People shift their demand with higher income more and more to products no longer directly relevant for their basic needs but which represent some sophistication. Especially the German industry is specialised for products like expensive cars for which a higher demand with higher income levels can be expected. Of course this applies only for a part of the population: Even at higher income levels there are many people who cannot afford expensive cars. The results obtained contribute to the explanation of differing paths for employment development between regions which cannot be addressed by conventional approaches of regional economics.

Table 16.3 Employment growth per region & industry (fixed effects for districts, IV)

	(1)	(2)	(3)	(4)
Interaction (Demand elasticity−1) * Productivity growth.	3.89*** (−14.40)	3.85*** (−14.29)	1.26*** (−4.38)	1.26*** (−4.38)
Interaction income Elasticity * Produc. Gr.		6.37*** (11.07)	6.81*** (11.76)	6.81*** (11.76)
Wage growth			−0.162*** (−33.39)	−0.162*** (−33.39)
Employment density				0.0573 (0.72)
Constant	2.426*** (20.13)	1.878*** (14.50)	2.647*** (20.83)	2.529*** (12.31)
N	367,693	367,693	367,693	367,693
adj. R^2	0.048	0.049	0.054	0.054
F	468.0	454.9	475.4	462.4

t statistics in parentheses $•p < 0.1$, $**p < 0.05$, $***p < 0.01$, data from the employment statistics

5   Conclusion

This article shows the relevance of the theorem on the employment effects of productivity increases in a general framework. The theorem holds under very general conditions, the assumptions made in its derivation are largely standard (see Blien and Sanner 2014). The theorem is potentially very important in explaining (regional) unemployment. We have shown some empirical analyses, which support the relevance of the theorem. The direction of the effect of technological progress depends on the elasticity of demand, i. e. whether the compensating or the substitution effect dominates. On the basis of this finding some positions of the current discussion about technology appear as being not refined enough. In some currently very popular positions, we called in the introduction the "technical theory of labour demand". There the production process is regarded as taking place in a technical system. If an element of this system is replaced, it is no longer needed. However, this view of the production process ignores some basic elements of a capitalist society. It ignores that the production is intermediated by markets and that is follows the calculation of an entrepreneur, who is interested in profit. Crucial economic variables are not regarded, especially the price effects of productivity increases, we focus upon.

Adding one final point, it is further possible to assess the political implications of the theorem on the employment effects of productivity gains. In doing this it is helpful to consider the expectations of economic agents. It has already been shown that the actors involved are normally not aware of the described mechanism concerning the emergence of unemployment. In the case of economic policy decisions such aspects play an indirect role at most. In a region, the "success recipe" for the political actors may be the support of a booming industry during a certain phase. An industry that is at the beginning of the product cycle will quickly create employment and the region in which it is located will benefit.

Once the stakeholders have become accustomed to this success recipe, the elasticity of demand for the industry concerned may shift. The promotion of investment, and thus of technical progress, has previously created employment, and now it is raising unemployment. In time and space (between regions) absolutely equally oriented promotion measures can have opposite effects on employment. The same factors, which initially determine the success of a region, are also decisive for its failure later. It is sufficient that in a region a specific product, a sector, a product conglomerate is established as the dominant one. In the cycle, this type of production can initially prove to be extraordinarily successful, but later it leads to crises. The sectors that initially establish the dominance of a region are later part of its decline. It must be very irritating for the actors, when the "success recipes" of the past change in time and space.

There are many examples which are candidates for the described processes. In Germany the Ruhr area was once one of the leading regions, the location of key industries. Today it is characterized by high unemployment rates and by the persistent structural problems of an "old" industrial region. Since the size of the demand elasticity is unknown to the actors, the decisive criterion for the distinction between the success prospects of measures is missing. In addition, it should be noted that the product cycle described above only provides some possibilities and does not describe any "regular" development. How quickly a shift of demand elasticities takes place and in which direction it goes is largely open. An important conclusion, therefore, is that empirical economies are burdened with considerable uncertainties in their development and unemployment can arise at any time due to structural distortions.

References

Appelbaum E, Schettkat R (1999) Are prices unimportant? J Post Keynes Econ 21(3):387–398

Autor DH, Dorn D (2013) The growth of low skill service jobs and the polarization of the U.S. labor market. Am Econ Rev 103(5):1553–1597

Autor DH, Levy F, Murnane RJ (2003) The skill content of recent technological change. An empirical exploration. Q J Econ 118(4):1279–1333

Blanchard O (2007) A Review of Richard Layard, Stephen Nickell, and Richard Jackman's unemployment: macroeconomic performance and the labour market. J Econ Lit 45(2):410–418

Blien U, Ludewig O (2016) Technological progress and (un)employment development. IAB Discussion Paper 22

Blien U, Sanner H (2006) Structural change and regional employment dynamics. IAB Discussion Paper 6

Blien U, Sanner H (2014) Technological progress and employment. Econ Bull 34(1):245–251

Brynjolfsson E, McAfee A (2011) Race against the machine. How the digital revolution is accelerating innovation, driving productivity, and irreversibly transforming employment and the economy. Digital Frontier, Lexington, MA

Brynjolfsson E, McAfee A (2014) The second machine age. Work, progress, and prosperity in a Timeof brilliant technologies. Norton, New York

Cingano F, Schivardi F (2004) Identifying the sources of local productivity growth. J Eur Econ Assoc 2(4):720–742

Combes P-P, Magnac T, Robin J-M (2004) The dynamics of local employment in France. J Urban Econ 56:217–243

Frey CB, Osborne MA (2017) The future of employment: how susceptible are jobs to computerisation? Technol Forecast Soc Chang 114:254–280

Gregory T, Salomons A, Zierahn U (2016) Racing with or against the machine? Evidence from Europe. ZEW Discussion Paper

Layard R, Nickell S, Jackman R (2005) Unemployment. Macroeconomic performance and the labour market, New edn, first edn 1991, Oxford University Press, Oxford

Möller J (2001) Income and price elasticities in different sectors of the economy. An analysis of structural change for Germany, the UK and the US. In: ten Raa T, Schettkat R (eds) The growth of the service industries. Edward Elgar, Northampton, MA

Neisser HP (1942) 'Permanent' technological unemployment. 'Demand for commodities is not demand for labor'. Am Econ Rev 32:50–71

Partridge MD, Tsvetkova A, Betz M (2016) Are the most productive regions necessarily the most successful? Paper of the Ohio State University

Piva M, Vivarelli M (2017) Technological change and employment: were Ricardo and Marx right? IZA Discussion Paper 10471

Rendall M, Weiss FJ (2016) Employment polarization and the role of the apprenticeship system. Eur Econ Rev 82:166–186

Schettkat R (1997) Die Interdependenz von Produkt- und Arbeitsmärkten. Die Wirtschafts- und Beschäftigungsentwicklung der Industrieländer aus der Produktmarktperspektive. Mitt Arbeitsmarkt Berufsforsch 30(4):721–731

Südekum J (2005) Increasing returns and spatial unemployment disparities. Pap Reg Sci 84(2):159–181

Printed by Printforce, the Netherlands